D1088097

100

Φ

Take 100 is an unprecedented compendium of the most promising emerging film directors from around the world. We asked the artistic directors of ten prestigious film festivals to each nominate ten of the best emerging film directors working today. The result: an exceptional look at global contemporary filmmaking. The 100 featured directors have all recently come to international attention for their contribution to cinema and represent countries as diverse as China, Israel, Mexico, Algeria, India, Romania, and Canada. The festival director-curators include: Cameron Bailey and Piers Handling (Toronto); Trevor Groth (Sundance); Kim Dong Ho (Pusan); Li Cheuk-to (Hong Kong); Frédéric Maire (formerly of Locarno); Marco Müller (Venice); Olivier Père (formerly of Cannes), Christoph Terhechte (Berlin); Azize Tan (Istanbul); and Sergio Wolf (Buenos Aires).

Whether you are a film professional or a casual moviegoer, *Take 100* will guide you through today's must-see films and directors not to miss. Some of the directors and their films are well-known—Sarah Polley (*Away from Her*), Ari Folman (*Waltz with Bashir*), Carlos Reygadas (*Silent Light*), Florian Henckel von Donnersmarck (*The Lives of Others*)—and others are just beginning to burst onto the scene—Gianfranco Rosi (*Below Sea Level*), So Yong Kim (*In Between Days*), Izumi Takahashi (*The Soup, One Morning*). *Take 100* is a must-have for anyone who loves film and wants to be the first to know who are the newest directors to watch, and what are the films making the biggest impact in the world of film today.

Arranged alphabetically by director, the book explores the work of each director through the close analysis of one key film featured on two spreads, providing the reader with detailed information about each film and its author through film stills, on-set photographs, posters, and an original essay written by the nominating curator. Ranging in genres from drama to crime, documentary to animation, big-budget studio films to one-man productions, the selected films are a cross-section of the most promising and daring cinematographic creations from around the globe. Additionally, each curator discusses one classic film which has influenced contemporary cinema, illustrated by its poster and a photograph of the director.

The directors and films featured in *Take 100* are pushing the boundaries in the field of filmmaking—whether through exploring taboo subject matter, inventing new animation technology, or combining an intelligent drama with a classic horror flick—these are films you won't want to miss, made by directors you'll be hearing about for years to come.

CAMERON BAILEY AND PIERS HANDLING

Cameron Bailey is the co-director of the Toronto International Film Festival and is responsible for all programming. He has been with the organization for over twelve years in various capacities, including programming the annual selection of films from Africa, South Asia, and the Philippines, and heading up the Perspective Canada series. He has twenty years' experience as a film critic in print and broadcast media, and made the essay film *Hotel Saudade*.

Piers Handling is the co-director and chief executive officer of the Toronto International Film Festival. He worked previously at the Canadian Film Institute, and joined the Festival in 1982. He has extensive international and Canadian film programming experience, has published numerous books and articles, and has served on many film juries. He is currently on the board of the Canadian Film Centre and serves on the Minister of Culture's Advisory Council. He is a Chevalier des Arts et Lettres.

TREVOR GROTH

Trevor Groth is the director of programming for the Sundance Film Festival in Park City, Utah. A native of Salt Lake City, Groth has been affiliated with Sundance since 1993, when he joined the programming staff. In 2003 he became a senior programmer and oversaw the narrative and documentary feature selection, as well as the festival's short film selection. He has also served as artistic director of the CineVegas Film Festival since 2002.

KIM DONG HO

Kim Dong Ho is the founding director of the Pusan International Film Festival, a showcase for emerging Asian and international filmmakers, established in 1996. He is considered an expert on modern world cinema, and has served on the juries of numerous prestigious festivals such as Rotterdam, India, and Venice. He published a book in 2005 entitled *History of Korean Cinema Policy*, and was instrumental in establishing the Asian Film Academy and Asian Film Market.

LI CHEUK-TO

Since 2004 Li Cheuk-to has served as the artistic director of the Hong Kong International Film Festival, where he previously served as a programmer for seventeen years. Born in Hong Kong, Li joined the editorial board of *Film Biweekly* in 1980 and was its editor-in-chief from 1983 to 1986. A founding member of the Hong Kong Film Critics Society, he served as its president from 1995 to 1999. He was a member of the official jury of the 48th Berlin International Film Festival in 1998.

FREDERIC MAIRE

Born in Switzerland, Frédéric Maire has been passionate about film since adolescence. In the early 1980s he began working as a director, programmer, and film journalist. In 1992 he founded the Magic Lantern with three friends, a film club for children, which remains well-known today in Switzerland and abroad. Since 1986 he has collaborated with the Locarno International Film Festival, where he held the position of artistic director from 2005 to 2009. Currently he is director of the Swiss Film Archive.

MARCO MULLER

Marco Müller is the director of the Venice International Film Festival. Born in Rome, Müller began his film career as a film critic and historian, authoring several books on cinema, and more recently has produced several films. From 1986 to 1989 he served as director of the International Exhibition of New Cinema in Pesaro, and from 1989 to 1991 was director of the International Film Festival Rotterdam. He directed the Locarno International Film Festival from 1991 to 2000, where, alongside the presentation of emerging directors, he promoted important film retrospectives. He has been with Venice since 2004, when he also took up the position of director of cinema for the Venice Biennale Foundation.

OLIVIER PERE

Olivier Père is the recently appointed artistic director of the Locarno International Film Festival, having been the director of the Cannes Directors Fortnight since 2004. Born in France, and educated at the Sorbonne, Père joined the French Cinémathèque in 1995, serving as a programmer. He has written about film for the publication *Les Inrockuptibles* since 1997.

AZIZE TAN

Azize Tan is the director of the Istanbul International Film Festival, a position she has held since 2006. Born in Istanbul, she received her MA from Bosphorus University, and has worked for the Istanbul Foundation for Culture and Arts since 1993. In 2003 she became the deputy director of the IIFF, and also organizes the Istanbul Autumn Film Week. She is a member of NETPAC and the Asia Pacific Screen Awards Nominations Council.

CHRISTOPH TERHECHTE

Christoph Terhechte has been head of the International Forum of New Cinema at the Berlin International Film Festival since 2001. Born in Münster, he studied political science and journalism at the University of Hamburg and worked as a film journalist since 1984. In 1991 he became film editor at the Berlin magazine *tip*, and in 1997 joined the selection committee of the Forum.

SERGIO WOLF

Born in Buenos Aires, Sergio Wolf is the artistic director of the Buenos Aires International Independent Film Festival, a position he's held since 2008. A critic, professor, screenwriter, and documentary filmmaker, Wolf is the author of numerous books and screenplays, including the 2002 book *Nuevo Cine Argentino*. He held the position of programmer at BAFICI from 2005 to 2007.

MAREN ADE
ASHIM AHLUWALIA
LISANDRO ALONSO
ÖZCAN ALPER
RABAH AMEUR-ZAIMECHE
JUDD APATOW
ANDREA ARNOLD
ADITYA ASSARAT
LIONEL BAIER
SOPHIE BARTHES
AIDA BEGIC
CHRISTOFFER BOE
BONG JOON-HO
JAN BONNY
SERGE BOZON
ANDREW BUJALSKI
YOON-CHUL CHUNG
DENIS COTE
PEPE DIOKNO
QUENTIN DUPIEUX
JAY AND MARK DUPLASS
NASH EDGERTON
EDWIN
FERNANDO EIMBCKE
PAZ ENCINA
PELIN ESMER
JIM FINN
RYAN FLECK AND ANNA BODEN
ARI FOLMAN
TOM FORD
CARY FUKUNAGA
CHRIS FULLER
JONATHAN GLAZER
MIGUEL GOMES

DOUGLAS GORDON
BRADLEY RUST GRAY
VALESKA GRISEBACH
LANCE HAMMER
MIA HANSEN-LØVE
FLORIAN HENCKEL VON DONNERSMARCK
JODY HILL
HIROMASA HIROSUE
HO YUHANG
JIANG WEN
RIAN JOHNSON
MIRANDA JULY
HUSEYIN KARABEY
FARAH KHAN
ERIC KHOO
SO YONG KIM
ULRICH KOHLER
ERAN KOLIRIN
ISAKI LACUESTA
PABLO LARRAIN
LIU JIAYIN
LIU JIE
LU CHUAN
LUCRECIA MARTEL
RAYA MARTIN
TOM MCCARTHY
STEVE MCQUEEN
BRILLANTE MENDOZA
CRISTIAN MUNGIU
RADU MUNTEAN
GERARDO NARANJO
SHIRIN NESHAT
NING HAO
NOH YOUNG-SEOK

VEIKO ÕUNPUU
ASLI ÖZGE
GYORGY PALFI
HO-CHEUNG PANG
SARAH POLLEY
CORNELIU PORUMBOIU
CRISTI PUIU
PHILIPPE RAMOS
KELLY REICHARDT
CARLOS REYGADAS
ENRIQUE RIVERO
JOAO PEDRO RODRIGUES
GYEONG-TAE ROH
AXELLE ROPERT
GIANFRANCO ROSI
ESTHER ROTS
WISIT SASANATIENG
JEAN-STEPHANE SAUVAIRE
LIEV SCHREIBER
ALBERT SERRA
ZACK SNYDER
AURAEUS SOLITO
IZUMI TAKAHASHI
TARIQ TEGUIA
SEYFI TEOMAN
HUGO VIEIRA DA SILVA
TAIKA WAITITI
HANS WEINGARTNER
HENNER WINCKLER
JONG-CHAN YOON
ZHANG LU
ANDREI ZVYAGINTSEV

100 DIRECTORS

Maren Ade's second film tells the story of Gitti and Chris (Birgit Minichmayr and Lars Eidinger), a couple on a holiday of secluded togetherness. Taking a leaf from the book of another couple they encounter, Chris tries to show his willful girlfriend who's boss, and she attempts to conform to his new ideal. But this playful experiment begins to destabilize their relationship. The film is a subtly humorous, cruelly meticulous study of the contradictory desires of a couple searching for their own identities and an intimate love story that plunges the depths of a relationship and reflects the emotional disorientation of an entire generation.

MAREN ADE
EVERYONE ELSE

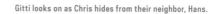
Gitti looks on as Chris hides from their neighbor, Hans.

Gitti tells Chris the makeup suits him.

Maren Ade first attracted attention with her thesis film, *The Forest for the Trees* (*Der Wald vor lauter Bäumen*, 2003), which tells the story of a young teacher starting a job in a new town, where she promises to "shake things up" a bit. Her efforts are met with little approval, however, but she only notices when it's much too late, having already put her foot in it right, left, and center. Ade achieves the feat of creating empathy for a less-than-engaging person; in the end, the viewer is able to practically take part the lead character's suffering, feeling mortified at every embarrassment that comes her way.

On the contrary, Ade does everything not to let us into her characters in her second feature, *Everyone Else* (*Alle Anderen*, 2009). The film is about a couple, who you might say are "having a crisis," although it's not entirely clear where their typical way of dealing with each other stops and the actual crisis begins. That's exactly what makes the film so exceptional: nothing dramatic occurs, there are no traumas to deal with, there's no tragic event calculated to catalyze emotional outbursts. Instead, all the tiny inconsistencies, irritations, moments of hurt, and transgressions simply pile up to such an extent that it can't possibly go on much longer. Or perhaps it can, but just not in the same way it has up until now.

Chris and Gitti–played by Lars Eidinger and Birgit Minichmayr–are both in their early thirties, and on vacation at Chris's mother's holiday home in Sardinia. The fact that they are on vacation and don't live there all the time is told by Ade only in passing. Equally casually, we discover that Chris is an ambitious architect still waiting for success to arrive and that Gitti works in the PR department of a major music company. Cool jobs, large houses, expensive cars, affluent parents; the whole setup isn't designed to impress, but rather is displayed in the same casual way that the protagonists themselves see it. How they speak to each other, play their different roles, act relaxed as if compelled to do so–it would all be simply unthinkable in any other milieu.

To begin with, the couple's sillinesses still come across as funny. But it soon becomes clear that Gitti's theatrical, extroverted temperament and Chris's inhibited, ironic manner are just ways of avoiding conflict, of overriding repressed feelings. Everything is said indirectly or ironically, everything is ridiculed, all attempts are made in only a semi-serious way so that retreat is always possible and the opposite can always be argued. Correspondingly, they spend all their time eyeing the other's behavior and gesticulations. At one point, Chris puts his arm around Gitti while out on a walk, leading her to burst out laughing, explaining, "You're just such a bad actor. You've never done that before."

Chris is a loner, Gitti is more adventurous. Instead of giving in to Gitti's demands and going to a club one night, they find themselves in his mother's room, a veritable treasure trove of kitsch, where he gives an exaggerated dance performance to a soft-rock song. The couple end up in bed anyway, where he's unwilling to respond to her "I love you," finally paying her a series of forced-sounding compliments that reach their crescendo with, "You were the most beautiful woman in the club." Everything that's said has to be followed by a partial retraction. Although the couple's little games do express a certain intimacy, the whole situation has a blatantly aggressive, disrespectful tone to it. You end up breathing a sigh of relief when at one point Chris asks, "Can't we just speak normally for a change?" It goes without saying that that goes wrong, too.

Perhaps the most astounding thing about the film is the way that Ade never puts her characters on show or condemns them. The film doesn't leave them alone for a single moment, even during their greatest torments, allowing the viewer to take turns trying to identify with them. This comes to a head when they are confronted with a mirror image of their relationship in the form of Hans, a more successful, overbearing, and patronizing architect, and his picture-book wife, Sana. They initially treat this likeness with contempt before beginning to emulate it unintentionally. It is precisely the misery of each having to play someone else that perversely unites them, meaning everything remains possible right up to the very end, an open outlook that is all the more gripping for it.

Everyone Else is often funny, but it isn't a comedy; it's serious for the most part, but is certainly no tragedy. Above all, it's the most complex, richly detailed, and imaginative film in a long time to deal with a couple's relationship and all the humiliations, secrets, spite, and lies both big and small that come along with it. Ade's precision, consistency, and objectivity are without comparison in contemporary European cinema.

Chris stands outside his home with a bloodied face after running into a glass door.

Year and place of birth
1976   Karlsruhe, Germany
—
Lives and works in
Berlin, Germany
—
Education
University of Film and Television
    Munich, Germany
—
Filmography
2000   Level 9 (Ebene 9) (short)
2001   Vegas (short)
2003   The Forest for the Trees
       (Der Wald vor lauter
       Bäumen)
2009   Everyone Else
       (Alle Anderen)
—

Director's awards
The Forest for the Trees
Cinema Jove – Valencia
International Film Festival
    (Best Feature, 2005)
IndieLisboa – International
Independent Film Festival
    (Grand Prize, Best Feature
    Film, 2005)
Newport International
Film Festival
    (Best Feature, 2005)
Sundance Film Festival
    (Special Jury Prize, World
    Dramatic Competition, 2005)
— —

Release date
2009
—
Country of release
Germany
—
Language
German
—
Running time
119 min.
—
Genre
Drama
—

Producers
Janine Jackowski,
Dirk Engelhardt, Maren Ade
—
Writer
Maren Ade
—
Cinematographer
Bernhard Keller
—
Key cast
Birgit Minichmayr: Gitti
Lars Eidinger: Chris
Hans-Jochen Wagner: Hans
Nicole Marischka: Sana
—

Filming location
Sardinia, Italy
—
Format
35 mm
—
Awards for Everyone Else
Berlin International Film Festival
    (Silver Bear – Grand Jury
    Prize, Silver Bear –
    Best Actress, Femina Film
    Prize – Best Production
    Design, 2009)
Buenos Aires International
Independent Film Festival
    (FIPRESCI Award,
    Best Director, 2009)
International Women's
Film Festival Dortmund
    (Best Director, 2009)

Love Is Folly International
Film Festival
    (Best Actor, 2009)
Ourense International
Film Festival
    (Best Actress, 2009)
— —

Gitti embraces Chris after he's injured.

Gitti asks Chris if he hates her.

GITTI: Are you sad? Hey.

CHRIS: No, just tired.

GITTI: You looked sad.
Can I ask you something?

CHRIS: No.

GITTI: Do you hate me sometimes?

CHRIS: What kind of question is that?

GITTI: For example, in the living room just now.
There was something in your eyes. That was hate.

CHRIS: We don't have to talk about everything.

Stretching the genre of documentary into something resembling science fiction, the film follows six Indians working in a Mumbai call center, where they answer calls from American customers. This seemingly futuristic world of adopted American aliases and simulated reality is not science fiction, but modern-day life. Avoiding the traditional approaches of cinéma vérité and character-based narrative, the film raises disturbing questions about the nature of personal identity in a twenty-first-century globalized world.

ASHIM AHLUWALIA
JOHN & JANE

Osmond at home on the telephone.

Glen and Raul get stoned at the swamp.

Behind the glittering blare of Bollywood, a new generation of filmmakers is at work in Mumbai. Where Bollywood dazzles, they pose questions. Where their city overwhelms with its barrage of everything at once, they craft small worlds that capture some of the complexity of what it means to be Indian today. Their ranks include Shivajee Chandrabhushan, Paromita Vohra, and Umesh Kulkarni—filmmakers with styles and subjects too radically varied to constitute a single movement. And yet there is one film that could be called the signature text for twenty-first-century alternative filmmaking in India's maximum city: Ashim Ahluwalia's *John & Jane*.

A sui generis artifact, this 2006 film defies categorization. It is a documentary but shot in carefully composed 35-millimeter images. It follows real people but evolves into something close to science fiction. It is set within the now-familiar world of outsourced Indian call centers, but its reach extends far beyond tired debates about globalization. Instead, Ahluwalia uses a formal style that pushes his theme past outsourcing's slippages of identity towards a wider existential abyss.

In vast, fluorescent-lit rooms, thousands of ambitious young Indians talk to people in Kentucky, California, or Idaho. Bridging continents by telephone, they pitch products and soothe the frayed nerves of customers. As they troubleshoot, they dream of America. As they dream, they change. Welcome to the world of offshore call centers.

John & Jane is an astonishing look at the souls of the outsourced. Composed and filmed with unsettling grace, this documentary finds an entirely original and fitting language to express the eerie dislocation of virtual work. The six lives it depicts are real, but the film's approach gives those lives the scope of speculative fiction. At a stroke, Ahluwalia recasts Mumbai as a spectral city, flooded not simply with masses of people and monsoon rains but with simulation upon simulation.

Two of the film's subjects, Glen and Sydney, have taken Western names, partly for the convenience of their customers and partly for their own pleasure. They sleep during the daytime and work in the middle of the night, following American business hours. Neither of them has ever left India. As part of their training, they learn what work, money, and God mean for Americans. In classes that could be read as satire or tragedy, they study shopping flyers as though they were textbooks. Some begin to adopt American values as their own. One dreams of buying his own Spanish-style villa. Another notes, "Everyone who's ever gone to America gets rich." When their shifts end, Glen and Sydney go back to traditional Indian homes, with simple amenities and mothers who urge them to eat.

Ahluwalia reveals the portraits of his six subjects in succession, each one building on the previous. The first worker, Glen, remains the most immersed in his local reality. By the time the film arrives at Naomi—born Namrata—it has lifted off into another dimension. With her bleached skin and dyed yellow hair, she strikes many viewers as a sad, constructed monster. "I'm totally naturally blond . . . I'm very Americanized," she insists in a strange affected American accent. And then, like a robot that has hit a programming glitch, she descends into non sequiturs. "I love to be the me of myself," she says. "I love to gather myself and to be just me." It sounds like nonsense, but her claiming of an utterly false me-ness may be the most direct statement of the film's intent. Mirroring all of cinema's sad cyborgs dating back to *Metropolis* (1927), Naomi embodies the dilemma of synthetic existence: how to be authentically false.

Born in 1972 in what was then still Bombay, Ahluwalia grew up in the old, "non-aligned" India that kept a rigorous distance from the enticements of American pop culture. In his youth, he recalls that there was no Coca-Cola in his country and only one black-and-white television channel. He left Bombay for Bard College in upstate New York, and upon returning to India in the 1990s, he found his country radically transformed by the power of new money, and his city renamed—by cultural and religious nationalists—Mumbai. Restlessly intellectual, Ahluwalia began to use filmmaking to probe the inevitable fault lines that develop in a rapidly shifting society.

He shot *John & Jane* in twenty days but took nearly two years to edit it, even designing the moody, electronic soundscape himself. "I was trying to get the balance between fiction and non-fiction right," he's said.

With its controlled aesthetic and immersion in the postmodern uncertainties of a globalizing Asia, *John & Jane* may have its most direct corollary in Jia Zhangke's *The World*. In constructing images that obliterate the conventional anchors of documentary truth, Ahluwalia has crafted something remarkable: a dystopia that fits India and America equally well.

At 3:43 a.m. a shift begins at the call center.

Year and place of birth
1972   Bombay, India
—

Lives and works in
Mumbai, India
—

Education
**Bard College,
Annandale-on-Hudson, N.Y., USA**
—

Filmography
1999   *Thin Air*
2006   *John & Jane*
—

Director's awards
Thin Air
**Film South Asia
  (Best Film, 1999)**
— —

Release date
2007
—

Country of release
USA
—

Language
English
—

Running time
83 min.
—

Genre
Documentary

Producer
Future East Film
—

Cinematographer
Mohanan
—

Score
**Masta'Justy, Minamo,
Thomas Brinkmann,
Metamatics, Signal Drift**
—

Key cast
**Glen Castinho: Glen
Sydney Fernandes: Sydney
Oaref Irani: Osmond
Vandana Malwe: Nikki
Nikesh Soares: Nicholas
Namrata Pravin Parekh: Naomi**
—

Filming location
Mumbai, India
—

Format
35 mm
—

Awards for *John & Jane*
**European Media Art
Festival Award
  (Best Film, 2006)
Los Angeles Asian Pacific
Film Festival
  (Special Jury Prize, 2006)
Belfast Film Festival
  (Maysles Brothers Award,
  2007)
Indian National Film Awards
  (Best Non-Fiction Film,
  2007)**
— —

Naomi goes shopping.

Nicholas's wife meets her husband between shifts at a McDonald's.

Naomi in a call center cubicle.

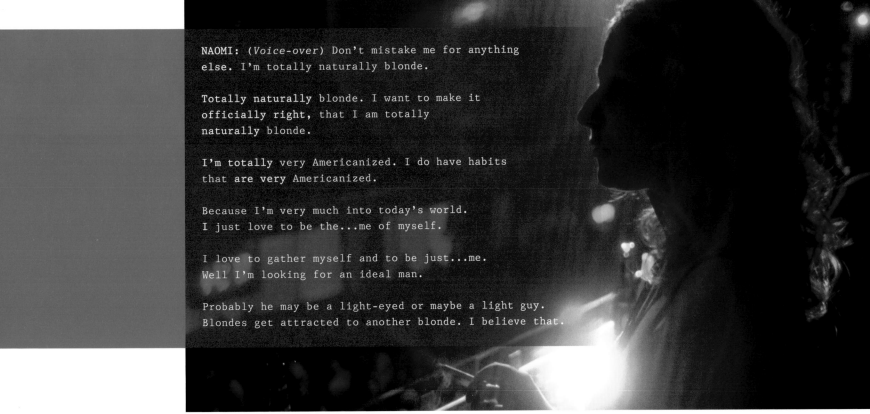

NAOMI: (*Voice-over*) Don't mistake me for anything
else. I'm totally naturally blonde.

Totally naturally blonde. I want to make it
officially right, that I am totally
naturally blonde.

I'm totally very Americanized. I do have habits
that **are very** Americanized.

Because I'm very much into today's world.
I just love to be the...me of myself.

I love to gather myself and to be just...me.
Well I'm looking for an ideal man.

Probably he may be a light-eyed or maybe a light guy.
Blondes get attracted to another blonde. I believe that.

Naomi in nightclub, searching for the perfect man.

Vargas (Argentino Vargas), a fifty-four-year-old man, has been released from jail in the province of Corrientes, Argentina. He wants to find his now adult daughter, who lives in a swampy and remote area. To get there, he must cross great distances in a small boat on the rivers, going deep into the jungle. Vargas, quiet and self-contained, possesses the restraint of those living close to nature. A deep mystery surrounds him, the people he encounters, and the places he goes through.

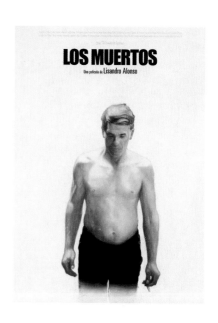

LISANDRO ALONSO
LOS MUERTOS

His last haircut in prison.

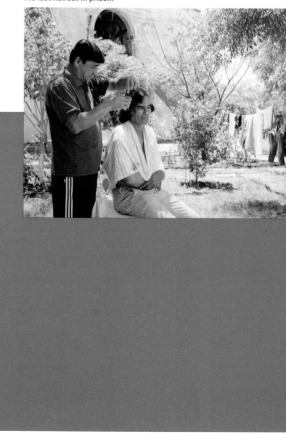

Vargas, with fellow inmates, sips tea on his last day in prison.

In the opening of *Los muertos* (2004), the camera floats smoothly through a forest, suggesting the subjective gaze of a character. Immersed in sounds so realistic they feel both tactile and dreamlike, we can see trees and catch glimpses of the sky that pierce the foliage like splinters. The shot progresses toward winding streams of murky water, only to reveal the bloody corpse of a child. Yet the camera moves on unwaveringly, even when somebody (whose face we don't see) passes carrying a large curved knife. It is as if nothing could stop the camera's ominous, measured movement, or as if nothing particularly attracts its attention, not even a second, possibly lifeless body lying sprawled on the leaves, almost hidden under a bush.

The mastery of this shot lies not in the virtuosity of its execution, but in that we see everything and don't know anything—or, rather, that we know only what we see. And although the next shot shows the main character, Argentino Vargas, sleeping in a squalid prison in Goya, Argentina, the film does not resolve whether the opening scene was a dream, the memory of an appalling killing, or any of several other possibilities.

The lack of distinction between the perspectives of the character, the director, and the film as a whole is based upon an approach called the free indirect subjective. Formulated by Pier Paolo Pasolini, the idea is the foundation of all modern cinema. In *Los muertos*, Lisandro Alonso integrates it into a system that is both narrative and poetic, governed by a concision that is deeply built into the film. Alonso considers almost all the methods used by conventional cinema to be obscene; he chooses to drop a character into the world at large, instead of creating a character and inventing a world for him. The film consequently gazes at Vargas without explaining him. We know nothing of his past, or why he went to prison, or how he came to gain his freedom and set off downriver by canoe (with the apparent aims of delivering a letter for another prisoner and, at the end of his journey, seeing his daughter).

It proves impossible to determine whether the film is based upon a character or a person. Are we watching Argentino Vargas the fictional character or Argentino Vargas playing himself? So, too, is it absurd to draw a line between fiction and documentary. In this sense, Alonso is responding to a style that has been imposed on contemporary cinema: the documentarization of fiction. In Alonso's "documentary fiction," shots are selected in real time, without any internal editing. Even when working within a system of clichés such as the road movie, he does not spotlight incidents that transform the protagonist; he shows him performing everyday activities or ones focused on survival. In the filmmaker's debut feature, *Freedom* (*La libertad*, 2001), he was already depicting the systematic actions of a lumberjack in such a way that we could observe exactly how a tree is chopped down, just as Argentino Vargas shows us, without the least didactic intent, how to navigate a river, how to find honey in the forest, and how to slaughter a baby goat. The viewer does not learn how to do these things, but rather has the feeling that he or she has done them before. And just as Argentino Vargas plays "Argentino Vargas," so does he replicate what he has done before.

With a story stripped of narrative progression and a protagonist devoid of psychological development, *Los muertos* advances instead by concentrating on the physical enigma of Argentino Vargas, without pretending to reveal anything. Words are no use, because Vargas is a monosyllabic character who only speaks when questioned or when he has no other option; verbal communication is replaced by his facial expressions, his silences, and, above all, his body. This is a body marked by time—whether on the alert like a crouching animal, or in action rowing down the river, or crudely satisfying his frustrated sexual desires with a prostitute. Vargas occupies the screen throughout the film, though we see only portions of his figure in the opening sequence and the similarly prolonged epilogue. In the latter shot, Vargas refrains from following a child into a house and goes off screen, his body replaced by a toy soccer player that has fallen to the floor. Once again we hear the strident sounds of nature, but it remains unclear whether following the boy would involve a repetition of the horrific opening scene.

Just as the film leaves all these questions to the viewer without offering the slightest trace of an answer, it also leaves unexplained the meaning of *los muertos* in the title. We don't know whether the dead are the bodies sprawled in the wood, the rural spaces we travel through, or simply all the film's characters, who seem to be alive but wander, silent and gloomy, like ghosts.

Vargas waits for the patrol car to arrive.

Year and place of birth
1975 Buenos Aires, Argentina
—

Lives and works in
Buenos Aires, Argentina
—

Filmography
2001 *Freedom (La libertad)*
2004 *Los muertos*
2006 *Fantasma*
2008 *Liverpool*
—

Director's awards
La libertad
Oslo Films from the
South Festival
    (FIPRESCI Prize, 2001)
International Film Festival
Rotterdam
    (FIPRESCI Prize – Special
    Mention, KNF Award –
    Special Mention, 2002)

Liverpool
Gijón International Film Festival
    (Grand Prix Asturias, 2008)
— —

Release date
2004
—

Country of release
Argentina
—

Language
Spanish
—

Running time
78 min.
—

Genre
Drama
—

Producers
Lisandro Alonso, 4L,
Fortuna Films, Slot Machine
—

Writer
Lisandro Alonso
—

Cinematographer
Cobi Migliora
—

Key cast
Argentino Vargas: Vargas
—

Filming location
Goya, Argentina
—

Format
35 mm
—

Awards for *Los Muertos*
Lima Latin American Film Festival
    (Critics Award, 2004)
Torino Film Festival
    (Best Film, 2004)
Viennale
    (FIPRESCI Prize, Reader Jury
    of the "Standard", 2004)
Karlovy Vary International
Film Festival
    (Independent Camera, 2005)
Yerevan International
Film Festival
    (Jury Special Prize, 2005)
— —

Vargas rides in the back of a truck after being released from prison.

Dropped off by truck drivers, Vargas begins the journey to find his daughter.

Varela provides Vargas with the boat Maria left for him.

VARGAS: Everything's fine,
it's fine.

VARELA: They told me you were
in jail there, that you killed
your brothers.

VARGAS: Yes, yes. But I've
forgotten it all, I'm over it now.
Do you have any water to give me?

VARELA: Yes, sure. Here you are
Vargas. Well...such a long time.
So then, you're off to the
island to meet up with Maria.

Sentenced to jail as a university student, Yusuf (Onur Saylak) is released on health grounds ten years later and returns home to his sick and elderly mother. In a tavern, Yusuf meets Eka (Megi Kobaladze), a beautiful young Georgian prostitute. Neither the timing nor circumstances are right for these two people from different worlds to be together. For all that, love becomes a final desperate attempt to grasp life and elude loneliness. With the 1990s as a backdrop, the film at once documents and criticizes a slice of recent history, exposing the irony, ruthlessness, and reality of the period.

ÖZCAN ALPER
AUTUMN

Yusuf plays with Onur, one of the only young people in the village.

Yusuf lies in his mother's garden after being released from prison.

How does one lie down to die? In *Autumn* (*Sonbahar*, 2008), young director Özcan Alper quietly recounts the state of mind of political prisoner Yusuf, who is released early because he is terminally ill. After serving ten years in jail for taking part in anti-government demonstrations when he was a university student, Yusuf returns home to his worried and affectionate elderly mother. The film takes December 19, 2000, in Turkey, as its starting point, when a bloody intervention took place against political prisoners who were protesting their isolation by fasting to the death. It is cruel and tragic that this intervention—during which thirty prisoners and convicts died alongside two soldiers—was dubbed "Operation Return to Life." As the film opens with archival video footage of this incident, we hear an official say to the prisoners, "Life is sweet." After this brief montage, the movie quickly jumps to Yusuf's release from prison and we follow him to his small mountain village east of the Black Sea, near the Georgian border.

In this context, *Autumn* picks up where Steve McQueen's *Hunger* (2008) left off. Both films revolve around the harsh lives of political prisoners. *Hunger* focuses on the final months of real-life figure Bobby Sands, an IRA martyr who went on a hunger strike that resulted in his death while imprisoned in 1970s Ireland. Challenging historical amnesia, *Autumn* was also inspired by real events and victims in Turkey. Both powerfully and skillfully shot, the films differ greatly in their cinematic presentations, though their interpretations are very similar. McQueen and Alper capture the essence of political stories and transfer them into a universal theme: the human condition under intense oppression. Both directors are concerned with how the human body relates to—and is tested by—the human psyche.

While *Hunger*'s brutality is at times unwatchable, *Autumn* is less horrific: it's as if Alper's story provides an alternate ending to *Hunger*, in which Bobby Sands survives and is released after all his deadly struggles. In Alper's vision, Yusuf is sinking slowly in a beautifully and calmly photographed landscape. He is quiet, as is the movie. Angel-like Eka, who shares Yusuf's interest in soulful Russian literature, describes him best: "You are very romantic, and it looks like you don't live in the present." A Georgian refugee who sells her body in order to support her family living across the border, she might have been a cliché in the hands of another director. But Alper's proposed possibility of love works on multiple levels, as he reflects on the clash of political idealisms and body politics.

The survival of these characters doesn't actually depend on the stamina of their bodies but of their hearts and minds—their souls. It is the soul that represents the permanent idea of resistance; the perishable body is disposable. However, the body is portrayed as a powerful weapon of resistance, especially when it is all one has. There is a desperation that drives Yusuf to take extreme control of his body, which is already damaged both physically and emotionally. In *Autumn*, we have to perceive Yusuf's silence as a symbol of resistance and integrity. At times, the silence is hard to bear, a cold wall that almost risks losing audiences, despite the film's gorgeous surroundings.

But with failing lungs, the inability to sleep, and the disconnect with his surroundings, Yusuf and his silence present a dignified melancholy from which all his old student-activist friends have moved on when they abandoned their socialist ideals. The film does not announce the death of idealism; on the contrary, it emphasizes the current sense of void, just as Yusuf's old comrade Mikail, who has built a safe life for himself in the village instead of dedicating himself to the cause, claims that "at least socialism existed back then." Yusuf, who is reminded by Eka that it's "such a shame" he's been "imprisoned in vain for socialism," doesn't bother to tell her that the developments in Turkey and Georgia in the early 1990s were completely different.

Meanwhile, as the film proves powerful in tackling the in-between state of hope and hopelessness, it also illustrates that the same seasons, the same struggles, prevail all around. The melancholic on-screen repentance by Uncle Vanya, claiming that "life is beautiful, no matter what," is a warning. Alper, who is renowned for his shorts and documentaries, recounts with a meditative cinematic narrative the trauma of a government's non-transparency. And at the same time, he reminds us of sacrifices made by those such as Yusuf and Bobby Sands, and softly states that struggle must not be futile.

Yusuf and Eka meet in a hotel room.

Year and place of birth
1975   Artvin, Turkey
—

Lives and works in
Istanbul, Turkey
—

Education
Istanbul University, Turkey
—

Filmography
2001   *Grandmother* (*Momi*)
         (short)
2002   *Voyage in the Time*
         With a Scientist
2005   *Rhapsody and Melancholy*
         in Tokai City (short)
2008   *Autumn* (*Sonbahar*)
— —

Release date
2008
—

Country of release
Turkey
—

Language
Turkish, Hemshin
—

Running time
106 min.
—

Genre
Drama
—

Producer
Serkan Açar
—

Writer
Özcan Alper
—

Cinematographer
Feza Çaldiran
—

Score
Yuri Ryadchenko, Ayşenur Kolivar
—

Key cast
Onur Saylak: Yusuf
Raife Yenigül: Gülefer
Megi Kobaladze: Eka
Serkan Keskin: Mikail
—

Filming locations
Hopa, Turkey
Çamlıhemşin, Turkey
—

Format
35 mm
—

Awards for *Autumn*
Adana Golden Boll Film Festival
     (Best Film, Best Supporting
     Actress, Special Jury Prize,
     2008)
Angers European First
Film Festival
     (Best Music, 2008)
Ankara International
Film Festival
     (Best Film, Best Director,
     Best Supporting Actress,
     Best Cinematographer,
     Best Editing, 2008)
Festival on Wheels
     (Silver Goose Award,
     SIYAD Award, 2008)
International Eurasia
Film Festival
     (NETPAC Jury Prize, 2008)

Locarno International
Film Festival
     (The Art & Essay CICAE
     Prize, 2008)
MedFilm Festival
     (Special Mention, 2008)
SIYAD (Turkish Film Critics'
Association) Awards
     (Best Film, Best Script,
     Best Actor, Best
     Cinematographer, 2009)
Sofia International
Film Festival
     (Best Director, 2009)
Tblisi International Film Festival
     (Silver Prometheus,
     Best Director, 2008)
Trento Film Festival
     (Best Film, 2009)
Yerevan International
Film Festival
     (FIPRESCI Prize, Special
     Jury Prize, 2009)
Yesilcam Awards,
Istanbul, Turkey
     (Turkcell Best Debut Film,
     Best Actor, 2009)
— —

EKA: You know, you seem like you don't live in
the present.

Silence for a while.

EKA: It's like you've walked off the pages
of a Russian novel.

Yusuf remains silent and Eka breaks the silence again.

EKA: Yusuf, you know what I've been thinking?
I wish I could leave everything behind and set
off on a long journey with you.

At end of the wooden pier, they stand as if they
have come to the edge of the world. The camera,
from afar, shoots them standing still while the sun
sinks over the sea.

Eka and Yusuf at the pier.

Yusuf meets an old friend and learns that his ex-girlfriend is married.

Mikail and Yusuf, on the mountains where they played as youths.

Yusuf walks along the pier on a cold autumn day.

In a rundown industrial park, Mao (Rabah Ameur-Zaïmeche), a Muslim boss, owns a small company that specializes in repairing trucks and pallets. Business is not doing well, so in order to maintain order among the other Muslim workers he decides to open a mosque. When Mao designates an imam without consulting his employees, he angers this small community and divides the workforce.

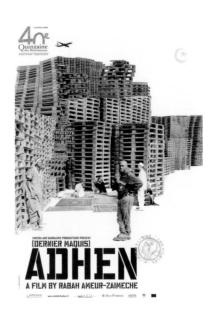

RABAH AMEUR-ZAIMECHE
ADHEN

A worker paints the pallets red.

Mao's pallet-repair company.

Adhen (*Dernier maquis*, 2008) is Rabah Ameur-Zaïmeche's third film, following *Wesh wesh, qu'est-ce qui se passe?* (2001) and *Back Home* (*Bled Number One*, 2006). He has established himself as one of the finest directors of his generation by offering political films that treat sensitive subjects such as religion, immigration, and employment without falling into a black-and-white view of the world or becoming explicit. The films express themselves through the quality of their direction and their poetic observation of the world around them.

Born in Algeria, Ameur-Zaïmeche grew up in a housing project on the outskirts of Paris. He set up his own company, Sarrazink Productions, in 1999, making films entirely of his own creation, serving as writer, director, and actor, a matter of both choice and necessity. His views of society and of making films, which sometimes clash with political correctness, resulted in timidity from financial backers. He makes guerrilla films, leading a small gang of collaborators to organize "pirate" shoots with a passion that makes up for a lack of money. One cannot help but admire artistic and human initiatives of this sort, especially when they're driven by such great talent.

Adhen is the story of a male community left high and dry in an industrial park on its last legs. Mao (Ameur-Zaïmeche) owns a small pallet-repair company. Business is bad, and the group's survival is threatened by the probable closure of the factory. All the employees are immigrants, from North or Sub-Saharan Africa. They are also all Muslims, and Mao relies on Islam to maintain social order,

suppress workers' demands, and increase productivity. He decides to build a mosque, and chooses one of his employees to be the imam. The lack of consultation provokes anger and division among the workers, and the crisis that shakes this little self-governing world is not only religious but also economic. When it becomes clear that Mao is going to close the garage, relations sour, leading to conflict and a strike. At the end of the film, Mao is alone in the deserted mosque.

Adhen is a film that had been in the director's thoughts since 2002. While writing the screenplay, he took a detour into painting as a way of preparing the project. The colors that would define the film soon declared themselves: yellow, and especially red, the color of the thousands of pallets that make up the film's spatial structure. To Ameur-Zaïmeche, red is the color of popular revolution, rebellion, and passion. It also has Communist associations that he doesn't try to hide. The boss's name, Mao, is both the diminutive of Mohammed, the prophet of Islam, and Mao Zedong, the leader of the Chinese revolution.

Like Jean-Luc Godard, Ameur-Zaïmeche aims to carry on a dialogue with cinema history, and with the other arts. *Wesh wesh, qu'est-ce qui se passe?* has a close relationship with language and speech, turning the courtyards of a housing project into real open-air theaters. *Back Home* was built around music and singing, and guitar solos played by the composer Rodolphe Burger in person form part of the development of the story.

The red pallets in *Adhen* do not, perhaps, have the same value as the little red books in Godard's

La Chinoise (1967), but they have a symbolic force that is both political and visual. They are a good example of Ameur-Zaïmeche's artistic and poetic treatment of the world he films. Some pallets were already present at the location where he chose to shoot; it was just a matter of adding more to expand the film's visual architecture. That's the underlying strength of Ameur-Zaïmeche's cinema; he creates a lyrical world from the concrete details of working lives. It's not a question of sacrificing beauty in the interest of didactic effectiveness. The film fits the setting, an industrial park, and not the other way around. The director and his crew invited themselves into an actual factory and worked side by side with its employees, who participated in the film as actors while continuing to do their usual jobs. This is a unique example of integrating an art project into a workplace.

Adhen is anything but a "do-good" film with a social conscience. On the contrary, Ameur-Zaïmeche's works express the complexity of human beings and their lives. He has produced a political film that addresses the crucial issue of the exploitation of Islam in the workplace without claiming to offer solutions or answers. The film has nothing to prove, and is hostile toward the smallest tendency to see things in black and white. In a film that celebrates those who are marginalized and oppressed, Mao is never presented as a bastard or an exploiter. He's a man who has to deal with the problems the owner of a small business faces. Ameur-Zaïmeche has borrowed Jean Renoir's saying: that all his characters have their reasons, and one cannot judge or condemn them.

Titi, recently converted to Islam, looks in the mirror before performing a self-circumcision.

Year and place of birth
1966   Beni-Zid, Algeria
—

Lives and works in
Montreuil, France
—

Education
**Sorbonne René Descartes,
    Paris, France**
—

Filmography
2001 *Wesh wesh, qu'est-ce qui
       se passe?*
2006 *Back Home
       (Bled Number One)*
2008 *Adhen (Dernier maquis)*
—

Director's awards
*Wesh wesh, qu'est-ce qui
se passe?*
**Prix Louis-Delluc
    (First Film, 2002)
Berlin International Forum
of New Cinema
    (Grand Prize, 2002)**

Back Home
**Cannes International
Film Festival
    (Un Certain Regard,
    Prix de la Jeunesse, 2006)**
— —

Release date
2008
—

Country of release
France
—

Language
French, Arabic
—

Running time
93 min.
—

Producer
Rabah Ameur-Zaïmeche
—

Writers
**Rabah Ameur-Zaïmeche,
Louise Thermes**
—

Cinematographer
Irina Lubtchansky
—

Score
Sylvain Rifflet
—

Key cast
**Rabah Ameur-Zaïmeche: Mao
Mamadou Kebe: Muezzin
Mamadou Koita: Village chief
Larbi Zekkour: Imam
Christian Milia-Darmezin: Titi
Salim Ameur-Zaïmeche, Abel
Jafri, Sylvain Roume:
    Mechanics**
—

Filming location
Villeneuve-le-Roi, France
—

Format
HD
—

Awards for *Adhen*
**Cannes International
Film Festival
    (Quinzaine des Réalisateurs,
    2008)
Dubai International Film Festival
    (Prix Spécial du Jury, 2008)**
— —

The industrial park where the men work.

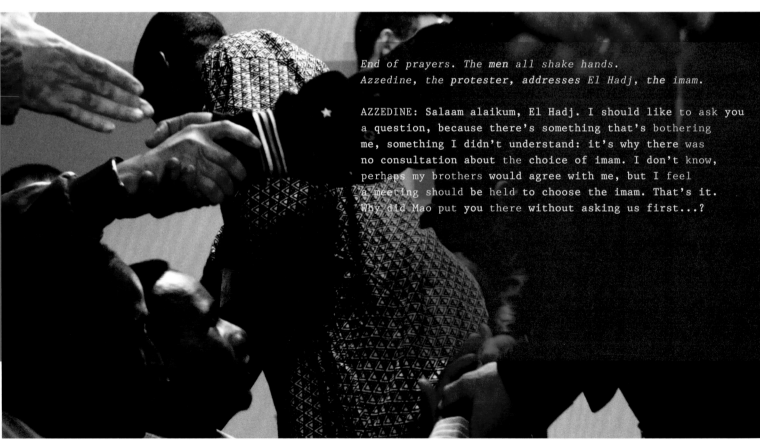

End of prayers. The **men** *all shake hands.
Azzedine,* the **protester**, addresses *El Hadj,* the **imam**.

AZZEDINE: Salaam alaikum, El Hadj. I should like to ask you
a question, because there's something that's bothering
me, something I didn't understand: it's why there was
no consultation about the choice of imam. I don't know,
perhaps my brothers would agree with me, but I feel
a meeting should be held to choose the imam. That's it.
Why did Mao put you there without asking us first...?

A worker expresses his disappointment over the imam selection.

Mao tries to keep the peace among his workers.

The mechanics would prefer Titi to be their imam.

George Simmons (Adam Sandler), a famous and wealthy funnyman, doesn't give much thought to how he treats people until a doctor delivers some shocking health news, forcing him to reevaluate his priorities with a little help from an aspiring stand-up comic, Ira Wright (Seth Rogen).

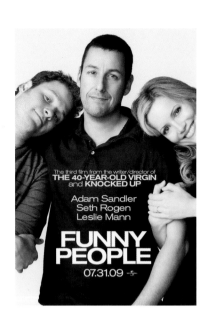

JUDD APATOW
FUNNY PEOPLE

George begins performing his stand-up again after the diagnosis.

George is leaving the doctor's office when a fan stops him for a photo.

There is what you might call an Apatow system. Judd Apatow is the most important comedy director to have emerged in American cinema in the 2000s. He's also a producer and screenwriter, and with his prolific contributions to film and television he has swiftly built up a list of humorous work with a new tone and style, ranging from parody to comedy of manners. Today's best comic actors gravitate toward him, and he has helped launched a whole new generation of funnymen: Jim Carrey, Ben Stiller, Will Ferrell, Steve Carrell, Seth Rogen, and Michael Cera.

Apatow has been fascinated by American comedy–from the Marx Brothers to *Saturday Night Live*–ever since childhood, when he began writing and performing his own sketches. He worked on many television series, including *The Ben Stiller Show* and *The Larry Sanders Show*. He also wrote and produced *Freaks and Geeks*, which was canceled after only eighteen episodes because of poor ratings. Yet it enjoyed great critical success, making Apatow a new comic director to watch.

When Apatow made the jump from television to cinema, he proved to be a skilled producer. He used television actors at the top of their game, giving them free rein to exercise their abundant imaginations and attitudes, encouraged by his laid-back, irreverent approach to schoolboy humor. Ben Stiller's *The Cable Guy* (1996), Adam McKay's *Anchorman: The Legend of Ron Burgundy* (2004), and Greg Mottola's *Superbad* (2007) swiftly became cult films, standout examples of the new American comedy.

Apatow's first two features as director, *The 40-Year-Old Virgin* (2005) and *Knocked Up* (2007), established him as the unrivaled voice of male friendship and trash humor. His characters are mainly immature young adults obsessed with sex, but who are at a loss when faced with the idea of settling down and starting a family. Yet that's often what happens to them in the end, reversions to the norm tinged with melancholy and disappointment. Apatow's heroes are ordinary people who dream about the things they don't have: love, sex, beauty.

Underlying tenderness, buried under a deluge of idiocies and scabrous gags, forms the heart of *Funny People* (2009), Apatow's third feature. His best and most ambitious work, it's also the strangest and most disconcerting, and both audiences and critics gave it a chillier reception than his previous films. They saw the somewhat deceptive film as disappointing, and as a sign that the director might be running out of steam. And it's possible that Apatow did go too far, delivering a nearly two-and-a-half-hour comedy that doesn't necessarily try to be funny and is stuffed with deliberately crude sketches, depressing themes, and characters who are often unsympathetic.

Funny People is Apatow's most autobiographical film to date, representing two points in his life: the young beginner and the celebrity in the grip of an existential crisis. George Simmons is a stand-up comedy star and a big name in Hollywood. He learns he has a rare illness and only a short time to live, but decides not to tell anyone. He attends a performance by Ira Wright, one of his admirers, and offers him the

opportunity to be his assistant and write sketches for him. It's a bonanza for the young man, who becomes the lonely star's friend and confidant. *Funny People* is the film that perhaps best represents Apatow's maturity, and his dialogue and actors blossom as well. Apatow has been criticized for his vulgar jokes, yet he is a craftsman of modern language, writing dialogue that is both realistic and scripted, close to Quentin Tarantino in this regard.

Apatow is remarkably successful at communicating the ambience of Los Angeles. His films are very contemporary but also create a subtle stylization of everyday life found in 1970s cinema. *Funny People* is strongly reminiscent of Hal Ashby's *The Last Detail* (1973), which, famous for its filthy dialogue, is one of Apatow's favorite films. The insider's view of the performer's world depicted in *Funny People* resembles the one found in Bob Fosse's films, while Sandler's character has something in common with the unbalanced, depressed antiheroes of Blake Edwards's most melancholy films. With *Funny People*, Apatow is looking above all for realism; the humor doesn't arise from funny situations but from the characters' views on life. Like *Superbad*, but in a more adult way, there is real tenderness and romanticism behind the cynicism.

Will the often misunderstood ambition of *Funny People* be followed up by a return to good commercial sense or by another more measured attempt at formal experimentation? Either way, it's safe to assume that Apatow's future work will include new, stimulating chapters, with life and nothing else being the source of the all-around filmmaker's inspiration.

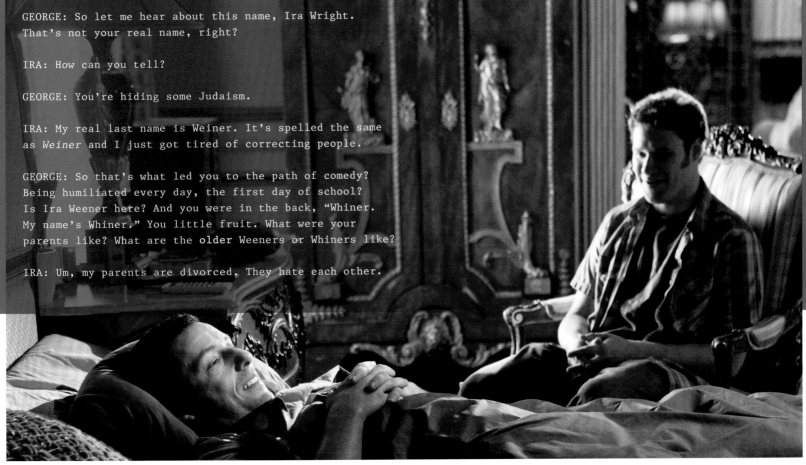

George insists that Ira talk him to sleep.

Year and place of birth
1967 Queens, N.Y., USA
—

Lives and works in
Los Angeles, Calif., USA
—

Filmography
2005 *The 40-Year-Old Virgin*
2007 *Knocked Up*
2009 *Funny People*
—

Director's awards
The 40-Year-Old Virgin
Critics' Choice Awards
   (Best Comedy Movie, 2006)

Knocked Up
People's Choice Awards
   (Favorite Movie Comedy,
   2008)
— —

Release date
2009
—

Country of release
USA
—

Language
English
—

Running time
146 min.
—

Genre
Comedy, Drama
—

Producers
**Judd Apatow, Barry Mendel,
Clayton Townsend**
—

Writer
Judd Apatow
—

Cinematographer
Janusz Kaminski
—

Score
**Jason Schwartzman,
Michael Andrews**
—

Key cast
Adam Sandler: George Simmons
Seth Rogan: Ira Wright
Leslie Mann: Laura
Eric Bana: Clarke
Jonah Hill: Leo Koenig
Jason Schwartzman:
   Mark Taylor Jackson
Aubrey Plaza: Daisy Danby
Maude Apatow: Mable
Iris Apatow: Ingrid
RZA: Chuck
Aziz Ansari: Randy
—

Filming locations
**Los Angeles, Calif., USA
San Francisco, Calif., USA
Sausalito, Calif., USA**
—

Format
35 mm
— —

Ira tries to help George, who starts to feel the effects of his disease.

After finding out he's sick, Laura tells George he was the love of her life.

Laura's husband Clarke, home early from a business trip, entertains George, Ira, and the kids over pizza.

Clarke attacks George for manipulating Laura with his illness.

Jackie (Kate Dickie) works as a CCTV (closed-circuit television) operator. Each day she watches over a small part of the world, protecting the people living their lives under her gaze. One day a man appears on her monitor, a man she thought she would never see again, a man she never wanted to see again. Now she has no choice—she is compelled to confront him.

April in the elevator at Red Road flats.

ANDREA ARNOLD
RED ROAD

An image on one of the security cameras of sunshine on the Red Road flats.

Andrea Arnold's striking debut, *Red Road* (2006), and her critically acclaimed second feature, *Fish Tank* (2009), have made the director heir to the realist tradition in British cinema. Think Ken Loach without the technical exercises and Alan Clarke with a sense of hope. Bringing a fresh spin to Brit-grit realism, Arnold boldly offers humanistic and intimate dramas about ordinary people without being overly sentimental.

Following the success of her Oscar-winning short, *Wasp* (2003), both her features focus on complex and conflicted female characters, and are set in council-estate ghettos in today's Britain; her films are about the struggles of love and personal loss in an indifferent society. In *Red Road*, the daily routine of Jackie, a lonely and emotionally disconnected CCTV operator, immediately generates a sense of insecurity and mystery. Dark in every way and resolute not to give plot away easily, the film works as a thriller with an escalating feeling that something more profound lies just beneath the surface. In the end, we are reminded that confronting tragedies can be tricky, and that grief can be a frightening emotional state.

A study of the post-pubescent female psyche, *Fish Tank* (2008) is a social-realism film that emphasizes fifteen-year-old Mia's struggles both at and away from home. In lieu of her previous dark visual style, for this movie Arnold lets the sunshine of summer days in. This choice highlights Mia's desert-like surroundings. Angry and neglected, she is inconsistent, confused, and in need of love like any other teenager. Along with the script's humor and agony, the film's shooting and editing style skilfully display those inconsistencies

in Mia's vulnerable existence. Her life in a ghetto can be equated to dancing alone on a slippery and restricted stage. In both of Arnold's films, the trigger of the action comes as a stranger, a man from the outside. In *Fish Tank*, it is her mother's handsome and charming new boyfriend, Connor, who arrives with the promise of a father figure. In *Red Road*, the identity of the man is more suspicious, in the spirit of a tense thriller.

Red Road is the first part of a projected trilogy under the Advance Party banner, a Scottish-Danish film concept, which emerged as an offshoot of the Dogme 95 movement started by Danish directors Lars von Trier and Thomas Vinterberg in the late 1990s. Despite the rules and possible limitations dictated by this new movement, Arnold expertly manages to make the film her own.

Arnold creates a hypnotic and insecure atmosphere in which the main character, a CCTV operator mourning the loss of her husband and child, floats in despair and remains distant to her surroundings. That is, until she detects a face on the screen—a man linked to her past. Jackie (superbly played by Kate Dickie) begins to spy on him using the surveillance system as her joystick, and ends up in Red Road, the high-rise tower blocks located in Glasgow. Neither the many cameras above Glasgow nor the grimy housing estate Red Road are fictitious. It's everyday Britain. Built in the 1960s, these towers were meant to be a welcome improvement in living conditions. Scheduled for demolition, these run-down towers, whose residents are now largely refugees from

Africa, Asia, and beyond, symbolize broken dreams and the fall of an empire.

While Jackie monitors this harsh neighborhood we share her experience through the CCTV cameras. The Orwellian Big Brother legacy is clear, but at some point our voyeurism shifts toward her. In an almost post-apocalyptic, sci-fi atmosphere, our curiosity is piqued by Jackie's mysterious obsession with Clyde. She meets him in a pub, and a passionate sex scene follows. Clyde eventually discovers that neither love nor lust is the motivation behind her actions. Both leads are very subtle yet brimming with emotion, even when those emotions are shut off. Alongside Dickie, Tony Curran as Clyde gives a nuanced performance, adding depth to his ex-convict character. This drama of obsession in a working-class setting succeeds as a meditation of loss and redemption.

Like *Red Road*, *Fish Tank* also becomes a tale of revenge, yet with a betrayed Mia still able to connect with her inner child just as the redemptive final note arrives. Arnold's conflicted, lonely, and vulnerable young women are powerful and willful, whether or not revenge drives their actions. Arnold's bold and beautiful approach makes her one of the most innovative British filmmakers working today.

Jackie looks around Clyde's flat.

Year and place of birth
1969　Erith, UK
—
Lives and works in
London, UK
—
Filmography
1998　*Milk* (short)
2001　*Dog* (short)
2003　*Wasp* (short)
2006　*Red Road*
2008　*Fish Tank*
—
Director's awards
Dog
Brief Encounters
　(The Jameson Award, 2001)
Regensburg Short Film Week
　(Jury Prize, 2003)
Videomedeja International
Film Festival
　(First Prize, 2003)

Wasp
Stockholm International
Film Festival
　(Best Short Film, 2003)
Cracow International Short
Film Festival
　(Principal Prize, Government
　Prize Best Film, 2004)
Palm Springs International
ShortFest
　(Best of Festival, 2004)
Worldwide Short Film Festival
　(Best Live Action Fiction
　Film, 2004)
Academy Awards
　(Best Live Action Short, 2005)
Sundance Film Festival
　(Jury Prize in International
　Short Filmmaking, 2005)

Fish Tank
British Independent Film Awards
　(Best Director, 2009)
— —

Release date
2006
—
Country of release
UK
—
Language
English
—
Running time
117 min.
—
Genre
Drama
—

Producer
Carrie Comerford
—
Writer
Andrea Arnold
—
Cinematographer
Robbie Ryan
—
Key cast
Kate Dickie: Jackie
Tony Curran: Clyde
Martin Compston: Stevie
Natalie Press: April
Paul Higgins: Avery
Andrew Armour: Alfred
—
Filming location
Glasgow, Scotland
—
Format
HD
—

Awards for *Red Road*
British Academy of Film and
Television Awards Scotland
　(Best Film, Best Actor,
　Best Actress, Best Director,
　Best Screenplay, 2006)
British Independent
Film Awards
　(Best Actor in a British
　Independent Film,
　Best Actress in a British
　Independent Film, 2006)
Cannes International
Film Festival
　(Grand Jury Prize, 2006)
London Film Critics'
Circle Awards
　(British Newcomer
　of the Year, 2006)
The Times BFI 50th London
Film Festival
　(BFI Sutherland Trophy
　for Most Original and
　Imaginative First Film, 2006)

British Academy of Film and
Television Awards
　(The Carol Foreman Award
　for Best Newcomer
　to British Film, 2007)
Göteborg International
Film Festival
　(The Ingmar Bergman
　Film Award, 2007)
Miami International Film Festival
　(FIPRESCI Prize, Special
　Jury Award, 2007)
Philadelphia Film Festival
　(Best First Time Director,
　2007)
— —

Jackie watches Clyde, April, and Stevie on camera.

Jackie goes to meet Clyde at the pub.

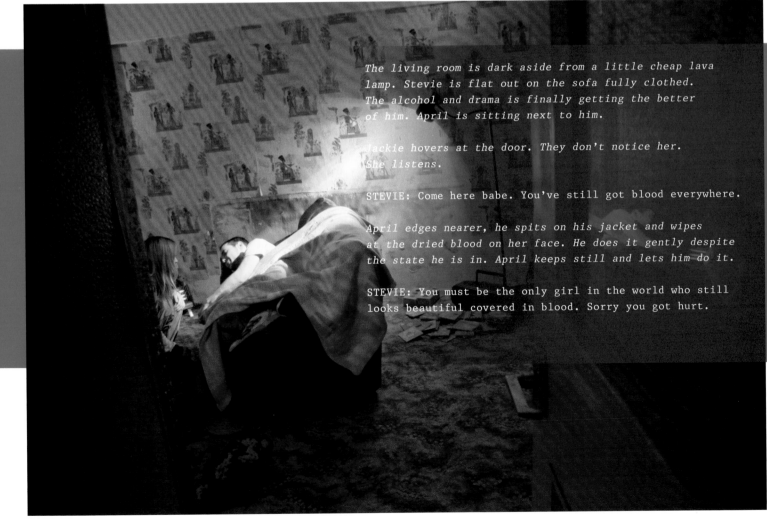

The living room is dark aside from a little cheap lava lamp. Stevie is flat out on the sofa fully clothed. The alcohol and drama is finally getting the better of him. April is sitting next to him.

Jackie hovers at the door. They don't notice her. She listens.

STEVIE: Come here babe. You've still got blood everywhere.

April edges nearer, he spits on his jacket and wipes at the dried blood on her face. He does it gently despite the state he is in. April keeps still and lets him do it.

STEVIE: You must be the only girl in the world who still looks beautiful covered in blood. Sorry you got hurt.

April and Stevie talk after the fight.

Takua Pa is a small town in the south of Thailand. Since the tsunami of 2004, it has become a town of sadness. Young people ride motorcycles in circles. Old people remember better times in the past. One day a stranger comes to town and falls in love with a woman who works at the hotel where he is staying. Their love is strong, but her brother disapproves, and trouble brews.

ADITYA ASSARAT
WONDERFUL TOWN

TON: Can I help you with this?

NA: Oh no, it's my personal things.

Ton walks over and picks up a pink shirt that has fallen off the laundry line. It is a sexy-looking shirt with spaghetti straps.

TON: Whose is this?

She hurries over and grabs it from him.

TON: It's the same color as your face.

She is embarrassed.

TON: Let me help you with this...

Ton and Na take down laundry on the roof of the hotel.

Thai filmmaker Aditya Assarat took the international film-festival circuit by storm with his fictional feature debut, *Wonderful Town* (2007). In Thailand, critics hailed it as the best feature film of the year, and Assarat was welcomed into the elite circle of leading Southeast Asian directors.

Wonderful Town was inspired by the region of Takua Pa, a district of Phang Nga Province nestled on the shores of the Andaman Sea in southern Thailand. The 2004 tsunami killed an estimated eight thousand people in the area. Assarat visited Takua Pa in 2006 and discovered to his surprise that, contrary to the images of destruction he had seen on the television news, the region was very peaceful and beautiful. The roads were clean, the houses had been rebuilt, and the coconut trees swayed in the breeze. It seemed to Assarat that, after the tsunami had swept everything away, the people of Takua Pa were trying their best to erase the memory of the devastation from their land.

Assarat dug deeper and found that, although the damage appeared to have healed on the surface, the locals of Takua Pa clearly bore the scars of the disaster. People still seemed to be walking around in a daze, as if they had suddenly awoken in a strange place and could not find their way home. As the process of rebuilding rolled on, emotions remained paralyzed. In this sense the title *Wonderful Town* is ironic, and Assarat illuminates the deep wounds left by the tsunami, drawing comparisons between the physical reconstruction outside and the emotional reconstruction slowly occurring within people.

The film concentrates on the interlaced relationships of three main characters: Ton, a young architect sent from Bangkok to help rebuild a beach complex in a devastated coastal town; Na, a local woman who runs the small hotel where Ton stays; and Na's brother Wit, who is the town's gang leader. Ton and Na begin a discreet love affair, and Wit carefully keeps an eye on them. One day Wit overhears Ton on the telephone with his old lover, telling her that he will leave Na and come back to her. Enraged, Wit is driven to commit murder, and the film's action ends with his dumping Ton's body into a river.

In essence, *Wonderful Town* portrays the despair and pain caused by circumstances beyond one's control, and how both old and new relationships are affected by suffering rooted in the past. Through the stark contrast of scenic imagery and the tragedy of a love story between a stranger and a local, the director portrays the lingering sadness of Takua Pa, a place where love or happiness can no longer blossom as they once did. The tragedies of the past prevent the couple from building a future.

In order to plumb the depths of sadness that lie beneath the sunny, laid-back atmosphere of Takua Pa, Assarat uses subtle camera movements to capture the quiet gazes of his characters. Often a static camera observes the serene village scenery, but the still perspective is then disturbed by a highly emotional encounter, such as when Ton and Na are making love. Ton is presented as an external catalyst who triggers buried emotions and is perhaps emblematic of the uncaring outside world. Na meanwhile is trapped inside this coastal town, where no one is allowed to escape. One of the most heartfelt moments of *Wonderful Town* is when Na attends a funeral. The camera focuses on her as she burns incense, while behind her the other mourners are kept out of focus, resembling hazy ghosts. The film is reminiscent of *The Stranger* by Albert Camus in its treatment of dramatic events as mundane or insignificant. Yet balancing this remove is the deep weariness caused by the weight of existentialist burdens present throughout the film.

Assarat received postproduction funding from the Pusan International Film Festival to finish *Wonderful Town*, which was shot in HD and transferred to film afterward. His visual style is subtle and introspective as he presents the beauty of nature in contrast to the town's sites of ruin and its suffocating customs. The result of the sensitively juxtaposed images and emotions is the potent sentiment that life continues on, despite what has been swept away.

Na rides a bicycle through town.

Ton and Na kiss on the roof of the hotel.

Year and place of birth
1972 Bangkok, Thailand
—

Lives and works in
Bangkok, Thailand
—

Education
**University of Southern
    California, Los Angeles,
    USA**
—

Filmography
2000 *Motorcycle* (short)
2002 *Raw Velvet*
2003 *Waiting* (short)
2004 *Boy Genius* (short)
2005 *The Sigh* (short)
2005 *3 Friends (Ma-Mee)*
2007 *Silencio* (short)
2007 *Wonderful Town*
2009 *Sawasdee Bangkok*
    (short)
2009 *Phuket* (short)
2010 *High Society*
—

Director's awards
Motorcycle
Chicago International
Film Festival
    (Gold Hugo – Best Student
    Narrative Short Film
    15 Minutes and Over, 2000)
Shorts International
Film Festival
    (Best Short Film –
    Student, 2000)
Aspen Shortsfest
    (Special Jury Award, 2001)
San Francisco International
Film Festival
    (Golden Gate Award –
    Bay Area Film & Video,
    Short Works, 2001)
— —

Release date
2007
—

Country of release
Thailand
—

Language
Thai
—

Running time
92 min.
—

Genre
Drama
—

Producers
**Soros Sukhum,
Jetnipith Teerakulchanyut**
—

Writer
Aditya Assarat
—

Cinematographer
Umpornpol Yugala
—

Score
Koichi Shimizu, Zai Kunung
—

Key cast
**Anchalee Saisoontorn: Na
Supphasit Kansen: Ton
Dul Yaambunying: Wit**
—

Filming locations
**Takua Pa, Thailand
Khao Lak, Thailand
Phang-Nga, Thailand**
—

Format
HD
—

Awards for *Wonderful Town*
Pusan International Film Festival
    (New Currents Award, 2007)
Deauville Asian Film Festival
    (Jury Prize, 2008)
Hong Kong International
Film Festival
    (FIPRESCI Prize, 2008)
IndieLisboa Film Festival
    (Grand Prize, 2008)
International Film Festival
Rotterdam
    (Tiger Award, 2008)
Las Palmas Film Festival
    (Jury Prize, 2008)
San Francisco Film Festival
    (Jury Prize, 2008)

Subhanahongsa Thailand
National Film Awards
    (Best Picture,
    Best Director, Best Script,
    Best Cinematography,
    Best Production Design,
    2008)
Taipei Film Festival
    (Jury Prize, 2008)
Yerevan International
Film Festival
    (Silver Apricot Prize, 2008)
— —

Ton and Na talk in the field as trouble builds around them.

Ton turns to look at the motorcycle gang following him.

The town of Takua Pa.

Ton walks on the beach.

When Lionel (writer/director Lionel Baier) learns by chance that his family originates from Poland, a chain of events is set off that will change his life forever. He and his sister, Lucie (Natacha Koutchoumov), make their way to Eastern Europe in a "borrowed" car, not completely sure if they are descendants of a Polish family. However, getting involved in a car chase in Slovenia is a sure thing, as is the stolen car, a white wedding, and false passports. The road to Warsaw turns into the adventure the siblings have been longing for. And somewhere in Poland, a horse drowns every night.

LIONEL BAIER
STEALTH

Lionel and Lucie arrive in Auschwitz, Poland.

Ewa, at the family picnic, as Lionel and his mother look on.

When Swiss cinema is the topic of conversation, every well-informed cinema buff will immediately mention the work of the Groupe Cinque, a nouvelle vague of sorts that emerged in French-speaking Switzerland in the 1960s and included Alain Tanner, Claude Goretta, and Michel Soutter. In the same way today, a new generation of francophone directors appear to be simultaneously making their mark on the screen: Jean-Stéphane Bron, with *Mais im Bundeshuus – Le génie helvétique* (2003) and *Mon frère se marie* (2006); Ursula Meier, with *Home* (2008); Frédéric Mermoud, with *Complices* (2009); Fulvio Bernasconi, with *Fuori dalle corde* (2007); and Lionel Baier.

Baier, born in Lausanne to Swiss parents of Polish extraction, turned to cinema at a very early age. By 1992 he was programming and co-managing the Cinéma Rex in Aubonne, a small town between Lausanne and Rolle. From 1995 to 1999 he studied literature at the University of Lausanne, and in 2002 he was appointed head of the film department of the Ecole cantonale d'art de Lausanne (known as ECAL), one of Switzerland's five professional schools, where many of his colleagues also trained.

His brilliant career as a cinephile eventually transformed into an equally remarkable one as a filmmaker. He started shooting as early as 1999, first making a short with the appropriate title *Mignon à croquer*, and following up in 2000 with a medium-length documentary, *The Pastor's (My Personal Vision of Things)* (*Celui au pasteur [ma vision personnelle des choses]*). As the title suggests, the film focuses on his experience as the (gay) son of a Protestant minister in the canton of Vaud, just as *The Parade (Our Story)* (*La Parade [notre histoire]* 2002) documents the 2000 Gay Pride march in Valais, a predominantly Catholic area.

After another short film that referenced his personal and cinema antecedents, *Mon père c'est un lion* (2002), whose title says it all, he made his first feature, *Stupid Boy* (*Garçon stupide*, 2004), which won him great critical acclaim and was well received in France. In 2006, he made *Stealth* (*Comme des voleurs [à l'est]*), a rite-of-passage comedy about origins, journeys, the pleasures of the quest, and the love of cinema, in which he plays the lead character.

In the film, Lionel, a thirty-year-old journalist, the son of a minister from Vaud, learns by chance that his family may have originally come from Poland. He starts questioning his father, who is evasive about their Slav origins. The idea of being from Poland offers Lionel the dimensions of fiction and exoticism that his life had seemed to lack. He learns the language, discovers Switzerland's Polish community, and trades General Guisan for Lech Walesa. He and his sister, Lucie, "borrow" a car from the radio station where he works and they go off "like thieves" in search of their roots. Heading eastward, to Slovakia, Silesia, and Warsaw, Lionel sets out on an adventure of some sort in this existential road movie, which is a journey into himself and, necessarily, into cinema.

In Baier's films there are (almost) always direct links to his own life story, as if at every stage an autobiographical thread is being woven between the filmmaker and his work, both in the elements that are real (the minister father, the name, homosexuality, and the love of writing) and those that are invented. "I don't want to say it's my story, because the character I play in the film isn't me, even if he has the same name as me. He's a fictional character, with whom I share a certain number of truths . . . And the film tells something about this merging. In [*Stealth*], the character Lionel Baier is a construction. It's an open question that belongs to the real Lionel. But that's true of all 'auteur' films that tell something about their maker. For my part, it's true that I really enjoy confusing the issue . . . "

Baier has since made a fourth feature film, *Another Man* (*Un autre homme*, 2008), a philosophical comedy that fared well in competition at the Locarno International Film Festival and has been enjoying success throughout the world. Baier was mentioned in the same breath as Alain Tanner (for his wit), François Truffaut (for his treatment of love), and Eric Rohmer (for his fondness of language). But his films also have something of Jean-Pierre Melville and Howard Hawks. As a great cinephile, Baier clearly draws nourishment from the history of the seventh art, but he does so in order to find a new, slightly tongue-in-cheek way to tell a life story.

In my opinion, Baier is unquestionably one of the best filmmakers in Switzerland (and beyond), a lover of cinema who also knows how to take a risk and make films for little or no money, out of the strength of his desire rather than in any expectation of security. It is precisely this way of making films "like a thief" that gives Baier's films their incomparable energy.

Lionel and Lucie look around the flea market.

Year and place of birth
1975   Lausanne, Switzerland
—
Lives and works in
Lausanne, Switzerland
Paris, France
—
Education
University of Lausanne,
    Switzerland
—
Filmography
1999   *Mignon à croquer* (short)
2000   *The Pastor's*
        (My Personal Vision of
        Things) (Celui au Pasteur
        (ma vision personnelle
        des choses))
2001   *The Parade (Our Story)*
        (La Parade (notre
        histoire))
2002   *Mon père, c'est un lion*
        (short)
2004   *Stupid Boy*
        (Garçon Stupide)

2006   *Stealth (Comme des*
        voleurs [a l'est])
2007   *Continuité nationale*
        (short)
2008   *Another Man*
        (Un autre homme)
2008   *Lausanne-Bellerive*
        (short)
—
Director's awards
Stupid Boy
The Barcelona International
Gay & Lesbian Film Festival
    (Diversity Award, 2005)
New European Film Festival
of Vitoria-Gasteiz
    (Best European Film Director,
    2005)
— —

Release date
2007
—
Country of release
France
—
Language
French/Polish
—
Running time
112 min.
—
Genre
Comedy
—

Producer
Robert Boner
—
Writer
Lionel Baier
—
Cinematographer
Séverine Barde
—
Score
Maurice Ravel, Dominique Dalcan
—
Key cast
Lionel Baier: Lionel
Natacha Koutchoumov: Lucie
Alicja Bachleda-Curus: Ewa
Stéphane Rentznik: Serge
Michal Rudnicki: Stan
Bernabé Rico: Liberto
Luc Andrié: Victor
Anne-Lise Tobagi: Madeleine
—

Filming locations
Paris, France
Trstená, Slovakia
Andalucia, Spain
Aubonne, Switzerland
Lausanne, Switzerland
Payerne, Switzerland
Ressudens, Switzerland
Krakow, Poland
Silesia, Poland
Warsaw, Poland
Zakopane, Poland
—
Format
DV
—

Awards for *Stealth*
Mannheim-Heidelberg
International Filmfestival
    (Special Award of the Jury,
    2006)
B-EST International Film Festival
    (Special Award of the Jury,
    2007)
Châtenay-Malabry Film Festival
    (Youth Prize, 2007)
Gardanne Film Festival
    (Youth Prize, 2007)
Zinegoak International Festival
of Gay and Lesbian Cinema
    (Best Feature Film, 2008)
— —

"Nasze zdrowie!" ("To us!")

At the Warsaw Archives, Lionel tells Lucie that someone has checked out the book they need.

Lionel and Lucie's farewell at the train station.

LIONEL: What are you going to do about your little guest?

LUCIE: What little...Oh...I don't know. It takes two...if I want to keep him from crossing Europe in a beat-up car...Afterwards, we'll see.

LIONEL: After what? Where are we headed?

LUCIE: Continue writing. This is just the beginning.

LIONEL: I'll miss you. Not because you're my sister, but because we both come from the bottom of the river. I love you. Don't let them take advantage of you.

In response to American consumerism comes Sophie Barthes's clever comedy in which souls are extracted and traded as commodities. Balancing on a tightrope between deadpan humor and pathos, reality and fantasy, the film presents Paul Giamatti as himself, agonizing over his interpretation of Chekhov's *Uncle Vanya*. He stumbles upon a solution via a company that promises to alleviate suffering by extracting one's soul. Giamatti enlists their services only to discover that his bears a close resemblance to a chickpea. Complications ensue when a talentless Russian soap-opera actress borrows Giamatti's soul, sending him on a wild goose chase to reclaim it.

SOPHIE BARTHES
COLD SOULS

Paul and Dr. Flintstein observe the replicas of some frozen souls.

I think it's safe to say that Sophie Barthes has established herself as a genuine writer and director of science fiction. However, we're not talking the H. G. Wells or Isaac Asimov variety. In fact, I'm not even sure that the award-winning Barthes would want to be classified as being within the confines of such a genre, but all the same, she deserves the mention. Showing an understanding of the work and teachings of Carl Jung, Anton Chekhov, Luis Buñuel, and even Woody Allen, Barthes has created not one but two intriguing takes on alternate reality in which the way we feel and act can easily be bought, sold, and borrowed.

Born in France, and raised in South America and the Middle East, Barthes's worldview was shaped at a very early age. This led her to study at Columbia University's School of International and Public Affairs before making her foray into filmmaking. Along with DP and director Andrij Parekh, Barthes first made a documentary about Yemen, followed by the short *Snowblink* (2005), which was shot in the Ukraine. Her third short, *Happiness* (2006), was my original intro-duction to Barthes, and proved to be a good testing ground for what inevitably came next in long form.

Happiness is about a middle-aged prophylactics factory worker who purchases a box of happiness, but soon returns it because she can't figure out how to use it. Shot in Boston, the film deals with abstractions—the obvious one being an actual box of happiness—and was met very favorably on the film-festival circuit, receiving laughs from audiences around the world. Barthes came to Park City to screen the film, and it was just a matter of time before she ended up as part of the Sundance family with her future feature endeavor: the Sundance selection, *Cold Souls* (2009).

The future of *Cold Souls* was cemented by the Sundance Screenwriters and the Directors Lab, which helped Barthes find direction for the piece, and encouraged her to write the best story possible. Starring Paul Giamatti as himself, the film centers on the neurotic actor who is confused and ultimately anxious over his interpretation of *Uncle Vanya*. Almost serendipitously, he reads a magazine article about a company that promises to alleviate suffering by deep-freezing one's soul, and, with some level of hesitation, he decides to have his own removed (which ends up resembling a measly chickpea). However, even with the absence of such a heavy "weight," Giamatti soon realizes that the soul has a lot more to do with his happiness than his aching pain, though not until hijinks ensue involving a Russian bully, a talentless soap actress, and a soul-trafficking "mule," all looking for a piece of his inner core.

Barthes pulls off *Cold Souls*' dystopian society by staying within the realms of reality. This isn't the distant future, or another world entirely, but rather a city with a few alterations—like a soul shop, for one. In some ways, this setup required Barthes to do some extra thinking about how tiny shifts ultimately affect the world and its inhabitants in sometimes the subtlest of ways. Unlike most science fiction fare, Barthes's script doesn't rely on heavy special effects or big-time plotting to cover up the absence of character. On the contrary, it tells a story fueled by personality, pathos, wit, and humor.

Originally spawned from a dream Barthes had in which Woody Allen loses his soul, her script was written expressly for Giamatti, who agreed to come on board shortly after reading it; eventually David Strathairn and other veteran performers followed suit. One can argue that Barthes had it easy working with such an expert cast, but for any first-time writer/director, there's a level of confidence that must be had to clearly communicate one's vision, and that was surely a daunting, albeit fruitful, task for Barthes.

Taking a cue from abstract theater and surrealist cinema, *Cold Souls* is stuffed with philosophical subtext and symbolism, if audiences dare to peel the layers back that far. Giamatti follows an arc, finding his life has a deeper meaning after all. It's Barthes's intelligence and perceptivity that keep the film in check by never providing easy or empty answers to the film's many questions—metaphysical and psychological; instead, it simply responds by posing another question. The film's level of interpretation remains pretty infinite thanks in part to its somewhat minimalist structure and style (it's a beautiful movie; it just doesn't rely on a lot of editing and lighting tricks).

All of this helps prove that Sophie Barthes is here to stay, and inevitably here to shine. The filmmaker not only knows how to capture an audience's attention but its imagination and philosophical prowess as well. And whether or not she sticks to this genre or ventures to another one altogether, her future work remains some of the most anticipated in the independent film community. You can almost feel the verity of her promise deep in the soul—chickpea-sized or not.

Nina lies in the Russian Soul Extractor machine, while Sveta checks the shape of a soul.

Year and place of birth
1974   France
—
Lives and works in
New York, N.Y., USA
—
Education
Columbia University School
   of the Arts Film Division,
   New York, N.Y., USA
Columbia University Graduate
   School of International
   and Public Affairs,
   New York, N.Y., USA
—
Filmography
2004   *Snowblink* (short)
2006   *Happiness* (short)
2009   *Cold Souls*
—

Director's awards
Happiness
British Academy of Film and
   Television Arts Los Angeles
   (Short Film Award, 2006)
Festival Internacional de Cine
Expresion en Corto International
   (Best Live Action Short, 2006)
Nantucket Film Festival
   (Showtime Tony Cox Award
   for Best Screenplay in a
   Short Film, 2006)
Palm Springs ShortFest
   (Best Live Action Short,
   2006)
— —

Release date
2009
—
Country of release
USA
—
Language
English, Russian
—
Running time
101 min.
—
Genre
Surreal Comedy
—

Producers
Daniel Carey, Elizabeth Giamatti,
Paul Mezey, Andrij Parekh,
Jeremy Kipp Walker
—
Writer
Sophie Barthes
—
Cinematographer
Andrij Parekh
—
Score
Dickon Hinchliffe
—

Key cast
Paul Giamatti: Paul
David Strathairn: Dr. Flintstein
Dina Korzun: Nina
Katheryn Winnick: Sveta
Lauren Ambrose: Stephanie
Emily Watson: Claire
—
Filming locations
New York, N.Y., USA
St. Petersburg, Russia
—
Format
35 mm
—

Awards for *Cold Souls*
Nantucket Film Festival
   (Showtime Tony Cox Award
   for Best Screenplay, 2006)
Hamburg International
Film Festival
   (Critics' Prize, 2009)
Karlovy Vary International
Film Festival
   (Best Actor, 2009)
— —

Paul explains to his wife, Claire, that his soul has been smuggled to Russia.

PAUL: A Russian actress who happens
to be the wife of some big shot
is toying with my soul. That's all
I know...

CLAIRE: Are you sure you don't
want to bring the lawyers or Steve
or Max?

PAUL: No lawyers, no managers,
no agent, no publicists. This is
no one's business.

Paul tells Nina that his soul is dried out.

Paul explores his soul and encounters strange androgynous creatures.

In Bosnia, 1997, only six women, one old man, and a few children live in the war-torn village of Slavno. Their families have been killed, though their bodies were never found. Living with the memories of their missing loved ones, the villagers have created a very special world, one in which the absent are still very much present. One day, two businessmen show up unexpectedly, demanding that the residents leave Slavno in return for money. But when a sudden storm traps them in town, it forces the outsiders to face something bigger than anticipated—the truth.

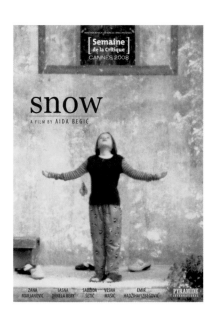

AIDA BEGIC
SNOW

Safija finishes her morning prayers.

Aida Begić was sixteen years old when the siege of Sarajevo, her hometown, began in 1992. The city was cut off from the outside world for nearly four years, hardly the typical way for a European teenager to grow up in the 1990s. Begić, however, says that those years turned out to be pivotal, enabling her to understand how art, culture, film, and theater become an essential form of sustenance for a populace living in such extreme conditions.

Following a series of internationally celebrated short films that bore witness to her rich talent for dark humor, *Snow* (*Snijeg*, 2008) is the young Bosnian director's feature debut, which allowed her to address the trauma of experiencing violence in an incisive and unsentimental way. Set in the fall of 1997, two years after the war ended, only six women, one old man, and a few children still live in the small east Bosnian village of Slavno. Their sons, fathers, and husbands have died in the war, although their exact fate still remains unclear. The charades that the women play, passing time by imitating their menfolk, and their entertaining the childish hope that they might somehow have survived and come back someday, keep the presence of the male villagers very much alive.

While prepping the film, Aida Begić and her team needed a long time to find a suitable location. Many of the ruined villages in eastern Bosnia are still full of mines, the dreamlike beauty of the landscape making it easy to forget that it was here, not far from Srebrenica, that the most brutal "ethnic cleansing" took place.

The women in the village are connected by their experiences and knowledge of such atrocities:

Alma, a young widow, wears a headscarf and fulfills her religious obligations; Nadija is afraid to tell her children that their father won't be coming home; Safija, Alma's mother-in-law, waits on the sofa for her own end to come; and Sabrina wants to get away as quickly as possible, motivated by the vague hope that a Swedish man once awoke in her.

The things they have experienced have bonded them together, and the film avoids using any grand words to convey this. Begić doesn't even attempt to address the indescribable and the unspeakable by means of dialogue, showing them instead through the strangely ritualized ways in which the characters behave: the way grandmother Jasmina silently weaves every piece of cloth she can find into the rag rug she's making; the way one little boy's hair grows every night before it is cut off again in the morning; the way Alma relentlessly puts bowl after bowl of plums though the meat grinder to make the chutney that she hopes will keep the village afloat. It seems as if the entire village is in a state of paralysis, caught in a deadlock from which no new dawn will break. The shots in the film are often static, the camera capturing individual details like a small still life. It's only the recurring shot of Alma's headscarf fluttering in the wind that needs slowing down via the use of slow motion.

It is two events that end up releasing the village from this numbness. Alma and Nadija meet Hamza, a truck driver who transports furniture for the Bosnians now returning from Germany and promises to take their produce to the nearest market, which may finally provide them with some income. Later, Jovanović,

a Serbian former neighbor of theirs, arrives with a negotiator, and offers the inhabitants a chance to sell their village to foreign investors, who are interested in setting up holiday homes there.

At one point, one of the characters asks, "What is a good life?"—a question to which the film gives no definitive answer. Should they sell their land, improve their financial situation, and turn their back on the ghosts of the past? Or should they, like Alma, commit themselves to staying, making a new start, and feeding half of Bosnia with their homemade produce?

While the villagers try to decide, the first snow begins to fall as if by magic, preventing the two Serbs, whose car won't start, from leaving. The small community symbolically uses plastic maps—upon which the insignia of the UN protection troops can be briefly seen—as shelter from the snow, despite the fact that they don't offer any real shelter. The night will reveal what happened to their relatives and where their mortal remains can be found. Begić manages to convey how important the past is in terms of the future in one brief moment that is as magical as it is beautiful: grandmother Jasmina unfurls her rag rug across the river and walks into the blue caves where the remains of the dead lie.

Cinema is actually capable of playing a unique role in revisiting the eternal question of how we live together in communities, of our history, becoming in the process an essential form of sustenance. By avoiding the pitfalls of the history book and by taking the necessary artistic liberties, this sustenance can even become a true delicacy, as is the case with *Snow*.

Alma and Nadija wait for someone to buy their products.

Year and place of birth
1976 Sarajevo, Yugoslavia

—

Lives and works in
**Sarajevo, Bosnia
and Herzegovina**

—

Education
**Academy of Performing Arts,
Sarajevo, Bosnia and
Herzegovina**

—

Filmography
**1995 Autobiography
(*Autobiografija*) (short)
1997 *Triumph of the Will*
(*Trijumf volje*) (short)
2001 *First Death Experience*
(*Prvo smrtno iskustvo*)
(short)
2003 *North Went Mad*
(*Sjever je poludio*) (short)
2008 Snow (*Snijeg*)
2009 *Bait* (*Mamac*)**

—

Director's awards
First Death Experience
**Archipelago New Media and
Short Film Festival
(Special Jury Prize, 2001)
Huesca Film Festival
(Critics' Award, 2002)
Ourense International
Film Festival
(Best Short, 2002)**

North Went Mad
**Göteborg International
Film Festival
(Best Short Fiction
Screenplay, 2002)**

— —

Release date
2008

—

Country of release
France

—

Language
Bosnian

—

Running time
99 min.

—

Genre
Drama

Producers
**Elma Tataragić, Benny Drechsel,
Karsten Stöter**

—

Writers
Aida Begić, Elma Tataragić

—

Cinematographer
Erol Zubčević

—

Score
Igor Čamo

—

Key cast
**Zana Marjanović: Alma
Jasna Ornela Bery: Nadija
Sadžida Šetić: Jasmina
Vesna Mašić: Safija
Emir Hadžihafizbegović: Grandpa
Irena Mulamuhić: Grandma
Jelena Kordić: Sabrina
Jasmin Geljo: Miro
Dejan Spasić: Marc
Alma Terzić: Lejla
Muhamed Hadžović: Hamza
Benjamin Đip: Ali
Nejla Keškić: Zehra
Mirna Ždralović: Hana
Emina Mahmutagić: Azra**

—

Filming location
Žigovi, Bosnia and Herzegovina

—

Format
35 mm

—

Awards for *Snow*
**Auteur Film Festival
(Freedom Award, 2008)
Cannes International Film
Festival – Semaine de la Critique
(Grand Prix, 2008)
Chungmuro International
Film Festival
(Special Jury Prize, 2008)
Festival du Nouveau Cinéma
(Special Jury Award, 2008)
Hamptons International
Film Festival
(Brizzolara Family Award
for Films of Conflict and
Resolution, 2008)
Reykjavik International
Film Festival
(Church of Iceland Award,
2008)**

Thessaloniki International
Film Festival
**(Women and Equity Award,
2008)**
Trieste Film Festival
**(Audience Award, Special
Mention, 2008)**
Fajr International Film Festival
**(Best Director, Best Movie,
Recognition of Ministry
of Culture, 2009)**
Golden Minbar International
Muslim Film Festival
**(Critics' Award,
Best Script, 2009)**
Prague International
Film Festival
(Grand Prix, 2009)
Prishtina International
Film Festival
(Best Film, 2009)
Tetouan Mediterranean
Film Festival
**(Special Jury Prize for Best
First Feature Film, 2009)**

— —

DAY, EXT. — IN FRONT OF
NADIJA'S HOUSE

*Hana comes out of the house.
It is early morning and there
is nobody around. She looks
at the sky and sees snow for the
first time in her life! It is
so light and beautiful. She puts
on slippers too big for her
little feet and walks slowly
towards the edge of the terrace.
Hana is amazed by the scenery,
she takes a deep breath and makes
a gesture like she will hug the
world saying...*

HANA: Snow...

Hana sees snow for the first time.

Alma counts how much money they could make by selling their products.

Lejla asks Miro if he has seen her father.

After a long absence, famous pianist Zetterstrøm (Ulrich Thomsen) returns from New York to his native Copenhagen on the occasion of a gala concert. A perfectionist by nature, he has one major personal flaw: he has lost the memory of his past. But when he is contacted by a messenger from a mysterious off-limits "Zone" in the middle of the city, he connects with what lies behind him and what made him run away: his love for the captivating Andrea (Helena Christensen). He hopes for the past to come back to him, but the Zone leads him to a challenging remembrance of things past.

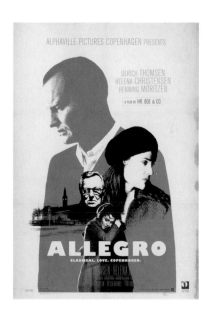

CHRISTOFFER BOE
ALLEGRO

Zetterstrøm and Andrea walk by the canal when she falls into the water.

Andrea reads a love letter from Zetterstrøm.

Christoffer Boe's 2003 debut, *Reconstruction*, thrilled the festival circuit and garnered him a fistful of awards, including the prestigious Caméra d'Or for best first feature. The film tells the story of a man who suddenly abandons his girlfriend for another woman. As a result, his universe dissolves, and his friends appear to forget who he is. In *Allegro* (2005), the Danish director's second film, the romantic premise is reversed, exploring notions of memory, love, and loss. Boe has said that *Allegro* is "not so much about a relationship ending. It's about a guy not accepting love. . . . It's very much a movie about melancholy."

The opening credits lead into the first of several animated sequences that punctuate the film. The protagonist, the concert pianist Zetterstrøm, is depicted as a guileless small child experiencing his first ice-cream and his first kiss. Then he hears a recording by Arturo Benedetti Michelangeli, a pianist renowned for his perfectionism. In the music Zetterstrøm feels a new "calmness," and, as he embraces his new obsession, he retreats from the real world.

The adult Zetterstrøm, played by Ulrich Thomsen, remains cold and aloof until he meets Helena Christensen's character, Andrea. An avuncular voiceover swiftly details their "happiness, sorrow, loss, and tenderness." Zetterstrøm confesses that it was only this relationship that could bring passion to his music; with her, he feels "almost human." But Andrea, unable to break through his detachment, leaves, and commits suicide after aborting or losing a baby. Failing to cope, Zetterstrøm effectively "erases" his past. But

"reality suddenly cracks," creating a mysterious area called "the Zone" in the heart of the city.

The idea of an impenetrable and unexplainable area, and indeed the term "the Zone," recalls Andrei Tarkovsky's *Stalker* (1979), in which a guide leads people through a mysterious region to a room that can grant their deepest wishes. Boe has confirmed in an interview that the reference is intentional: "If I hadn't called it 'the Zone,' I'm not sure people would have made the strong connection between this movie, which is whimsical . . . and also has a great melancholy, which owes a great debt to Tarkovsky, who is maybe the greatest melancholic filmmaker of all time."

Besides *Stalker*, *Allegro* also has parallels in its production design with another science fiction story, Godard's *Alphaville* (1965), filmed on Parisian streets without special effects or futuristic props. Boe's admiration of the movie is no secret: his production company is called Alphaville Pictures Copenhagen, in tribute to the film. Indeed, the filmmaker is adamant that he draws more on the French New Wave director than his closer contemporary Lars von Trier and his Dogme cohorts: "There would be no modern cinema without Godard, and I think that the whole New Wave of the sixties is everything that Dogme was and more. It was handheld cameras and small crews, it was natural settings, it was out in the street, and it was by young people who love cinema."

Ten years after the break-up, Zetterstrøm is persuaded to return to his native city by a faux interviewer working for the narrator, who announces, "Your past has been kidnapped and is now in the

Zone." On his arrival in Copenhagen, he receives a letter containing pictures of his old house and of Andrea that he does not recognize. The narrator invites him to enter the Zone; to do so, he must go through the ladies' restroom of a local bar. On the labyrinthine shifting streets of the Zone, Zetterstrøm meets the narrator, a wheelchair-bound man by the name of Tom. He witnesses a woman's body being pulled from the canal and the gory extraction of a live baby from the corpse's torso. After returning to the real world, he discovers he can no longer play the piano. The pianist has unwittingly left his talent in the Zone. He must return and untangle his lost memories from its mystery.

Although undeniably dark at times, the movie is playful with its methods of narrative, without taking itself too seriously. In many ways, the film is like a children's story or a fairy tale, even beyond the animated segments of Zetterstrøm as a child. The narrator's dialogue and indeed the very presence of a narrator echoes fairytale tropes, and C.S. Lewis's *The Lion, the Witch and the Wardrobe* is referenced in the film's doorways to secret worlds and to a forest. Furthermore the impregnability of the Zone is illustrated by showing children playing ball against its invisible wall. These associations with childhood allow audiences more sympathy with the essentially closed-up Zetterstrøm and let Boe provide vivid context with a few broad strokes.

Allegro is full of striking ideas about the tricks people play on themselves to escape pain and suffering. Boe has made a fascinating yarn that offers explorations of narrative structure and filmmaking, but also the very nature of memory and emotion.

Andrea and Zetterstrøm share a last embrace.

Year and place of birth
1974 Rungsted Kyst, Denmark
—

Lives and works in
Copenhagen, Denmark

Education
University of Copenhagen, Denmark
National Film School Of Denmark, Copenhagen, Denmark
—

Filmography
1999 *Obsession* (short)
2000 *Virginity* (short)
2001 *Anxiety* (short)
2003 *Reconstruction*
2004 *Visions of Europe* ("Europe Does Not Exist")
2005 *Allegro*
2006 *Offscreen*
2008 *Follow the Money: Riskaer*
2010 *Everything Will Be Fine*
—

Director's awards
Anxiety
Syndicat Français de la Critique de Cinéma (Prix Découverte de la Critique Français, 2002)

Reconstruction
Cannes International Film Festival (Caméra d'Or, Prix Regards Jeunes, 2003)
Norwegian International Film Festival (Amanda Awards – Best Nordic Newcomer, 2003)
San Sebastián International Film Festival (FIPRESCI – Director of the Year, 2003)
Sofia International Film Festival (Grand Prix, 2004)

Offscreen
Venice Film Festival (Young Cinema Award-Alternatives, 2006)
Austin Fantastic Film Festival (Jury Prize – Best Film, 2007)
— —

Release date
2005
—

Country of release
Denmark
—

Language
Danish
—

Running time
88 min.
—

Genre
Drama, Romance
—

Producer
Tine Grew Pfeiffer
—

Writers
Christoffer Boe, Mikael Wulf
—

Cinematographer
Manuel Alberto Claro
—

Score
Thomas Knak
—

Key cast
Ulrich Thomsen: Zetterstrøm
Helena Christensen: Andrea
Henning Moritzen: Tom
Niels Skousen: The cook
Ellen Hillingsø: Clara
Nicolas Bro: Terence Sander
Ida Dwinger: Simone
Benedikte Hansen: Piano teacher
Svetoslav Korolev: Young Zetterstrøm
Tommy Kenter: Professor
—

Filming locations
Copenhagen, Denmark
New York, N.Y., USA
—

Format
35 mm
—

Awards for *Allegro*
Danish Film Academy Awards (Robert for Best Cinematography, 2006)
— —

Zetterstrøm tries to find the portal to the Zone.

ZETTERSTRØM: (*Interrupting*) I'm interested in hearing more about this woman.

TOM: I understand – but I can't help you there. It's up to you.

ZETTERSTRØM: How is it up to me?

TOM: Well, if it isn't up to me, then it must be up to you. Perhaps the Zone can help. It's a wonderful place to seek help – if you're in doubt.

ZETTERSTRØM: I'm not in doubt – I don't need any help.

Zetterstrøm wants to know more about the Zone but Tom wants to play games.

Tom and his chef have stolen Zetterstrøm's talent and keep it in a container.

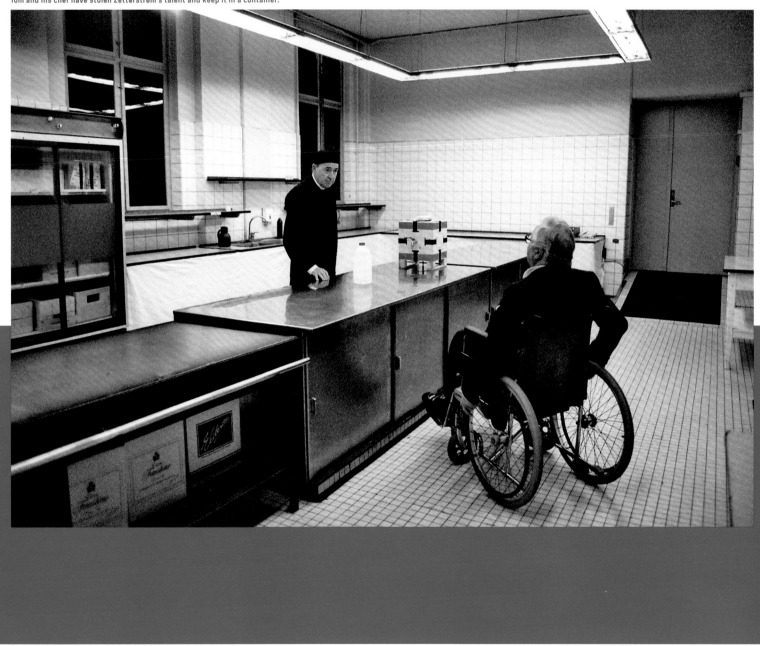

A crowded river bank in Seoul is turned into an inferno when a creature suddenly attacks and devours people, and Gang-du (Song Kang-ho), a half-witted father, loses his beloved daughter to the creature before his eyes. His ex-anti-government, out-of-work brother; his sister, a National Bronze medalist in archery; and his elderly father, join forces for the revenge.

BONG JOON-HO
THE HOST

Hie-bong prepares a dish for a customer outside his shop.

Gang-du, asleep on the job.

Bong Joon-ho represents how contemporary Korean film has diversified since 2000. What distinguishes Bong is that he has managed both to smash Korean box-office records and to become a favorite at Cannes and other prestigious film festivals. This is a reflection of not only the distinctive qualities of Korean film but Bong's incredible capacity to balance these two sides of cinema.

This balance is grounded in the use of genre and is significant for two reasons. First, the rapid growth of the Korean film industry after 2000 created a unique environment in which films that appealed to the masses were in high demand. Audiences found genre films more accessible, and this led to an increased interest among young directors in exploring different types of movies. Second, genre films produced in Korea were able to maintain a style distinct from those made in Hollywood, even as they tapped into the same traditions. The practice of manipulating old forms to create new ones is apparent in the work of many Korean directors, and reflects both the fascination with and resistance to Hollywood's product.

The combination of these two opposing elements—broad and artistic appeal—has resulted in a wide-ranging reception of Bong Joon-ho's films. For example, *The Host* (*Gwoemul*, 2006) ranked third on a list of the year's best movies in *Cahiers du Cinéma*, the esteemed French film magazine. *The Host*, which recounts one family's experiences when a monster shockingly appears in the Han River, follows the tradition of Hollywood action-adventure while introducing its own innovative twists and turns. Bong's

film was recognized for its success in taking advantage of genre in order to create something new.

Such positive reactions recall the reevaluation of Hollywood directors who worked with genre in the 1940s and 1950s, and also applied cinematic conventions while developing individual styles. *The Host* introduces added complexity by addressing the U.S. military's discharge of toxic chemicals into the Han River and by metaphorically expressing Korea's political state through chaotic scenes of a virus spreading. The timid approach of the government in the film, and the solidarity shown among socially marginalized people (such as the homeless people who fight the monster), allow for even more political interpretations.

Crucially, these unexpected elements are made possible within the boundaries of the genre. Bong Joon-ho once used an analogy to expound on the logic behind using such visual narratives:

"Imagine that there is a tour bus at Kwang-hwa-moon, the gate of Seoul. The bus attendant gathers people, telling them that the bus goes all the way to the Cheongryangri train station, and the gathered group anxiously awaits the moment the bus will take off. In the beginning of course the bus takes a route familiar to all. But then it slowly departs from the direct course and diverges into a more roundabout route. The passengers are perplexed at first, but the driver offers them a chance to see a side of Seoul that is often missed, all the while as he displays his ability to smoothly operate the ride. . . . When the bus finally stops, a bit further off from its original destination,

hardly anyone complains because they had a refreshing and unexpected tour. Obviously, the bus represents the film and the passengers, the viewers."

Setting is also an important factor in Bong Joon-ho's films. In *The Host*, the Han River reflects the inherent characteristics of Korea as a nation. The massive river runs directly through the heart of the capital and has been a symbol of modernization and development in Seoul. What is distinctive about Bong's filmmaking is how deeper meanings are illuminated as his unique characters enter and engage in the setting. The participation of distinctly Korean actors, such as Song Kang-ho and other well-known faces, results in images that can express Bong's interpretation of Korean society. In this way, Bong is able to work as a filmmaker with both Korea's national identity and the forms of the genre. In short, he calls for stretching the boundaries of genre films, which also reflect the diverse desires of today's audiences.

Each new film by Bong Joon-ho is greatly anticipated because of this ability to handle a wide scope of issues while maintaining his rich perspective. Like many other Asian directors, Bong is also a movie addict, but what distinguishes him is his ability to fearlessly unleash his own narrative on top of the visual images he has absorbed over the years. This talent has captured the attention of audiences not only on a national scale but throughout the Asian film industry. Yet Bong adds prestige to his status as a commercially successful director by both continuing to make something new out of the old and maintaining a carefully crafted style that is all his own.

TV REPORTER:
Mr. Yoon's body...

HYUN-SEO: That's gross.

TV REPORTER: *...without the lower half was discovered from Han River.*

GANG-DU: Turn to 505. The sports channel...

HIE-BONG: Oh, it's started!

HYUN-SEO: Nam-joo is on. You gonna watch?

GANG-DU: Gold medal time!

HIE-BONG: I can't watch my daughter's matches.

Gang-Du and his daughter Hyun-seo watch TV as the grandfather looks on.

Year and place of birth
1969   Seoul, South Korea
—

Lives and works in
Seoul, South Korea
—

Education
Yonsei University,
    Seoul, South Korea
Korean Academy of Film Arts,
    Seoul, South Korea
—

Filmography
1994   *White Man* (short)
1994   *Memories in My Frame*
       (short)
1995   *Incoherence* (short)
2000   *Barking Dogs Never Bite*
       (*Flandersui gae*)
2003   *Memories of Murder*
       (*Salinui chueok*)
2004   *Sink and Rise* (short)
2004   *Influenza* (short)
2007   *The Host* (*Gwoemul*)
2008   *TOKYO!* (short: "Shaking
       Tokyo")
2009   *Mother* (*Madeo*)
—

Director's awards
Memories of Murder
San Sebastián International
Film Festival
    (Best Director, Altadis:
    New Director Award,
    FIPRESCI Award, 2003)

Barking Dogs Never Bite
Hong Kong International
Film Festival
    (FIPRESCI Award, 2000)
— —

Release date
2008
—

Country of release
South Korea
—

Language
Korean
—

Running time
119 min.
—

Genre
Science Fiction

Producer
Choi Yong-bae
—

Writer
Bong Joon-ho
—

Cinematographer
Kim Hyung-goo
—

Score
Lee Byung-woo
—

Key cast
Song Kang-ho: Gang-du
Byun Hie-bong: Hie-bong
Park Hae-il: Nam-il
Bae Doo-na: Nam-joo
Ko A-sung: Hyun-seo
—

Filming location
Seoul, South Korea
—

Format
35 mm
—

Awards for *The Host*
Hawaii International
Film Festival
    (Audience Award, 2006)
SITGES International Fantastic
Film Festival of Catalonia
    (Best Special Effects, 2006)
Brussels Film Festival
    (Golden Crow Award, 2007)
Fantasporto: Oporto
International Film Festival
    (Best Director, 2007)
— —

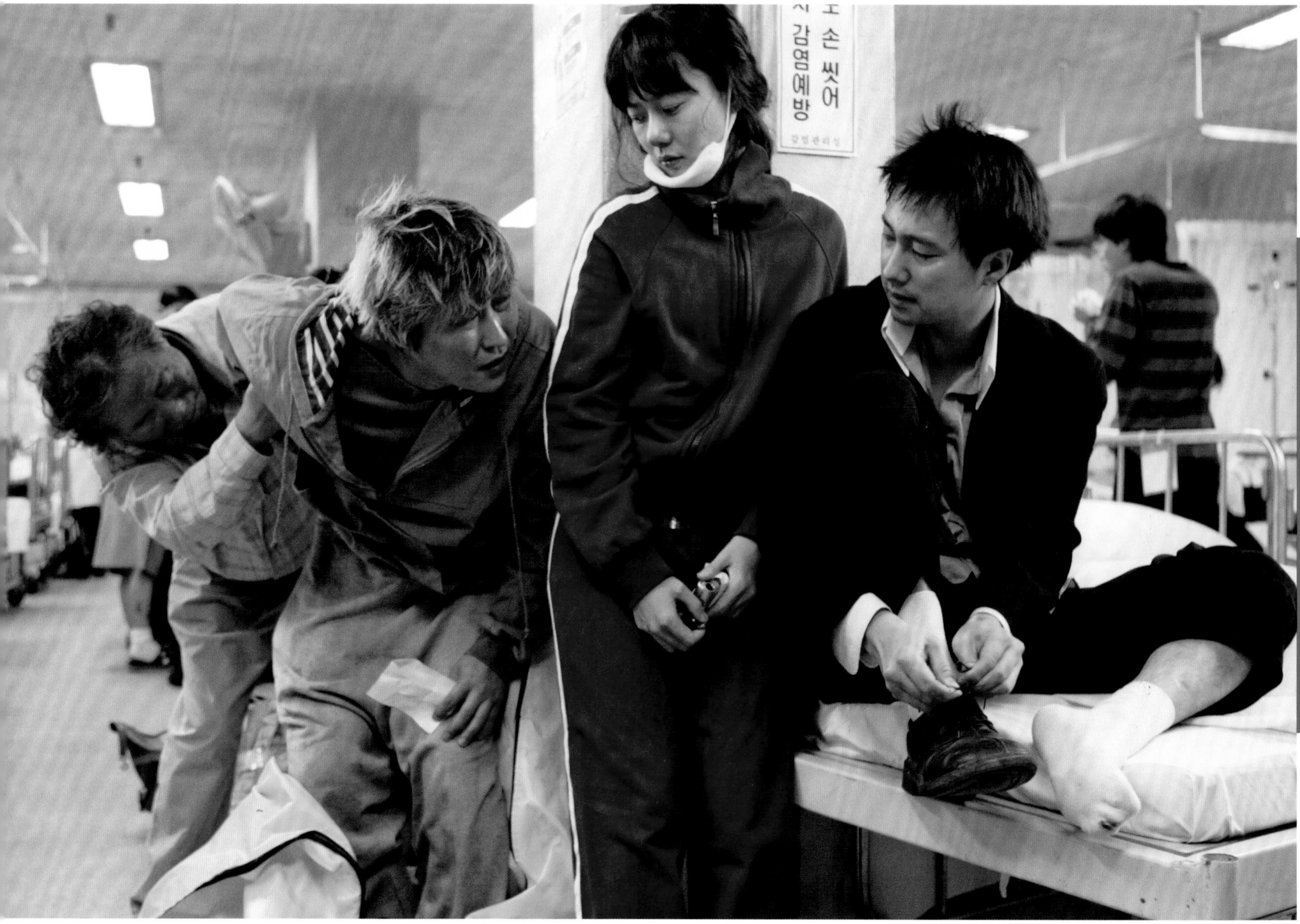

Gang-du is told he must undergo numerous tests after being exposed to the monster.

Nam-joo tries to track down the monster.

Facing the monster head-on under a bridge.

Police officer Georg (Matthias Brandt) is very popular among his colleagues for being calm and cool-headed. His partner, Michael (Wotan Wilke Möhring), also admires him for his seemingly harmonious marriage to Anne (Victoria Trauttmansdorff), an attractive primary-school teacher. After Georg is promoted, he begins to lose control over the carefully maintained façade of his "intact" family life. One Christmas, the conflicts that have been dominating the couple's lives for years start to surface. Anne struggles for recognition, Georg attempts to suit everyone's needs, and their children helplessly look away from the physical violence that can no longer be hidden.

JAN BONNY
COUNTERPARTS

Anne reassures her husband, Georg, after her father chides them about work and money.

In the 2000s, young German directors made films of exceptional vitality and intelligence. Maren Ade, Angela Schanelec, Christoph Hochhäusler, Ulrich Köhler, and a number of others are the avant-garde of what may be called a renaissance in German auteur cinema. Jan Bonny's name must now be added to this list of talented newcomers. He has directed only one feature film to date, but has made his mark as a very promising director, showing an impressive mastery of his subject and the resources at his disposal.

Bonny made one short film and a number of commercials before directing and co-writing *Counterparts* (*Gegenüber*) in 2007. Like most of his cohort, Bonny deals with the themes of marriage and the nuclear family, but does so in a way that is genuinely surprising and shocking, without falling into sensationalism. *Counterparts* tackles the sensitive subject of domestic violence in a way that is very unsettling for the viewer, far from the black-and-white positions of an "issue" film or social drama. The unusual nature of the situation creates a sensation of unease and takes the film in the direction of a psychological thriller.

The film is shot in a highly realist style, following the characters at close quarters. Bonny doesn't employ a sophisticated style of direction; there aren't any shots, camera movements, or lighting effects that are pleasing to the eye. On the contrary, the characters all inhabit rather dreary urban settings, and everything seems sad and ugly, from the police station to the Hoffmanns' modest apartment, as if the drama had rubbed off on the environment, or the other way around. From

the camera held on his shoulder, Bonny studies his characters' most minute reactions. His direction rests essentially on the precise handling of actors and the subsequent mind-blowing performances of the two leads, Victoria Trauttmansdorff and Matthias Brandt.

Georg Hoffmann is a policeman, his wife, Anne, a teacher. They have two grown-up children who have left home. They are liked and respected at work, and are a seemingly happy couple. But this calm, reassuring facade hides a marital hell. Anne is dissatisfied and unstable, and blames Georg for everything. She slaps and beats him, and Georg submits with resignation to these outbursts of violence. The gravity of the situation, revealed gradually at first and then gathering momentum, places the audience in an uncomfortable position. We are neither voyeurs nor judges as we try to understand how this couple functions. Bonny works elliptically at first, showing Georg treating his injuries without our knowing what has caused them, before revealing their source. Anne's repeated attacks become increasingly violent, and Georg is taken to a hospital. Christmas, a time usually reserved for family reunions, makes the abuse to which Georg is subjected even crueler.

The film offers a psychological explanation for their marital conflict. Anne is frustrated by her need for recognition, caused by the crushing contempt of her father, a cold, arrogant man who has never treated his daughter lovingly and who still belittles her— by infantilizing her husband at family gatherings, and by constantly reminding them of the money he lent the couple so that they could buy an apartment.

The couple's respective jobs and the dichotomy between their social and private lives make the drama seem symbolic and almost absurd. Georg's role as a policeman is to protect but also to react to violence. After intervening to save a colleague's life, he is rewarded for this act of bravery with a promotion. Anne, as a teacher, shows her pupils how to interact peacefully, and calms them down when they can't control their anger. This couple who "discipline and punish"– to borrow Michel Foucault's title–society on a daily basis, express, in an ironic reversal, their inability to conduct a normal relationship in private.

But what is a normal relationship? Psychological explanations aside, the film demonstrates the unique nature of every love story, a mixture of irrationality and tacit agreement. Anne and Georg are not in opposition but make an extraordinarily strong couple. This complicity is connected not only with a shameful secret but also with the meeting of two neuroses, two kinds of insecurity. Anne suffers from being a "weak" woman (and even from still being a little girl in her father's eyes), and makes her husband pay the price. Georg suffers from being a man, and from having to assume a virility that is wanted neither at home nor at work. He tries to have a platonic relationship with a young woman, but fails in this attempt to evade his responsibilities and return to adolescence.

Counterparts is an extraordinary dissection of marriage and the petite bourgeoisie, but also a remarkable character study and original portrait of an impenetrable man whose extreme submission is almost as disturbing as his wife's violence.

Anne has sunk down to the floor, Georg is on his knees.

GEORG: Anne, please!

ANNE: I thought we would have a nice evening, for a change.

GEORG: But we can still have a nice evening.

ANNE: Yes, sure. With your dumb wife who you can't talk to in a normal way.

GEORG: Look at me.

Georg holds Anne as they try to discuss their problems.

Year and place of birth
1979 Düsseldorf,
West Germany
—
Lives and works in
Cologne, Germany
—
Education
Academy of Media Arts
Cologne, Germany
—
Filmography
2004 *2nd and A* (short)
2007 *Counterparts* (*Gegenüber*)
— —

Release date
2007
—
Country of release
Germany
—
Language
German
—
Running time
96 min.
—
Genre
Drama

Producer
Bettina Brokemper
—
Writers
Jan Bonny, Christina Ebelt
—
Cinematographer
Bernhard Keller
—

Key cast
Victoria Trauttmansdorff:
Anne Hoffmann
Matthias Brandt:
Georg Hoffmann
Wotan Wilke Möhring:
Michael Gleiwitz
Susanne Bormann: Denise
—
Filming location
Essen, Germany
—
Format
16 mm
—

Awards for *Counterparts*
Cannes International
Film Festival – Quinzaine
des Réalisateurs
(Special Mention, 2007)
Förderpreis Deutscher Film
(Best Script, 2008)
Munich Film Festival
(The Young German Cinema
Award for Best Screenplay,
2007)
— —

Anne avoids going home to Georg.

Marie tells Anne to get a dog.

Anne hugs Georg after he shares the news of his promotion.

Michael playfully promotes Anne as well.

Georg and Michael discuss marriage.

In the autumn of 1917, World War I is raging. Camille (Sylvie Testud) eagerly awaits news from her husband at the front, but one day she receives a note ending their relationship. Distraught and determined, she disguises herself as a man to search for him, and heads for the front. In a forest, she comes across a small group of soldiers who do not suspect her true identity. She follows them, embarking on a new life, and discovers what she could never have imagined, what her husband had never told her, and what her new companions will avoid revealing to her: France.

SERGE BOZON
LA FRANCE

The battalion walks toward the river.

The lieutenant asks about Camille's motivations.

Ezra Pound wrote that a classic is something beautiful we hold onto. Taking the poet's line of thought one step further, how might we define the idea of genre? Certainly, a genre is something familiar, employing elements we have already seen, know well, and expect to see again. But genres also require some variation, lest every movie turn out to be identical. Fortunately, very little about contemporary film is easy to define. And so it is with Serge Bozon's *La France* (2007), a work that tests the outermost limits of what we understand as genre.

For Bozon, movie genres are more than an opportunity for provocation. He doesn't take them apart to show us what "real" filmmakers should do. Rather, Bozon understands their power and allure, and plays with them. He shows how liberating it can be to work with and around them, dissolving one into another as if tinkering with a chemistry set. In other words, Bozon wants to move beyond a cinema of taxonomies; the fewer the categories, the further cinema is from becoming a science. *La France*, then, is his obsessive attempt at gathering various genres and distilling them to their purest essence.

La France is set in the final stages of World War I. A young French woman named Camille receives a letter from her husband at the front. He says that he has decided to leave her and tells her to forget about him. But Camille leaves home immediately to find him and save her marriage to the man she loves. In order to track him down, she dresses like a man and joins a wandering battalion of soldiers as they make their way towards the front. The soldiers almost never encounter the enemy on their patrols. Instead, they spend their moments of rest singing and playing the musical instruments that they prefer to their guns. Thus the first two-thirds of the movie has already jumped from a historical genre to an epistolary one, then on to romance, comedy, war movie, and, finally, musical.

What is original about *La France* is how it belongs to all these genres and how Bozon transcends their customary role of fulfilling expectations. In other words, Bozon returns genre to the realm of art: something never before seen, totally unknown, and completely unexpected. As a result, the film is relentlessly unpredictable, pulling the viewer into a game of guessing where it will go next. Bozon avails himself of genres that have never before been used to narrate a film or resolve its plot as they are here. *La France* manipulates genres with the same innovative touch as Bong Joon-ho's *The Host* (*Gwoemul*, 2006), which coincidentally came out the same year. But whereas Bong tries to reinvent genre by synthesizing its forms and contexts, from folklore and mythology to science and politics, that is only the starting point for Bozon. *La France* is relentless in its drive for totality, its need to incorporate everything. In that sense, it is like a vampire that feeds off the old in order to stay young. But its expansiveness, and the sheer permeability that enables it, is also a sign of how current the film is. *La France* absorbs almost everything, but from that apparently promiscuous appetite comes a refreshing sense of cohesion that is all too rare in cinema.

Bozon has always been something of a chameleon. As an actor, he has appeared in many of the movies that marked the renaissance of French cinema over the past decade, including films by director Sandrine Rinaldi and screenwriter Axelle Ropert. But he is also an accomplished composer and DJ. Perhaps these multiple personalities explain the strange and intense convergence of different materials and moods in *La France*.

But Bozon is not simply plucking genres off the shelf at the supermarket. What guides *La France* is the very contemporary ambition of using the past to invent the present. Bozon plays with existing materials but is conscious of their legacies; in order to revive them, he must rewrite them. Far from engaging in what people hastily and vulgarly write off as postmodernism, Bozon's techniques rescue all that is most enjoyable in modern film: a playfulness with conventions that combines fragile and self-conscious characters with strange locations; brusque changes of tone that oscillate between tenderness and violence; errant plotlines; unstable divisions between the political and the private; a delightful confounding of masculine and feminine; long, wide shots in natural light; and songs, recorded live and often outdoors. In short, everything that reminds us how movies transform our memories into a pure present, in which the past is nonetheless at hand.

When cinema as we know it is long dead, and an anthropologist from Jupiter arrives on Earth to research its remains, he could do no better than to find a copy of *La France*. For in it he would find everything: all that was and all that could have been. And from there, he could begin to build it all over again, while gazing deep into Camille's eyes.

The lieutenant explains to Camille the death of a fellow soldier.

Year and place of birth
1972   Lyon, France
—
Lives and works in
Paris, France
—
Education
Université Paris, France
—
Filmography
1998   *L'Amitié*
2003   *Mods*
2007   *La France*
—
Director's awards
Mods
Entrevues Belfort International
Film Festival
**   (Prix Léo Scheer Award, 2002)**
— —

Release date
2007
—
Country of release
France
—
Language
French
—
Running time
102 min.
—
Genre
Drama
—

Producers
David Thion, Philippe Martin
—
Writers
Axelle Ropert, Serge Bozon
—
Cinematographer
Céline Bozon
—
Score
Medhi Zannad (Fugu),
Benjamin Esdraffo
—

Key cast
Sylvie Testud: Camille
Pascal Greggory: Le Lieutenant
Guillaume Verdier: Le cadet
François Negret: Jacques
Laurent Talon: Antoine
Pierre Léon: Alfred
Benjamin Esdraffo: Pierre
Didier Brice: Jean
Laurent Lacotte: Frédéric
Guillaume Depardieu: François
—
Filming locations
La Brenne, France
Fontainebleau forest, France
Sénart forest, France
—
Format
35 mm
—

Awards for *La France*
Mexico International
Film Festival
**   (Best Director, 2007)**
Prix Jean Vigo
**   (2007)**
— —

A cadet dies in Camille's arms.

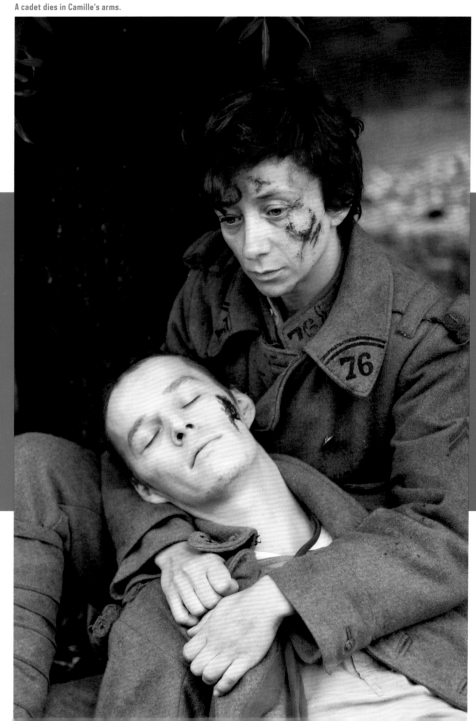

The battalion moves ahead.

Soldiers from the battalion are exhausted.

Twin sisters Jeannie and Lauren (Tilly and Maggie Hatcher) are roommates in Austin, Texas. Jeannie, who's in a wheelchair, runs a vintage clothing store with an increasingly estranged partner who's threatening to sue. In her time of crisis, Jeannie turns to an ex-boyfriend, Merrill (Alex Karpovsky), who's recently graduated from law school and is all too eager to try to fix her problems as a way of ignoring his own. Director Andrew Bujalski's third film is a story about how we depend on families—the ones we're born into and the ones we build for ourselves.

ANDREW BUJALSKI
BEESWAX

Amanda and Jeannie sign bank papers.

Jeannie works at Storyville, a thrift store she owns with her friend Amanda.

Oddly enough, there's one thing that both fans and detractors of Andrew Bujalski's work seem to agree on: nothing actually happens in his films; they're "aimless," "modest," or "lacking in plot." But is that really the case? Bujalski's debut, *Funny Ha Ha* (2002), explores the fairly existential questions of love and work in a highly insightful way. Shot in Boston, the film follows a young woman bouncing from one job to another, while her romantic advances are rejected just as comprehensively as she rejects those of a former colleague. When an American distributor finally picked it up in 2005, it had long achieved cult status and Bujalski was already putting the finishing touches on his second film, *Mutual Appreciation* (2005), about a young musician trying to find his feet in Brooklyn.

His films were vigorously advertised by critics under the banner of Mumblecore, a term used lovingly and dismissively in equal measure, and struck a nerve for a whole generation of young adults whose high level of education still didn't offer any sort of perspective. If these films' proximity to real life mean that they appear to lack a plot, then it would seem that having a plot implies turning your back on real life. Bujalski's merit lies in his refusal to stick to the bigger-than-life doctrine that is so pervasive in American cinema.

His work has been compared with that of many important directors: John Cassavetes, Mike Leigh, Eric Rohmer, Yasujiro Ozu. Although the Ozu comparison might be the most overblown, it is perhaps the least misleading. Bujalski's films are patient, attentive, precise; they're interested in the things that make up

actual life, the moments that are too often dismissed as banal in films. It shouldn't come as a surprise that Belgian director and artist Chantal Akerman was his thesis advisor at Harvard.

Bujalski's third feature, *Beeswax* (2009), revolves around twin sisters Lauren and Jeannie, played by Maggie and Tilly Hatcher. Jeannie is down to earth; Lauren is flighty. Jeannie wants to save her business; Lauren is looking for adventures further afield. Jeannie is in a wheelchair; Lauren is able-bodied. Jeannie runs a small boutique and is worried about being sued by her business partner, Amanda, who's become increasingly distant of late.

Although Bujalski describes the film as a "legal thriller" with a fair degree of irony, there's a certain seriousness to that description. Whether Amanda will actually sue Jeannie or not remains a question until the end, thus providing *Beeswax* with its external drama. The protagonists of Bujalski's most recent film are a few years older and a bit more mature than their predecessors, who were still in a state of shock at having suddenly become adults. Now they've finally gotten there.

That the film is set in Austin, Texas, also represents a departure from the milieu of Bujalski's previous films—there's even a trip to the country. The 16 mm widescreen format enables Bujalski to open up new spaces and new colors. The wealth of color in Jeannie's boutique comes across as positively strident, particularly in comparison to the black-and-white *Mutual Appreciation*. The camera takes in the setting by staying at Jeannie's eye level, following her

wheelchair move through different spaces with agility and surprising speed.

On a verbal level, the film's characters are awkward more often than not, constantly struggling to retain their composure. None of them can fully express what really moves them, their lack of confidence leading them to beat around the bush, sometimes behaving like jerks without meaning to. It's easier to tell what they really mean from their body language rather than what they're saying. *Beeswax* is all about how one really speaks: about looking for words whether or not they can be found, saying the wrong thing, being forced to end a conversation abruptly. Few directors have captured this as naturally as Bujalski, who avoids ever ridiculing his characters. After all, is anyone ever really as quick-witted and poised as a movie star?

Bujalski also avoids using a composed film score. It's therefore all the more surprising when you realize how many songs actually appear in the film. They melt into the sound of the voices and the noises all around, forming what the director refers to as genuine film music, subtly creating a form of cinematic magic. When Corinne, the new shop assistant, remarks acerbically to her boss that she could be run over by a bus at any time, they are both shocked by the sound of a squealing tire at that exact moment. Or when Lauren asks Jeannie's ex Merrill how many people he knows who are dead, the bang of a light bulb burning out seems to suggest that their ghosts are replying from the ether. And the best thing is that it's no longer possible to tell what has been staged and what is just a strange coincidence.

Jeannie plays nervously with her straw on a date with her ex-boyfriend.

Year and place of birth
1977 Boston, Mass., USA
—

Lives and works in
Austin, Tex., USA
—

Education
**Harvard University,
 Cambridge, Mass., USA**
—

Filmography
2002 *Funny Ha Ha*
2005 *Mutual Appreciation*
2009 *Beeswax*
—

Director's awards
Funny Ha Ha
**Black Point Film Festival
 (Best Feature Film, 2004)**
**Independent Spirit Awards
 (Someone to Watch Award,
 2004)**

Mutual Appreciation
**Newport International
Film Festival
 (Jury Award for Best
 Screenplay, 2005)**
— —

Release date
2009
—

Country of release
USA
—

Language
English
—

Running time
100 min.
—

Genre
Comedy, Drama
—

Producers
Dia Sokol, Ethan Vogt
—

Writer
Andrew Bujalski
—

Cinematographer
Matthias Grunsky
—

Key cast
**Tilly Hatcher: Jeannie
Maggie Hatcher: Lauren
Alex Karpovsky: Merrill
Anne Dodge: Amanda
Katy O'Connor: Corinne
Janet Pierson: Sally
Christy Moore: Paula**

Filming location
Austin, Tex., USA
—

Format
Super 16 mm
— —

Merrill, Lauren, and Jeannie catch up upon Lauren's return from her trip.

The girls look at some photos with their mother.

Lauren gives Jeannie a lift.

LAUREN: You think you can do this path?

JEANNIE: Looks kind of like a trap...

Jeannie puts the strap to her camera between her teeth and puts her arms over Lauren's shoulders. Lauren stands up quickly, lifting Jeannie who pops up in the air and hoots, like a cowgirl hanging onto a bronco.

As a child, Cho-won (Seung Woo Cho) would throw tantrums, bite himself, and refuse to communicate with anyone. His mother, Kyung-sook (Misook Kim), never gave up on him and was determined to prove to the world that her child could be normal. As Cho-won gets older he begins to find a passion for running and his mother, and coach, are right there to encourage him.

YOON-CHUL CHUNG
MARATHON

Cho-won and his mother after a 10-kilometer race.

Cho-won, the central character of Yoon-chul Chung's *Marathon* (2005), is a young man with autism who seems trapped in his own world. As a child, he refuses to eat meals at the table and prefers to eat chocolate pies in front of the television, mesmerized by programs showing zebras. But as he grows older, he blossoms into a promising runner, which gives his mother, Kyung-sook, hope for his future.

Cho-won's achievements provide inspiration about human potential, but his childlike qualities also provide the film with comic moments. Cho-won farts without reserve and uses a polite form of speech towards his younger brother that would be more appropriate for speaking to his teacher. On top of this, his curiosity causes mishaps throughout the film. Even at the age of twenty, he behaves like a five-year-old, and he relies on his mother for support in his day-to-day life. Kyung-sook devotes herself to the goal of helping Cho-won finish a marathon in under three hours and throws all her energy into making it happen.

Chung frequently uses fantasy as a way of creating a sense of solidarity with his audience. During his training, Cho-won often fantasizes that he is running through endless African plains. Chung avoids the danger of making a formulaic success drama by stylistically melding Cho-won's fantasies with his deeply felt joy of running. A disabled character running a marathon sounds like a cliché recipe for a box-office hit, but Chung instead emphasizes Cho-won's physical sensations of bliss, as viscerally experienced with his body—his heart, hands, and feet—while he trains at the Han River Park. By playing up the sensory experience

of the character, the film overcomes the potential limitations of a popular genre movie. The effect is twofold: *Marathon* is a success story of an individual overcoming his own disability, but it also breaks down the binary of pain and bliss.

In his choice of style, Chung refrains from dramatizing one-dimensional emotions, and instead attempts to engage viewers deeply with Cho-won in the act of running. Far from denying the pain of reality, Chung aims to pull us into the young man's inner world and create a space for introspection. Interestingly, as the film progresses, Chung portrays Cho-won's circumstances and Kyung-sook's despair more forcefully in order not to suggest a sense of hope that is artificially separated from pain.

After Cho-won takes third place in a ten-kilometer race, a reporter asks Kyung-sook what she most wants to do. Her initial response during the interview is calm and collected, but later, after an incident at the pool, she confesses that her wish is to die the day after Cho-won does. The emotional resonance of this moment comes out in the remorseful tears shed by Kyung-sook, as she contemplates her life as a flawed protector of her twenty-year-old son, to whom she gave birth at the age of twenty. Her tears are a condensation of all the years she suffered under the double burden of contempt from onlookers and her own guilt over ignoring the needs of the rest of her family. This is the moment when the wall between Kyung-sook and the world crumbles.

The devastation Kyung-sook experiences when it becomes clear that Cho-won will not be able to

finish the marathon in time reflects not only a mother's despair but also the great sense of loss that anyone might feel. Indeed, her despair clashes with the image of maternal figures in many Korean films, women who willingly and lovingly sacrifice themselves for their families. Kyung-sook by contrast undergoes an emotional evolution in pursuing her obsessive passion. The film expresses rage against societal ignorance when she confronts a woman who treats Cho-won like an idiot. Yet later in the film, Kyung-sook finds herself on the receiving end of rage. When Cho-won's coach, Jung-wook, gets fed up with her all-consuming determination, his outburst is pointedly directed at her: "You think running is so noble? Then why don't *you* run and see if it's really true."

Jung-wook's words underline the fact that Kyung-sook is not the angelic, self-sacrificing mother she thinks she is. She is also a mother who ignores the needs of her younger son, Jung-won, and her husband, thus driving them away emotionally and physically. Through the opposing, splintered aspects of Kyung-sook's character, the film interweaves the varieties of indignation that different characters express and experience. This web of human relationships and emotions is what makes the film so rich. Jeong has made his mark by exploring the gulf between the individual and society, the cracks within the family structure, and the social issues that pose new challenges every day. Like the American director Frank Capra, Jeong provokes an engagement with the diverse humanistic concerns that are universal to us all.

Kyung-sook asks the coach to train Cho-won for the marathon.

Year and place of birth
Seoul, South Korea
—

Lives and works in
Seoul, South Korea
—

Education
**Hanyang University Film
& Theatre
Seoul, South Korea
Yong In University Film School,
South Korea
Australian Film & TV Radio School
Sydney, Australia**
—

Filmography
**1997 *Memorial Photographing*
(short)
1999 *Hibernation* (short)
2005 *Marathon*
2007 *Skeletons in the Closet*
2008 *A Man Who Was Superman***
— —

Release date
2005
—

Country of release
**South Korea, Japan, France,
Singapore, Hong Kong**
—

Language
Korean
—

Running time
75 min.
—

Genre
Drama
—

Producer
Chang-whan Shin
—

Writers
Yoon-chul Chung, Jin ho Yoon
—

Cinematographer
Hyuk-joon Kwon
—

Score
Joon-sung Kim
—

Key cast
**Seung Woo Cho: Cho-won
Misook Kim: Kyung-sook
Ki-young Lee: Jung-wook**
—

Filming location
Seoul, South Korea
—

Format
35 mm
—

Awards for *Marathon*
**Golden Bell Film Festival
(Best Film Award, 2005)
Blue Dragon Film Festival
(Best Film Award, 2005)**
— —

The coach shows Cho-won how to run well in a funny way.

Cho-won feels the rain on his hand.

Cho-won lets his coach feel his heart beat.

*After running together for the first time, Cho-won
and his coach, Jung-wook, are relaxing their tired bodies.
Cho-won puts a hand to his chest with deep breathing.*

CHO-WON: My heart...it's racing. Cho-won's heart is going
pitter pot.

JUNG-WOOK: Pounding is more like it.

CHO-WON: Pounding...

JUNG-WOOK: Say it. "It's pounding like hell!"

CHO-WON: It's pounding like hell!

JUNG-WOOK: How does it feel with your heart pounding?

CHO-WON: Good!

The coach and Cho-won lie on the grass after a run.

On a stretch of secondary road in a thoroughly isolated village, an ex-Mafioso (Normand Lévesque) and his rebellious daughter-in-law, Coralie (Eve Duranceau), seek resolution for their dead-end lives and chronic financial problems. Desperate and deeply affected by the recent death of the woman who acted as wife and mother, respectively, the pair hope to find peace of mind for him and freedom for her.

DENIS COTE
ALL THAT SHE WANTS

Pierrot nervously awaits the visitor's arrival.

Coralie is saddened by the state of things.

Denis Côté, born in New Brunswick, Canada, in 1973, has an air of cowboy about him; as a filmmaker he's nothing if not quick on the draw, and often works with exiguous budgets. He has roots in journalism and the underground music scene, and studied cinema in Montreal before founding nihilproductions in 1993 and making a number of essay films and shorts. He is a presenter and critic on Montreal's independent radio, and wrote the weekly cinema column for the now-defunct magazine *ici*.

His first full-length feature, *Drifting States* (*Les états nordiques*, 2005), won the Golden Leopard in the Video Competition at the Locarno International Film Festival and was shown throughout the world. The documentary-style film about a man helping his terminally ill mother die is impressive for its visual impact as well as its keen observations about human solitude and the natural world.

Using video and minimal resources again, he shot *Our Private Lives* (*Nos vies privées*, 2007), an edgy romance set in the forests of Quebec that displays touches of fantasy and horror. No surprise, given that Côté himself says, "When I was growing up, I gorged on horror films. In my teens I was a walking encyclopedia on the subject, until I discovered Godard and Pasolini. Then I binned all that and turned into a serious movie buff. My role models change all the time, but I think my world is definitely that of a cinephile. But you can go from George Romero to Ernst Lubitsch without making 'copy and paste' versions of their films."

Next, with a slightly bigger budget, he made *All That She Wants* (*Elle veut le chaos*, 2008), a rather dark work with the twilight feel of a modern western. It's a tragic, open-ended film that gives the impression that it begins after some catastrophic event has occurred, and features characters who all seem to expect something from life, without knowing quite what. As Côté says, "I find it very hard to explain where my projects come from. In this case, it was listening to 'La Man,' a song by the famous French singer Christophe, that you hear in the film, that sparked off the story. I pictured a world of lost souls, with a solitary girl at its center, a female figure taking revenge on a male world. And the character of the Frenchman, played by Laurent Lucas, highlights a certain inward-looking tendency in Quebec society. It's a tendency that leads to a sort of unspoken, passive xenophobia: a fear of being robbed of our French, a fear of our American or British invaders. Pierrot therefore quickly becomes "the Frenchman," someone who comes out of prison and is going to cause trouble. At the same time, I wanted the landscape and the sound, for example, to become characters in their own right."

Here Denis Côté explains: "I'm not a very good storyteller. My aim isn't to tell a moving, shocking, or amusing story. I like to conceal information from the audience. If they miss something, they won't understand anything else; things are only shown once. My aim is to make purely cinematographic creations, to ask myself questions about the use of sound and image."

All That She Wants was shot at a crossroads in the Quebec countryside, and its framing and direction are very deliberate. "In contrast to *Les états nordiques* [*Drifting States*], which relied heavily on improvisation, this time there was considerable preparatory work," says Côté. "That's what comes of having a large budget and a crew of twenty-five. My meeting with Josée Deshaies, director of photography, was perhaps the most extraordinary aspect of the project. She works mainly in Paris, often on Bertrand Bonello's films, and it was in association with her that I opted for black and white, which she was using for the first time. And in any case, I don't feel my characters in any way deserve color . . . "

All That She Wants was shown at Locarno in 2008, as part of the International Competition, where it easily took the Best Director Prize. Côté's work is both extremely rigorous and nourished by a great love of cinema. His films are highly sophisticated, with a wide range of references, links to a rich cinematographic heritage, and a conscious, meticulous use of every possible cinematic resource, specifically framing, sound, sets, and language. But this sophistication never appears on the surface; on the contrary, it has the effect of giving audiences the impression of great sincerity, of "truth" in emotions and sensations, like some of the best westerns and genre films do. In this respect, Denis Côté is a very modern filmmaker who draws on the work of his predecessors to find new ways of telling a story.

Côté has since made his fourth feature, *Carcasses* (2009), which was selected for the Directors' Fortnight at Cannes. It's a film that borders on documentary and fiction, and was again made on a shoestring and shot in the depths of a forest. And it's more than likely that by the time you read this, he will have finished making another!

Yelena waits for orders from her boss.

Year and place of birth
1973   Perth-Andover, N.B.,
Canada
—

Lives and works in
Montreal, Que., Canada

Education
Collège Ahuntsic, Montreal,
Que., Canada
—

Filmography
2005   Drifting States
(Les états nordiques)
2007   Our Private Lives
(Nos vies privées)
2008   All That She Wants
(Elle veut le chaos)
2009   Carcasses
—

Director's awards
Drifting States
Locarno International
Film Festival
(Golden Leopard–
Video Competition, 2005)
Jeonju International
Film Festival
(Woosuk Award, 2006)
— —

Release date
2008
—

Country of release
Canada
—

Language
French
—

Running time
105 min.
—

Genre
Drama

Producers
Denis Côté, Stéphanie Morissette
—

Writer
Denis Côté
—

Cinematographer
Josée Deshaies

Key cast
Eve Duranceau: Coralie
Normand Lévesque: Jacob
Réjean Lefrançois: Alain
Nicolas Canuel: Spazz
Olivier Aubin: Pic
Laurent Lucas: Pierrot
—

Filming location
Contrecœur, Que., Canada
—

Format
HD
—

Awards for *All That She Wants*
Locarno International
Film Festival
(Best Director, 2008)
— —

Coralie accompanies Alain to the cornfield to talk.

CORALIE: Are you ok? Why the gun?

ALAIN: There are groundhogs.

CORALIE: Forget the groundhogs.
They won't steal your corn.
(*Pause*) I hear you have visitors
at your place. Girls.

ALAIN: Yeah.

CORALIE: You don't want to talk?

ALAIN: You let Hélène leave? (*Pause*)
Got anything to eat?

CORALIE: We manage. (*Pause*) I gotta go.
(*Pause*) Somewhere else.

Pic watches Yelena and Katerina's dance routine.

Coralie is desperate for a way out of Spazz's truck.

Inspired by true events, this film tells the story of Richard (Felix Roco) and Raymond (Daniel Medrana), two teenage brothers on opposite sides of a gang war. Richard is the leader of the Bagong Buwan (New Moon), while Raymond is just being inducted into the rival Batang Dilim (Children of the Night). Complications arise at a midnight *engkwentro* (clash) when Raymond is assigned the task of killing his older brother. All the while, the City Death Squad, a vigilante group allegedly backed by the omnipresent Mayor Danilo Dularte Suarez (Celso Ad Castillo), is hunting Richard down. Will they take his brother, too?

PEPE DIOKNO
CLASH

Raymond is told to kill his older brother, Richard, in order to gain acceptance to the gang.

Richard is a teenage gangster running away from the vigilantes of the City Death Squad.

For his debut feature, the twenty-one-year-old Filipino film student Pepe Diokno spared no effort in rendering his story about a gang member in a fix—several fixes, to be exact. *Clash* (*Engkwentro*, 2009) is a vivid look at slum-dwelling teen Richard (Felix Roco, son of movie star Bembol). He faces a tough-talking enemy gang looking to squash his small crew, a younger brother threatening to drop out of school, a girlfriend he wants to run away with, and the looming specter of vigilante death squads.

It's a story that would be nerve-wracking in any case, but Diokno raises the bar by choosing a technique that does not spare a single second of Richard's life on the run. *Clash* unfolds in what appears to be a single unbroken shot; the camera cruises through the alleys and byways of the youth's neighborhood without the finality of an editing cut. There is action (beatdowns) and inaction (idle chatter), ensuring a variety of rhythms. As in Gus Van Sant's *Elephant* (2003), the movie's perspective trapezes from one person to the next—Richard, his little brother, Raymond, the rival gang members—in recounting a day in the life of Richard and his woebegone neighborhood.

Yet one need not look beyond Diokno's contemporaries for comparisons: overwhelming immersion in what Renoir might have called "the lower depths" has practically become a proud house style of Philippine cinema. From the work of Brillante Mendoza through individual films like Jeffrey Jeturian's *Kubrador* (2006) or *Cavite* (2005) by expats Neill dela Llana and Ian Gamazon, his fellow filmmakers have aligned themselves with the approaches of socially conscious traditions, past and present, foreign and domestic. But another way of looking at it is far simpler: they are merely rendering what is out there, in a country whose tumultuous history has had lingering painful results.

Though his treatment of the gangs inevitably carries a certain entertaining frisson, Diokno situates his film firmly in the service of a social issue. An opening title announces that 814 people have been killed by vigilante death squads, whose crime fighting has been the subject of Human Rights Watch alerts. A montage of government slogans and photo ops follows and establishes the complicity of the bellicose, rabble-rousing prime minister. Richard lives under the constant threat of execution, and Diokno manifests this menace through the prime minister's macho radio addresses, which pop up on the soundtrack throughout the movie. Though the problem of vigilante killings has mushroomed in the Philippines recently, the character of the prime minister also recalls the specter of dictatorship in a country that has experienced it; in fact, Diokno's grandfather was a famous human rights defender and senator who was imprisoned for a time.

A further measure of grounding in fact comes from Diokno's source for the material. While working on a documentary about prisons, he met two young brothers who were certain that after release they would be murdered by death squads. The plight of Richard and of Raymond, who joins a gang that asks him to kill his own brother, therefore feels all too possible, even as it joins a long cinematic tradition of double binds dating back through Neorealism and earlier urban-set American silent film. Visually, Diokno enhances the sense that there is no way out for these spirited but benighted characters by avoiding bright light when night falls, leaving the camera to wander through the intimidating darkness. Entire gang fights occur in a murkiness that rivals *The Blair Witch Project* (1999), though the horror of what the movie depicts is real.

And yet, *Clash* is of course a work of fiction, and Diokno's approach is an aesthetic decision—a fact the rhetoric of realism that is so popular in criticism can obscure. What also gets obscured, however, is the effort involved in creating what looks like a whirlwind widescreen tour through a Davao slum. Diokno's efforts included the construction of an enormous set, the employment of hundreds of extras, a gradual switch from a Steadicam-esque flow to a hectic handheld hustle, and, perhaps most stunning of all, the use of digital manipulation to create the illusion of a continuous tracking shot. The average audience may not even be aware of the technical achievement involved, but Diokno recognizes that the feeling of being suspended in the present tense is something viewers can simply sense, however it was created.

The making of *Clash* thus underlines the irony of so much cinema: a mass orchestration intended to produce the illusion of a story that is unfolding naturally, out of anyone's control. But that's just another way of expressing Diokno's dedication to the medium as a spectacle that shows us rather than shields us. And having started his career so early, Diokno, and audiences, can benefit from many years of attentive filmmaking to come.

Batang Dilim leader Tomas wants to kill Richard to snag his girlfriend, Jenny-Jane.

Year and place of birth
1987 Manila, Philippines
—

Lives and works in
Manila, Philippines
—

Education
**University of the Philippines
Film Institute,
    Manila, Philippines**
—

Filmography
**2006 *No Passport Needed*
        (short)
2009 *Clash (Engkwentro)***
— —

Release date
2009
—

Country of release
Philippines
—

Language
Filipino, Cebuano
—

Running time
61 min.
—

Genre
Drama
—

Producer
Pepe Diokno
—

Writer
Pepe Diokno
—

Cinematographer
Emman Pascual

Key cast
**Celso Ad Castillo: Mayor Danilo
    Dularte Suarez
Felix Roco: Richard
Daniel Medrana: Raymond
Zyrus Desamparado: Tomas
Eda Nolan: Jenny-Jane
Moises Magisa: Father
Bayang Barrios: Mother
Jim Libiran: Hitman**
—

Filming location
Manila, Philippines
—

Format
HD
—

Awards for *Clash (Engkwentro)*
**Cinemalaya International
Film Festival
    (Special Citation, 2009)
Venice International Film Festival
    (Luigi De Laurentiis Award
    for a Debut Film, 2009)**
— —

"Batang Dilim, untouchables!" Tomas brags.

Jenny-Jane tries to raise money for Richard's escape.

Richard discovers Raymond is joining a gang.

Richard stands up and takes the gun. He points it at an unconscious Tomas and cocks it. A pause. Then, he fires. Richard turns around and looks at his younger brother. Raymond still has the "samurai" sword drawn but he is trembling. There is anger in Raymond's face.

RICHARD: That's what'll happen to you! That! Everything — fuck — I did everything for you to see. Do you want to be like me — is that what you want? Or be like him? Fuck you, Raymond! Fuck you.

Tomas orders Raymond to behead his older brother.

When Blaise (Eric Judor) is released from a psychiatric hospital after seven years for a crime he didn't commit, he enters a futuristic, sci-fi world, one where young men undergo cosmetic surgery to fit in. Dress codes and speaking styles have completely changed and Blaise has difficulty navigating the new culture. His old friend Georges (Ramzy Bedia) has joined a gang of Botox-injecting, milk-drinking rich bullies and Blaise wants in. Even if it means performing his own face-lift.

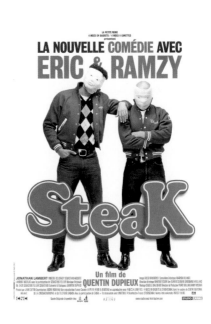

QUENTIN DUPIEUX
STEAK

Dr. Schmidt persuades Georges to undergo cosmetic surgery.

Georges kills a group of schoolmates.

When it came out in France in June 2007, *Steak* was a commercial flop, but what was most marked was the way the majority of audiences and critics misunderstood it, to the extent that the relatively big-budgeted and widely promoted film was referred to as an industrial accident, even a minor artistic scandal. And that's always a good sign.

The big mistake was to try to sell *Steak* as a mass-market comedy, on the strength of the names Eric Judor and Ramzy Bedia, comedians whose stage and television work was very popular among young audiences, and who had already appeared in a number of successful screen comedies. Many who like *Steak* discovered it later, mainly on DVD, and it now has fervent admirers who consider it one of the best French-language films of recent years.

Steak was the first "official film" by Dupieux, who as a musician was already well known on the electro house scene under the pseudonym Mr. Oizo. The movie might be described as a science-fiction comedy set in a world that resembles our own but with codes and customs that don't quite add up. Following a misunderstanding, Blaise has spent seven years in a psychiatric hospital, sentenced for the murder of three high-school students, a crime that was in fact committed by his friend Georges. When Blaise gets out, he's faced with a totally different world. Ways of talking and dressing have changed and cosmetic surgery is a normal part of life, especially among young people. On campus, a gang of "tough" boys have invented ridiculous ways of living and thinking. They drink only milk, inject themselves with Botox

in class, and only date girls with breast implants. Georges decides to join the gang, even if it means remodeling his face to look like a Michael Jackson clone. The return of Blaise, who doesn't understand this weirdness, is just another obstacle in his way.

From the opening scenes, audiences feel they're in a make-believe world; the cinematography makes ordinary places look unreal, creating a purely cinematic, science fiction world. The whole film takes on the tone of a highly original kind of depressive burlesque, with few normal reactions or situations with which the audience can identify. There is no doubt that difficulties on the set and conflicts with the producers impaired the project, and the director has admitted that he toned down the film's violence and took it in a more neutral direction. But this neutrality is what makes it such a unique film, one of the strangest and most difficult in recent French cinema. Dupieux appears to have directed the film according to a principle of rejection: rejection of psychology, narrative continuity, and cinematic or theatrical acting styles, whose mannerisms he detests. What we have here is a kind of wild antinaturalism, made even more striking by the restraint of the direction and a mind-blowing electronic soundtrack by some rising stars of "French touch" house music.

Dupieux also objects to the idea of tight directorial control. Films usually need a screenplay and many weeks' preparation, but *Steak* came into being as the antithesis of professional filmmaking. An inexperienced director found himself in charge of a comparatively large production, shot in Canada

without a proper screenplay, writing scenes as shooting proceeded. Dupieux could be compared to a chemist more interested in experiments than results. He sometimes includes scenes in which the details didn't work out as intended, highlighting his interest in awkwardness, embarrassment, even failure.

"A film is made up of nothing but small mistakes," says the director, who, with his first feature, seems to have tried to smash the expensive toy that is cinema. It would be wrong, however, to see *Steak* as a self-destructive "happening." Dupieux succeeds in portraying strangeness without resorting to bizarre framing or outlandish camera movements. It's often the beauty of his shots, and their visible calm or very slow zoom-ins, that create a sense of unease. A long fixed-angle shot of a car interior, in which Georges, his face bandaged following cosmetic surgery, tries to explain the "new humor" to Blaise, is the film's best sequence. *Steak* also isn't a tabula rasa exercise or a calculated affront to cinema history. Dupieux refers very subtly to some of the films and directors he admires: Luis Buñuel's *The Phantom of Liberty* (1974), Gus Van Sant's *Elephant* (2003), Blake Edwards, David Cronenberg, and Stanley Kubrick. A lover of collage and juxtaposition, he also confesses to being influenced by a number of French comedies of the 1980s that never really rated high with critics or film buffs.

Dupieux represents a countercurrent to French and international auteur cinema and has succeeded in subverting the genre of film comedy with a disquieting lunatic quality, one whose future manifestations we await with impatience.

Georges, post-surgery, and the Chivers gang in the schoolyard.

Year and place of birth
1974   Paris, France
—

Lives and works in
Paris, France
—

Filmography
2001   *Non Film*
2007   *Steak*
2010   *Rubber*
— —

Release date
2007
—

Country of release
France
—

Language
French
—

Running time
85 min.
—

Genre
Comedy
—

Producers
Thomas Langmann, Jean Cottin
—

Writer
Quentin Dupieux
—

Cinematographer
Riego Van Werch
—

Score
Mr. Oizo, Sebastien Tellier,
SebastiAn
—

Key cast
Ramzy Bedia: Georges
Eric Judor: Blaise
Jonathan Lambert: Serge
Vincent Belorgey: Dan
Sébastian Akchoté: Félix
Laurent Nicolas: Max
Sébastien Tellier: Prisme
Vincent Tavier: Doc Brown
Jacky Lambert: Doc Schmidt
—

Filming location
Montreal, Que., Canada
—

Format
35 mm

Georges explains to Blaise what it means to be a Chiver.

The Chivers play a violent ball game on the tennis court.

Dan throws the square ball.

SERGE: Me!

Serge runs and picks up the ball.

SERGE: 100!

Max hits Serge hard with his paddle in the stomach.

MAX: Indeed.

DAN: OK, back in position. C'mon! The mystery...
is 523 plus 412.

SERGE: Me!

Serge runs and picks up the ball.

Matt (Ross Partridge), Catherine (Elise Muller), Chad (Steve Zissis), and Michelle (Greta Gerwig) are four friends and out of work actors who retreat to the country for a weekend to write a collaborative screenplay with roles for them to star in. One night, when Michelle thinks she sees someone in the woods, the group decides it's the perfect inspiration for their screenplay. As the film ensues, they become increasingly spooked that they're not alone out there.

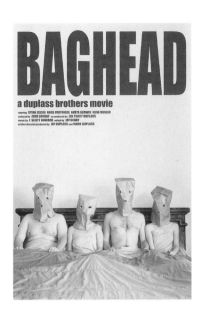

JAY AND MARK DUPLASS
BAGHEAD

Chad avoids scriptwriting and sings a song with Michelle instead.

"Independent cinema," translated literally, means mainstream movies with no budget, no stars, and no studio. The films made by the Duplass Brothers—with Jay and Mark assuming, in some variety, the roles of director, actor, writer, and producer—are truly independent, yet offer more laughs and humanity than most big-budget romantic comedies manage to.

The real cliché of moviemaking is that you need a giant camera, a huge crew, professional actors, and a traditional story to make something of note. The brothers threw this out the window and went into their kitchen. Jay grabbed a mini-DV camera and turned it on Mark as he tried repeatedly, and desperately, to record a satisfactory outgoing message on his answering machine. The resulting short film, *This Is John* (2003), is sad and hilarious, and taps into life's problems we can all relate to, and hopefully laugh at.

Jay and Mark were off and running. They followed up with the short, *Scrapple* (2004), which starts off as a friendly game of Scrabble and descends into a nasty battle of wits. (The Duplasses don't pretend to know why we do stupid things in our relationships, but they seem to get when and how it happens.) Their third short solidified this fly-on-the-wall style: *The Intervention* (2005) portrays a group of twenty-somethings who accuse a friend of being in the closet, and badger him into recalling those possibly gay moments in his life, insisting they'll love him no matter what. The notion of a gay intervention is a signpost of our 1970s-born, '80s-raised generation, accepting of anything and everyone, determined to show the hippies just whose generation is kinder.

In their first feature, *The Puffy Chair* (2005), manchild-hipster Josh hangs on the thread of his practically non-existent music career. For his dad's birthday, he buys a puffy recliner chair on eBay that resembles one from his childhood. The trip to deliver it, however, turns from road fun to group therapy when his girlfriend, Emily, and his hippie brother, Rhett, worm their way into the van. Comedy shenanigans ensue, including Rhett impulsively marrying a girl the same day he meets her. Things, of course, don't go well.

Having firmly established their mode of ultra-realism that finds humor and insight in the everyday, the Duplasses ventured outside of their comfort zone (sort of) with their second feature, the fiendishly clever *Baghead* (2008). It is a horror film conceptually, but still employs the same down-home look and feel they honed in their prior work. *Baghead* follows a group of aspiring actors/filmmakers being terrorized in the woods, though it's truly about making movies in a self-obsessed culture. Opening with a pretentious post-screening Q&A and ending with two friends working out a work-induced betrayal, the film brings the Duplass Brothers full circle as they dare to question their own milieu. The film pokes merciless fun at the very same DIY aesthetic that called it into existence, pondering whether there's a certain creative bankruptcy to a bunch of friends getting together and deciding to make a movie.

Ross Partridge, Steve Zissis, Greta Gerwig, and Elise Muller play four such friends who head off into the woods for a weekend, where their brainstorming session devolves into futile drunken babbling, yielding not a single good idea. Their little project finally finds some life when Muller dreams (or does she?) about an intruder with a bag on his head. From there, an excited Partridge takes the lead in turning the baghead concept into a *Blair Witch*–style horror thriller, complete with a loose structure and improvised dialogue reminiscent of the Duplass Brothers' past productions. The situation is complicated by some relationship issues among the quartet, most of them involving Gerwig, who bats away the clumsy advances of Zissis and instead takes a romantic interest in Partridge. When a fifth figure, who just may be an actual baghead killer, starts stalking the friends at their cabin, the film suddenly lurches into real horror.

Much of the fun of *Baghead* is that it's unclassifiable, with elements of moviemaking satire, relationship comedy, and kids-in-the-woods slasher film. The Duplass brothers are self-aware filmmakers who are serious about their craft yet don't take themselves too seriously. They flesh out simmering conflicts with both wit and a vérité facade camouflaging scenes that wouldn't seem any more structured even had they been storyboarded. Roving camera angles and sublime reaction shots detail the sometimes awkward byplay between the characters as their true feelings and foibles rise to the surface. *Baghead* is a slight movie by design, but it goes further than expected in pushing the boundaries of no-budget independent filmmaking. It's a good argument for picking up a camera and shooting away—even if your last name isn't Duplass.

Michelle sees a baghead in the middle of the night.

Michelle realizes she's had too much to drink.

Year and place of birth
Jay Duplass
1973 New Orleans,
     La., USA

Mark Duplass
1976 New Orleans,
     La., USA
—

Live and work in
Los Angeles, Calif., USA
—

Education
University of Texas, Austin, USA
—

Filmography
Jay Duplass
2002 *The New Brad* (short)
2003 *This Is John* (short)
2005 The Intervention (short)
2005 *The Puffy Chair*

Jay and Mark Duplass
2004 *Scrapple* (short)
2008 *Baghead*
—

Directors' awards
The Puffy Chair
BendFilm Festival Jury Prize
    (Best Screenplay, 2005)
South by Southwest Film Festival
    (Emerging Vision Award,
    2005)

Scrapple
Florida Film Festival Grand
Jury Award
    (Best Narrative Short, 2004)
— —

Release date
2008
—

Country of release
USA
—

Language
English
—

Running time
84 min.
—

Genre
Horror, Comedy, Drama
—

Producers
Jay Duplass, Mark Duplass,
John E. Bryant
—

Writers
Jay Duplass, Mark Duplass
—

Cinematographer
Jay Duplass
—

Score
J. Scott Howard
—

Key cast
Ross Partridge: Matt
Steve Zissis: Chad
Greta Gerwig: Michelle
Elise Muller: Catherine
—

Filming locations
Smithville, Tex., USA
Austin, Tex., USA
—

Format
HD
— —

A baghead prepares to scare Matt and Michelle in the house.

CHAD: That's him! That's him!

CATHERINE: Let's go back inside.

MICHELLE: I agree.

CATHERINE: Matt!

MATT: Hey man, what do you want? You are on private property. You better leave. I'm going to bash your fucking head in, man. You better go.

MICHELLE: No, I think we should just...I don't think you should do that...

Michelle and Catherine tag along with Matt and Chad to scare off a baghead.

Escaping the monotony of a loveless marriage, Ray (David Roberts) becomes entangled with the beautiful and troubled Carla (Claire van der Boom). His moral limits are tested when she presents him with the proceeds of her controlling husband's latest crime. This is their chance: take the money and run. If only it were that simple. The seed is planted, and Ray, fearing he will lose his love, engineers the plan, which threatens to go horribly wrong. Alarm bells sound and suspicions are raised, yet miraculously the dust looks to settle. Then the first blackmail note arrives . . .

NASH EDGERTON
THE SQUARE

Carla faces herself in the mirror.

Eddie plays poker at Smithy's house.

Independent film is often considered a tonic to action-driven Hollywood movies. The works of Nash Edgerton, however, suggest that the two don't have to be mutually exclusive. With a slew of terrific shorts and one accomplished feature, he has established a distinctive style fueled by adrenaline and mind-blowing stunts, enriched by a deep understanding of character and nuance.

I first met Edgerton in 1999 when I was asked by the Australian Film Institute to curate a program of American short films that were to be screened along Australia's East Coast. I was lucky enough to tag along on the tour, where I met a raw and electrifying filmmaker's collective called Blue-Tongue Films. They consist of Edgerton, his brother Joel (then an emerging actor, now one of Australia's most prolific), and Kieran Darcy-Smith. Their intense short film *Bloodlock* (1998) offered a glimpse of things to come. Nash was already an established stuntman, and he applied those skills to making a collection of bombastic shorts that were marked by scintillating action scenes and well-developed characters—for the genre, anyway. The stunts were not low-budget trickery, but full-on heart-stopping insanity that had to be seen to be believed.

So why are Edgerton and crew considered independent and not Hollywood pretenders? Their answer would have to be their tone. During a blow-out action movie, audiences usually connect with the characters on a less personal level; Edgerton provides someone to believe in with just a few stylish touches. The couple in his short film *Fuel* (2003) are young, happy, and expecting a child. But when they run out

of gas in the middle of nowhere en route to a vacation getaway, the movie unpredictably shape-shifts into a gnarly monster flick.

With less reliance on plot, Edgerton also blew audiences away with the short *Lucky* (2005), about a man who wakes up in the trunk of a car. He frees himself to find that the car is going ninety miles an hour without a driver. Over the next few breakneck minutes the guy rips and tears his way into the driver's seat in order to save himself. Edgerton really came into his own as a director with the short film *Spider* (2007), which takes the age-old words of wisdom "it's all fun and games until someone gets hurt" and runs with them. This tale, forged from the blackest of black comedy, screened at hundreds of film festivals and has been viewed millions of times online.

After mastering the art of walloping audiences with shocks and thrills in thirty minutes or less, Edgerton expanded his filmmaking repertoire with *The Square* (2008). His feature debut follows a married construction company owner, Ray, whose very bad financial decisions result in an accidental death he tries to cover up. Ray is having an affair with Carla, who's also married. One fateful day Carla discovers a bag of money and sees it as their ticket to a fresh start. She proposes they take the money and run, but as is the case with most plans driven by lust and greed, it seems destined to crash and burn.

Co-written by Edgerton's brother Joel, who also appears in the film, and Matthew Dabner, *The Square* has roots in classic noir but is imbued with a vividly distinct sensibility that is all Edgerton. Utilizing their

trademark stunts to full effect, the brothers fashioned an intense thriller with dramatic elements of equal impact thanks to fully realized performances by the ensemble cast. Edgerton's visual style meshes perfectly with the taut, engrossing story. His seductive camerawork lures viewers down a foreboding path, but they are compelled and thrilled to be on it. Bursts of gallows humor adroitly break up the tension, allowing momentary relaxation for the viewer. As accomplished as his filmmaking is, he also brought out the best in his cast: David Roberts, as Ray, shows the resolve and fragility of a man whose judgment is tragically clouded by desire, while Claire van der Boom, in the role of Carla, radiates as the femme fatale.

Nash's direction focuses on storytelling, and his command of the material is total. He builds tension and intrigue almost flawlessly, making audiences pay attention by not spelling everything out. For example, when a TV broadcaster talks about an armed robbery—which is where the stolen money came from—he presents it as a throwaway following another news item that is crucial to the scene. *The Square* presents everyday people in extreme situations, and pushes them to the dark outer recesses of human facility. All the major characters in its multi-strand plot must make good on their murky intents, with all forced to discover just how far they'll go in pursuit of what they desire.

The Square is as stylish as it is unsettling, and its ever-building momentum will grip you and leave you breathless—as much from the film as from knowing that you're witnessing the swift emergence of directorial force coming up from Down Under.

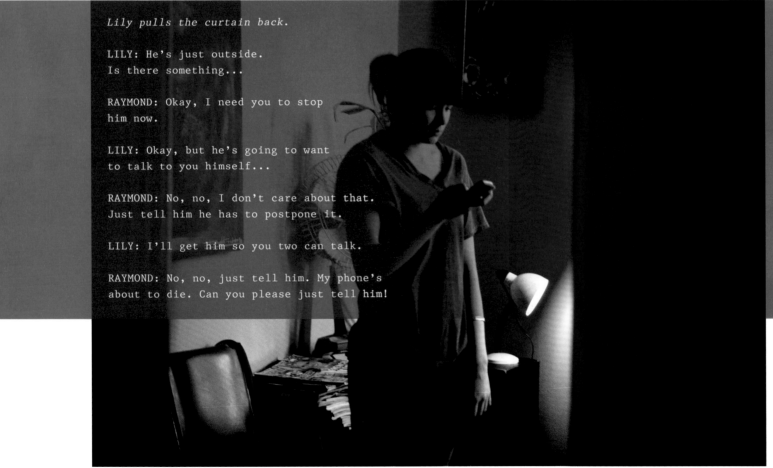

Lily on the phone with Ray.

Year and place of birth
1973 Sydney, Australia

—

Lives and works in
Sydney, Australia

—

Filmography
1996 *Loaded* (co-directed
        with Kieran Darcy-Smith)
        (short)
1997 *Deadline* (short)
1998 *Bloodlock* (co-directed
        with Kieran Darcy-Smith)
        (short)
2001 *The Pitch* (short)
2003 *Fuel* (short)
2005 *Lucky* (short)
2007 *Spider* (short)
2008 *The Square*

—

Director's awards
Fuel
Eyescream Short Film Festival
    (Runner-Up, 2005)
Flickerfest International Short
Film Festival
    (Most Resourceful
    Production, 2005)

Lucky
Cabbagetown Short Film &
Video Festival
    ("Golden Cabbage" People's
    Choice Award, 2005)
Chicago International REEL
Shorts Festival
    (Best Action Film, Audience
    Choice Award, 2005)

St. Louis International
Film Festival
    (Best Short Short, 2005)
Tropfest
    (Second Prize, 2005)
Cleveland International
Film Festival
    (Best Live Action Short
    Film, 2006)

Spider
AFI Fest
    (Grand Jury Award for Best
    Short Film, 2007)
Prague Short Film Festival
    (Audience Award for Best
    Short Film, 2007)
Sydney Film Festival
    (Audience Award for Best
    Short Film, 2007)
Aspen Shortsfest
    (Best Comedy, Hard C High-
    Five to Lo-Fi Award, 2008)
Calgary Underground
Film Festival
    (Jury Award for Best
    Narrative Short, 2008)
San Sebastián Horror & Fantasy
Film Festival
    (Jury Award, Audience Award,
    2008)
Sundance Film Festival
    (Honorable Mention in Short
    Filmmaking, 2008)
— —

Release date
2008

—

Country of release
Australia

—

Language
English

—

Running time
105 min.

—

Genre
Drama, Thriller

—

Producer
Louise Smith

—

Writers
Joel Edgerton, Matthew Dabner

—

Cinematographer
Brad Shield

—

Score
François Tétaz, Ben Lee

Key cast
David Roberts: Raymond Yale
Claire van der Boom: Carla Smith
Bill Hunter: Gil Hubbard
Kieran Darcy-Smith: Barney
Anthony Hayes:
    Greg "Smithy" Smith
Damon Herriman: Eddie
Brendan Donoghue: Leonard Long
Joel Edgerton: Billy
Hanna Mangan-Lawrence: Lily

—

Filming location
Sydney, Australia

—

Format
35 mm

—

Awards for *The Square*
Australian Film Critics'
Association Film Awards
    (Commended for Best
    Australian Film, 2008)
Film Critics Circle of
Australia Annual Awards for
Australian Film
    (Best Original Screenplay,
    2008)
— —

Smithy at the police station after the fire at his home.

Carla waits for Ray in their hotel room.

Leonard attacks Ray.

Lily, upset at the consequences of not telling Billy the truth.

This series of vignettes follows Linda (Ladya Cheryl), a young Chinese woman in Indonesia, and the people around her, all trying to become someone else. Linda rekindles her friendship with childhood friend Cahyono (Carlo Genta); Linda's father, a blind dentist, wants to convert to Islam and take a new, younger wife; Salma (Andhara Early) appears on the show *Planet Idol*; and Romi (Wicaksono) and Yahya (Joko Anwar) practice performing penetrative sex. The film depicts a fragile but panoramic vision of a community that is not at ease with itself, and hopes that can never be truly fulfilled.

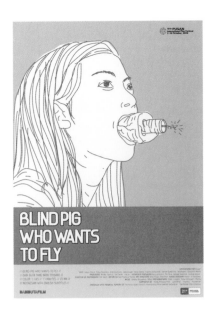

EDWIN
BLIND PIG WHO
WANTS TO FLY

Cahyono walks around in a daze after being beaten up.

Linda demonstrates lighting a firecracker in her mouth on the Cesa Show.

A blind pig, tied to a wooden stake, would apparently prefer to fly than to see again. After all, what good is being able to see if you're not free? Freedom being a greater commodity than knowledge is a concept that manifests itself again and again in *Blind Pig Who Wants to Fly* (*Babi buta yang ingin terbang*, 2008).

Trying to describe what Edwin's film is actually about is like pulling teeth. Maybe that's why he chose to put a dentist at its center, functioning as a liaison between all the characters whose fragmented stories are presented in a non-linear, episodic manner. Although these fragments end up forming distinct plot threads, they are never beholden to an overarching narrative logic.

Most of the characters are united by their Chinese roots. They are all looking for a foothold in Indonesia and are met with a resistance that seems to span all generations—the different stages of a failed assimilation process. There's the dentist's wife, who used to be an Indonesian national badminton player. And the couple's daughter, who, since childhood, has put fireworks in her mouth and lit them. Previously a means of protecting herself from assault, it is now just an entertaining stunt to be paraded on sensationalist TV shows. Her childhood friend, also a victim of ethnically motivated repression, goes on to become a TV director—possibly forming a kind of autobiographical reminiscence. Last but not least, there's the gay male couple who represent the Indonesian military and try to compensate for their fear of coming out by allowing themselves to be sexually repressed when in the dentist's chair—an expression of the brutal repression inherent to a hypocritical political system.

Blind Pig is not focused on the narration in the foreground but the central principles attached to it: ethical and political conflict and the integration and discrimination of minorities. In the same way the pig would like to fly, the characters all look to be something else, anything other than Chinese. And they are doomed to fail, because the time of discrimination and repression is by no means over.

The film addresses these weighty themes with a light touch and some grotesque humor. And it isn't just the humor that's black here; what is possibly the film's most important object is also black: the pair of sunglasses the dentist has worn since going blind. His ethnic background has left him with only one possible yet improbable course of action: to change the shape of his eyes via surgery to achieve integration. The dentist's constant renditions of Stevie Wonder's hit "I Just Called to Say I Love You" represent the only moments of freedom open to him, which count for far more than either sight or knowledge—something the pig has already taught us.

Edwin expresses regional concerns in a universal language by drawing on some easily accessible clichés: the pig as a Chinese metaphor for luck (and, by contrast, as an unclean animal in a predominantly Muslim society), the melody of the Stevie Wonder song, and a remarkable opening scene that sets the film's tone. In silence, we observe a face-off between two badminton players, one from China, the other from Indonesia. It is a competitive match that represents the struggle between two different political and cultural systems—a metaphor that's nearly too overt. But Edwin demonstrates his cinematic intelligence by subverting the very clichés he employs, exposing the stereotypes at the same time he uses them. In keeping with this idea, he uses slow motion to inject a sense of alienation into the match, placing the focus on the dynamic that sets a process in motion rather than on the process itself.

Blind Pig addresses both the discrimination against the Chinese minority in Indonesia and the ways in which it's carried out. Edwin contradicts the ostensible superficiality of his images with ambiguity: silent answers instead of verbal messages. The young Indonesian director has already proven himself to be a master of irony with his highly unusual short films. And this first feature reveals him as a moralist who's never overbearing. The wooden badminton rackets don't just smash birdies but solidify clichés. Edwin's singular form of hybrid cinema, which at first glance comes across as a chaotic mixture of underground and pop-culture aesthetics, very much has method to its madness. He works with the same accuracy that the women must have on the badminton court, and uses alienation techniques to create a snapshot of his country. Edwin, who goes by his first name only, could very well be given the surname Brecht.

At the end of the story, the wooden stake is all alone, the pig has disappeared. And Stevie Wonder's song becomes the order of the day: "No summer's high / No warm July / No harvest moon to light one tender August night / No autumn breeze / No falling leaves / Not even time for birds to fly to southern skies."

Salma, the dentist's assistant who becomes Halim's second wife, sings on *Planet Idol*.

Year and place of birth
1978 Surabaya, Indonesia
—

Lives and works in
Jakarta, Indonesia
—

Education
Petra Christian University,
    Surabaya, Indonesia
Jakarta Institute of the Arts,
    Faculty of Film and
    Television, Indonesia
—

Filmography
2002 *A Very Slow Breakfast*
    (short)
2004 *Dajang Soembi, the
    Woman Who Was Married
    to a Dog (Dajang Soembi,
    perempoean jang
    dikahwini andjing)* (short)
2005 *Kara, Daughter of a Tree
    (Kara, anak sebatang
    pohon)* (short)
2006 *A Very Boring
    Conversation
    (Percakapan yang
    membosankan)* (short)

2006 *Songs from Our Sunny
    Homeland (Nyanyian
    negeri sejuta matahari)*
2007 *Misbach: Di Balik Cahaya
    Gemerlap* (short)
2007 *Trip to the Wound* (short)
2008 *Hulahoop Soundings*
    (short)
2008 *Blind Pig Who Wants
    to Fly (Babi buta yang
    ingin terbang)*
—

Director's awards
*Dajang Soembi, the Woman
Who Was Married to a Dog*
Jakarta International
    Film Festival
    (Second Prize for Best
    Short Film, 2004)

A Very Boring Conversation
Jogja NETPAC Asian Film Festival
    (Best Short Film, 2007)

Hulahoop Soundings
Asian Hot Shots Berlin
    (Second Prize for Best Short
    Film, 2009)
— —

Release date
2008
—

Country of release
Indonesia
—

Language
Indonesian
—

Running time
77 min.
—

Genre
Drama
—

Producers
Meske Taurisia, Sidi Saleh,
Edwin
—

Writer
Edwin
—

Cinematographer
Sidi Saleh
—

Score
Windra Benyamin

Key cast
Ladya Cheryl: Linda
Pong Harjatmo: Halim
Andhara Early: Salma
Joko Anwar: Yahya
Carlo Genta: Cahyono
Clairine Baharrizki: Little Linda
Darren Baharrizki: Little Cahyono
Wicaksono: Romi
O K T: Opa
Elizabeth Maria: Verawati
—

Filming locations
Mount Bromo, Indonesia
Jakarta, Indonesia
Surabaya, Indonesia
—

Format
35 mm

Awards for *Blind Pig Who
Wants to Fly*
International Film Festival
Rotterdam
    (FIPRESCI Prize, 2009)
Singapore International
Film Festival
    (Special Mention, 2009)
— —

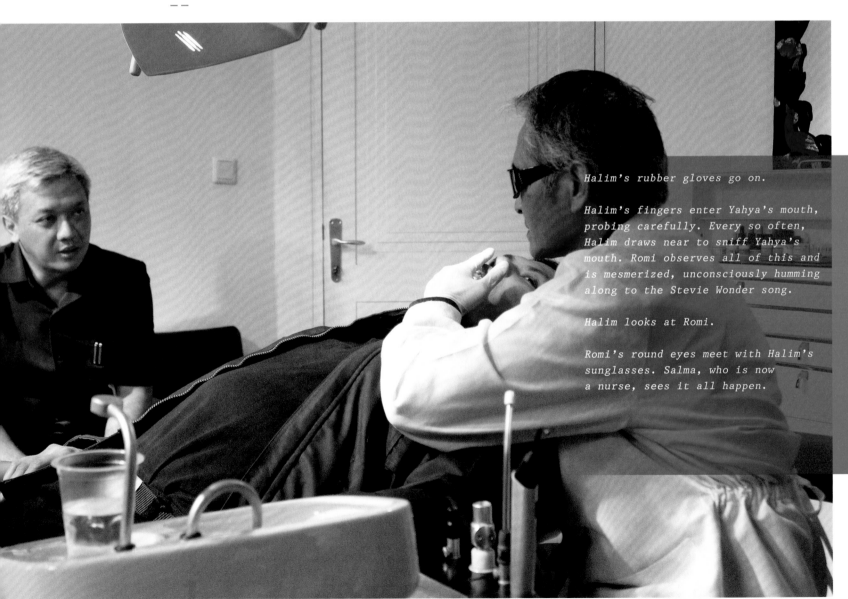

Halim's rubber gloves go on.

Halim's fingers enter Yahya's mouth, probing carefully. Every so often, Halim draws near to sniff Yahya's mouth. Romi observes all of this and is mesmerized, unconsciously humming along to the Stevie Wonder song.

Halim looks at Romi.

Romi's round eyes meet with Halim's sunglasses. Salma, who is now a nurse, sees it all happen.

Romi watches Halim work on his partner, Yahya.

Linda picks at her scars.

In an attempt to escape from a home where sorrow reigns, sixteen-year-old Juan (Diego Cataño) crashes the family car into a telephone pole on the outskirts of town. Scouring the streets searching for help, he meets Don Heber (Héctor Herrera), a paranoid mechanic who promises to fix the car as soon as Juan can find the necessary part. He encounters an eclectic mix of characters along his one-day journey, during which he will come to accept an event as natural and inexplicable as death.

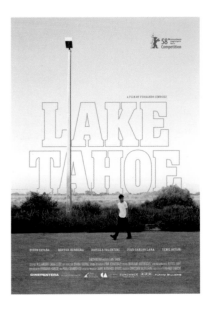

FERNANDO EIMBCKE
LAKE TAHOE

The outskirts of town.

Young Mexican director Fernando Eimbcke's body of work is further evidence of the recent revival of Latin American cinema. Simple on the surface, rich in detail, and subtle in their comedic effects, his films successfully hit the minor key of adolescent yearning. His two features so far, *Duck Season* (*Temporada de patos*, 2004) and *Lake Tahoe* (2008), tenderly tell the stories of youth in limbo, their desperation and frustration often masking personal grief.

Shot in black and white, *Duck Season* unfolds as two best friends plan a lazy Sunday at one's apartment while his parents are out. As their emotions, dreams, and disappointments are revealed, the apartment becomes a stage for the boys, and the events of the day come to represent their pre-adulthood states of mind. Distractions from the outside are therefore unavoidable. At the beginning, they prepare to endure another boring Sunday of their boring adolescence with bottles of soda, video games, porn magazines, and pizza. Then, two additional young souls join their environment: a beautiful neighbor who wants to use the apartment's oven to bake a cake, and the eleven-seconds-late pizza-delivery boy who refuses to leave without being paid. Then the power goes out.

Eimbcke demonstrates his strength as a director by depicting these distractions as ordinary occurrences, both frustrating and alluring. With Eimbcke's subtle, slow-building sense of black humor, these incidents initially appear as unfortunate coincidences for the characters, before triggering them to express their adolescent confusion on a broader scale. They talk about issues like parents' divorces, loneliness, love, and friendship. And even though the film is almost entirely set in one confined space, the apartment seems somehow empty. Perhaps because of the absence of adults.

In *Lake Tahoe*, that absence is the key to almost everything. Teenager Juan crashes the family car on the way to his small Mexican harbor hometown, and spends the rest of the day trying to get it fixed. It's a hot day. The streets are empty and reminiscent of a ghost town, and nobody seems to be working, indicating that it's probably a Sunday. As Juan continues trying to find help, the camera simply follows his transitions between home, the shop, and the car. The whole world seems to have closed in, and Eimbcke depicts this with dreamlike, colorful long takes interrupted by black-screen pauses. Juan comes across a variety of eccentrics: a grumpy old man with a dog, a single-teen mother, a friendly kung-fu fanatic. Once again, with his subdued, oddball characters, reminiscent of those found in a Jim Jarmusch film, and stone-faced gags, Eimbcke also generates a sense of hidden sorrow. It gradually becomes clear that Juan is not only searching for a mechanic but also for some closure to an unmentioned loss, communicated only through his silence. Eimbcke's characters implode with a loss of speech instead of releasing an explosion of emotions. And the stark visuals emphasize the open space of this Yucatan town, implying something vital is missing or dead.

Eimbcke works with minimal material, and chooses not to show some key events of the story. For instance, we never see the car crash or Juan's father's death, although they are subtly alluded to later on in the form of sounds, such as a Bruce Lee fight, which might suggest Juan's suppressed anger and despair. Eimbcke also avoids using dialogue whenever possible, causing viewers to pay greater attention to the characters and their surroundings. Funny and moving, both his films symbolize possibilities of new departures. Maybe too obvious, but still tender, the painting of ducks on the wall in *Duck Season* signifies that the boys are on their migratory paths out of childhood. In *Lake Tahoe*, we see a bumper sticker on the car for this famed American resort town—representing wealth, leisure, time spent with family—a place where Juan wanted to go with his father in the past. Stopping short of sentimentality, *Lake Tahoe* emerges as a moving elegy to Juan's past, and as a preface to his future.

EXT. ROAD ON THE OUTSKIRTS OF THE CITY — MORNING
A road in a deserted place and the only things in sight are light posts and brightly colored houses in the horizon. From a distance you can hear the sound of a car motor, then after a few seconds a red Tsuru enters the frame and crashes into one of the light posts.

FADE TO BLACK
The name of the film appears in white letters against a black title card.

EXT. ROAD ON THE OUTSKIRTS OF THE CITY — MORNING
Juan, 13 years old, gets out of the crashed car and appears vulnerable. Juan is wearing black pants and shoes and a white dress shirt. He has puffy eyes and his hair is a mess.

Juan looks at the crash and after letting out a sigh, hits his head with his right hand. Juan walks out of frame.

Juan looks at his father's car after crashing it into a light post.

Juan calls a friend and asks for money to fix the car.

Year and place of birth
1970   Mexico City, Mexico
—
Lives and works in
Mexico City, Mexico
—
Education
Centro Universitario de Estudios Cinematográficos, Universidad Nacional Autónoma de México, Mexico City, Mexico
—
Filmography
1993   *Reaching a Star (Alcanzar una estrella)* (short)
1993   *Sorry for the Inconvenience (Disculpe las molestias)* (short)
1994   *Excuse me? (¿Perdón?)* (short)
1995   *Not Everything is Permanent (No todo es permanente)* (short)
2002   *Weightwatch (La suerte de la fea...a la bonita no le importa)* (short)
2003   *Don't Be Bad (No sea malito)* (short)
2003   *The Look of Love* (short)
2004   *Duck Season (Temporada de patos)*
2005   *Goodbye to the Traps (Adiós a las trampas)* (short)
2005   *Dog That Barks (Perro que ladra)* (short)
2008   *Lake Tahoe*
—

Director's awards
Duck Season
AFI Fest
      (Special Prize of the Jury for Best Feature Film, 2004)
Guadalajara International Film Festival
      (Best Feature Film, Best Screenplay, Best Director, FIPRESCI, JVC Prize, 2004)
Mostra Internazionale del Nuovo Cinema di Pesaro
      (CinemAvvenire Prize for Best Feature Film, 2004)
Thessaloniki International Film Festival
      (Best Director, 2004)
Academia Mexicana de Artes y Ciencias Cinematográficas
      (Best Feature Film, Best Screenplay, Best Director, 2005)
Encuentro Latinoamericano de Cine
      (Best First Feature Film, 2005)
Festival Iberoamericano de Cine
      (Tatú Tumpa Award for Best Film, 2005)
Mar del Plata Film Festival
      (Best Latin American Film, 2005)
Paris Cinema International Film Festival (Special Prize of the Jury, 2005)
— —

Release date
2008
—
Country of release
Mexico
—
Language
Spanish
—
Running time
81 min.
—
Genre
Drama
—

Producer
Christian Valdelièvre
—
Writers
Fernando Eimbcke, Paula Markovitch
—
Cinematographer
Alexis Zabé
—
Score
Los Parientes de Playa Vicente
—
Key cast
Diego Cataño: Juan
Héctor Herrera: Don Heber
Daniela Valentine: Lucía
Juan Carlos Lara: David
Yemil Sefami: Joaquín
—

Filming location
Yucatán, Mexico
—
Format
35 mm
—
Awards for *Lake Tahoe*
Berlin International Film Festival
      (Alfred Bauer Prize, FIPRESCI Prize, 2008)
Cannes International Film Festival–International Critics' Week
      (Revelation of the Year FIPRESCI, 2008)
Guadalajara International Film Festival
      (Best Director, 2008)
Transilvania International Film Festival
      (Special Jury Prize, 2008)

Academia Mexicana de Artes y Ciencias Cinematográficas
      (Best Director, Best Film, 2009)
Cartagena International Film Festival
      (Best Film, Best Screenplay, Best Photography, 2009)
Pune International Film Festival
      (Best Film, 2009)
3 Americas Film Festival
      (Best Film, 2009)
— —

Juan with Don Heber, an old mechanic who will help Juan if he takes his dog for a walk.

Joaquín, Juan's little brother, asks him where he was.

As they wait for David, Lucía sings a song.

Juan is back home, but something is still missing.

The time is June 14, 1935, and yet much later. In a remote place in Paraguay, an elderly peasant couple, Cándida and Ramón (Georgina Genes and Ramón Del Río), await their son's return after going off to fight in the Chaco War. They are also waiting for the rain and wind to come, for the unseasonable heat to break, and for the dog to stop barking—none of which happens. In short, they are waiting for better times to come. Eternal waiting is found between the "before" and the "after" of time.

PAZ ENCINA
PARAGUAYAN HAMMOCK

RAMON: What's wrong with you?

CANDIDA: What's wrong with me?

CANDIDA: I can't go on like this, Ramon, changing the place of the hammock all the time, waiting for the dog to stop barking... It's too much.

RAMON: But why do you put the hammock closer to the dog then?

CANDIDA: What else can I do? There is no other shade.

RAMON: Why didn't you leave it where it was since it was further away? Answer me...

Cándida and Ramón wait for the dog to stop barking.

Paz Encina studied cinema in college and made a number of short films, beginning in 1997, before becoming a teacher herself at the Catholic University of Asunción and the Instituto Paraguayo de Artes y Comunicación (IPAC). In a country with no film industry and very few filmmakers, she felt she had a special responsibility: before her first feature, *Paraguayan Hammock* (*Hamaca Paraguaya*, 2006), was released, the country's last film to be shot in 35 mm and shown in theaters was made in 1970. Explaining her motivations, Encina says, "What I'm trying to do is to portray my people. Sometimes I believe that to make a portrait of the Paraguayan condition is my destiny. Sometimes I see it as fate, at other times as a blessing. I believe that if given the opportunity, Paraguayan cinema could acquire an identity of its own and could be known and acknowledged throughout the world." In 2000, she made a short video, also entitled *Paraguayan Hammock*, which won prizes at various festivals and enabled her to recruit a number of leading independent European producers, including Marianne Slot, Ilse Hughan, José María Morales, and one Argentinian, Lita Stantic.

It's 1935, and in an isolated area of Paraguay, Cándida and Ramón, an old peasant couple, are awaiting the return of their son, who has gone to the front. They're also waiting for the rain, which threatens but never arrives; the wind, which never blows; a break in the heat, which continues unabated; and for the dog to stop barking. But it goes on barking. . . . In short, they're waiting for better days. Each of them waits differently: the father is hopeful, while the mother is convinced that their son is dead and this waiting is pointless.

At the edge of the forest, next to a cane field, hangs a hammock. The two characters meet and talk there. The audience observes them in static shots filmed from a distance, hearing stories about the everyday reality of people who work the fields, a tough life, and a poverty-ridden society. It's a world of silence, too, and therefore of things unsaid. With this very radical directorial device, Encina has created a new way of cinematic thinking that is both harshly political and deeply poetic.

When it was shown in Cannes in 2006, in the Un Certain Regard section, *Paraguayan Hammock* was a revelation. It's far removed from the kind of Latin American cinema that hides a very conventional product behind a politically correct form of language, and this young Paraguayan director uses sound and image to their greatest advantage for her modern reading of cinema.

In the tradition of some Argentine directors (Lisandro Alonso and Lucrecia Martel come to mind), Encina fully exploits the possibilities of long shots, timing, rhythm, and framing, constantly pushing back the limits of traditional narrative. "Ever since I conceived the temporal aesthetics of *Paraguayan Hammock*, I decided that each image would last as long as necessary to fully express itself, and not as long as others needed to look at it. In each shot small, actions last as long as they need to last: the beginning and end of a breath, a fan that takes its time to refresh the air, the chirping of a cicada, an orange peeled and eaten at just the right moment. My main interest is that each image captures not only the beauty of things but also the precise moments evoked by a perfect detail emanating from each action that lasts until it is truly seen. Ever since I started to conceive this film, I had the certainty that this is the way I see things; this is the way I see my hometown and my people, and the perception of time that I propose is the one that I feel we are living in."

The film became part of New Crowned Hope, an innovative project organized in Vienna by the stage director Peter Sellars to celebrate the 250th anniversary of Mozart's birth. It's a festival that brought together artists from many fields in celebration of the composer's creative genius. To Sellars and his producers, Simon Field and Keith Griffiths, *Paraguayan Hammock* was like a new interpretation of the "requiem": "A requiem for a lost son but also a requiem for a country and generations of its people. It is about remembering the dead and coming to terms with loss, but in its restraint and its ambiguity of time, it is about the present as much as the past and about so much that lies offscreen."

Encina acknowledges this musical dimension: "When I wrote *Paraguayan Hammock*, it was like writing a score. I tried to do it with the same care, and, unconsciously, the notes slid onto the computer in the form of letters. Crotchets, quavers, and especially minims and semibreves . . . and silence, much silence. I only thought about the time, about the rhythm of the words, and about how two people, with words, could sing a funeral repose. I wanted this to happen, for two peasants to mourn their distress, singing, as their voices are extinguished by passing time."

Cándida peels manioc and Ramón tries to see the birds.

Ramón works in a sugar cane plantation.

Year and place of birth
1971   Asunción, Paraguay
—
Lives and works in
Asunción, Paraguay
—
Education
Universidad del Cine,
    Buenos Aires, Argentina
—
Filmography
1997   The Siesta (La siesta)
       (short)
1998   The Charms of the
       Jasmine (Los Encantos
       del Jazmín) (short)
2000   I Knew You Were Sad
       (Supe que estabas triste)
       (short)
2000   Paraguayan Hammock
       (Hamaca Paraguaya)
       (short)
2006   Paraguayan Hammock
       (Hamaca Paraguaya)
—

Director's awards
The Siesta
Buenos Aires Art Festival
    (2nd Award, 1997)

I Knew You Were Sad
Asunción, Paraguay
Genesis Award
    (Best Sound, Best
    Direction, 2001)
— —

Release date
2006
—
Country of release
Paraguay
—
Language
Guaraní
—
Running time
78 min.
—
Genre
Drama
—

Producers
Lita Stantic, Marianne Slot,
Ilse Hughan
—
Writer
Paz Encina
—
Cinematographer
Willi Behnisch
—
Score
Oscar Cardozo Ocampo
—
Key cast
Ramón Del Rio: Ramón
Georgina Genes: Cándida

Filming locations
Mbocayaty and Yataity,
    Departamento Del Guairá,
    Paraguay
Caacupe, Departamento de
    Cordillera, Paraguay
—
Format
35 mm
—

Awards for Paraguayan Hammock
International Film Festival
Rotterdam
    (Prince Claus Fund Film
    Grant, 2005)
Brussels Film Festival
    (Prix de l'Age d'Or, 2006)
Cannes International
Film Festival
    (FIPRESCI Prize – Un Certain
    Regard, 2006)
São Paulo International
Film Festival
    (Critics Award –
    International, 2006)
Federación Iberoamericana
de Productores de Cine y
Audiovisuales
    (Luis Buñuel Award for
    the Best Ibero-American
    Film, 2006-7)
Göteborg International
Film Festival
    (Viewer's Feature Film
    Choice, 2007)
Lima Latin American Film Festival
    (Best First Work – Special
    Mention, Critics Award, 2007)
Mexico City International
Contemporary Film Festival
    (Best Latin American Film,
    2007)
— —

Ramón finds out that the war is over.

Ramón rests after working in the plantation.

Cándida gently holds the dead butterfly.

Cándida mourns the butterfly next to the tatakuá (brick and clay oven).

For Mithat (Mithat Esmer), a passionate collector, Istanbul is as vast as his collections. For Ali (Nejat Isler), the concierge of his building, it doesn't extend beyond a few blocks around the building. When it's revealed that the old building will be torn down, Mithat's struggle to save his collections begins. The building becomes the common ground for these two lonely men, whose relationship begins with the collaborative effort to keep their homes and then changes track as they involuntarily alter each other's fate.

PELIN ESMER
10 TO 11

For Mithat, clocks are one of the most important collection items.

Mithat starts his day under the Galata Bridge, hunting for new items.

How can the continuity of life, generations, and culture be sustained? Young Turkish director Pelin Esmer addresses this question in *10 to 11* (*11'e 10 kala*, 2009) from the perspective of an old collector, Mithat, and the young concierge in his apartment building, Ali. A film about the clash of values and the decadent age we live in, *10 to 11* takes an intimate peek at the dynamics between two lonely people.

Esmer blurred the border between fact and fiction in her debut feature-length film, *The Play* (*Oyun*, 2005), which portrays a group of women from a rural Turkish village putting on a play. In *10 to 11*, Esmer tells the story of her real-life uncle, the eighty-three-year-old collector Mithat Esmer, also the subject of her 2002 documentary short, *Koleksiyoncu: The Collector*. This time, though, Esmer has strategically placed fictional characters and incidents around Mithat.

Mithat is such an interesting character that he outshines the fictional ones. He values the notion of preserving history by recording and archiving cultural objects from the Turkish Republic. At the beginning of the film, we see Mithat shopping in several districts of Istanbul, at antiquarian bookshops and from peddlers. Mithat is not your ordinary collector; he doesn't specialize in any single thing, which we understand once the camera enters his home. The daily newspapers, alcohol, clocks, toys, photographs, encyclopedias, and sounds (yes, sounds) that he collects are emblematic of the diversity of Istanbul. The sounds he records accompany the images the camera captures as it wanders around the house. Although it looks like a hoarder's trash-filled mess, the place is actually like life itself: a collection of personal history and the history of one's city and country.

Mithat may seem lonely, but he stubbornly proves otherwise. He lives in a building with a large assortment of characters, including Ali. Unlike Mithat, Ali is overwhelmed by Istanbul; Mithat considers the entire city to be his own, while Ali, who comes from the countryside, rarely leaves the building where he works. The two become united when it's announced that the building will be torn down due to an earthquake regulation.

Esmer approaches the film with both humor and sad reminiscences. In one scene, Mithat tests the recording device at the repair shop; the tape plays the voice of Turkish nationalist leader Alparslan Türkeş announcing the military coup of 1960. Mithat, trying to fix the recorder, grunts ironically, "Doesn't it rewind?"

Mithat's curiosity rubs off on Ali, who slowly begins to experience Istanbul and life outside his building. But Ali is not fully able to appreciate the value of collected experiences. Perhaps Mithat's efforts are deemed impossible by those around him because the end to his collecting is nowhere in sight: objects and information are endless. The title of the film refers to an encyclopedia series on Istanbul collected by Mithat that is missing only the eleventh volume. Mithat isn't presented as an elitist, though he takes pleasure in sharing his extensive knowledge about Ottoman culture with a student, and embraces modern Istanbul, even collecting cheap Chinese items sold on the street.

Esmer's film portrays trust as part of a lost set of values. While Mithat relies on the security of his old apartment building, most inhabitants want to move to more modern places. Mithat conducts some research that proves the building's safety, but in the age of fast and temporary solutions, his voice goes unheard. One of the most crucial points in the film arrives when the manager decides that Mithat is an excessive hoarder and calls in the municipal police. This act of intervention is depicted with finesse. Mithat quietly protests, "I am actually being disturbed," exhibiting a fragility as he desperately tries to avoid eviction and save his collection. Ali, meanwhile, is trapped in his moldy basement apartment. But the instant Ali discovers that what he perceived as trash is actually worth something, his own personal history begins.

10 to 11's story is not limited to the Turkish Republic, or hindered by class or culture gaps. Esmer is after a subject as old and ordinary as humanity: the interaction between two people. For example, Mithat goes to Ali's apartment and learns that it's the first-ever visit from one of the tenants. They prepare a cocktail using vodka taken from Mithat's collection and Ali's stewed fruit, and we witness the joyous joining of two lonely souls in a dim, almost empty apartment that practically announces their confinement.

The building is eventually demolished and the encyclopedia set is never completed. The film ends with a message of resistance to decadence, as Mithat, looking frail and battered, hangs on to his manual-powered lamp. In her film, Esmer sheds light on the dark emotions of our age with a multilayered story of two locals in a unique metropolis that couldn't be any more universal.

Each night in his basement, Ali speaks to his wife and daughter, who live in his home village.

Ali collects the trash from Mithat.

Year and place of birth
1972 Istanbul, Turkey
—

Lives and works in
Istanbul, Turkey
—

Education
Bogazici University,
    Istanbul, Turkey
—

Filmography
2002 *Koleksiyoncu: The
    Collector* (short)
2005 *The Play (Oyun)*
2009 *10 to 11 (11'e 10 kala)*
—

Director's awards
Koleksiyoncu: The Collector
    Rome Independent Film
    Festival (Best Documentary,
    2002)

The Play
Adana Golden Boll Film Festival
    (In Memoriam Yilmaz Güney
    Award, 2006)
Bucharest International
Film Festival
    (Best Film in the Black Sea
    Region, 2006)

Boston Turkish Film Festival
    (Best Documentary, 2006)
CMCA
    (Best Mediterranean
    Documentary, 2006)
Créteil International Women's
Film Festival
    (Best Documentary, 2006)
Punto de Vista International
Documentary Film Festival
of Navarra
    (Audience Award, 2006)
Nürnberg Film Festival
    (Special Prize of the Jury,
    2006)
Tribeca Film Festival
    (Best New Documentary
    Filmmaker, 2006)
Trieste International
Film Festival
    (Best Documentary, 2006)
Turkish Cinema Writers
Association Awards
    (Special Prize, 2006)
Vitoria New European
Film Festival
    (Human Rights Award, 2006)
— —

Release date
2009
—

Country of release
Turkey
—

Language
Turkish
—

Running time
110 min.
—

Genre
Drama
—

Producers
Tolga Esmer, Nida Karabol
Akdeniz, Pelin Esmer
—

Writer
Pelin Esmer
—

Cinematographer
Ozgür Eken
—

Key cast
Nejat Isler: Ali
Mithat Esmer: Mithat Bey
Tayanc Ayaydin: Omer
Laçin Ceylan: Feride Hanim
Savas Akova: Ruhi Bey
Sinan Düğmeci: Old book seller
—

Filming location
Istanbul, Turkey
—

Format
35 mm
—

Awards for *10 to 11*
Adana Golden Boll Film Festival
    (Best Film, Best Screenplay,
    2009)
Istanbul International
Film Festival
    (Special Prize of the Jury,
    2009)
Middle East International
Film Festival Abu Dhabi
    (Best New Middle Eastern
    Director, 2009)
— —

Ali tries to find the last missing volume of the Istanbul Encyclopedia for Mithat.

After a long day's search for the encyclopedia, Ali takes a rest, and enjoys Istanbul for
a change.

Helping Mithat opens the door to a new life for Ali.

MITHAT: What about the
missing paper?

ALI: The missing one...I asked at four or
five places but I couldn't find it anywhere.

MITHAT: But we have to find it. We can't have
it missing. Or else the collection will be ruined.

ALI: I asked at lots of places, but they all said
the same. The papers had been returned.

MITHAT: I told you so. Did you get to the library?

ALI: Yes, but I didn't make it in time. It had been
shut down. The system.

MITHAT: So what did you do all afternoon?

Mithat is not content with Ali's work.

This recreation of one day at the Canto Grande prison in Peru follows women guerrillas in the Maoist Shining Path movement from their morning marches to their bedtime chants. Isolated in cellblocks, the guerrillas refuse to acknowledge that they have been imprisoned. The cells are viewed as another front in the so-called People's War and are known as the "shining trenches of combat." The film depicts the belief system and intense indoctrination of a brutal Latin American insurgency.

JIM FINN
LA TRINCHERA LUMINOSA
DEL PRESIDENTE GONZALO

The prisoners behind bars.

Camarada Ileana leading the morning march to begin the day at the Canto Grande prison.

What does it mean to make political cinema? One might define the practice as thinking about cinematic forms from a political standpoint. Forty years ago, Jean-Luc Godard questioned the films of Costa-Gavras, such as *The Confession* (*L'Aveu*, 1970), which examined the reality of socialism in Czechoslovakia. Godard claimed such work reproduced the dramatic and narrative models of conventional cinema while addressing political subjects. Today, the field of political cinema has opened up in a thousand directions, but the strategy is to avoid the forms that have hardened into conventions and lost their subversive power.

These include counter-hegemonic cinema, with its simplistic authoritarianism; investigative reports, with their slanted statistics; ethnographic cinema, which gives a voice to the oppressed but from a paternalistic position devoid of critical viewpoint; the first-person documentary, in which barely concealed narcissism overwhelms any individual experience; horror or science fiction films that employ political allegory; and films that advocate on behalf of minorities with an opportunistic militancy consisting solely of specific demands. All these approaches have been stripped of any capacity to unsettle or surprise. Appearing tame to the average audience, they are incapable of shaking things up with any remedial effect.

Accordingly, Jim Finn's *La trinchera luminosa del Presidente Gonzalo* (2007) must be considered one of the most provocative political films of the decade. By questioning dogma that preaches to the converted, the film induces a crisis in the viewer who is in search of comfort and speedy comprehension. Finn seeks to retrace the challenging paths which political films once traveled but which have now become overcrowded freeways. The modernity of *La trinchera* lies in how Finn stays away from the tried and true without resorting to forms from ten, twenty, or even thirty years ago, ones that are often presented as novel but in practice amount to amnesia. Finn draws on these forms from the past but twists them around.

La trinchera is the second part of a trilogy on communism that Finn began with *Interkosmos* (2006) and completed with *The Juche Idea* (2008). The film is set entirely in a prison run by the Shining Path, the Peruvian guerrilla group. Here women are trained in the art of savage, unconventional war against capitalism and bourgeois democracy. The prisoners/apprentices are instructed and give instruction partly following the precepts of Marxist-Leninism and Maoism but primarily according to the dictates of "Chairman Gonzalo"–the movement's leader who was imprisoned in the late 1980s. It is unclear whether the women, who are of various ethnic origins and mostly very young, have been incarcerated because of shortcomings in their military prowess or have come of their own free will.

As if reproducing the strict rules of the prison guards, the action in the film never crosses the boundaries marked out by the cells and an exercise courtyard painted with murals and political slogans. Discipline is also imposed on the narrative structure through the depiction of theoretical-practical training rituals: readings from texts, rehearsals of military parades, first-aid classes for treating wounded combatants, and even a people's court for debating the revisionist stances adopted by two of the prisoner-students. Interspersed throughout are interviews with the women. An off-screen interviewer asks questions in a dispassionate monotone; the women repeat slogans learned by rote, clichés about militant orthodoxy, and defenses of the group's cruel armed engagements.

Lacking any explicit stylization, *La trinchera* resembles an agitprop home video and has the anonymous starkness of a political communiqué. But the question arises as to how Finn and his camera gained access to such a forbidden bastion. The film doesn't offer an answer till the credits, and Finn ultimately explodes any assumption that we are watching a documentary or a perfect fictional reconstruction without the slightest hint of mockumentary. This exploration of the tricky territory at the borders of irony is the director's great accomplishment. Finn has drawn on Godard's work with the Dziga Vertov Group but has discarded their meta-language, quotations, artifice, and burlesque theatricality. In *La trinchera*, there are no actors, just ordinary people; no set, just a natural location; and, instead of pop as counterculture, only the precisely replicated tics of targeted, single-viewpoint Latin American documentaries. Finn copies forms while inverting their sense, instead of deceiving the viewer by passing off a fiction film as a documentary. In this way, he lets the film itself, and not any explanatory voiceover, produce doubt about what we are watching, leaving us to fill in the gaps.

Comandante Rebeca explains the difference between revolutionary error and excess in the Escuela Popular (People's School).

Year and place of birth
1968   St. Louis, Mo., USA
—

Lives and works in
Troy, N.Y., USA
—

Education
Rensselaer Polytechnic Institute,
    Troy, N.Y., USA
University of Arizona,
    Tucson, Ariz., USA
—

Filmography
2006   Interkosmos
2007   La trinchera luminosa
        del Presidente Gonzalo
2008   The Juche Idea
—

Director's awards
The Juche Idea
Ann Arbor Film Festival
    (Honorable Mention, 2008)
Chicago Underground
Film Festival
    (Best Narrative Feature,
    2008)
— —

Release date
2007
—

Country of release
USA
—

Language
Spanish/Navajo
—

Running time
60 min.
—

Genre
Experimental narrative

Producer
Jim Finn
—

Writer
Jim Finn
—

Cinematographer
Dean DeMatteis, Jim Finn
—

Score
Jim Becker, Colleen Burke
—

Key cast
Magali Arreola:
    Comandante Laura
Rebeca Mayorga: ·
    Comandante Rebeca
Gabriela Mayorga:
    Camarada Gabriela
Lisandra Tena:
    Camarada Lisandra
Isabela Montes:
    Camarada Isabela
Sophina James: Camarada Maria
—

Filming location
Albuquerque, N.Mex., USA
—

Format
Hi-8
— —

Camarada Lisandra reading aloud the poetry of Chairman Gonzalo.

Camarada Daisy and Comandante Rebeca sing in unison.

A mural based on an action taken by a group in Lima in the early 1980s.

Camaradas Maria and Ileana denounce the unrepentant excommunicated member of the group at the end of the criticism session.

Miguel Santos, aka Sugar (Algenis Perez Soto), a Dominican pitcher, struggles to make it to the big leagues and pull himself and his family out of poverty. Miguel finally gets his break when he advances to the United States' minor league system. He travels from his tight-knit community in the Dominican Republic to a small town in Iowa, where he and a couple of Latin American teammates are the only Spanish-speaking people. As Miguel struggles with the new language and culture, he's faced with an isolation he has never before experienced. When his play on the mound falters, he begins examining the world around him and his place within it, and ultimately questions the single-mindedness of his life's ambition.

RYAN FLECK AND ANNA BODEN SUGAR

Miguel practices his knuckle curve as his teammates on the Kansas City Knights, a Dominican baseball academy, observe.

Miguel and his friends hanging out by the Malecon in San Pedro de Macoris.

If filmmaking was a horse race, then you could say that Ryan Fleck and Anna Boden hit the Sundance trifecta right out of the gate. They had a short film at the festival, attended the Screenwriters Lab, and showed their first feature as part of the U.S. Dramatic Competition. It's not only impressive that they managed to achieve this at such young ages, but that they did it with their relationship intact. A real-life couple, they form a dynamic duo whose works examine the fragility of the human condition with graceful humor and keen insight. Their latest, *Sugar* (2008), has established them as filmmakers truly worth watching.

Their first trip to Sundance came when *Gowanus, Brooklyn* (2004) screened in the short film competition. The story revolves around a young girl and a teacher with whom she strikes up an unusual but necessary relationship. They are both out of place in their lives, and are hiding something from the world. The setup veers dangerously close to the familiar, but the obligatory conflicts don't unfold. Instead, lingering camera takes and meaningful glances transport viewers not into an artificial film world but a world of real people dealing with real problems. *Gowanus, Brooklyn* went on to win the Sundance Jury Prize in Short Filmmaking, helping the writing team earn a place in the Sundance Screenwriters Lab, where they developed the short into a feature version called *Half Nelson* (2006).

Half Nelson is also about an idealistic young Brooklyn teacher who falls into a friendship with the wise, wary, and hurting female student who uncovers his secret that he is a crack addict. The film neither condemns nor condones the actions of its characters, who wrestle with various aspects of themselves as well as their roles in the larger world. The film won rave reviews at Sundance and showed off the filmmakers' deft ability to work with actors both experienced—like Ryan Gosling, who injected his character with layers and dimensions rarely seen in film—and inexperienced, like Shareeka Epps, who displayed both wisdom and innocence in her phenomenal breakout performance. Gosling went on to be nominated for an Academy Award, and *Half Nelson* launched Fleck and Boden's careers. But because *Gowanus, Brooklyn* and *Half Nelson* were versions of each other, and both set in a world familiar to the filmmakers, it was possible to assume that the team might face a sophomore slump if that was their one story to tell—but they proved it's best not to assume anything.

For their follow-up to *Half Nelson*, Fleck and Boden busted out of their comfort zone and swung for the cinematic fences by crafting a baseball movie that doubles as an immigrant story. By fusing these two genres they created another searing exploration of alienation that spanned such weighty topics as idealism, class, and race relations, and were observed through the lives of their finely wrought, ever-human characters. Fleck and Boden's talent matched their ambition with a home run of a film that proved they would not be one-hit wonders.

Sugar follows the story of Miguel Santos, aka Sugar, a Dominican struggling to make it to the big leagues and to pull his family out of poverty. He gets his break at age nineteen when he advances to the United States' minor league system and travels from his tight-knit community to a small town in Iowa. Miguel struggles with the new language and culture despite the welcoming efforts of his host family. When his play on the mound falters, he begins to examine the world around him and his place within it more closely, and ultimately questions the single-mindedness of his life's ambition.

What begins as a classic rags-to-riches sports story turns into a much more complex and realistic examination of what it means for these young athletes to chase their dreams. Algenis Perez Soto shines in the lead role, delivering a multifaceted performance that is both natural and absorbing. Set against the disparate backdrops of the Dominican Republic, rural Iowa, and New York City, Sugar explores a fascinating side of America's pastime and what it means to people outside of America.

Ryan Fleck and Anna Boden are a soft-spoken couple who carry a big moviemaking stick. They display an uncanny ability to draw exceptional performances from their actors, to burrow into the core of humanity, and to illuminate the complexities of life. They followed through on their early promise with a film far removed from the world of their prior two, but one which shares the same extremely high level of craft. Their insights into the human condition, and their facility in transferring them to the screen intact, pack a mighty punch that enlightens as much as it entertains. With *Half Nelson* and *Sugar* under their belts, the duo is out in front of the pack and sure to be standing in the winner's circle for years to come.

The waitress returns with French toast and another plate with samples of different eggs.

WAITRESS: Okay. This is scrambled. Scrambled.

MIGUEL: Scrambled.

WAITRESS: (*Pointing to plate*) Over easy.

MIGUEL: Over easy.

WAITRESS: (*And finally*) This one's tricky... Sunny-side-up.

The waitress helps Miguel with his order of eggs.

Year and place of birth
Ryan Fleck
1976   Berkeley, Calif., USA

Anna Boden
1979   Newtown, Mass., USA
—

Live and work in
Brooklyn, N.Y., USA
—

Education
Ryan Fleck
New York University, USA

Anna Boden
Columbia University,
    New York, N.Y., USA
—

Filmography
Ryan Fleck and Anna Boden
2003   *Have You Seen This Man?*
    (short)
2005   *Young Rebels*
2008   *Sugar*

Ryan Fleck
2004   *Gowanus, Brooklyn*
    (short)
2006   *Half Nelson*
—

Directors' awards
Have You Seen This Man?
Cinequest Film Festival
    (Audience Award, 2003)
Independent Film Festival Boston
    (Audience Award, 2003)

Gowanus, Brooklyn
Aspen Shortsfest
    (Special Jury Recognition,
    2004)
Independent Film Festival Boston
    (Special Jury Prize, 2004)
Sundance Film Festival
    (Jury Prize in Short
    Filmmaking, 2004)

Half Nelson
Boston Society of Film
Critics Awards
    (Best New Filmmaker, 2006)
Dallas-Fort Worth Film Critics
Association Awards
    (Russell Smith Award, 2006)
Deauville Film Festival
    (Jury Prize, Most Promising
    Newcomer, 2006)
Gotham Independent Film Awards
    (Best Feature, Breakthrough
    Director, 2006)
Locarno International
Film Festival
    (Special Jury Prize, 2006)
New York Film Critics
Circle Awards
    (Best First Film, 2006)
Philadelphia Film Festival
    (Best Director, 2006)
San Francisco International
Film Festival
    (FIPRESCI Prize, 2006)
— —

Release date
2008
—

Country of release
USA
—

Language
English, Spanish
—

Running time
114 min.
—

Genre
Drama

Producers
Paul Mezey, Jamie Patricof,
Jeremy Kipp Walker
—

Writers
Anna Boden, Ryan Fleck
—

Cinematographer
Andrij Parekh
—

Score
Michael Brook
—

Key cast
Algenis Perez Soto:
    Miguel "Sugar" Santos
Rayniel Rufino: Jorge
Andre Holland: Brad
Michael Gaston: Stu
Ellary Porterfield: Anne Higgins
Richard Bull: Earl Higgins
Ann Whitney: Helen Higgins
Jaime Tirelli: Osvaldo
Joendy Pena Brown: Marcos
Kelvin Leonardo Garcia: Salvador
Teodosia Sanchez Reyes: Carmen
Emmaneul Nanita Carvajal: Reyes
Walky Alvarez: Sofia

Filming locations
Consuelo, Dominican Republic
San Pedro de Macorís,
    Dominican Republic
Phoenix, Ariz., USA
Davenport, Iowa, USA
Burlington, Iowa, USA
Bronx, N.Y., USA
—

Format
35 mm
— —

Miguel and his teammates pay their respects during the national anthem.

Miguel joins his Iowa host family, Helen and Earl Higgins, at church.

During a road trip, Miguel overhears a teammate call home to the Dominican Republic.

Exploring the horrors of war using life-like animation techniques, director Ari Folman recalls his time in the Israeli Army during the Lebanon War in the early 1980s. Based on interviews with friends and comrades, the film explores the mysteries behind an old friend's recurring nightmare in which he is chased by twenty-six vicious dogs. Folman needs to discover the truth about that time and about himself, memories that have long been forgotten or repressed. As he delves deeper and deeper, his memories begin to creep up in surreal images.

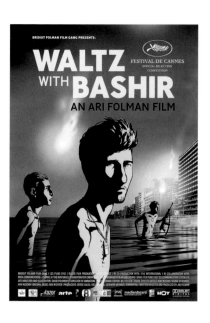

ARI FOLMAN
WALTZ WITH BASHIR

Ari, at the Tel Aviv promenade, reminisces about the Lebanon War for the first time.

Dogs terrorize the streets of Tel Aviv.

Waltz with Bashir (*Vals Im Bashir*, 2008) begins with the recollection of a relentless nightmare: in a bar, Boaz tells his friend Ari Folman of his nightly dreams about a pack of ferocious dogs. These imaginary images have come to replace real memories of his military service during Israel's 1982 armed incursion into Lebanon, which culminated with the massacre in Sabra and Shatila. Although imagination appears to have softened the impact of the events by turning real life into a dream, it has in fact created an obsession, which is spread by this casual conversation like a virus. From then on, Folman is infected, triggered by his own memories that he thought he had banished. He is driven to find out why he suppressed this past and whether there is any sense in recapturing it.

The massacre has left an indelible mark that does not allow the tragedy to be washed away. The work of bringing it to light—of making it return like a zombie rising from the grave—reflects Folman's commitment to the era through which he lived. But he is not a conventional militant director aspiring to make a purely functional film that exists only to ratify his fidelity to certain ideals. Folman's real commitment is to his art and to the challenges of the present as well as the past. How can one react, artistically, to the contemporary world's invasion of homogeneous images? What is the alternative to a documentary-like style that would only make the film resemble a war dispatch and turn the massacre—unique when seen from an individual viewpoint—into just another episode in a series or another genre movie?

As *Waltz with Bashir* shows, the story of this massacre can only be told by avoiding generalization and emphasizing the individual viewpoint, and so Folman could not work within genres except to appropriate them. But in doing so, he demonstrates that no major work can avoid interweaving with the fabric of those genres. *Waltz with Bashir* is, for one thing, a detective story, because it chronicles an investigation (by somebody who will end up discovering himself). At the same time, it is a war movie, because Folman understands that the one indispensable element in depicting a war is the lives of the soldiers who fight it. It is also a fantasy, in which hallucinations make reality feel only more real.

What is surprising and subversive is how Folman builds a road for future cinema by heading toward the past. Like many of today's best movies, Folman's film exhibits an awareness that the subjective dimension is just as real as so-called reality. The answer he gives to the conundrum of how to treat reality is paradoxical: the real is something that exists or existed for some-body, and its traumas must be viewed both subjectively and collectively, but this requires a degree of distance. Therefore, even though the director preserves the actual voices and stories of the participants questioned by his stand-in character, he chooses not to shoot them documentary style, which would put them literally and brutally on display. Such an approach would have been tantamount to declaring that the real was taking place right then and there, during the filming, without the gap in time that helped blur the memories. The witnesses' vulnerability in the face of the events would

have been exposed, when the premise of this film is rather its position on the frontier between the real and the imaginary.

The use of animation in *Waltz with Bashir* plants the film precisely on this borderline by including the participants' voices and physical appearances, and by mediating the latter through drawn renderings that lend an unreal quality. Beyond rejecting traditional forms of documentary, Folman also found that contemporary approaches in animation, such as rotoscoping, were insufficient for his purposes. He invented his own set of stylized techniques that take into account the reality of people and places but also make them feel phantasmagorical. The paradoxical result: animated documentary.

What makes *Waltz with Bashir* so radically modern, however, is its rebuttal of Marcel Proust's work, in which a small everyday detail can spark. In Folman's film, memories cannot be recaptured, because they persistently slip out of one's grasp. Rather than burst onto the scene, remain elusive; they are only fragmentary and never precise. Whereas *Citizen Kane* (1941) ushered modernity into cinema with its multiple viewpoints, *Waltz with Bashir* is the height of modernity because any unified perspective dissolves in the multiple characters' viewpoints. The film's ironic stance on psychiatry is to suggest that these memories are shared by everybody without ceasing to belong to each of them individually. If Proust was the chronicler of the imaginative world of the nineteenth century, and Orson Welles of the twentieth century, perhaps Folman does the same for the twenty-first.

Ari meets his friend Carmi to find out what happened on the night of the massacre.

Year and place of birth
1962 Haifa, Israel
—

Lives and works in
Tel Aviv, Israel
—

Education
Tel Aviv University, Israel
—

Filmography
1991 *Comfortably Numb* (short)
1996 *Saint Clara*
2001 *Made in Israel*
2008 *Waltz with Bashir*
(*Vals Im Bashir*)
—

Director's awards
Comfortably Numb
**Israeli Academy Awards
(Best Documentary, 1991)**

Saint Clara
**Israeli Academy Awards
(Best Film, Best Director,
1996)**
— —

Release date
2008
—

Country of release
Israel
—

Language
Hebrew
—

Running time
87 min.
—

Genre
Animated documentary
—

Producers
**Ari Folman, Serge Lalou,
Yael Nahlieli, Gerhard Meixner,
Roman Paul**
—

Writer
Ari Folman
—

Art director and illustrator
David Polonsky
—

Director of animation
Yoni Goodman
—

Score
Max Richter
—

Key cast
**Ari Folman: Himself (voice)
Ori Sivan: Himself (voice)
Ronny Dayag: Himself (voice)
Shmuel Frenkel: Himself (voice)
Ron Ben Yishai: Himself (voice)
Dror Harazi: Himself (voice)
Zahava Solomon: Herself (voice)
Yehezkel Lazarov: Carmi Cna'an
(voice)
Miki Leon: Boaz Rein-Buskila
(voice)**
—

Format
35 mm, 2D Animation
—

Awards for *Waltz with Bashir*
**Asia Pacific Screen Awards
(Best Animated Feature Film,
2008)
Israeli Academy Awards
(Best Movie, Best Director,
Best Screenplay, Best
Artistic Design, Best Editing,
Best Sound Design, 2008)
Israeli Film Critics Awards
(Best Israeli Film, 2008)
Los Angeles Film Critics
Association
(Best Animation, 2008)
National Society of Film Critics
Awards (USA)
(Best Picture, 2008)
Tokyo FILMeX
(Grand Prize, 2008)
British Independent Film Awards
(Best Foreign Independent
Film, 2009)**

**Broadcast Film Critics'
Association Awards (USA)
(Best Foreign Language Film,
2009)
César Awards
(Best Foreign Film, 2009)
Cinema Eye Awards
(Outstanding Achievement
in Direction, Graphic
Design and Animation, Music
Composition, International
Feature, 2009)
Directors Guild of America
(Outstanding Achievement in
Documentary, 2009)
Golden Globe Awards
(Best Foreign Language Film,
2009)
Writers Guild of America
(Documentary Screenplay
Award, 2009)**
— —

Carmi's dream of the woman who will redeem him.

Young Ari tells the soldier to "just shoot and pray."

Ari and another soldier evacuate bodies.

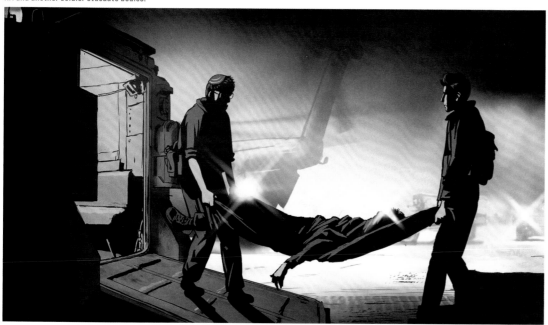

Ari is standing in front of the large windows opposite the remnants of the large Boeing aircraft. There are soldiers running behind him and the sound of helicopters in front of him. The sky is painted red.

ARI: ...That's when I start hearing the sounds, the voices and the shelling in the city. I realize where I am and start getting scared of what is about to happen.

Young Ari in the Beirut airport terminal.

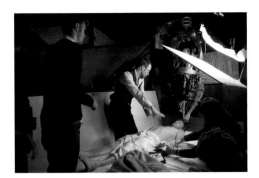

George (Colin Firth) struggles to find meaning in his life after the death of his partner, Jim (Matthew Goode). He dwells on the past as we follow him through a single day, where a series of events leads him to decide if there is a meaning to life after Jim. George is consoled by his closest friend, Charley (Julianne Moore), who is wrestling with her own questions about the future. A romantic tale of love interrupted, the film focuses on the isolation that is an inherent part of the human condition, and ultimately the importance of the seemingly smaller moments in life.

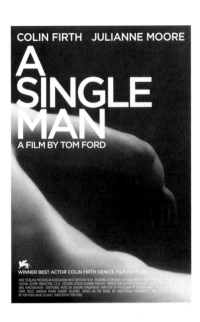

TOM FORD
A SINGLE MAN

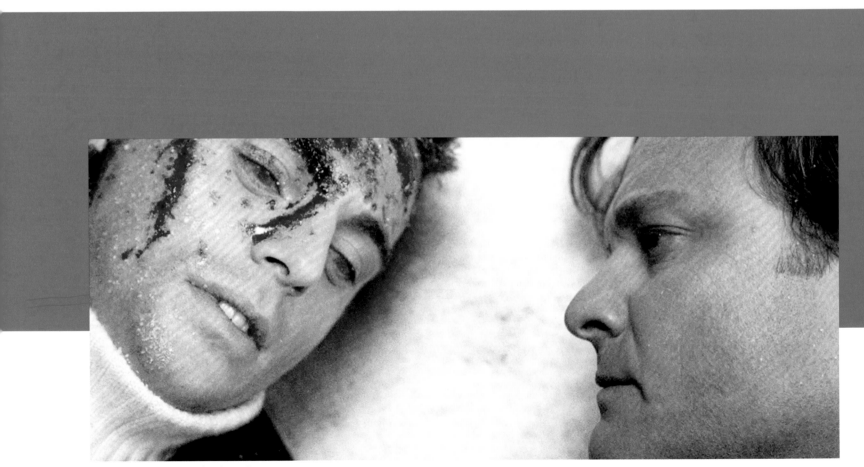

In his dream, George finds Jim after the accident.

In the past decade, the roster of first-time filmmakers who hail from other creative pursuits has ranged from installation artists Steve McQueen and Miranda July to rockers Fred Durst and Rob Zombie. Like the 1980s art star and director of *The Diving Bell and the Butterfly* (2007) among others, Julian Schnabel—an early, influential pioneer in the recent tradition of such artistic bilingualism—fashion transplant Tom Ford in his debut, *A Single Man* (2009), possesses a painterly eye for color and design, and an interest in the heady rush of transcendent emotion.

But Ford, of course, stands on his own two feet. Formidable as both an arbiter of style and an entrepreneur, he achieved fame and notoriety while the creative director for Gucci and Yves Saint Laurent and the highly visible head of his own name-brand lines. Predictably, and pleasurably, his first feature, a long-cherished dream realized, demonstrates exquisite design and the sort of confidence that comes with the comfort of past mastery in another field.

Perhaps nowhere is that confidence on display as much as in Ford's choice of material: the groundbreaking 1964 novel by Christopher Isherwood, which Edmund White has called "one of the first and best novels of the modern gay liberation movement." Adapting its subtle tone and interior-monologue structure for the screen would pose a challenge for even a seasoned filmmaker, but Ford demonstrates a willingness to experiment that marks the most effective translations from written page to screen. Not unlike a designer in dialogue with his public, he finds a way to create something that fulfills and confounds expectations from diverse audiences—in this case, a love story both highly specific in its closeted-gay milieu and universal in its aching depiction of devotion and longing.

In the film, George Falconer is an English professor at a California college who, years after his lover Jim's death in a car accident, remains preserved in his grief as if in amber. In the role, Ford smartly casts Colin Firth, that talented icon of buttoned-down romance, and sharpens George's pain by introducing to Isherwood's nimble text the specter of suicide. The single, neat-as-a-pin, sad man must be dislodged from his spiral, whether by his longtime friendship with a blowsy divorcée, the flattering attention of a flirty undergraduate, or by taming the memories that swirl across the film in flashbacks.

Set in the early 1960s, *A Single Man* describes the painful interplay between inside and outside, and it is powerfully evoked not only by Firth's breathtakingly restrained performance but by the notion of sensual surfaces. The production design is executed by the team responsible for the television show *Mad Men*, who maintain the characteristic color and line of the period, with all the accompanying dissonances between style and repression. But Ford goes one step further through a striking coloration technique embedded in the filmmaking itself: moments of heightened emotion are infused with the saturated hues associated with the Technicolor of classic melodrama.

Far from a superficial flourish, the surge of colors that are periodically unleashed on the muted palette bring us deeper into George's mind and heart, because they allow us to see the world as he feels it. The look that one critic compared to a mix of David Hockney and Hong Kong sensualist Wong Kar-wai suggests a fragile suspension, disturbed by recollections of both romantic rapture and domestic stability. George's ironic wit is still present, but so is the ache of loss, and the feeling of being marooned by his sadness in day-to-day encounters with neighbors or strangers.

Not many filmmakers are capable of, much less interested in, sustaining such a roil of emotions for an entire movie, but Ford is faithful to George's inner states. Far from lingering on paralyzing grief, the emotional terrain includes the sensitive and rare depiction of male-female friendship, in George's visits with the floundering Charley, played by Julianne Moore, trapped too by her own past. There's also a flashback to the night George and Jim met in a crowded bar, oblivious to those around them. Or, unforgettably, the phone call in which George receives news of, first, Jim's death, and then the fact that he will not be invited to the funeral.

It's that justly praised scene that can silence even knee-jerk skeptics of a fashion designer turned to cinema. Between Firth's interpretation of the moment, wisely left without directorial interference, and its echo with jarring sociopolitical realities across the decades, the scene confirms that Ford has more on his mind than George's tailored suits or the precise placement of a dazzling *Psycho* billboard in the background of a scene. And since the freshly minted filmmaker has voiced his intention to direct again, it should not be long before *A Single Man* proves to be the first in a line of visually and emotionally stirring films.

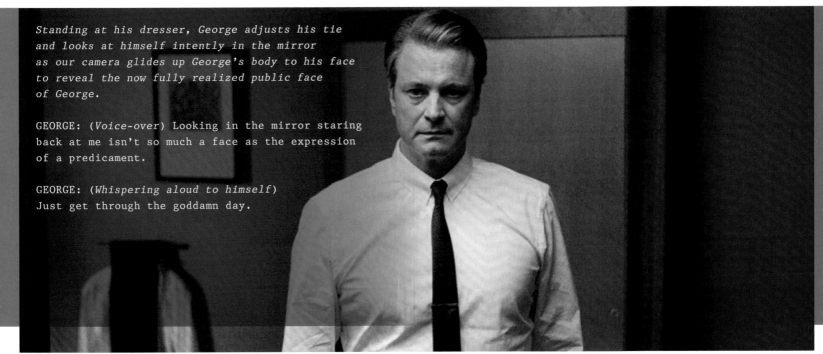

Standing at his dresser, George adjusts his tie and looks at himself intently in the mirror as our camera glides up George's body to his face to reveal the now fully realized public face of George.

GEORGE: (*Voice-over*) Looking in the mirror staring back at me isn't so much a face as the expression of a predicament.

GEORGE: (*Whispering aloud to himself*) Just get through the goddamn day.

George talks to himself as he prepares for a new day.

Year and place of birth
1961 Austin, Tex., USA
—

Lives and works in
Los Angeles, Calif., USA
London, UK
—

Education
New York University, USA
Parsons The New School for
Design, New York, N.Y., USA
—

Filmography
2009 A Single Man
— —

Release date
2009
—

Country of release
USA
—

Language
English
—

Running time
99 min.
—

Genre
Drama
—

Producers
Tom Ford, Chris Weitz,
Andrew Miano, Robert Salerno
—

Writers
Tom Ford, David Scearce
—

Cinematographer
Eduard Grau
—

Score
Abel Korzeniowski
—

Key cast
Colin Firth: George
Julianne Moore: Charley
Nicholas Hoult: Kenny
Matthew Goode: Jim
Jon Kortajarena: Carlos
—

Filming locations
Pasadena, Calif., USA
Glendale, Calif., USA
Leo Carillo State Beach,
Calif., USA
Santa Monica, Calif., USA
—

Format
35 mm
—

Awards for A Single Man
Venice International Film Festival
(Best Actor, 2009)
— —

Charley in her dressing room, before George comes over.

George visits his best friend Charley.

Jim and George, in a flashback, at Joshua Tree State Park.

Charley and George dance and reminisce about the old days.

George runs into his student Kenny at a bar.

Seeking the promise of America, a beautiful young Honduran woman, Sayra (Paulina Gaitan), joins her father and uncle on an odyssey to cross the gauntlet of the Latin American countryside en route to the United States. Along the way she crosses paths with a teenage Mexican gang member, El Casper (Edgar Flores), who is maneuvering to outrun his violent past and elude his unforgiving former associates. Together they must rely on faith, trust, and street smarts if they are to survive their increasingly perilous journey toward the hope of new lives.

CARY FUKUNAGA
SIN NOMBRE

Casper and Smiley walk back into La Confeti.

Willy, aka Casper, lies in bed with Martha Marlene.

Sin Nombre (2009) was a long shot to succeed. Or that's easily how it could have been interpreted by those who knew little or nothing of director Cary Fukunaga. How could an American first-time filmmaker, barely thirty years old, manage to lead a cast of mainly nonprofessional actors and crew through Central America, provide honest insight into Mexican gang culture, and then captivate Sundance audiences? These types of cinematic miracles simply don't happen, but this film, one of the most authentic and gripping tales ever made on the subject of immigration plight, proved to be an exception.

When *Sin Nombre* first screened at the Sundance Film Festival, there was much talk that it was the perfect independent film: one that not only displayed a fresh breed of talent but also deftly combined a character-based story with a more expansive examination of Latin American immigration culture. Heralded by festivalgoers up and down Park City, and bestowed with awards for its direction and cinematography, the film was later released to critical acclaim by Focus Features and solidified Fukunaga as one of the most exciting and spirited voices to hit the independent film scene.

The birth of *Sin Nombre* came as a harrowing and moving short film called *Victoria para Chino* (2004) that Fukunaga made as an NYU Tisch graduate student. In 2003, Fukunaga read a tragic headline about how seventeen of eighty-one illegal immigrants perished while locked inside an abandoned tractor-trailer en route to crossing the border. The resulting 35 mm short earned an invitation to screen in competition at 2005's Sundance (where I became aware of him), several prizes and accolades on the festival circuit, and a silver medal at the Student Academy Awards.

It was an obvious path for Fukunaga to take part in both the Sundance Screenwriters and Directors Labs, and it was there that he honed his story about two young nomads seeking refuge in the United States by traveling across Mexico via jungle, river, and train top. One of the travelers plans to meet her Honduran family in New Jersey, while the other flees from a dangerous past that includes a broken brotherhood with the Mara Salvatrucha gang, haunted memories of a fallen love, and his dutiful yet questionable connection to a twelve-year-old recruit. The two strangers end up uniting in their travels and seeking a common goal of a better life beyond borders.

It's safe to say that in anyone else's hands (with perhaps the exception of Gregory Nava, whose *El Norte* [1983] bears some familiarity), this tale would not have worked. Fukunaga brings to the story a rare unfiltered, untainted authenticity, which never allows the audience to doubt its honesty. And no thought is given to Fukunaga being a gringo, which perhaps serves as the ultimate tribute to the type of fearless and dedicated director he is.

In order to research the film, Fukunaga wanted to see it all with "his own eyes." He traveled to Chiapas, in southern Mexico, to meet with immigrants, immigrant-rights organizations, and gang members, before finally taking the dangerous train journey himself. What came from these travels was an extremely confident voice that spoke of such a ride not only from an informed point of view but also a highly sophisticated one. The results speak for themselves.

When Fukunaga speaks about the making of the film, it's very clear how that same sort of confidence and experience could lead a cast and crew to success. It was by no means an easy shoot, yet Fukunaga turned nonperformers into legitimate thespians and a character-based story into a visceral trek across the Mexican countryside. Through imagery, one sees the tireless, dangerous journey the characters are on. Through writing, and an ability to communicate, one senses the emotional stakes at hand.

In current indie cinema, especially among filmmakers Fukunaga's age, there's a trend— a respectable one, don't get me wrong—in which the camera acts mainly as a voyeuristic tool. *Sin Nombre* employs a kind of documentary style, but it never comes from a place of ego or irrelevance. And through traditional storytelling, and strong emphases on all aspects of cinema, including cinematography, sound, and editing, the camera almost seems to function as an integral character in the film. It's not uncommon to see this sort of attention to story and craft from a director who has hit his or her stride with film five or six, but on a first feature? Simply put, Fukunaga is the real deal.

He is certainly setting himself up to be a leading director, whether or not that is his intention. Universal Studios is already on board for his next film, and it'll be fascinating to see where he goes with it in terms of content and scope. There's a lot of expectation about how high Fukunaga can fly, and it might just be beyond anyone's imagination.

Lil' Mago, Casper, and Smiley wait to jump onto the train.

Sayra, Horacio, and Orlando learn the train will not be departing.

Year and place of birth
1977   Oakland, Calif., USA
—
Lives and works in
New York, N.Y., USA
London, UK
—
Education
UC Santa Cruz, Calif., USA
Tisch School of the Arts,
    New York University, USA
—
Filmography
2003   *Kofi* (short)
2004   *Victoria para Chino*
    (short)
2009   *Sin Nombre*
—
Director's awards
Victoria para Chino
Austin Film Festival
Audience Award
    (Best Narrative
    Student Short, 2004)

Woodstock Film Festival
    Jury Prize
    (Best Student Short, 2004)
Aspen Shortsfest BAFTA/LA
Award for Excellence
    (Honorable Mention, 2005)
BendFilm Festival Jury Prize
    (Best Student Film, 2005)
Gen Art Film Festival
    (Audience Award: Best Short,
    Best Short Film, 2005)
Milan International Film Festival
    (Best Short, 2005)
Nashville Film Festival
    (Best College Short, 2005)
Student Academy Awards, USA
    (Narrative Silver Medal,
    2005)
Sundance Film Festival
    (Short Filmmaking Award –
    Honorable Mention, 2005)
— —

Release date
2009
—
Country of release
Mexico
—
Language
Spanish
—
Running time
96 min.
—
Genre
Drama
—

Producer
Amy Kaufman
—
Writer
Cary Fukunaga
—
Cinematographer
Adriano Goldman
—
Score
Marcelo Zarvos
—

Key cast
Edgar Flores: Willy/El Casper
Paulina Gaitan: Sayra
Kristian Ferrer: El Smiley
Tenoch Huerta Mejia: Lil' Mago
Luis Fernando Peña: El Sol
—
Filming locations
Mexico City, Mexico
Veracruz, Mexico
Chiapas, Mexico
—
Format
35 mm

Awards for *Sin Nombre*
Deauville American Film Festival
    (Prix du Jury, 2009)
Edinburgh Film Festival
    (Skillset New Directors
    Award, 2009)
Sundance Film Festival
    (Directing Award, Excellence
    in Cinematography, 2009)
— —

Casper contemplates his future while heading north through Veracruz.

WILLY: Hurry up and get in the water, girl.

Sayra undresses to her underwear quickly, puts her clothes in a plastic bag and slips into the water. Leche grabs onto a rope tied to the black inner-tube and pulls Sayra into the current of the river. Sayra watches Willy as she's pulled further into the river, there is a sadness in his eyes. She suddenly understands why he's not getting ready. A tattooed face appears in a clearing. She barely has time to warn him when he raises a chimba, BAM! A bullet whizzes over Willy's head. Willy ducks. Willy darts back into the hedgerow tunnels.

SAYRA: Willy!

Sayra crosses the Rio Bravo with her belongings in a trash bag.

Adolescents come to terms with their lives following the 1996 race riots in St. Petersburg, Florida. Jason (Travis Maynard), a pierced and inked skinhead, takes impulsive and self-destructive chances with everyone and everything around him, while his mechanic friend Cale (Chris Fuller, under the name Lewis Brogan) embarks on a fleeting romance with Nicole (Kayla Tabish), a promiscuous diner waitress.

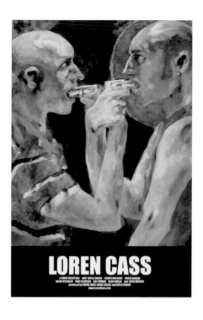

CHRIS FULLER
LOREN CASS

The Fight Kid and friends savagely attack Jason on the street.

Jason sits outside his home.

Loren Cass (2006), shot in just fourteen days in 2004, has a long, strange history. Its director, Chris Fuller, was born in Florida in 1982 and started writing the screenplay when he was in his mid-teens. In Fuller's words: "The adventure of *Loren Cass* began when I was fifteen years old. At that time, St. Petersburg, where I live, was a battleground, in the aftermath of the race riots. The city was divided into two, and you could literally cross one of its streets, Central Avenue, and find yourself in a completely different world. As soon as I wrote a screenplay about it, I was able to exorcise all the tension and destructiveness in which I had grown up."

With the screenplay under his belt, Fuller went in search of funding. He quit college and spent nights writing proposals in the hope of securing meetings and financial backing. He finally managed to begin principal photography in May 2004, and then spent over eighteen months reshooting sequences, editing, and generally polishing the film in postproduction.

Loren Cass is set in 1997. Its central characters are three teenagers—Cale Mitchell, Jason Ambrose, and Nicole Hayes—residing in St. Petersburg, Florida, a city in the grip of riots sparked by the killing of a young African-American by a white police officer. At their high school, the principal has a drinking problem, a boy loads a .357 in a bathroom stall, and Jason and Cale stir up old quarrels in the parking lot with their black classmates, which soon turn violent. Cale meets Nicole at the garage where he works after school and they start a relationship to overcome their boredom. Traveling home on the bus, Jason loses himself in dark, despairing daydreams, full of fires and graves. He tries to commit suicide, but fails. Even death seems to offer no solution to this grim cycle of violence and destruction.

"There is nothing literally autobiographical about the film, but it is intensely personal at the same time," says Fuller, who also appears as Cale, under a pseudonym. "All our efforts have been focused on making *Loren Cass* a totally new kind of film about young people, one whose soundtrack and visual language lie somewhere between dream and experimentation. It explores the mind of a teenager at a time of great tension and chaos. To me, it's a film that rests more on moods and feelings than on a clearly defined plot or narration. It's a celebration of unpleasant things."

The film's dialogue is succinct and laconic, and its fragmented, almost anecdotal plot plays out against news clips and commentary by individuals who took part in these events, people Fuller patiently sought out and interviewed. Shot in desolate urban locations whose emptiness reflects its characters' despair, *Loren Cass* is a very tough, aggressive portrait of a certain section of American youth, numbed by violence. Like an X-ray of the loss of innocence—which nothing can restore—this uncompromising film leaves its mark.

While there are dozens of films with similar themes—one need only mention Gus Van Sant's Palme d'Or-winning *Elephant* (2003)—rarely are they free of a somewhat mannered quality, or a desire to explain and simplify the phenomena that unfold. It is easy to film young people; it is extremely difficult, however, to express at a deep level what's missing from their lives. With a keen eye, Chris Fuller, benefiting from being young himself, has succeeded in doing just that. His inspired direction is almost abstract in its narrative style, but is very real in its violence.

Variety's Robert Koehler, who was struck by the film's energy, wrote: "A starkly radical film debut of uncommon power and artistic principle, Chris Fuller's *Loren Cass* announces a genuinely original filmmaking talent who literally pulls no punches in his depiction of teen angst and racial warfare on the streets of 1997 St. Petersburg, Fla. Suffused with pessimism and an overarching sense of the loneliness of modern American life, the pic affirms a vital alternative to the usual adolescent drama, making even Larry Clark look tame by comparison."

Finally, *Loren Cass* has enjoyed resounding success at many film festivals around the world. Its first public screening took place in 2007 at Dennis Hopper's CineVegas Film Festival, and two months later had its international premiere as a selection of the Locarno International Film Festival's Cinéastes du présent (Filmmakers of the Present) Competition. And in some countries the film has found remarkably wide distribution, by independent standards anyway. Because of its radical form—and uncompromising message—it continues to disturb and often provoke extreme reactions. And that's not the least of its power.

Jason and Cale talk outside the auto shop where Cale works.

Year and place of birth
1982   St. Petersburg, Fla., USA

—

Lives and works in
St. Petersburg, Fla., USA

—

Filmography
2006   *Loren Cass*

— —

Release date
2009

—

Country of release
USA

—

Language
English

—

Running time
83 min.

—

Genre
Drama

—

Producers
**Frank Craft, Chris Fuller,
Kayla Tabish**

—

Writer
Chris Fuller

—

Cinematographer
William Garcia

—

Score
Jimmy Morey

—

Key cast
**Kayla Tabish: Nicole
Travis Maynard: Jason
Lewis Brogan aka Chris Fuller:
  Cale
Jacob Reynolds: The Suicide Kid
Mike Glausier: The Punk Kid
Din Thomas: The Fight Kid**

—

Filming location
St. Petersburg, Fla., USA

—

Format
Super 16 mm

—

Awards for *Loren Cass*
**EntreVues, the Belfort
International Film Festival
(One+One Music Award,
2007)**

— —

Jason sits in the diner where Nicole works.

EXT. THE CLOCK RESTAURANT — NIGHT

We follow Nicole through the parking lot and inside.

*It's an all-night restaurant. Only a few people are
scattered around the place. She throws on an apron, grabs
a pen and a pad of paper, and heads to Jason's booth.*

NICOLE: What can I get ya?

JASON: Is it okay if I just sit here?

*He just needs a clean, well-lighted place. She nods
and goes about her night.*

The Fight Kid and Cale slug it out for the second time on the Sunshine Skyway Pier.

The Suicide Kid scans the crowd at a party in St. Petersburg, Florida.

Nicole stares out her window with Cale waiting below.

Ten years after the untimely death of her husband, Anna (Nicole Kidman) is tentatively emerging from her grief and taking steps to begin afresh. She agrees to marry Joseph (Danny Huston), who has patiently courted her for three years. Life seems to hold promise again, but then a ten-year-old boy (Cameron Bright) appears, claiming to be her husband reincarnated. Something about the boy, with his pervasive certainty, calm uncontainable force, and unquestionable memories, disrupts her on a profound level. She can't get him out of her mind, and against all her logic, sanity, and intelligence, she begins to be convinced.

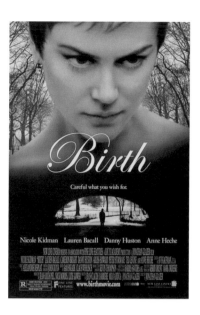

JONATHAN GLAZER
BIRTH

Sean meets Anna at the place where he says his previous life ended.

Anna and Joseph at their engagement party.

Contemporary British and American cinema, whether independent or mainstream, rarely offers films as adult, ambitious, and stylish as *Birth* (2004), a spellbinding work that explores mental and emotional depths from which no spectator will return unchanged.

Two films have marked Jonathan Glazer as the most original British director of recent years. His first, *Sexy Beast* (2000), was accomplished and full of promise, but it was his second, *Birth*, that revealed a filmmaker who set high standards. At the turn of the millennium he was highly regarded for his commercials and music videos for groups like Radiohead, Blur, and Massive Attack, and was seen as a pacesetter of the British audio-visual industry, a field known all too well for its cynicism and mediocrity. It wasn't so surprising, then, that he would make such an extraordinary impact when he turned to cinema.

Sexy Beast followed the tradition of British crime films; its screenplay and direction were adapted to cater to contemporary tastes, but was too intelligent to be seen as just another "cool" thriller. Set beside *Birth*, a visibly more ambitious work, *Sexy Beast* seems more like a psychological study than a simple genre film. In both, Glazer gives us a glimpse of his obsessions with psychological alienation, intrusions into enclosed and self-protective worlds, and the inner conflicts of neurotic characters divided between their fantasy lives, the desire for new beginnings, and fear of the unknown.

In *Birth*, a decade after her husband's sudden death, Anna (played by Nicole Kidman)—with the approval of her mother, a New York matriarch—is about to marry a rich man who has been wooing her for years. But then a young boy comes to her home claiming to be the reincarnation of her first husband and tries to dissuade her. *Birth* is more than surprising; unusual in both form and intention, and at first sight chic and somewhat bland (like its opulent New York interiors), it becomes increasingly disturbing. But despite its premise, *Birth* is not a horror film. Not to denigrate genre cinema, but anyone who sees the film as a derivative of M. Night Shyamalan's *The Sixth Sense* (1999), with which the director's style became an imitable brand, is failing to see *Birth*'s originality. It contains no sly narrative tricks, no last-minute revelations, but is like one movie hidden behind another, a story of reincarnation that for much of its length conceals the nub of the problem: the heroine's neurosis and her mental projections.

As a fiction of psychological disturbance, *Birth* draws on all the rich possibilities of perversion. Glazer co-wrote the screenplay—his first—with French scriptwriter Jean-Claude Carrière, a close collaborator of Luis Buñuel, whose presence is evident in the film's evocation of an airless upper-class milieu and its stifling rituals, which imperceptibly disintegrate as social conventions and characters' emotional repression are blown apart. If only in the film's midsection, the young boy plays the same role as the monkey in Nagisa Oshima's *Max My Love* (*Max mon amour*, 1986), which Carrière also scripted.

Birth is the portrait of a woman being slowly suffocated and gradually taking leave of reality, searching for a solution to her suffering. Glazer's direction is beautiful, with entrancing long shots that capture Anna's confusion, helplessness, and subtle mood changes. Particularly inspired is the stunning continuous shot during the opera sequence that freezes on her distraught face. Glazer acknowledges Stanley Kubrick's influence insofar as the kind of framing and camera movements he uses. He even references a key sequence from *Barry Lyndon* (1975) when Anna's fiancé corrects the child, his rival, in the middle of a private music recital, destroying order and propriety in an explosion of jealous rage. By allowing a brief moment of chaos to erupt, the fixity and symmetry of the frame are broken.

Birth, an urban, wintry film, gives great importance to its Central Park locations, beginning with a superb long opening sequence (a man filmed from behind runs through the snowy park, then collapses under the arch of a bridge). The way nature, dark and indomitable, survives in the heart of even the most sophisticated city gives *Birth* the quality of a psychoanalytical fairy tale. The film benefits from the sumptuous cinematography of Harris Savides, who's responsible for some of the most beautiful images in contemporary American cinema, in films for David Fincher, Gus Van Sant, Ridley Scott, James Gray, and Sofia Coppola. Glazer's admiration for Kubrick is also apparent in the extremely precise, reserved way he directs actors, and in his casting, which is uniformly excellent. Five years after Kubrick's *Eyes Wide Shut* (1999), Kidman is once again brilliant, giving one of her best performances to date.

In a theater, Anna considers the possible reincarnation of her dead husband, Sean.

Year and place of birth	Director's awards	Release date	Producers	Key cast	Filming location
1965 London, UK	*Sexy Beast*	2004	Nick Morris, Lizzie Gower	Nicole Kidman: Anna	New York, N.Y., USA
—	British Independent Film Awards	—	—	Cameron Bright: Sean	—
Lives and works in	(Best Director, 2001)	Country of release	Writers	Danny Huston: Joseph	Format
London, UK	National Board of Review	USA	Jean-Claude Carrière,	Lauren Bacall: Eleanor	35 mm
—	(Special Recognition, 2001)	—	Milo Addica, Jonathan Glazer	Anne Heche: Clara	—
Education	Toronto Film Critics Association	Language	—	Peter Stomare: Clifford	Awards for *Birth*
Middlesex Polytechnic,	(Best First Feature, 2001)	English	Cinematographer	Arliss Howard: Bob	Sitges – Catalonian International
London, UK	— —	—	Harris Savides	Alison Elliott: Laura	Film Festival
Trent Polytechnic,		Running time	—	Ted Levine: Mr. Conte	(Citizen Kane Award for
Nottingham, UK		100 min.	Score	Cara Seymour: Mrs. Conte	Best Directorial Revelation –
—		—	Alexandre Desplat	Joe M. Chalmers: Sinclair	Special Mention, 2004)
Filmography		Genre	—	Novella Nelson: Lee	— —
2000 *Sexy Beast*		Drama, Romance		Zoe Caldwell: Mrs. Hill	
2004 *Birth*		—		—	
—					

CLIFFORD: How can I help?

ANNA: Well I don't want...I don't want to fall in love again with "Sean." I don't want to fall in love with this little boy. Do you understand what I'm saying?

CLIFFORD: Sure.

ANNA: But that's what's happening. And I need you to come and help me. I need you to talk to him. I need you to tell him to go away.

CLIFFORD: Sure.

ANNA: Because I can't do it.

Anna goes to see her dead husband's brother Clifford and his wife Clara to tell them that her husband has been reincarnated as a ten-year-old boy.

In an echo of intimacy from another life, Sean and Anna bathe together.

Sean attempts to kiss Anna on the street.

Newlyweds Anna and Joseph on their wedding day.

In the heart of Portugal, amid the mountains, the month of August is abuzz with people and activity. Emigrants return home, set off fireworks, fight fires, sing karaoke, hurl themselves from bridges, hunt wild boar, drink beer, and make babies. In a cross between documentary and fiction, we witness the relationships of a father, daughter, and nephew in a traveling band develop against the vibrant landscape of a carnivalesque Portugal.

MIGUEL GOMES
OUR BELOVED
MONTH OF AUGUST

Torroselo's Philharmonic Band marches in the parade.

Filmmakers have been self-conscious about cinema from its earliest days, at least since Buster Keaton poked fun at the artifice and arbitrariness of editing in *Sherlock Jr.* (1924). As the century progressed, the movies stopped being merely a medium for storytelling and became a possible subject. Cinema began to explore the relationship between moviemakers and the money that went into their productions: from Vincente Minnelli's *The Bad and the Beautiful* (1952), to Jean-Luc Godard's modern masterpiece, *Contempt* (*Le Mépris*, 1963), to Joel Coen's parody about classic films, *Barton Fink* (1991).

This self-referentiality also made it possible for directors to do new things with their movies, such as engaging in film criticism by other means (Brian De Palma rewriting Alfred Hitchcock), converting successive movies into chapters of a single work in progress (Abbas Kiarostami's Koker trilogy), or defending the idea of art in a world full of harsh realities (the films of Victor Erice or Nanni Moretti). Either way, looking back at this history and bearing in mind that every movie inevitably makes a statement about cinema, we must ask ourselves: what new insight could *Our Beloved Month of August* (*Aquele Querido Mês de Agosto*, 2008) possibly bring?

Yet the film, by Portuguese director Miguel Gomes, does yield something new. For Gomes, the only way to think about movies is by substituting certainties with conjectures. Cinema is no longer something we search out, but rather something we might stumble upon. This sense of possibility—instead of the convincing affirmation normally provided by

a movie—is the theme of *Our Beloved Month of August*. One summer, in the town of Arganil, Portugal, a small crew led by Gomes tries to make a movie about an incestuous family and its melodramas. But shortly after shooting begins, the relationships among the actors also start to get complicated, to the point where the fiction they act out for the camera and the reality of the production itself mirror one another and become practically indistinguishable. Suddenly, we find ourselves watching an infinite loop in which the boundaries between fiction and reality are practically impossible to distinguish.

This imperceptible transformation is Gomes's great breakthrough. We don't know when or even how the lines between fiction and reality become blurred in the first place. In the classical era of cinema, there were rules that defined what was relevant and possible on screen. But in *Our Beloved Month of August*, there is no longer any guide helping us to distinguish drama from documentary, fiction from reality, nor are there any genre signposts to make sense of the story. As in François Truffaut's *Day for Night* (*La Nuit américaine*, 1973), the two territories—fiction and reality—cannot be separated. Instead, there is a pure continuity between the two in which Gomes wants us to get lost.

Gomes has described his film as a movie about our desire for fiction and the impulse to become stars even for a moment. Yet from the beginning, the film shows interviews with locals, as well as normal occurrences (religious processions, people camping) that would be happening even if the director's camera were not present. Thus *Our Beloved Month of August*

is composed of many different movies, and not in any particular order. It is not only an ethnographic documentary about a particular time and place, but also a documentary about making a movie. And when that documentary does not pan out, it becomes yet another documentary about local bands playing music all summer long. But at the same time, it is a fictional story about a handful of actors who try to make a romantic drama and the townspeople who sing and try to mix with the crew. Perhaps this is a crucial difference between Gomes's film and *Day for Night*: while Truffaut's film is essentially two movies in succession, Gomes's is many movies unfolding all at once.

It's no small irony that Gomes has given his film such a nostalgically Portuguese title, even though the movie refuses to pine for the long lost days of classical cinema. The wistful air of the title contrasts with the happiness of the characters singing in the movie, just as the simplicity of the songs contrasts with the sophistication of the mise-en-scène. For Gomes, there is no nostalgia for what has been lost, and a filmmaker's job is no longer to conjure a convincing scene but to propose an idea. The story is just an idea that the director lets develop but does not force, because reality is always lurking behind fiction, ready to ambush it. Fiction may survive, Gomes argues, but only if reality does not take its place. And when reality replaces fiction, these two enemies—thought to be irreconcilable—become confused, like brothers separated at birth that one day reunite and discover their inherent similarities.

LUIS MARANTE: *The after-hours bar*
A known nightspot
Place of ill-repute
With doors open all night
Anyone can go in
Yet on this night
Without expecting it
A lady entered
I was shocked
Because this lady was my wife

She got tired of sleeping alone
Waiting for me
And that night decided to put an end
To her long and wretched wait
She no longer wanted
To lead the life of the honored wife
If in truth

Luís Marante sings "Sound of Crystal."

Year and place of birth
1972   Lisbon, Portugal
—

Lives and works in
Lisbon, Portugal
—

Education
**Escola Superior de Teatro e
    Cinema, Amadora, Portugal**
—

Filmography
1999 *Meanwhile (Entretanto)*
        (short)
2000 *Christmas Inventory
        (Inventário de Natal)*
        (short)
2001 *Thirty-One Means Trouble
        (Trinta Um)* (short)
2002 *Kalkitos* (short)
2003 *Pre-Evolution Soccer's
        One-Minute Dance After
        a Golden Goal in the
        Master League* (short)
2004 *The Face You Deserve
        (A Cara Que Mereces)*
2006 *Canticle of All Creatures
        (Cântico das Criaturas)*
        (short)
2008 *Our Beloved Month
        of August (Aquele Querido
        Mês de Agosto)*
—

Director's awards
Meanwhile
Vila do Conde International
Short Film Festival
    (Best Director, 1999)
International Short Film Festival
Oberhausen
    (City Award, 2002)

Christmas Inventory
Entrevues Belfort International
Film Festival
    (Jury's Special Mention,
    2001)

Thirty-One Means Trouble
Vila do Conde International Short
Film Festival
    (Jury's Special Mention,
    2002)

The Face You Deserve
Covilhã Film Festival
    (Special Mention, 2004)

Canticle of All Creatures
Vila do Conde International Short
Film Festival
    (Best Portuguese Film, 2006)
Coimbra Film Festival
    (Best Portuguese Short Film,
    2007)
— —

Release date
2008
—

Country of release
Portugal
—

Language
Portuguese
—

Running time
150 min.
—

Genre
Drama
—

Producers
**Luís Urbano, Sandro Aguilar,
Thomas Ordonneau**
—

Writers
**Miguel Gomes, Mariana Ricardo,
Telmo Churro**
—

Cinematographer
Rui Poças
—

Score
Mariana Ricardo
—

Key cast
**Sónia Bandeira: Tânia
Fábio Oliveira: Hélder
Joaquim Carvalho: Domingos
Andreia Santos: Lena
Armando Nunes: Gomes
Manuel Soares: Celestino
Emmanuelle Fèvre: Fátima
Diogo Encarnação: Eric
Bruno Lourenço: Baixista
Maria Albarran: Rosa Maria
Nuno Mata: Médico**
—

Filming locations
**Arganil, Portugal
Góis, Portugal
Oliveira do Hospital, Portugal
Pampilhosa da Serra, Portugal
Tábua, Portugal**
—

Format
35 mm
—

Awards for *Our Beloved
Month of August*
São Paulo International
Film Festival
    (Critics Award, 2008)
Valdivia International
Film Festival
    (Best International
    Film Award, 2008)
Viennale
    (FIPRESCI Award, 2008)
Buenos Aires International
Independent Film Festival
    (Best Film, 2009)
— —

Hélder and Tânia go for a swim.

Domingos hugs his daughter Tânia.

Tânia and Helder goof off in Tânia's bedroom.

Tânia sings "To Die of Love."

During an entire Real Madrid versus Villarreal match, before 80,000 fans at the Santiago Bernabéu stadium, seventeen movie cameras were placed around the playing field, focusing solely on Zinédine Zidane. The film, which set out to get up close and personal to one of the sports world's untouchables, offers Zidane's private reflections and observations expressed through subtitles that act as soliloquy, and all the drama and excitement of a soccer genius at work in stunning detail.

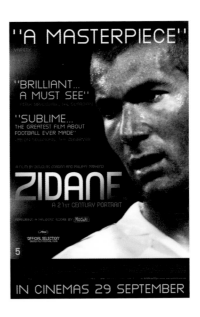

DOUGLAS GORDON
ZIDANE: A 21ST CENTURY PORTRAIT

Zidane surveys the field.

What makes a portrait? Must it be a formal rendering of a man, woman, or family sitting in a studio, or perhaps a traditional candid of a passerby in the street, captured unawares by a roving photographer? Or can it be, as video artists Douglas Gordon and Philippe Parreno propose over the course of ninety-one minutes in *Zidane: A 21st Century Portrait* (2006), a cubistic seventeen-camera production undertaken during a soccer game in front of thousands of spectators?

The artistic ambition of their endeavor is heralded by the presentation of the title in the credits: the letters ZIDANE appear superimposed like Da Vinci's iconic multiple-pose drawing *Vitruvian Man*. And in the extraordinary film that follows, the French-Algerian soccer superstar Zinédine Zidane is indeed captured in multiple poses—walking, waiting, turning, shooting, and forever watching, watching, watching. He is almost always the focus of the frame, often to the exclusion of the game at large between his Real Madrid and Villarreal, which took place at Madrid's Santiago Bernabéu Stadium on April 23, 2005.

The result is an unconventional portraiture, at once artwork and outsized sports photography. Gordon and Parreno cut between close-ups, full-body shots, and occasional panoramas, while also varying the sound we hear: crowd noise, Zidane's "hey"s and rustles, kibitzing Spanish announcers, and a serene guitar soundtrack specially done by the Scottish band Mogwai. Zidane's acute strategic eye is on display more than tactical derring-do, as he observes and weighs situations. Yet even at rest, he cuts a riveting, almost godlike figure: brutally handsome, tall, and rigidly poised, his sculpted shaved head often pouring sweat. And far from a star hyped up by spectacle, he is a body with all the vividness of real-time: at minute 11:00, he looks worried; at 12:55, he walks backwards in close-up, falling at 13:40; at 47:00, he checks out a fallen foe; and, finally, at hour 1:02, he eludes four defenders and cross passes to his teammate Ronaldo, who head-butts the ball into the goal.

The counterintuitive bravura of *Zidane* is typical of the work of Douglas Gordon, best known as an installation artist. The Glasglow-born Gordon specializes in appropriating art and media and re-mediating our experience of them through temporal and other distortion. In his career-making *24-Hour Psycho* (1993), the Hitchcock classic is slowed down to a geological pace, unspooling its psychological twists one frame at a time over the course of the day; *Déjà-Vu* (2000) projected the count-down noir classic *D.O.A.* at different speeds on three screens. The technique allows the viewer to inhabit a movie in new ways, uncover strange feelings in repose, and pay fresh attention to the sensual qualities of the image and its blown-up detail.

Zidane is a different sort of experiential dilation altogether—equally indebted to Andy Warhol and ESPN. As the soccer match unfolded, Gordon and Parreno directed their team of international star cameramen (overseen by Darius Khondji) from a trailer outside the stadium, thereby joining the unsung ranks of TV sports control-room mavens who have stitched together improvised coverage for the past several decades. Equipped with footage, the filmmakers went on to edit it together with rhythms that felt attuned to Zidane's ebb and flow, while also retaining an artisanal fluidity. Lest the project seem the acme of artistic pretention, it's worth noting that the film has in fact been repackaged by a German soccer-fan magazine as part of an eleven-part DVD series of televised games. (Hellmuth Costard's *Soccer As Never Before* [1971] would be the proper artistic precursor: similarly, an entire film focused on a star, George Best, in a match between Manchester United and Coventry City.)

Though *Zidane* properly falls within a tradition of portraiture in film and other media, it is amusing to note its arrival in festivals after a spate of biopics in mainstream cinema. And as one critic pointed out, a conventional record of Zidane would have mentioned his upbringing in a poor quarter of Marseille, or his crucial head-butt goals in the 1998 World Cup final. And while Gordon and Parreno are interested in aestheticizing Zidane—the play of pixels in certain shots makes him twinkle with life—they also provide glimpses into his internal monologue through quotations that appear at the bottom of the screen. In these he describes how he is focused exclusively on the game and capable of noticing any sound in the stadium.

These insights, together with Zidane's thoughtful grace and the strains of Mogwai's loping chords, achieve a lyrical serenity. It is an amazing accomplishment: stolen moments during a massive spectator event, self-conscious and unguarded, both embedded deep inside the game and abstracted into pure movement. With *Zidane*, Gordon and Parreno truly do put themselves forth as a portraitists of the twenty-first century—of both its men and its media.

When you are immersed in the game, you don't really hear the crowd. You can almost decide for yourself what you want to hear. You are never alone. I can hear someone shift around in their chair. I can hear someone coughing. I can hear someone whisper in the ear of the person next to them. I can imagine that I can hear the ticking of a watch.

Jumping to catch a pass.

Year and place of birth
1966   Glasgow, UK
—

Lives and works in
Berlin, Germany
—

Education
Glasgow School of Art, UK
The Slade School of Fine Art,
   London, UK
—

Filmography
2006   *Zidane: A 21st Century*
   ***Portrait* (co-directed**
   with Philippe Parreno)
— —

Release date
2006
—

Country of release
France
—

Language
English, French
—

Running time
91 min.
—

Genre
Documentary
—

Producers
Sigurjon Sighvatsson, Anna
Vaney, Victorien Vaney
—

Cinematographer
Darius Khondji
—

Score
Mogwai
—

Key cast
Zinédine Zidane: Himself
—

Filming location
Santiago Bernabéu Stadium,
   Madrid, Spain
—

Format
35 mm
—

Awards for *Zidane: A 21st*
Century Portrait
Copenhagen International
Film Festival
   (New Vision Award, 2006)
Edinburgh International
Film Festival
   (Best of the Fest, 2006)
— —

Zidane contemplates the Villareal defensive line.

The lights of Santiago Bernabéu Stadium.

Intercepting the ball from Villareal.

Zidane yells at an opponent, while attempting to capture the ball.

Twenty-year-old Ivy (Zoe Kazan) heads home
to New York for spring break with a fresh romance
in her heart. When her best friend Al (Mark Rendall)
can't find a place to stay, she asks her mother
to take him in. Spending time in the city together
strengthens their friendship, while Ivy's boyfriend
grows more distant. Although troubled, Ivy keeps
her emotions in check, until her feelings become
something she can't control.

BRADLEY RUST GRAY
THE EXPLODING GIRL

Ivy on the subway, home on break from college.

It's unlikely that many filmmakers could work as symbiotically as Bradley Rust Gray and So Yong Kim do. They produce each other's films, their production company is called soandbrad, and they share editing responsibilities, all of which they nearly always speak about in the first-person plural. Gray even refers to his second feature *The Exploding Girl* (2009) as a B-side to Kim's 2006 *In Between Days* (alluding to the single of the same name by The Cure, the B-side of which was called "The Exploding Boy"). And yet his films do differ noticeably from those of his partner. They are more romantic, more playful, more dreamy. Gray's first film, *Salt* (2003), is a love story, a road movie, almost a fairy tale. Gray has a thing for the fantastic; he's been developing a werewolf movie called *Jack and Diane* for years now. The lengthy gestation of the project can be attributed to *The Exploding Girl*. Gray and actress Zoe Kazan decided they wanted to work together although they didn't even have a rough sketch for a story, just the name of the main character: Ivy.

It was only when Mark Rendall came on board as the second lead that the story began to take shape, a sort of love triangle in which the third person remains absent. Al has been friends with Ivy for years, but has recently begun to see her as more. At the same time, Ivy is still very much hung up on her boyfriend, Greg, although she's no longer sure if her feelings are entirely reciprocated. The story begins with a journey back to New York from college for spring break. Upon arrival, it emerges that Al can no longer stay at his parents' place, leading him to move in with Ivy and her mother. Ivy's attention, though, is paid to her cell phone and Greg's nonexistent calls.

The way Al cautiously courts Ivy is just as touching as Ivy's patience with Greg, whom she never seems able to reach. Again and again, she gets his voicemail, and when he does end up calling, he just palms her off with lazy excuses. "Miss you" thus becomes the only declaration of love the two of them ever make. Al is aware of Ivy's distress, despite that she never mentions it directly. This makes cracks appear in their intimacy, as they play cards with Ivy's mother, go to parties, listen to music in the sun-dappled park, take walks, and visit a cousin who's just had a baby. When the baby's father asks Al how long Ivy and he have been together, Al explains, embarrassed, that they're just friends. Ivy pretends not to hear. She often comes across as detached anyway, strangely calm, as if she were watching her own life from a distance. This calmness is no coincidence, for Ivy is an epileptic, always prepared for her condition to break out once again—the second explanation for the film's unusual title.

When Ivy gently presses Al to start a relationship with another girl, Al turns the tables on her and asks for love advice in the hope that it will arouse her jealousy and thus her desire in the process. We wait impatiently for the moment when this will finally happen, although this involves looking at their faces and reading between the lines, for the big events that normally get things moving are absent from the film. One of these is the car accident that Greg is involved in. Ivy hears about it on the telephone, finding out at the same time that there was another woman in the car with him. The other is the epileptic fit that Ivy suffers after drinking too much beer at a party. We hear more of the seizure than we see of it, as everything happens at the rear of the frame, kept out of view by objects in the foreground.

There is clearly a method to this approach; the film's excellent camerawork relies on a large focal length to follow the actors at a distance, observing them on the street or on the subway in the midst of other people in an almost documentary style. The viewer is not a participant in the action but more of an interested observer. There are almost always obstructing objects in the foreground, the shallow depth of field emphasizing the isolation of the protagonists and intensifying the feeling of unreality generated by a warm New York spring. At times, it almost feels claustrophobic, creating a yearning for wide spaces, for a horizon.

The film only allows this to occur toward the end, when, sitting on the roof of an apartment building, Ivy gives free rein to her emotions and lets Al comfort her as swarms of pigeons fly overhead, the flapping of their wings suddenly rendering words superfluous. The film's subtle sound design contributes a great deal to its hypnotizing effect throughout.

The Exploding Girl ends as it began, with a car journey. Ivy and Al in the backseat. Her hand approaches his. His head is lying on her shoulder, hers leans against his. Suddenly, she opens her eyes and stares into the distance. The camera moves down to their hands, which are now firmly in each other's grip.

Ivy lies in bed the morning after she and Al hang out at a party.

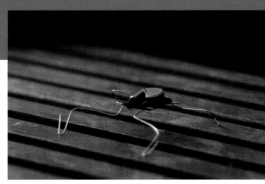

The robot Al made for Ivy.

Year and place of birth
1971   Kettering, Ohio, USA
—

Lives and works in
Brooklyn, N.Y., USA
—

Education
University of Southern
   California, Los Angeles,
   USA
British Film Institute,
   London, UK
The School of the Art Institute
   of Chicago, Ill., USA
Icelandic College of Arts and
   Crafts, Reykjavik, Iceland
Auburn University, Ala., USA
—

Filmography
2000   hITCH (short)
2003   Salt
2009   The Exploding Girl
—

Director's awards
Salt
Berlin International Film Festival
   (Caligari Film Prize, 2003)
Rouen Nordic Film Festival
   (Young European Audience
   Award, 2003)
Skip City International
D-Cinema Festival
   (Best New Director, 2004)
— —

Release date
2010
—

Country of release
USA
—

Language
English
—

Running time
79 min.
—

Genre
Drama
—

Producers
So Yong Kim, Karin Chien,
Ben Howe, Bradley Rust Gray
—

Writer
Bradley Rust Gray
—

Cinematographer
Eric Lin
—

Score
múm
—

Key cast
Zoe Kazan: Ivy
Mark Rendall: Al
Maryann Urbano: Mom
Franklin Pipp: Greg
—

Filming locations
Brooklyn, N.Y., USA
New York, N.Y., USA
—

Format
4K Digital
—

Awards for The Exploding Girl
Santiago International
Film Festival
   (Best Film, 2009)
Tribeca Film Festival
   (Best Actress, 2009)
— —

Al tells Ivy about a girl he likes at school.

Ivy starts to feel ill on the street, and Al tries to comfort her.

GREG: This isn't going to be easy to say. But,
I think we should break up. I mean, we kinda need to.

Ivy stops.

IVY: Why?

GREG: Cause...I like Rebecca still. It's like
I got back and realized I never stopped liking
her...you know.

Pause. Ivy doesn't answer.

GREG: You still there?

IVY: Yeah.

Silence. Ivy swallows.

Greg breaks up with Ivy over the phone.

In a village near Berlin, Markus (Andreas Müller), a metalworker, is married to Ella (Ilka Welz), a domestic servant. One day Markus visits a nearby town to attend a training course with the volunteer fire brigade of which he is a member. In the evening there is a lot of drinking, laughing, and dancing. The next morning, Markus wakes up in the apartment of a waitress, Rose. He can't recall much of what happened. When he tries to find out, it is the beginning of a love to which he is unaccustomed, yet which does not seem to affect his love for his wife.

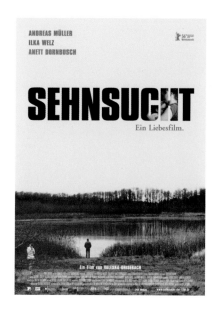

VALESKA GRISEBACH
LONGING

Markus dancing at the firemen's ball to a song by Robbie Williams.

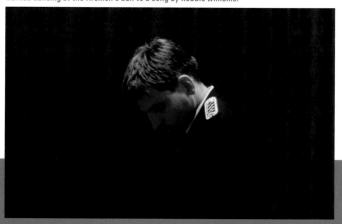

Markus and Ella sleeping in an embrace.

There was a time when characters in movies were meant to put viewers at ease from the moment they appeared on screen. Their social, cultural, and emotional status would all be immediately identifiable, lest the viewer get confused or frustrated. Next to the work of Valeska Grisebach, however, such older movies are little more than dinosaurs, plodding along slowly and predictably. Grisebach's films have the light and enigmatic touch of a director who is not out to prove what she already knows but to discover something yet unknown.

In her debut, *Be My Star* (*Mein Stern*, 2001), two teenagers, Nicole and Schöps, adopt the romantic rhetoric of adults without actually having experienced love, as if fast-forwarding into their predestined societal roles. While making the movie, Grisebach carefully observed the young duo and their interactions, but without putting them under a microscope. She tried to capture the innocence of adolescence by letting the actors add their own lines and ideas. The result was an air of informality, a sense of levity that remains even in the movie's most difficult and dramatic moments.

Grisebach is a master of observation, but her skill goes well beyond the director's proverbial "eye for detail." Her true talent is the ability to capture the lives of her characters without judging them. By avoiding the imposition of prejudices and opinions, she steers clear of unnecessary explanations, which in turn frees her characters of clichés.

Grisebach's power of observation is even more refined in her second feature, *Longing* (*Sehnsucht*, 2006), which in a way picks up where *Be My Star* left off. Markus, a metalworker and voluntary firefighter, and his wife, Ella, have an apparently happy life; at first glance, they resemble Schöps and Nicole, twenty years later. Although Grisebach's films both touch on the fragility of love, the similarities between them quickly end. For one thing, whereas *Be My Star* is set in the city, *Longing* unfolds in the countryside. When suicide tears apart a couple whom Markus and Ella know, the death is like an earthquake that opens a chasm between them and sends their marriage crumbling. The suicide is an omen of things to come, and the threat grows steadily until the movie's pivotal scene. Markus travels to a nearby town for a firefighters' meeting, where his perfect love for Ella begins to crack. After dinner, drinks, and dancing, he wakes up the next morning in bed with Rose, a local waitress, with no idea what happened the night before.

Therein lies Grisebach's greatest gamble: she redefines what it means to be a spectator. The moment that *Longing* withholds—Markus's suspected infidelity—becomes a mental prison cell for the viewer, who is forced to work to understand the film. Whereas cinema originated as a mass diversion to occupy leisure time, Grisebach takes the moviegoer in a different, more challenging direction. Her spectator is a product of modernity and therefore no longer a passive child but an active adult, who must work to supply the missing pieces necessary for the film to make sense. The uncertainty inevitably recalls the beginning of the film and raises another question: could Markus have saved the man who killed himself? But Grisebach also holds a tremendous surprise in store, closing the movie with a bang as startling as the opening scenes were deceptive.

Grisebach substitutes subtle looks for explanations, but the absence of unnecessary dialogue—which connects her characters to those of Bruno Dumont and, to a lesser extent, the Dardenne brothers, all obvious influences—does not make her characters simple or one-dimensional. Instead, the sparse dialogue makes us work to understand them. We never understand Markus better than when he sings "Feel" by Robbie Williams and dances to the music. Markus's performance is shown in real time, and the momentary deviation from the plot reveals the movie's key secret: rhythm. The pacing of *Longing* is measured yet variable, allowing for surprises that turn its length into a virtue rather than a burden. And as Markus suddenly escapes from the storyline, his dance captures the strange, sensual, and offbeat movements not of Markus but of the actor, Andreas Müller.

It is as if Grisebach realized at this moment that her movie was more of a documentary about its actors than a drama about Markus and Ella. This long, hypnotic sequence underlines the extraordinary and genuine interest that the latest German directors have in their countrymen. At the same time, the scene suggests the connections between two generations of filmmakers: on one hand, Christian Petzold, Andreas Dresen, Thomas Arslan, and Angela Schanelec; and on the other, their younger colleagues, Maren Ade and Valeska Grisebach. Clearly, leaving the moviegoer with plenty of questions is not a bad way to make a film.

MARKUS: It was a nice day.

ELLA: I have to think of you so often. Of us. When I look at you like this it takes my breath away. I imagine things we don't normally do. Looking at each other when we touch, talking when we have sex. I desire you so much.

MARKUS: Ella.

ELLA: Sleep with me.

Markus and Ella make love upon his return.

Year and place of birth
1968   Bremen, West Germany
—

Lives and works in
Berlin, Germany
—

Education
Vienna Film Academy, Austria
—

Filmography
1995   *Speaking and
       Nonspeaking (Sprechen
       und Nichtsprechen)*
       (short)
1997   *In the Desert of Gobi
       (In der Wueste Gobi)*
       (short)
1999   *Berlino* (short)
2001   *Be My Star (Mein Stern)*
2006   *Longing (Sehnsucht)*
—

Director's awards
Be My Star
First Steps Award
       (Best Feature Film Under
       60 Minutes Length, 2001)
Toronto International
Film Festival
       (FIPRESCI – Special Mention,
       2001)
Torino Film Festival
       (International Feature Film
       Competition – Best Film,
       2002)
— —

Release date
2006
—

Country of release
Germany
—

Language
German
—

Running time
88 min.
—

Genre
Drama
—

Producer
Peter Rommel
—

Writer
Valeska Grisebach
—

Cinematographer
Bernard Keller
—

Key cast
Andreas Müller: Markus
Ilka Welz: Ella
Anett Dornbusch: Rose
—

Filming location
Brandenburg, Germany
—

Format
35 mm
—

Awards for *Sehnsucht*
Brussels Film Festival
       (Prix l'Age d'Or, 2006)
Buenos Aires International
Independent Film Festival
       (Special Jury Award, 2006)
Copenhagen International
Film Festival
       (Alice Award, 2006)
Gijón International Film Festival
       (FIPRESCI Jury Award –
       Best Film, 2006)

Ludwigshafen German
Film Festival
       (Art of Film Award, 2006)
Pesaro Film Festival
       (Best Film, 2006)
Warsaw International
Film Festival
       (Special Jury Award, 2006)
— —

Firemen in the village have lit a fire to celebrate Easter.

Markus takes some time alone.

A grieving Markus holds onto the rabbit in his garage.

A single mother and her embattled son struggle to
subsist in a small Mississippi Delta township.
An act of violence thrusts them into the world of
an emotionally devastated store owner, awakening
the fury of a bitter and long-standing conflict.

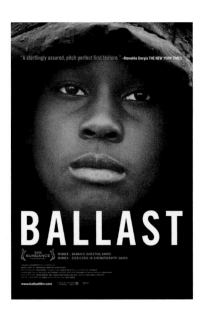

LANCE HAMMER
BALLAST

Marlee has returned from work and discusses the day with James before putting him to bed.

James wanders about the new property.

In traditional practice, movies were made by coming up with the characters and plot, and then choosing where to shoot the film and set these elements into motion. But modern filmmakers from Michelangelo Antonioni to Tsai Ming-Liang have turned that convention on its head by putting location first. The setting is allowed to determine the story. The characters can no longer be separated from their surroundings, because everything that happens to them stems from the part of the world to which they belong. Cinema, one might say, becomes "site-specific."

This is precisely how Lance Hammer conceives his feature-length debut, *Ballast* (2008). When the camera first sweeps over the Mississippi Delta, we are already left with the impression that something important has happened. Here, death and tragedy lurk, encircling a family that might politely be called dysfunctional: Lawrence, his late brother's widow Marlee, and her child, James. Through ellipses in time and space Hammer keeps us from putting together their story until the very end, as if hiding pieces of a puzzle. As a result, the drugs, suicide, violence, solitude, joblessness, and insanity of their lives engender a sense of discomfort more than desolation.

Hammer's bleak, devastated characters are like modern updates of William Faulkner's creations, as discovered by an anthropologist after a hurricane. But instead of Hurricane Katrina, these Southerners have been ravaged by the hurricane of capitalism. The wind took more than their houses, jobs, and personal belongings; it took away their sense of who they are. *Ballast* is, among other things, a movie about the destruction of people as the agents of their own lives. The characters are defined not only by their weathered faces and bodies, but above all by the places they wander: harsh, empty environments at once unignorable and uninhabitable. These spaces become extensions of the characters' states of mind, in a kind of symbiosis. Even though Hammer makes the extraordinary decision to use close-ups that hide the context of each scene, the locations speak loud and clear. And they speak because they capture the underlying theme of the movie: the hardship of life.

The privation in the story does more than smother and strangle the characters. It is a force that quietly shapes their lives too. An economy that is both political and verbal is evident in the images and sounds of the film. Hammer prefers to show rather than tell; he withholds the gestures of his actors and never presents his conflict using words. The light that falls seems an extension of the opaque expressions of his sad, hopeless creatures, while their words are mere sounds as well as a form of communication.

But if Hammer denies his characters an ease of communicating through words, this devaluation of language reflects his broader approach to sound and, more importantly, its absence. The director creates silence that is never completely silent, but rather an omission that allows us to hear something else, a sensation that evokes a low murmur, sad and insistent, or a slow, painful cry. It is the sound of a requiem for something lost, or never possessed in the first place, as if the world itself were expressing its discomfort.

Ballast is a movie about survival, but not because it depicts survivors. In order to survive, you must believe that something will last, but these characters do not look toward the future with optimism. They know quite well that all they have are their feelings. Rather, Hammer's movie is about survival because it escaped the collapse of what was once called American independent film, or at least the homogenizing effect wrought by the 1990s on the following ten years. *Ballast* does belong to a certain tradition, but that does not make the film a hostage to the past. Hammer's drama is conscious of what came before while also being aware that it is impossible to go back. What most makes *Ballast* a survival story is thus this stubborn recognition of the past, as opposed to the "independence" customarily sought by other artists working in independent film. Yet Hammer, like his own protagonists, refuses to yearn for some lost paradise, let alone attempt to build a new one. Instead, he asks whether it is even possible to save something that has already been destroyed. In the end, the question of what can be rescued from the past and the movie's own poetic vision are one and the same.

Lawrence, James, Juneau cross the road and proceed into the field. They walk for awhile in silence. Deeper into field now, James is several yards ahead of Lawrence.

JAMES: If you're almost the same person and have the same feelings as my dad, did you love my mamma too?

LAWRENCE: No.

JAMES: Did she love you?

LAWRENCE: No.

JAMES: Why not, if you're the same as him?

LAWRENCE: We're not exactly the same.

James walks in the field with his uncle, Lawrence.

Year and place of birth
1967   Ventura, Calif., USA
—
Lives and works in
Los Angeles, Calif., USA
—
Education
**University of Southern
    California, Los Angeles,
    USA**
—
Filmography
2008   *Ballast*
— —

Release date
2008
—
Country of release
USA
—
Language
English
—
Running time
96 min.
—
Genre
Drama
—
Producer
Lance Hammer
—
Writer
Lance Hammer
—
Cinematographer
Lol Crawley
—

Key cast
**Micheal J. Smith, Sr.: Lawrence
JimMyron Ross: James
Tarra Riggs: Marlee
Johnny McPhail: John**
—
Filming location
The Mississippi Delta, Miss., USA
—
Format
35 mm
—
Awards for *Ballast*
**Buenos Aires International
Independent Film Festival
    (FIPRESCI Prize, Directing
    Award, SIGNIS Prize, 2008)**

**Cinema City International Film
and New Media Festival
    (Grand Prix, 2008)
Deauville American Film Festival
    (Jury Prize, Cartier Newcomer
    Award, 2008)
Durban International
Film Festival
    (Directing Award, 2008)
Gijón International Film Festival
    (Best Actor, Best Actress,
    2008)
Gotham Independent Film Awards
    (Breakthrough Director
    Award, 2008)
Independent Film Festival Boston
    (Grand Jury Prize, 2008)
Ljubljana International
Film Festival
    (FIPRESCI Prize, 2008)**

**Provincetown International
Film Festival
    (John Schlesinger Award,
    2008)
San Francisco International
Film Festival
    (FIPRESCI Prize, 2008)
Sundance Film Festival
    (Dramatic Directing
    Award, Excellence in
    Cinematography Award,
    2008)
Toronto Film Critics Association
    (Best First Feature, 2008)
IndieLisboa International
Independent Film Festival
    (Grand Prize, 2009)
Mexico City International
Contemporary Film Festival
    (Grand Prize, 2009)**
— —

James takes refuge in Juneau.

Lawrence returns to the radio station.

Lawrence drags James into the field demanding to know where the bullets are.

Marlee stops the car to observe Lawrence.

Victor (Paul Blain) lives in Vienna with Annette (Marie-Christine Friedrich) and their young daughter, Pamela (Victoire Rousseau). He avoids work by spending his days, and sometimes his nights, away from home. Annette trusts that he will get his act together once they move back to Paris, but he doesn't. After a violent argument, he moves in with a junkie with whom he has fallen in love. Annette leaves Victor and disappears with Pamela. Eleven years later, Pamela (Constance Rousseau), now seventeen and living in Paris with her mother, learns that her father lives nearby and decides to see him again.

MIA HANSEN-LØVE
ALL IS FORGIVEN

Victor, soon after Annette tells him she is taking Pamela to Vienna for the holidays.

Annette and Pamela at a friend's house on Pamela's birthday.

It's a rare film (especially a first film) that succeeds in expressing feelings as profound as those surrounding separation, absence, and bereavement with as much subtlety and style as Mia Hansen-Løve's *All Is Forgiven* (*Tout est pardonné*, 2007). Confirming the remarkable narrative and aesthetic mastery that this young director demonstrated in her debut feature, is a second film, *Father of My Children* (*La père de mes enfants*, 2009), which is elegance itself. Hansen-Løve, born in 1981, received a Master's degree in German philosophy before making a number of short films. She also acted in Olivier Assayas's *Late August, Early September* (*Fin août, début septembre*, 1998) and *Sentimental Destinies* (*Les Destinées sentimentales*, 2000).

All Is Forgiven tells a story that is both simple and painful, based, it would seem, on the director's own memories. Victor lives in Vienna with Annette, a beautiful Austrian woman, and their daughter, Pamela. Victor would like to be a writer, but most of the time he avoids work: he plays with Pamela, visits Annette's parents, and hangs out with drug dealers. Annette, deeply in love with him, believes he will get it together once they return to Paris. Back in France, though, Victor resumes his bad habits and takes increasing amounts of drugs. One evening, Annette and Victor, who is jealous and violent under the influence of alcohol, have a fight. Victor leaves the family home and has an affair with a young addict, who dies of an overdose. Annette leaves for Vienna with Pamela. Eleven years later, Pamela is seventeen and living in Paris with her mother, who has made a new life with another man. One day, Pamela learns that her father is also living in Paris and decides to see him again.

The film is divided into sections ("Vienna 95," "The return to Paris," "One month later," "Pamela," "11 years later"), giving it a literary quality. These chapters also enable the director to insert gaps into the story; not everything is narrated and these ellipses give the lives of the characters an element of mystery. Life continues in these "holes"; missing things and missing people are as important as those that are seen. Cinema is more a matter of time than of image. *All Is Forgiven*, which resuscitates moments of a past story, is based on selection, constructed around emptiness, absence, and loss, divided between two cultures, two languages, two cities. But at the same time, the feeling engendered by the film's outlook is one of harmony, not rupture. It has a subtle modernity, closer to that of Robert Bresson than Antonioni. The father's disappearance is not like Anna's in *L'avventura* (1960); it is neither absolute nor the manifestation of an ontological crisis.

Though taking a traditional cinematic route by making a first, autobiographical film—a genre in itself in French cinema since François Truffaut's seminal *The 400 Blows* (*Les quatre cents coups*, 1959)—Hansen-Løve has found a tone, a style, and a way of handling a story that belongs only to her, very far from the conventional approaches and awkwardness that often mar directors' early efforts. She films adolescence as an age of wisdom and intelligence, not of anger and rebellion, as the clichés would have it. Before she forgives her father, Pamela tries to understand him. Their exchange of letters at the end, which concludes their brief reacquaintance, is upsetting because it expresses, despite the shock of sudden death, the possibility that Pamela can really make a new start in life.

In this perfectly controlled first film, whose very delicacy is a kind of strength, the director seems to have carried within herself not only its subject but also her personal style, the beauty of her vision of the world, and the rightness of her decisions in directing her actors, most of them little known or newcomers to the screen. The choice of Paul Blain to play Victor subverts expectations. He hasn't appeared in many French films, but his rare performances reveal an intense, gentle presence reminiscent of the Bresson-inflected films made by his father, Gérard Blain, whom Paul "plays" in *Ainsi soit-il* (2000). *All Is Forgiven* is dedicated to Humbert Balsan, a French producer on the film who committed suicide while it was being made. Hansen-Løve drew inspiration from Balsan and his sudden death when she made *Father of My Children*, another story about families and bereavement. This second film, equally as beautiful and accomplished as the first, attests to the talent of a director who creates moving work, with the qualities of a novel, out of personal experience.

Several young French female directors have recently made films that demonstrate great talent, courage, and stylistic ambitions. To the names of Hansen-Løve, Isild Le Besco, Aurélia Georges, and Axelle Ropert, Rebecca Zlotowski will soon be added. They are interested in stories from the past, their own and others', and in the worlds of children, adolescents, and adults. The future belongs to them.

Pamela and Victor embrace upon her return from Vienna.

Year and place of birth
1981   Paris, France
—

Lives and works in
Paris, France
—

Education
Paris Drama Conservatory,
France
—

Filmography
2003 *Après mûre réflexion*
      (short)
2004 *Un pur esprit* (short)
2007 *All Is Forgiven*
      (Tout est pardonné)
2009 *Father of My Children*
      (Le père de mes enfants)
—

Director's awards
Après mûre réflexion
Bordeaux International Festival
of Women in Cinema
     (Special Mention Short Film,
     2004)

Father of My Children
Cannes International
Film Festival
     (Un Certain Regard Special
     Jury Prize, 2009)
— —

Release date
2007
—

Country of release
France
—

Language
French, German
—

Running time
105 min.
—

Genre
Drama
—

Producers
David Thion, Philippe Martin
—

Writer
Mia Hansen-Løve
—

Cinematographer
Pascal Auffray
—

Key cast
Paul Blain: Victor
Marie-Christine Friedrich:
     Annette
Victoire Rousseau:
     Pamela as a child
Constance Rousseau:
     Pamela as a teenager
Carole Franck: Martine
Olivia Ross: Gisèle

Filming locations
Paris, France
Vienna, Austria
—

Format
35 mm
—

Awards for *All Is Forgiven*
Gijón International Film Festival
     (Best Actress, 2007)
Prix Louis-Delluc
     (First Film, 2007)

PAMELA: So Victor wouldn't recognize me?

MARTINE: Yes, of course he would. You know, he lives nearby.

PAMELA: He does? I thought he lived in China.

MARTINE: In China? What a strange thought. He never left Paris. Did Annette tell you that? She's got some nerve. What do you know about Victor?

PAMELA: Not much. Just what Mom told me. That he got really sick, they broke up and he just disappeared.

MARTINE: She left with you! You two disappeared!

Pamela meets her aunt, Martine, and learns that her father lives in Paris.

Victor and Pamela meet for the first time in eleven years.

Pamela shows Victor's final letter to her best friend.

East Berlin, November 1984. Five years before its downfall, the former East German government ensures its claim to power with a ruthless system of control and surveillance. Party loyalist Captain Gerd Wiesler (Ulrich Mühe) hopes to boost his career when given the job of collecting evidence against playwright Georg Dreyman (Sebastian Koch) and his girlfriend Christa-Maria (Martina Gedeck). What he doesn't anticipate, however, is that immersion in the world of the target has effects on the surveillance agent as well. Wiesler becomes acutely aware of the meagerness of his own existence and discovers a new way of life that he has trouble resisting.

FLORIAN HENCKEL VON DONNERSMARCK THE LIVES OF OTHERS

Christa-Maria and Georg at the premiere party of Georg's play.

Wiesler interrogates a prisoner of the Stasi.

The stylish and morally complex debut feature of the German director Florian Henckel von Donnersmarck is about history and the role of the individual. The setting is East Germany in the 1980s, but made as it was in 2006, and concerning as it does surveillance of one's fellow citizens, *The Lives of Others* (*Das Leben der anderen*, 2006) has deeper implications in the context of 9/11. It is a film that elegantly speaks to both past and present, while also acknowledging the dystopian masterpieces of literature and film—Orwell and Huxley, *Alphaville* (1965) and *The Trial*. For such is the world that the director enters in his remarkably rich, almost scientific study of one part of his country.

Henckel von Donnersmarck places individuals at the center of the film's concerns, in a tightly woven, intricate web of relationships, and proceeds to brilliantly dissect their motivations and, by implication, what drives the society in which they live. The portrait is relentless and unforgiving but rarely judgmental—a delicate balance for a film of this nature, but one that this filmmaker achieves with remarkable maturity.

The film attempts a painstaking re-creation of East Germany in the 1980s. Every object is an original, every set a scrupulous facsimile. The color scheme, a drab ensemble of grays and browns, underlines the mood and feel of the era. This rigorous attention to detail is as controlled as the narrative structure in which the characters play out their individual dramas. The film never feels over-schematized, yet closer examination reveals it is scrupulously mapped.

Set in 1984, *The Lives of Others* both acknowledges Orwell's literary masterpiece and summons up the moment just before Gorbachev grabbed the reins of power a mere year later and shook apart the sclerotic Communist system. Henckel von Donnersmarck's intent is both to castigate that system and to examine the cracks and schisms within it. The East Germany of his film is a Stasi-controlled police state, where surveillance is an extension of state power, and fear and intimidation are tools of control.

To probe more deeply into this haunted society, Henckel von Donnersmarck posits a culture of opposing values: artists versus state officials—creativity countered by control. Each group is highly suspicious of the other, but each needs the other for various reasons. The cast of characters form a studied expression of this bifurcation. On the one hand there are the bureaucrats: a sleazy government minister, Hempf, and a Stasi colonel, Grubitz. On the other, the artists: two well-known playwrights, Dreyman (who is in favor with the regime) and Jerska (disgraced and blacklisted), and their outspoken friend, Hauser.

What turns the film from prosaic into sublime, however, is the pair of deeply complex characters at the heart of the film: a cold state automaton, Wiesler, and a conflicted, self-doubting actress, Christa-Maria. The two represent opposing poles of state and art in the starkest of ways. But the transformation and exchange of roles that they undergo are brilliantly conceived and speak eloquently to the contradictions in a society that believed in the perfectible human being.

The Stasi captain, Wiesler, brilliantly played by Ulrich Mühe (whose life story provided the basis for the film), is a pure specimen of Stalinist social engineering: a zealot and a loner—unmarried, abstemious, and virtually sexless. A highly trusted functionary in the Stasi, he is ordered to eavesdrop on Dreyman and find incriminating evidence so that the sleazy Hempf can have the playwright's attractive girlfriend to himself. The woman in question is Christa-Maria, and she is everything Wiesler is not. An actress and artist, she is warm, open, tender, sexual, in touch with her feelings and body. Living with Dreyman, she is embedded in the world of artists but has her own secrets and weaknesses that compromise her loyalties and place in this world.

The act of surveillance contains the seeds of their transformations. Wiesler is humanized (and finally referenced by name as opposed to being simply "Captain"), Christa-Maria dehumanized. The lonely Stasi captain, by listening in on Dreyman and Christa-Maria, discovers the beauty of art, which releases reveries that touch his soul. Conversely, Christa-Maria, grappling with her demons and insecure about her talent, compromises herself and is coerced into the role of informer. She becomes the fallen angel.

Their journeys express something deep within each of us: the desire to do the right thing, and the realization that we may not. Cutting deeply into this compromised society, Henckel von Donnersmarck explores what it means to take responsibility for one's actions. *The Lives of Others* is a profoundly moral film, laying bare the differences between those who compromise and those who do not. It stands as a stark warning to those democracies who currently employ surveillance methods in the name of state security.

After Georg's birthday party, he unwraps a script for a play with Christa-Maria.

Year and place of birth
1973　Cologne, Germany
—

Lives and works in
Berlin, Germany
Los Angeles, Calif., USA
—

Education
New College, Oxford University,
　UK
—

Filmography
1997　*Mitternacht* (short)
1998　*Das Datum* (short)
1999　*Dobermann* (short)
2002　*The Crusader*
　　　(*Der Templer*) (short)
2006　*The Lives of Others*
　　　(*Das Leben der Anderen*)
— —

Release date
2006
—

Country of release
Germany
—

Language
German
—

Running time
137 min.
—

Genre
Drama
—

Producers
Quirin Berg, Max Wiedemann
—

Writer
Florian Henckel
von Donnersmarck
—

Cinematographer
Hagen Bogdanski
—

Score
Gabriel Yared, Stéphane Moucha
—

Filming location
Berlin, Germany
—

Format
35 mm
—

Key cast
Martina Gedeck:
　Christa-Maria Sieland
Ulrich Mühe:
　Captain Gerd Wiesler
Sebastian Koch: Georg Dreyman
Ulrich Tukur:
　Lieutenant Colonel
　Anton Grubitz
Thomas Thieme:
　Minister Bruno Hempf
Hans-Uwe Bauer: Paul Hauser
Volkmar Kleinert: Albert Jerska
Matthias Brenner: Karl Wallner
—

Awards for *The Lives of Others*
European Film Awards
　(Best Film, Best Actor,
　Best Screenwriter, 2006)
German Film Awards
　(Best Film, Best Director,
　Best Actor, Best Supporting
　Actor, Best Cinematography,
　Best Production Design,
　Best Screenplay, 2006)
Academy Awards
　(Best Foreign Language Film,
　2007)
César Awards
　(Best Foreign Film, 2008)
Independent Spirits Award
　(Best Foreign Production,
　2008)
— —

Christa-Maria returns home to Georg instead of meeting with Stasi Minister Hempf.

Wiesler confronts Christa-Maria.

From the window, Lieutenant Colonel Grubitz sees Christa-Maria lying on the street.

Jody Hill's first film is the story of Mr. Simmons (Danny McBride), a small town taekwondo instructor, who relishes the power that comes from being the master of a small kingdom. Mr. Simmons considers himself the "king of the demo" but can't seem to nail a demonstration to save his life. The man in control is hit hard when he discovers that his wife, Suzie (Mary Jane Bostic), has cheated on him with her new boss, sending Mr. Simmons into a downward spiral.

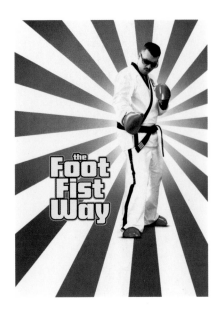

JODY HILL
THE FOOT FIST WAY

Fred and his assistant Julio lead a taekwondo class.

Fred Simmons instructing a student.

There must be something in the water (or just one heck of a film school) in North Carolina because it has churned out a disproportionately high number of gifted filmmakers in recent years, including David Gordon Green, Aaron Katz, Jeff Nichols, Paul Schneider, and Craig Zobel. In addition, there's another who has created a name for himself: Jody Hill, known for his raucous and bombastic but ultimately humanistic comedies. Recognizing the funny in the everyday, Hill also has the skills to transfer it to the screen. He recently made *Observe and Report* (2009), starring Seth Rogen and Anna Faris, and co-created the hit HBO series *Eastbound & Down* (2009). His partners in crime are Ben Best and Danny McBride, both from North Carolina as well, who together have not only launched themselves into the upper echelon of Hollywood comedy but are reinventing what's acceptable for mainstream audiences to swallow.

The film that began it all was *The Foot Fist Way* (2006). Made for $70,000, it was launched at the Sundance Film Festival, where it caught the eye of Will Ferrell. He helped it secure distribution from Paramount, which makes it one of the smallest-budget studio releases of all time. But what it lacked in budget was more than made up for in talent.

The Foot Fist Way is the literal translation of taekwondo, the greatest of all martial arts according to Fred Simmons, a small-town taekwondo instructor who has neither the meditative contemplation nor physical prowess associated with being a kung fu master. What he does have, however, is a thin moustache, a red Ferrari, and a boastful attitude.

The film portrays Simmons as earnest in his endeavor to be the greatest taekwondo instructor in the world—which he already is in his own mind. When a young student asks him who would win in a fight between him and Chuck "The Truck," the eight-year undefeated kickboxing champion, he answers that it's a little too close to call. He relishes the power that comes from being the master of a small kingdom, and when he discovers that his wife Suzie has cheated on him, it hits him hard, launching him on a downward spiral that causes him to abuse his loyal students and make a general fool of himself. Simmons turning his impotent rage on his class provides some of the film's funniest and most affecting moments, particularly when he targets little Stevie Fisher, whose father Simmons believes had a fling with his wife. A man beating up on a seven-year-old shouldn't be amusing, but the scene's use of slapstick and its shuddering denouement are both harrowing and hilarious, and exemplify the total car crash that Simmons's life has suddenly become. For scenes best viewed through your fingers, it's hard to top when Simmons clumsily hits on a pretty new student who couldn't be less interested. When he attempts to kiss her, McBride plays the scene perfectly, unleashing the best worst-screen-kiss of all time.

Still messed up emotionally, Simmons goes on a road trip with his buddy, Mike, and two of his students, Henry and Julio, to a kung fu expo to marvel at their hero, Chuck "The Truck" Wallace. After an inauspicious introduction, things take a turn for the better when the rag-tag group is invited

to a party in Chuck's hotel room. This sets the stage for a delightfully awkward rendezvous. There's no question it's going to go poorly, and eventually the guys are so ridiculed that it brings out years of suppressed rage in Henry as he annihilates an alt-rock asshole who had been harassing him with a hateful ballad. But Hill takes a familiar scene and turns it on its ear by having their actions win Chuck and his buddies over—and one of the all-time greatest party montages ensues. The friendship doesn't last, though, and Simmons is forced to confront his hero, which leads to the kind of climax we've come to expect from every kung fu movie, no matter how unorthodox.

The Foot Fist Way is a film that demands repeat viewing so that the hilarious one-liners have a chance to sink in. Hill remains loyal to the people and places he portrays. He looks at martial arts as it exists in the real world, and, more pointedly, in the southern U.S. The film creates hilarity through real-life emotions and reactions rather than mockery. But the best comedic bits come from Danny McBride's staggeringly funny performance. He fleshes out his character in such a way that it is propelled from cartoonish to comic genius. His ability to deliver the most outrageous lines with the utmost sincerity is a divine gift that puts him in a rare class of comedians. McBride and Hill understand that the funniest moments are ones the audiences can relate to. Small in scope but big in laughs, *The Foot Fist Way* marked the emergence of another Tar Heel filmmaker with a black belt in funny.

Fred's students prepare to spar.

Year and place of birth
1976 Norfolk, Va., USA
—

Lives and works in
Los Angeles, Calif., USA
—

Education
University of North Carolina,
Winston-Salem, USA
—

Filmography
2006 The Foot Fist Way
2009 Observe and Report
— —

Release date
2006
—

Country of release
USA
—

Language
English
—

Running time
85 min.
—

Genre
Comedy
—

Producers
Jody Hill, Erin Gates, Robbie Hill,
Jennifer Chikes
—

Writers
Jody Hill, Danny McBride,
Ben Best
—

Cinematographer
Brian Mandle
—

Score
Pyramid, Dynamite Brothers
—

Key cast
Danny McBride: Fred Simmons
Mary Jane Bostic: Suzie Simmons
Ben Best:
    Chuck "The Truck" Wallace
Spencer Moreno: Julio Chavez
Carlos Lopez IV: Henry Harrison
Jody Hill: Mike McAlister
Collette Wolfe: Denise

Filming location
Concord, N.C., USA
—

Format
16 mm
—

Awards for The Foot Fist Way
Austin Film Critics
Association Awards
    (Breakthrough Artist, 2008)
— —

CARLOS: Yeah, I just passed the bar exam and um, I'm working for Williams Williams and Turner. And it was all thanks in part to the GI Bill.

SUZIE: Oh, that's great. And look at you Connie, he is quite a catch.

FRED: Suzie, why don't you just chill out for a minute. Stop flirting. Connie is sitting right here next to you.

SUZIE: I wasn't flirting.

FRED: Carlos you better watch out. I've got my eye on you. (Pause) I'm just kidding, dude, relax. Take it easy, dude. I'm joking.

Suzie's co-worker brings a date over for an awkward dinner.

Fred fights Chuck "The Truck" after catching him with his wife.

Fred shows up late— and sporting a black eye—to the belt ceremony.

Ryo (Akie Namiki) is an eighth-grade teacher. Her workday should be as ordinary as any other, but instead she finds herself mediating a tense atmosphere between students and faculty. When Ryo is subjected to the unique viciousness of fourteen-year-olds, her troubled past is exposed. By coincidence she encounters Koichi (Hiromasa Hirosue), a familiar face from her schooldays. Koichi is an average salary man who is tutoring one of Ryo's students in piano. Ryo and Koichi share a newfound connection as adults, and, reliving their adolescent traumas, discover that the fourteen-year-old within them still smolders just beneath their "grown-up" facade.

HIROMASA HIROSUE
FOURTEEN

Ryo and Koichi meet again after 12 years.

Koichi goes to meet his new piano student and the student's mother.

It's not easy to separate Hiromasa Hirosue's film work from Izumi Takahashi's. Together they developed their style collaborating on numerous shorts and features, for which Takahashi sometimes also served as script-writer and Hirosue as actor. Although their work appears thematically and stylistically homogenous, both have managed, almost as if taking turns, to establish themselves independently as directors unique to their generation in Japan.

Fourteen (*Ju-yon-sai*, 2007) is the second feature directed by Hirosue. A grant from the PIA Film Festival, which has been committed to promoting Japanese independent cinema for more than three decades, enabled Hirosue to shoot his most elaborate film thus far. It is the only one shot on 35 mm and the only one in which the cast of friends he normally uses is joined by professional actor Teruyuki Kagawa.

There are few films that don't completely divulge their secrets even on second viewing. This is certainly the case for those, like *Fourteen*, that deal with familiar themes. Puberty, teenage angst, conflicts with authority, and school violence are all common subjects in Japanese independent cinema. But Hirosue's film couldn't be further away from such formulaic tropes. He resists cheap epiphanies and déjà-vu effects, remaining mysterious and unsettling, choosing instead to seduce the viewer with a highly individual aesthetic that never feels ordinary.

The film employs extreme close-ups: shots of necks, hands, feet, or parts of faces; conspicuous sounds of footsteps, pens on paper, or someone cracking a candy; visual compositions pared down to complete abstraction, like gray school corridors whose emptiness seems claustrophobic; rapid cuts between long, calm sequences that feel like an explosion; and often impatient, hard-to-register camera movements, which give the impression of being about to take a leap. All of these aesthetic techniques serve only one goal: to draw up a complex psychological profile of a group whose information is conveyed to the viewer via sensory impressions.

Fourteen tells the story of two people forced to confront their own adolescence in the face of the young people surrounding them. Ryo Fukatsu (the versatile Akie Namiki, also known for her fearless performances in Takahashi's films) is a young junior-high teacher who resists the authoritarian climate at school. Koichi Sugino (played with stoic reserve by Hirosue himself) works in a job he describes as being too boring to talk about and has recently started teaching piano to one of Ryo's students. The shock generated by the accidental meeting of these two adults leads them to reconsider their repressed pasts and why both are failures in the present. When Ryo was accused of arson at age fourteen, she ended up ramming a pencil into her teacher's neck in front of Koichi. Did Ryo become a teacher only to protect the fourteen-year-old still inside her? And why did Koichi give up a career as a pianist for an inconspicuous existence as a simple employee?

As in all of Hirosue and Takahashi's films, *Fourteen* deals with the abuse of power, psychological dependencies, how norms are pushed to the limit and eventually violated, and so-called deviant behavior. The portrayal of bullying, of physical violence, of how the weaknesses of both adolescent and teacher are brutally exposed, is often hard to endure. *Fourteen* does not, however, denounce familial, social, or school violence, and refuses to bow to either sensationalism or emotionality. It is from this radical sobriety that the film draws its shocking impact. The shots are chosen with great care, with a noticeably large number of people's backs shown, underlining the indifference of both the perpetrators and the victims. The schoolchildren come across as if playing a violent game in a strangely detached manner, a game whose rules they only understand in an intuitive way, while astounding themselves with their potential for aggression.

The boundaries between aggression and auto-aggression are nearly always fluid, showing them that they are no different from the adults. In a highly oppressive scene at the end of the film, the authoritarian teacher, Makato Kobayashi (played by the prolific Teruyuki Kagawa), chastens a defiant student by slapping him again and again. As the punishment reaches a crescendo, a change in the camera perspective reveals that the teacher has, in a mysterious reversal, actually switched to slapping himself.

As minimalist-introspective members of the avant-garde, Hirosue and his cohort Takahashi have infused Japanese independent cinema with new vigor. They resist the twin temptations of sentimentality and kitsch in an unwavering manner, confronting their society with an analytical preciseness and sharp eye for detail.

Ryo speaks to her psychiatrist about her childhood.

Year and place of birth
1978   Muroto, Japan
—

Lives and works in
Tokyo, Japan
—

Filmography
2005   The Lost Hum
         (Hanauta dorobo)
2007   Fourteen (Ju-yon-sai)
—

Director's awards
The Lost Hum
International Film Festival
Rotterdam
     (NETPAC Award, 2006)
— —

Release date
2007
—

Country of release
Japan
—

Language
Japanese
—

Running time
114 min.
—

Genre
Drama
—

Producer
Mayumi Amano
—

Writer
Izumi Takahashi
—

Cinematographer
Kiyoaki Hashimoto
—

Score
Hideki Ikari
—

Key cast
Akie Namiki: Ryo Fukatsu
Hiromasa Hirosue: Koichi Sugino
Teruyuki Kagawa:
     Makato Kobayashi
—

Filming location
Sagamihara, Japan
—

Format
35 mm
—

Awards for *Fourteen*
International Film Festival
Rotterdam
     (NETPAC Award, 2007)
— —

Taiki asks Koichi if he should continue playing.

Ryo and Koichi talk about the past.

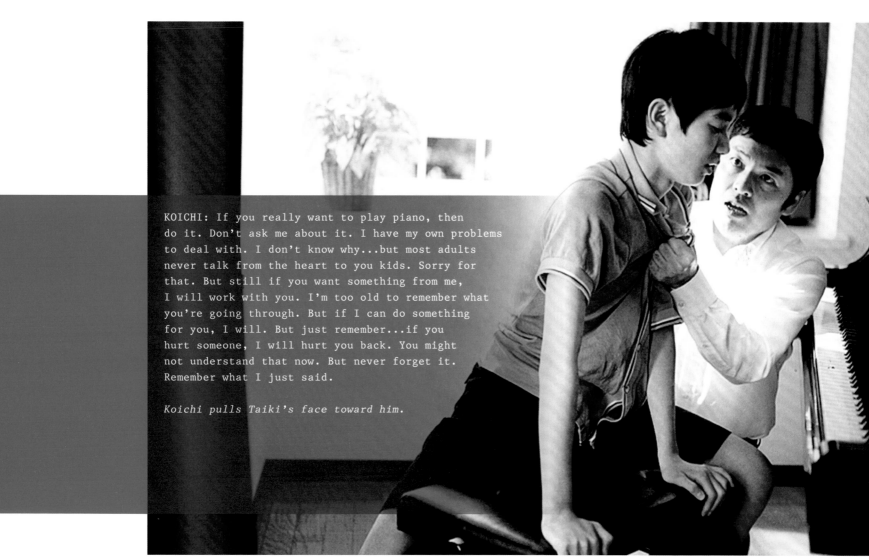

KOICHI: If you really want to play piano, then
do it. Don't ask me about it. I have my own problems
to deal with. I don't know why...but most adults
never talk from the heart to you kids. Sorry for
that. But still if you want something from me,
I will work with you. I'm too old to remember what
you're going through. But if I can do something
for you, I will. But just remember...if you
hurt someone, I will hurt you back. You might
not understand that now. But never forget it.
Remember what I just said.

Koichi pulls Taiki's face toward him.

Koichi lectures Taiki.

When Tung (Kuan Choon Wai)—a nineteen-year-old Malaysian living with his aging mother in a small town—sets out to meet his older brother in Kuala Lumpur, little does he know that a journey of self-discovery lies directly ahead. Guileless and overconfident, Tung soon finds himself drawn into a world full of deceit, treachery, violence, and loss, where the only lesson to be gleaned from his sudden coming-of-age is just how difficult adulthood can make it for any of us to ever go home again.

HO YUHANG
RAIN DOGS

Tung goes to the city to look for his brother, who is involved in criminal activities.

Malaysia's film scene is a genuine phenomenon within Southeast Asian culture. Even without a rich cinematic tradition to draw from, an extraordinarily productive movement has emerged in Kuala Lumpur over the past decade, which has also become a talking point worldwide. Of all the young filmmakers working in this scene, including Woo Ming Jin, Tan Chui Mui, Liew Seng Tat, and the highly original documentarian Amir Muhammad, it is Ho Yuhang who now enjoys the highest profile following his four feature films, with *Rain Dogs* (*Tai yang yue*, 2006) representing his international breakthrough.

Rain Dogs is more than just a film from Malaysia; it's a film about Malaysia, characterized to a greater extent by its setting than its characters or plot. The film deals with farewells and new starts, with how shifting locations lead to life phases ending or beginning. The nineteen-year-old Tung returns to his village and mother's house three times over the course of the film, with each return symbolizing a new step in his life.

At the beginning of the film, this shy young man arrives in Kuala Lumpur. His attempts to make contact with his older brother, Hong, fail, while a group of pimps manage to relieve him of his money in a sleazy motel. Hong's ex-girlfriend helps him find his brother, who spends his time in pool halls and betting clubs with a group of unsavory figures. Disillusioned, Tung makes his way back home, robbed yet again, this time of the money given to him by his brother to support their seamstress mother.

It is now that the film changes its palette of colors, with the luscious tropical green of the country becoming dominant. We suddenly experience Tung as a self-confident grown-up, almost on equal footing with his mother, whom he tries to move to Kuala Lumpur, away from her untrustworthy boyfriend. One day, Tung finds a police car waiting in front of the house as the rain falls. The next shot takes us back to Kuala Lumpur, where, in a dark hospital corridor, Tung learns that his brother has been fatally stabbed. Smoke rises from a crematorium, followed by a close-up of an urn, which Tung takes to Hong's girlfriend. The sequence ends with a wide shot of a cemetery; as the camera pans out, the image is framed through a mesh fence. The entire film is told with the same sense of economy. And the more tragic the events, the more restrained they're depicted. There's no doubt that Ho has been influenced by Taiwanese master Hou Hsiao-hsien (whose editor, Liao Ching-song, edited *Rain Dogs*).

Even when his brother's murderers receive a mauling from Hong's friends, Ho refrains from using the sort of stirring dramatic approach that might be expected. It is only Tung's cold, obdurate gaze that gives any indication of what's going on inside him. A few days later, on his brother's motorbike, he returns to his village for the second time. He's no longer the naive, reserved boy we initially met. The ghostly landscape shots, completely devoid of people, accompanied by blues legend Odetta singing "Motherless Child," represent the metamorphosis that has occurred in a world now hostile and without refuge. It is only now, thirty-eight minutes in, that the film's title, *Rain Dogs*, appears on the screen.

A town in the north of the country becomes Tung's next attempt at getting his bearings. His aunt (played by Malaysian director Yasmin Ahmad, before her tragic death in 2009) and her family seem like a friendly mirror-image of his own home life. Tung suddenly finds himself taking on the role of the older brother to his small cousin Yuk, while he sees in his uncle the father he never had. And he flirts with sisters Hui and Chui, who keep him at arm's length. Despite all this, he is still unable to reconnect with the carefree nature of his childhood. At some point, a pistol appears and shots are fired—a warning, nothing more. Tung beats up a local punk who is bothering Chui. His uncle turns out to be a heavy drinker.

Ho relates all this through incredibly precise visuals and economical dialogue. The film avoids any sense of redundancy, demanding the audience's attention, but in return providing a suitable reward. The film is never misleading or puzzling, never content to bask in its own aesthetics. Every image is a single tile in the mosaic that tells the story of Tung's coming-of-age, whereby landscapes and corridors become metaphors for mental states and developments. And, much like the work of Hou Hsiao-hsien, events come to a head in recurring images of the same locations, which are assigned new meanings to reflect the various stages of the protagonist's development.

Finally, Tung returns to his mother for a third time. A single, short scene shows the two of them together: Tung changes a lightbulb that had clearly burnt out several days before. His mother's boyfriend has gone. Tung is going to stay.

GU: Give it a try.

Tung, drunk as he is, recognizes that it's a gun.
He shakes his head. Gu fires a shot to the sky
and puts the gun in Tung's hand.

GU: Come on, try it!

Tung aims straight ahead, but he doesn't dare
pull the trigger. Gu takes the gun back. Then his
mobile phone rings.

GU: Hey, I'm taking a shower, got a problem with
that? Not free, okay? Make sure that joker calls me.

Gu hangs up. He looks at Tung in a funny way.
He slaps his cheek lightly.

The drunken Gu brings Tung to a deserted field to shoot his gun.

Year and place of birth
1971 Petaling Jaya, Malaysia
—
Lives and works in
Petaling Jaya, Malaysia
—
Education
Iowa State University, USA
—
Filmography
1999 *Camera Degree Zero*
       (short)
2001 *Good Friday at the Zoo*
       (short)
2001 *Not Far from Here* (short)
2003 *Min*
2004 *Sanctuary*
2006 *Rain Dogs (Tai yang yue)*
2007 *As I Lay Dying* (short)
2009 *At the End of Daybreak*
       (*Sham moh*)
—

Director's awards
Min
Festival des 3 Continents
    (Special Jury Award, 2003)
Cinemanila International
Film Festival
    (NETPAC Award, 2004)

Sanctuary
International Film Festival
Rotterdam
    (NETPAC Award, Tiger Award –
    Special Mention, 2005)
Pusan International Film Festival
    (New Currents Award –
    Special Mention, 2004)
— —

Release date
2006
—
Country of release
Malaysia
—
Language
Cantonese, Mandarin
—
Running time
94 min.
—
Genre
Drama
—

Producers
Lorna Tee, Ho Yuhang
—
Writers
Ho Yuhang, Lim Lay Kuen,
Too Set Fong
—
Cinematographer
Teoh Gay Hian
—

Key cast
Kuan Choon Wai: Tung
Cheung Wing Hong: Hong
Liu Wai Hung: Ah Gu
Yasmin Ahmad: Min
Pete Teo: Fook
Chua Thien See: Chui
Lai Fooi Mun: Hui
—
Filming locations
Petaling Jaya, Malaysia
Kuala Lumpur, Malaysia
Temoh, Malaysia
Tapah, Malaysia
Kuala Sepetang, Malaysia
Taiping, Malaysia
—
Format
35 mm
—

Awards for *Rain Dogs*
Festival des 3 Continents
    (Best Director, 2006)
Hong Kong Asian Film Festival
    (New Talent Award, 2006)
— —

Sisters Chui and Hui on a break from work at the barber shop.

Tung's aunt, Min, helps her son, Yuk Chai, with homework but he falls asleep.

Chui tells Tung that she prefers being alone to dating a boy.

Jiang Wen's third directorial work weaves the stories of four narratives, set in 1958 and 1976 in a Yunan village, a college campus, and the Gobi Desert. The first tale tells the story of a widow, played by Zhou Yun, who goes mad and abandons her son (Jaycee Chan). In the second story, college professor Old Tang (Jiang Wen) has an affair with the campus doctor (Joan Chen), who longs for Young Liang (Anthony Wong). Old Tang and his wife (Kong Wei) meet the abandoned son from the first tale in part three, and in the fourth act, the characters and stories are woven together in the Gobi Desert.

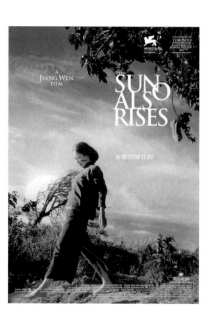

JIANG WEN
THE SUN ALSO RISES

Mother watches her son leave.

Jiang Wen found fame earlier than most of the filmmakers featured in this book. He blazed his way into directing back in 1994 with his debut, *In the Heat of the Sun* (*Yangguang Canlan de Rizi*). Six years later, his second feature, *Devils on the Doorstep* (*Guizi lai le*), won the Grand Prix at Cannes. For failing to obtain permission from the proper authorities to submit it to the festival, however, he was banned from making any film in China for five years. Hence the late arrival of *The Sun Also Rises* (2007).

Jiang, born in 1963, is remarkably talented. He starred in *Hibiscus Town* (*Fu rong zhen*, 1986) and *Red Sorghum* (*Hong gao liang*, 1988) in his early twenties. At thirty, he took up directing, and his artistic ambition and sensitivity set him apart from the other generations of filmmakers. For this, he was hailed as China's Orson Welles. Coming after years of enforced inaction, *The Sun Also Rises* represents the culmination of his creative energies, boasting a scope so broad and an imagination so boundless that the movie takes everybody by surprise.

The film is divided into four parts; the first three take place in 1976. In part one, "Madness," a widow in a misty Yunnan village goes mad after losing a pair of shoes. Her son discovers a stone igloo that she has built, where he finds things that have gone missing from home. The mother then disappears; her lost shoes and clothes are found floating in the river. In "Amour," Old Tang, a college teacher, carries on an affair with the campus doctor, Lin. Lin harbors a secret longing for Old Tang's buddy, Young Liang. One summer evening, Young Liang is detained under the suspicion of fondling a young woman during an outdoor film show. Old Tang and Lin go out of their way to prove his innocence. In "Rifle," Old Tang and his wife arrive in Yunnan on the same day that the mother from "Madness" disappears. They are met by the mother's son, a junior brigade leader. Old Tang spends his days hunting until he discovers that his wife has become the brigade leader's prey.

"Dream," the final section of the film, sets the clock back to 1958. Old Tang's wife and the mother from "Madness," pregnant with her future son, are traveling on camels in the Gobi Desert. The mysterious past of the mother is revealed, and we learn more about the heady younger days of the Tangs and Liang, Indonesian émigrés returning to build a "New China." A floodgate of emotions opens and brings the film to an inspiring, passionate conclusion. The mother's newborn, who is born on a train, seems to represent the optimism of the new republic, while the death of his father at the hands of Soviet border guards suggests the deterioration of Sino-Soviet relations. And when Old Tang shoots the young brigade leader who is after his wife, the act can be read as an allegory of the demise of idealism during the Cultural Revolution. But a new beginning is in sight, symbolized by a tent that appears to rise up like the sun. Life goes on, the film asserts, even as Jiang summons the soul of a bygone era.

The filmmaker has lost none of his flair since his earlier works. *The Sun Also Rises* is visually sumptuous, in sharp contrast to the stark black and white of *Devils on the Doorstep*. The film is also full of playful fantastical touches, as when five women cooks combine the task of mixing flour with a dance show. Joe Hisaishi, who composed the score, uses a marching tune for the theme music, which fits the sheer splendor of the film. Small wonder that *The Sun* has been compared to the works of Emir Kusturica, which are similarly charged with frenzied excitement even as they engage with history, politics, and culture.

Perhaps because of the ban triggered by *Devils on the Doorstep*, Jiang cannot help being cautious. *The Sun Also Rises* does not name its four sections on screen or specify the time and place of the story; these details are found only in the press releases provided to reviewers. Jiang goes so far as to say that the story "could have happened anywhere and anytime." It is fairly clear that the mother in "Madness" is a subtle symbolic reference to the Chinese Cultural Revolution, but the depiction of sexual repression and the mob hysteria surrounding Young Liang receive a more innocuous, farcical treatment in "Amour."

Absolutely dedicated to his artistic vision, Jiang took the trouble of transporting production materials (an old train car, red earth) over long distances. The total production cost was ten million dollars, while the box office returns were a mere thirty million yuan. In contemporary Chinese industry circles, where marketability trumps all other considerations, Jiang remains uncompromising with his artistic integrity. Naturally, he falls out of favor with viewers whose sensitivity was developed from daily doses of TV dramas, but as a film that goes against popular taste, *The Sun Also Rises* offers an invaluable comment on the vulgarity of the age.

Son carries his mother on his back.

Son swims to an unknown place.

Year and place of birth
1963   Tangshan, China
—

Lives and works in
Beijing, China
—

Education
**Central Drama Academy,
   Beijing, China**
—

Filmography
1994   *In the Heat of the Sun*
          (*Yangguang Canlan
          de Rizi*)
2000   *Devils on the Doorstep*
          (*Guizi lai le*)
2007   *The Sun Also Rises*
          (*Tai yang zhao chang
          sheng qi*)
2009   *New York, I Love You*
          ("Jiang Wen")
—

Director's awards
In the Heat of the Sun
Golden Horse Film Festival
   (Best Director, Best Film,
   Best Screenplay, 1996)

Devils on the Doorstep
Cannes International
Film Festival
   (Grand Prix, 2000; France
   Culture Award – Foreign
   Cineaste of the Year, 2001)
Hawaii International Film Festival
   (NETPAC Award, 2001)
Kinema Junpo Awards
   (Best Foreign Language
   Film Director, 2003)
Mainichi Film Concours
   (Best Foreign Language
   Film, 2003)
— —

Release date
2007
—

Country of release
China
—

Language
Mandarin
—

Running time
116 min.
—

Genre
Drama

Producers
Albert Lee, Jiang Wen
—

Writers
**Shu Ping, Jiang Wen,
Guo Shixing, Ye Mi**
—

Cinematographers
**Zhao Fei, Mark Ping-bin Lee,
Yang Tao**
—

Score
Joe Hisaishi

Key cast
**Jiang Wen: Teacher Tang
   ("Old Tang")
Joan Chen: Dr. Lin
Zhou Yun: Mad Mother
Jaycee Chan: Son
Anthony Wong: Teacher Liang
   ("Young Liang")
Kong Wei: Tang's Wife**
—

Filming locations
**Yunnan Province, China
Gansu Province, China
Beijing, China**
—

Format
35 mm
—

Awards for *The Sun Also Rises*
**Golden Horse Film Festival
   (Best Editing, 2007)
Asian Film Awards
   (Best Production Designer,
   Best Supporting Actress,
   2008)
Changchun Film Festival
   (Golden Deer – Best
   Cinematography, 2008)**
— —

Teacher Liang in the hospital.

Tang's wife and Son flirt with one another.

Doctor Lin holds a string-net
bag full of food in one hand and
arrives at Old Tang's doorstep.
She straightens her clothes and
hair and tap dances on the floor —
rhythmically knocking with her
feet—TATATATA!

The sound is delicate and pleasant.

Old Tang and Teacher Liang, seeing
this, suddenly burst out laughing.

Old Tang and Teacher Liang peek down the corridor at Doctor Lin approaching.

A high-school loner, Brendan (Joseph Gordon-Levitt), navigates the surreal underworld of his California hometown in search of the truth about the death of his ex-girlfriend, Emily (Emilie de Ravin). His pursuit leads Brendan to intrude upon the dark lives of classmates who belong to tightly knit social circles.

RIAN JOHNSON
BRICK

Laura holds court at her "Halloween in January" party.

Brendan gets a desperate call from an old flame.

Rian Johnson's first feature film, *Brick* (2005), shouldn't ever find trouble in the face of obscurity. Unlike the many independent titles that struggle to keep away from the shelves and find a way into an audience's conscience, *Brick* continues to be celebrated since making its debut at the 2005 Sundance Film Festival, and subsequently being distributed by Focus Features, for capturing imaginations with its fresh take on film noir.

Made for $500,000, and taking Johnson over six years to complete, the movie has followed an interesting lifespan so far: it was produced with (relatively) little money yet made a pretty big splash. Film-school kids devour it for its craft—a blend of classic cinema with contemporary youthful dramatics—and it's the kind of work aspiring filmmakers or film students look to after watching a film like *Double Indemnity* (1944) and just hoping to make something even half as cool. Less industry-minded audiences hang on to the film's perceptivity of high-school culture, which is heightened in its style but accurate in terms of its take on schoolyard significance.

Inspired by the novels of Dashiell Hammett, such as *The Maltese Falcon* and *The Glass Key*, Johnson's story features a high-school boy (played by the very talented Joseph Gordon-Levitt) who pieces together a series of clues in the wake of his ex-girlfriend's mysterious demise. Along with his brainy friend, he must confront a drug kingpin (an "old" guy of twenty-six years who lives in his parents' basement), stay clear of the law (in this case, the principal's office), and unveil the true intentions of the femme fatale who's become involved in the pursuit. Johnson combined his love of the genre with the throes of high school—classic noir dialogue and tone meet flashy design and an exciting young fleet of actors. The end result: certainly hip, assuredly cool, and very, very fresh.

It would have been easy for Johnson to fail. With such an obvious hook, the film was at risk of being hokey or way too high concept. However, Johnson successfully delivered by finding the pieces that fit best for such a hybrid. While he wrote the dialogue as old school, he didn't do the same with the overall look. Instead of paying homage entirely to an older style of filmmaking, he kept the visuals contemporary. In the same respect, Johnson never dipped the film into teenage melodrama—it's a bubblegum-free story filled with high stakes and life-and-death consequences.

Most of this was possible because Johnson didn't attempt to create a believable reality. The film's world isn't supposed to mirror any type of actual high-school hierarchy, but rather it touches upon life situations by its level of exaggeration. The details may seem to be a product of the imagination, but the overall themes come across as accurate, poignant, and powerful. Crushes, bullies, school, and suburban myths already feel like dire scenarios to a teenager, and Johnson kicks the action into higher-gear fun by also throwing in huge levels of adult danger.

Using imagery, sound, and style (something Johnson no doubt mastered at the prestigious USC School of Cinematic Arts), the director makes SoCal suburbia look like the most dangerous place on earth. And because of strong characterization and a likable lead (a credit to Johnson's casting and direction), we don't just care for our protagonist, we can also relate to him: we've all felt love and heartbreak, we either were or wanted to be the loner, the bully scared the hell out of us, and the adult world seemed so close yet still pretty mysterious. For this, Johnson knows his audience well . . .

It's no wonder that with such a fresh voice, Johnson has made an impact in the industry. And it took him a lot of rejection to get to this point. After more than half a decade of "No"s while trying to convince people to make *Brick* happen, he finally pulled together some financing from family and friends. The old Hollywood mantra is "write what you know." Johnson also shot it in a place he knew: his home city of San Clemente.

Met with very favorable reviews, and a Special Jury Prize for Originality of Vision at Sundance, the film almost immediately transitioned Johnson from an obscure name to an industry favorite. People wanted to work with him, or watch him work, and the road ahead seemed exciting to all involved. And for good reason: *Brick* has a unique voice that is by no means a fluke, and it is a sincere and stimulating first film that just screams of promise.

For his follow-up, Johnson secured a bigger budget and made *The Brothers Bloom* (2008), a globe-trotting caper movie starring Adrien Brody, Mark Ruffalo, and Rachel Weisz. Judging from Johnson's ability to make big things from limited resources, I can only imagine what type of ride this will allow him to take audiences on—undoubtedly an exhilarating one.

Dode gets knocked around by Brendan.

A scrap of a clue.

Year and place of birth
1973 Silver Spring, Md., USA
—

Lives and works in
Los Angeles, Calif., USA
—

Education
University of Southern
    California, Los Angeles,
    USA
—

Filmography
2005 Brick
2008 The Brothers Bloom
— —

Release date
2005
—

Country of release
USA
—

Language
English
—

Running time
110 min.
—

Genre
Mystery
—

Producers
Mark G. Mathis, Ram Bergman
—

Writer
Rian Johnson
—

Cinematographer
Steve Yedlin
—

Score
Nathan Johnson
—

Key cast
Joseph Gordon-Levitt: Brendan
Nora Zehetner: Laura
Emilie de Ravin: Emily
Lukas Haas: The Pin
Noah Fleiss: Tugger
Noah Segan: Dode
Meagan Good: Kara
Matt O'Leary: The Brain
Brian J. White: Brad Bramish
Richard Roundtree:
    Assistant VP Trueman
—

Filming location
San Clemente, Calif., USA
—

Format
35 mm
—

Awards for Brick
Sundance Film Festival
    (Special Jury Prize for
    Originality of Vision, 2005)
Austin Film Critics
Association Awards
    (Best First Film, 2006)
Central Ohio Film Critics
Association Awards
    (Best Screenplay – Original,
    Best Overlooked Film, 2006)
Chicago Film Critics Association
Awards
    (Most Promising Director,
    2006)
Cognac Police Film Festival
    ("New Blood" Award, 2006)
San Francisco Film Critics
Circle Awards
    (Best Original Screenplay,
    2006)
SITGES International Fantastic
Film Festival of Catalonia
    (Citizen Kane Award for Best
    Directorial Revelation, 2006)
— —

Brendan finds he is too late to save Emily.

The Brain in his element, the school library.

Vice Principal Trueman wants a word with Brendan.

INT. OFFICE
Brendan sits with an ice pack against his head in a tiny office. A man in his early thirties behind a wood colored desk and name plate, "GARY TRUEMAN, ASSISTANT VICE PRINCIPAL" plays with a pencil.

TRUEMAN: You didn't know this boy?

BRENDAN: No sir, never seen him.

TRUEMAN: And he just hit you?

BRENDAN: Like I said, he asked for my lunch money first. Good thing I brown bagged it.

Trueman trains a good natured dubious eye on Brendan.

TRUEMAN: Alright Brendan. I've been looking to talk to you.

Christine (Miranda July) is a lonely artist and "Eldercab" driver who uses fantastical artistic visions to draw her objects of desire closer to her. Richard (John Hawkes), a newly single shoe salesman and father of two boys, is prepared for amazing things to happen. But when he meets Christine, he panics. Meanwhile, Richard's seven-year-old son Robby (Brandon Ratcliff) is having a risqué Internet romance with a stranger, and Robby's fourteen-year-old brother, Peter (Miles Thompson), has become a guinea pig for two neighborhood girls.

MIRANDA JULY
ME AND YOU AND
EVERYONE WE KNOW

Christine uses static to make the sound of ocean waves.

When Andy Warhol and Gerard Malanga founded *Interview* magazine, they summoned artists like Miranda July into being. Stunningly self-aware, slyly provocative, and fluently bilingual in high and low culture, July is the party guest who stands just to the edge of the action, asking necessary questions. When *Interview* actually did approach the multidisciplinary artist for its July 2009 issue, it found exactly the right format. A guest list that included filmmakers Spike Jonze and Michel Gondry, visual artist Cindy Sherman, and musician Chan Marshall (aka Cat Power) sent questions to July via email. She answered in the style that has become her hallmark, no matter what the medium: cryptic, illuminating, and, more often than not, funny.

Many moviegoers first discovered July through her debut feature, *Me and You and Everyone We Know* (2005). But her voice had been developed and honed since adolescence. She began writing and performing plays as a teenager in Berkeley, California, and has retained even in her mature work an air of the precocious. Consistent with her videos, performances, and writing, *Me and You and Everyone We Know* is playful, willful, and wise, like the questions of a child who already holds degrees in art theory and sociology.

In the film, July plays Christine, a video artist struggling to attract interest from a gallery as she earns a living driving elderly residents on errands. She meets a shoe salesman, Richard, who has recently broken up with his wife and who marked the occasion by setting his hand on fire. His two sons, teenage Peter and seven-year-old Robby, find themselves adrift in their neighborhood, each one passing the time in diffident but sexualized encounters.

Although the gossamer flirtation between Christine and Richard could form the heart of a quirky romantic comedy, the film is as interested in the young people as the adults. In fact, one plotline involving Robby and a seducer he finds on the Internet hints at the charm, humor, and danger of July's enterprise.

Sex is unknown and inconceivable to the child, so when his interlocutor types leading questions, he responds with the only taboo he knows. "I want to poop back and forth," he writes. "You poop into my butthole, I poop into your butthole, back and forth forever." It's a hilarious and shocking collision of innocence and experience. But there is not a hint of exploitation here. In conceiving this scene and directing Ratcliff in such a winsome performance, July accomplishes something extraordinary: she transforms one of the most incendiary modern taboos into an arena of wonder and humor.

Me and You and Everyone We Know is a network narrative, roving among several characters with sometimes tenuous connections. But unlike *Short Cuts* (1993) or *Magnolia* (1999), in which Robert Altman and Paul Thomas Anderson approach the sudden connections of urban life with grand bombast, July illustrates her connections in delicate miniature. This is likely not a question of budget or even of gender. Instead, there is in July's character portraits a sense of wonder and optimism. She finds marvels and high philosophy in small rituals, whether the subject is the death of a goldfish or the prospect of a new romance.

Similarly, the style of the film emphasizes clean compositions, minimal camera movement, and a focus on performance rather than visual technique. Much of the film looks and feels as if it could easily work installed within the white walls of a gallery, if it didn't also move so well as a film narrative. It's a reminder that July has been consistent as an artist, dating back to her early work incorporating performance, video, slide projections, and music. Pitched between introversion and fearlessness, her work became known for cultivating a mood of awkward, self-reflexive humor, which remains the tonal hallmark of twenty-first-century alternative pop culture. It is to July's moment what irony was to the 1990s.

There are two teenage girls in the film who torment Peter but also flirt with a spectral man who leaves dirty notes for them on his window. When they finally knock on his door, he hides. They are his ultimate fantasy, and yet he hides. This is what is most potent in July's work. Her art shows us the fragility of human connection, how desire and the reactions it provokes are always sad and always funny, moving back and forth, forever.

In that interview in *Interview*, writer George Saunders asks July, "What is the purpose of making art, in your view?" Her answer: "I'm just gonna go for broke on this one and say that we do it because life is so ridiculously gorgeous, strange, heartbreaking, horrific, etc., that we are compelled to describe it to ourselves, but we can't! We cannot do it! And so we make art."

Richard sells shoes to one of Christine's Eldercab clients, Michael.

Year and place of birth
1974 Barre, Vt., USA
—

Lives and works in
Los Angeles, Calif., USA
—

Filmography
1998 *The Amateurist* (short)
2000 *Nest of Tens* (short)
2001 *Getting Stronger*
          ***Every Day* (short)**
2005 *Me and You and Everyone*
          We Know
— —

Release date
2005
—

Country of release
USA
—

Language
English
—

Running time
90 min.
—

Genre
Comedy, Drama
—

Producer
Gina Kwon
—

Writer
Miranda July
—

Cinematographer
Chuy Chávez
—

Score
Michael Andrews
—

Key cast
John Hawkes: Richard Swersey
Miranda July:
      Christine Jesperson
Miles Thompson: Peter Swersey
Brandon Ratcliff: Robby Swersey
Carlie Westerman: Sylvie
Hector Elias: Michael
Brad William Henke: Andrew
Natasha Slayton: Heather
Najarra Townsend: Rebecca
Tracy Wright: Nancy Herrington
JoNell Kennedy: Pam
Ellen Geer: Ellen
Colette Kilroy: Sylvie's Mom
James Kayten: Sylvie's Dad
—

Filming location
Van Nuys, Calif., USA
—

Format
HD
—

Awards for *Me and You and
Everyone We Know*
**Cannes International
Film Festival**
      **(Critics Week Grand Prize,
      Caméra d'Or, Prix Regards
      Jeune, Young Critics Award
      for Best Feature, 2005)**
**Chicago Film Critics
Association Awards**
      **(CFCA Award for Most
      Promising Performer, 2005)**

**Newport International
Film Festival**
      **(Audience Award for
      Best Feature, Jury Award
      for Best Director, 2005)**
Philadelphia Film Festival
      **(Best First Time Director,
      2005)**
**San Francisco International
Film Festival**
      **(Audience Award for
      Best Narrative Feature,
      SKYY Prize, 2005)**
Stockholm Film Festival
      **(Best Directorial Debut,
      2005)**
Sundance Film Festival
      **(Special Jury Prize for
      Originality of Vision, 2005)**
— —

Robby types))<>((to the person he's chatting with.

Richard tells Christine he's too tired to walk.

Robby looks for the source of the "tapping noise."

Christine wants to give her tape to Nancy, the museum curator.

Ayça (Ayça Damgaci) is a Turkish actress who lives in Istanbul. On a film set in Western Turkey, she meets Kurdish actor Hama Ali (Hama Ali Khan) and they fall in love. Following the shoot, Ayça returns to Istanbul and Hama to Suleymaniye, in Northern Iraq. But Ayça can't bear the distance between them and decides to go to him. However, getting into a country at war turns out to be just as difficult as getting out.

HUSEYIN KARABEY
GITMEK: MY MARLON AND BRANDO

Ayça on the way to her theater.

How far would you go for love? Turkish actress Ayça Damgaci left her flat in Istanbul for the Iraqi border when American bombs began falling on Baghdad in March 2003. The object of her affection, the Kurdish actor Hama Ali Khan, was on the other side of the border. This real-life romance became the inspiration for *Gitmek: My Marlon and Brando* (*Gitmek: Benim Marlon Ve Brandom*, 2008), a semi-fictional movie directed and co-written (with Damgaci) by the young Hüseyin Karabey. The lead actors appear as themselves, the heroes of a story, which, against the common current, moves from West to East, in search of happiness. But for Ayça, a woman in her thirties, this journey of passion into hellish wartime becomes even more dangerous, both physically and emotionally. What makes this statement on war, human rights, and borders a personal voyage both unique and universal lies in its contradiction: the movie toys with the cliché that the world is getting smaller and so interconnected that it is becoming one place. Yet, on the other hand, the more Ayça travels east of Turkey toward the Iranian border, the commonality of human concern becomes clearer in spite of the transforming geography.

Regarded as one of Turkey's most promising emerging talents, Karabey made his mark by handling challenging subject matter in many of his previous documentaries, short films (such as *Boran* [1990], which, by merging fact and fiction, explored the disappearance of 5,000 political activists in Turkey during the 1990s), and in his feature-length docudrama *Silent Death* (*Sessiz ölüm*, 2001). All are significant examples of his response to humanitarian issues through filmmaking. But more importantly, they reveal his ability to cinematically retell actual events with a poetic and emotional touch, while managing to stay true to his subjects, as he does in his first fiction feature, *Gitmek: My Marlon and Brando*.

A love story in the foreground and a history of a war-stricken place and its people in the background, the film is perhaps most powerful in the sequences in which Karabey makes use of his documentarian reflexes, while recounting the obstacles stage actress Ayça Damgaci tries to overcome in her quest to reunite with the Iraqi Hama Ali Khan, whom she met and fell in love with on a film set in Turkey. Watching Damgaci on the screen, as she re-enacts some of her own personal experiences, doesn't evoke a sense of forced intimacy. On the contrary, the excessive sentimentality of her highly poetic letters—in which she compares her lover to the stars, the moon, and Marlon Brando, punctuated with quotes by Diego Rivera and Gabriel García Márquez—makes us the witnesses of an almost-surreal or magical narrative.

The Superman spoofs and the general humorous quality of the video letters sent by Hama Ali, as well as his theatrical personality, are further catalysts of the sense of surreal. Hama Ali, who doesn't even go to Istanbul to see his girlfriend before the war erupts, is like a faithless lover who appears only in dreams or visions. In fact, it is the war that sets their love in motion, sets Ayça in motion; the war, ironically, allows them to explore their relationship. A star of alternative plays performed at a run-down theater, Damgaci doesn't take on parts any longer, though she did participate in anti-Bush demonstrations along with the rest of the world. Although possessing more vibrancy and buzz than other Western megalopolises, Baghdad's crowds further emphasize Ayça's distinctive solitude, and her independence within a dictated modern lifestyle further reinforce her loneliness. She therefore has nowhere in the world to turn but to her lover. As such, this road movie that is built upon a "broken" love story relates an obligation to create idealism and the need to consistently apply this idealism to real life. In this sense, the title, *Gitmek* (literally "to go" in Turkish), takes on another meaning. Avoiding radical political statements, this humanist docudrama reveals glimpses into the lengths Karabey's career could likely go.

Ayça is talking to Hama Ali in her head, composing her own love letter, in her rudimentary English.

AYÇA: (*Voice-over*) Dear love, I never stopped loving and dreaming of you. You are my Diego Rivera, you are stars, you is the moon in clouds, you is F-16 in the news, you is the body in my red bed, you is the left cigarettes in my wardrobe, you is the big dark green velvet jacket that I cover myself, you is the man that I want to fly to just like a bird, you are Iran, you are Suriye, you are the soldier in the border Habur...

Ayça, on the bus, thinks of Hama Ali.

Year and place of birth
1970   Istanbul, Turkey
—

Lives and works in
Istanbul, Turkey
—

Education
**Marmara University,
    Istanbul, Turkey**
—

Filmography
1996 *Etruch Camp* (short)
1997 *1 May 2 Film* (short)
1997 *Bachelors Inns* (short)
1997 *Dialogue* (short)
1998 *Lost People and
    the Street* (short)
1999 *Judgement* (short)
1999 *Boran* (short)
2001 *Silent Death
    (Sessiz ölüm)*
2003 *Gift to Nazim Hikmet Ran*
    (short)
2004 *Pina Bausch Istanbul
    "Breath"* (short)
2005 *Dialogues in the Dark*
2006 *I Missed My Rendez-vous
    with Death* (short)
2008 *Gitmek: My Marlon and
    Brando (Gitmek: Benim
    Marlon Ve Brandom)*
—

Director's awards
Boran
Antalya Altın Portakal
Uluslararasi Kisa Film Festivali
    (Culture Minister Special
    Award, 1999)
Corto Imola Festival
Internazionale Cortometraggio
    (Special Jury Prize, 2000)
Festival Chileno Internacional
del Cortometraje
    (Best Film, 2000)
Tel Aviv International Student
Film Festival
    (Best Film, 2000)
Ismailia International
Film Festival
    (Special Jury Prize, 2001)
Festival Internacional Tres
Continentes del Documental
    (Special Jury Prize, 2002)

Silent Death
Ankara International
Film Festival
    (Best Documentary, 2001)
— —

Release date
2008
—

Country of release
Turkey
—

Languages
**Turkish, Kurdish, English,
Arabic, Farsi**
—

Running time
92 min.
—

Genre
Drama
—

Producers
**Hüseyin Karabey, Lucinda
Englehart, Sophie Lorant**
—

Writers
Hüseyin Karabey, Ayça Damgaci
—

Cinematographer
Emre Tanyildiz
—

Score
**Kemal Sahir Gürel, Hüseyin Yildiz,
Erdal Güney**
—

Key cast
**Ayça Damgaci: Ayça
Hama Ali Khan: Hama Ali
Savas Emrah Ozdemir: Soran
Cengiz Bozkurt: Azad
Volga Sorgu Tekinoglu: Sah Havan**
—

Filming locations
**Istanbul, Turkey
Diyarbakir, Turkey
Silopi, Turkey
Van, Turkey
Hakkari, Turkey
Urmiye, Iran
Suleymaniye, Iraq
Zaho, Iraq
Erbil, Iraq**
—

Format
HDV
—

Awards for *Gitmek: My Marlon
and Brando*
Adana Golden Boll International
Film Festival
    (Best Actress, 2008)
Antalya Golden Orange
Film Festival
    (Best Supporting Actor,
    2008)
Borderlands International
Film Festival
    (Best Film Prize of
    Borderlands, 2008)
International Film Festival
of Kerala
    (Best Debut Film Award,
    NETPAC Award, 2008)
Istanbul International
Film Festival
    (Best Actress, 2008)
Jerusalem International
Film Festival
    (FIPRESCI Award, 2008)

Sarajevo International
Film Festival
    (Best Actress, 2008)
Tokyo International Film Festival
    (Best Asian-Middle Eastern
    Film Award, 2008)
Tribeca International
Film Festival
    (Best New Narrative
    Filmmaker, 2008)
Yerevan International
Film Festival
    (FIPRESCI Award – Ecümenlik
    Jury Special Award, 2008)
Ankara International
Film Festival
    (Special Jury Prize, 2009)
Festival International du Cinéma
Méditerranéen de Tétouan
    (Best Actress, 2009)
International Debut Film
Festival Spirit of Fire
    (Best 3rd Film Award, 2009)
Sofia International Film Festival
    (Best Balkan Film, 2009)
— —

Ayça, dancing at a Kurdish wedding near the border between Iraq and Turkey.

Ayça's bus going to Iran.

Ayça speaks with her Iranian taxi driver.

Ayça, desperate to hear news about Hama Ali, while in a small Iranian village.

Om Prakash Makhija (Shahrukh Khan) works as a junior artist in Bollywood in the 70s. He is madly in love with the superstar of that time, Shanti Priya (Deepika Padukone). His dreams and aspirations to become a superstar and be with his lady love are thwarted as he witnesses the brutal murder of his beloved Shanti by a mercenary producer, Mukesh Mehra (Arjun Rampal). Om Prakash dies trying to save Shanti, but destiny has something else in store when "Om Prakash" returns as "Om Kapoor," the superstar of 2007.

FARAH KHAN
OM SHANTI OM

Om cheering from the audience on the set of *Karz*.

If each film genre ranges in execution from the classical to the baroque, Farah Khan's *Om Shanti Om* (2007) must be considered the ultimate baroque Bollywood movie. Shuttling between parody and sincerity, Khan's sophomore feature is maximum Bollywood in the way that *Singin' in the Rain* (1952) is Hollywood squared. Self-reflexive to a dizzying degree and expressing a deep fluency in India's commercial cinema, it represents the high point to date from one of the world's most surprising popular auteurs.

Before turning to directing, Khan was best known in the West as a choreographer on crossover productions like Mira Nair's *Monsoon Wedding* (2001) and *Vanity Fair* (2004). To Bollywood fans, she was the woman behind dazzling dance sequences in hits such as Aditya Chopra's *Dilwale Dulhania Le Jayenge* (1995) and Mani Ratnam's *Dil Se* (1998), featuring the megastar Shahrukh Khan (no relation). The "Chaiyya Chaiyya" dance sequence atop a moving train in *Dil Se* made her instantly famous, and she choreographed three more key films featuring Shahrukh, all directed by Karan Johar, who serves as a useful reference point for Farah Khan. If he is the George Cukor of Indian cinema, Khan is its Stanley Donen. Donen had Gene Kelly; Khan has arguably the most adored movie star on the planet, Shahrukh Khan.

Her first feature as director, *Main Hoon Na* (2004), starred Shahrukh as an army major who goes undercover as a college student to thwart a terrorist and find his long-lost half-brother. If the plot strains credibility, it's hardly the point. Khan works with much larger forces here, showing a rare ability to rouse audiences with a combination of vigorous action, broad comedy, pan-national politics, and the irresistible tug of filial duty. She and Shahrukh, who produced the film with his wife, Gauri, had set out to make a full-on masala movie designed to appeal to all segments of the South Asian audience. It worked.

Om Shanti Om was Khan's next step, although she also choreographed eleven feature films in the meantime. Where *Main Hoon Na* aimed to recapture the spirit of the great Bollywood films of the 1970s, *Om Shanti Om* is actually set in that era and in the movie business. Shahrukh Khan returns, this time as Om, a struggling bit player in 1970s Bollywood who falls in love with Shanti (Deepika Padukone), the star of a production he's working on. Desperate both for her love and for leading man status, he attempts to pry her away from her scheming producer husband (Arjun Rampal), only to see her die in a fire on set. Through a magical bit of contrivance, the movie's second half sees Om reincarnated thirty years later as a massive star, now scheming to avenge Shanti's death.

The story's moviemaking milieu sets Khan free to plunge into a riot of self-reference. The film-within-a-film is also called *Om Shanti Om*, and the lead characters submit to endless plays on the religious and narrative echoes conjured by their names. At the same time, Khan layers the film with a blizzard of asides and in-jokes aimed at Bollywood initiates. One set piece riffs on the persona of veteran actor Manoj Kumar, while the musical number "Deewangi Deewangi" features no fewer than thirty-one stars from four decades of Indian cinema.

The flow of overlapping allusions seems at first comparable to Quentin Tarantino's work in *Kill Bill* (2003–4) or *Grindhouse* (2007), but there is a generosity that sets Khan's work apart. The effect of *Om Shanti Om*'s elaborate "movieness" is shared pleasure rather than the fanboy intimidation that often accompanies Tarantino. Even those who have never seen a single Indian film are let in on the jokes. The use of repetition, familiar narrative tropes, and even the very broadness of its humor welcome a much wider range of viewers.

Perhaps the most pleasurable scene of all comes while the final credits roll. As in *Main Hoon Na*, the film ends with not just the cast but the entire crew on screen for one last dance. This has become a kind of signature for Khan, gathering together the film, its filmmakers, and its audience in one embrace. Given the rigid hierarchies of both film production and Indian society, the sight of lowly cable technicians and carpenters sashaying up the same red carpet trod by stars and famous creative talent can produce a momentary euphoria. It is a fantasy of democracy, of course, but a glorious one. It's also an image that Stanley Donen and Gene Kelly might have loved.

"What is saving Indian cinema from being engulfed by Hollywood," Khan once said, "is our song and dance routines, because they just can't imitate that." With several much-imitated innovations in Indian pop choreography to her name, including the use of slow motion and fast editing, Khan must be acknowledged as the prime creative force at the heart of what makes Bollywood Bollywood. She is its pulse.

OM: Pappu you're sure I will become a hero?

PAPPU: Of course! You will definitely become a hero.

OM: My mom also says that.

PAPPU: I bet every comedian's mother says that to her son as well Omi.

OM: Really?

PAPPU: Yes, that's how mothers are.... But there is just one thing standing between you and your stardom.

OM: What's that?

PAPPU: Your name!

Om isn't certain he will make it in the movies, but Pappu never fails to bolster his dreams.

Year and place of birth
1965 Mumbai, India
—

Lives and works in
Mumbai, India
—

Education
**St. Xavier's College, Mumbai,
  India**
—

Filmography
2004 *Main Hoon Na*
2007 *Om Shanti Om*
—

Director's awards
Main Hoon Na
**International Indian Film
Academy Awards
  (Best Debut Director, 2005)
Screen Weekly Awards
  (Best Debut Director, 2005)
Zee Cine Awards
  (Most Promising Debut
  Director, 2005)**
— —

Release date
2007
—

Country of release
India
—

Language
Hindi
—

Running time
162 min.
—

Genre
Musical
—

Producers
Gauri Khan, Shahrukh Khan
—

Writers
**Farah Khan, Mayur Puri,
Mushtaq Sheikh**
—

Cinematographer
V. Manikanand
—

Score
Sandeep Chowta
—

Key cast
**Shahrukh Khan: Om Prakash
  Makhija / Om Kapoor
Deepika Padukone:
  Shanti Priya / Sandhya
Arjun Rampal: Mukesh Mehra
Shreyas Talpade: Pappu
Kirron Kher: Bela Makhija**
—

Filming location
Mumbai Film City, India
—

Format
35 mm
—

Awards for *Om Shanti Om*
**Asian Film Awards
  (Best Composer, 2008)
International Indian Film
Academy Awards
  (Best Lyrics, Best
  Art Direction, Best Special
  Effects, Best Costume
  Design, Best Makeup, 2008)
National Film Awards
  (Best Art Direction, 2008)
Neuchâtel International
Fantastic Film Festival
  (Best Asian Film, 2008)
Zee Cine Awards
  (Popular Award for Best Actor
  in a Negative Role, 2008)**
— —

Om dances on set as an extra.

Om tries to save Shanti from the fire.

The burned set reappears in Om's next life, thirty years later.

The film ends with a lavish dance number.

A tapestry of stories is woven around the themes of love, hope, and destiny. The film centers on characters leading separate lives but bound by a common desire: to be with their loved ones. The protagonists in the movie are fictitious except for Theresa Chan, a courageous deaf and blind woman whose life story is the inspiration behind the film.

ERIC KHOO
BE WITH ME

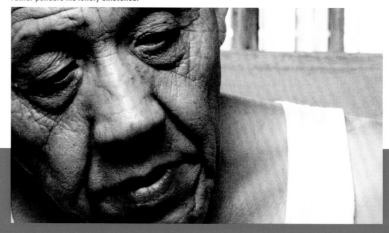

Father ponders his lonely existence.

Jackie and Sam share a special moment.

The highly respected filmmaker Eric Khoo frequently depicts the beauty and ailments of contemporary Singaporean society. This unique city-state became wealthy after going through rapid development during the 1980s. However, there is a dark side to Singapore's prosperity, because an authoritarian government was behind the achievement of this growth. Since 1959, when the People's Action Party seized power, the country has had an autocratic government.

Because of Singapore's past, its films often voice feelings of rebellion. Eric Khoo's first two features, *Mee Pok Man* (1995) and *12 Storeys* (*Shier lou*, 1997), are no exception. Dissent is expressed in both films through wandering ghost-like characters that repeatedly appear. These beings move through the same space and time, yet are not aware of their shared connection. On a deeper level, the two films reflect how sudden prosperity and rapid modernization have created a heterogeneous society that has severed itself from its traditions and consciousness, increasing the disconnect between generations.

Eric Khoo's third and best-known film, *Be With Me* (2005), explores the isolation and longing that arises from this loss of tradition. The film is dedicated to Theresa Chan, a woman who overcame her hearing impairment and became a teacher for children with disabilities. Chan actually appears in the film, and her real-life story unfolds in the film alongside fictitious characters, such as a man who is supposed to be Chan's old lover. *Be With Me* demonstrates Khoo's ability to break down the barrier between opposing elements such as documentary and drama, reality and fiction.

He does so to paint a portrait of Singapore's modern-day people who long for intimacy and love. This breaking down of barriers is also the director's method of melding Singapore's history and culture to bring about a greater understanding of hope and love. In an interview, Khoo once mentioned that his works are always hopeful, although they may seem bleak on the surface. This optimism is explored through the central theme of intimacy and the process through which intimacy is developed in his films.

Be With Me begins with a love affair between two teenage girls. As the heat of their affair cools down, an old man enters the story. He goes shopping, prepares food with love, and delivers the meal to his wife, who is in the hospital. Instead of focusing on dramatic moments, Khoo delves into these mundane activities to draw his viewers into the lives of his characters. He intends his viewers to contemplate the history of Singapore through the present-day reality of the film, which resembles the contemporary world the viewers themselves inhabit.

In the film, the son of the old man is a volunteer who helps Chan during her outings. When the wife of the old man dies, he gives the food he prepared to his son, and the son in turn gives the food to Chan. It becomes the seed for a new relationship to blossom. Later on, two scenes make especially poignant use of setting: first, the restaurant kitchen where Theresa works; and, second, the public swimming pool where two disabled older women swim. It is revealed that the pool is actually located in the same building where Elizabeth, another disabled woman who

teaches Theresa how to swim, was tortured as a girl by Japanese soldiers during the World War II occupation. As the scene demonstrates, Singapore is a city-state pockmarked by sites of historical suffering.

The interrelationships between the characters and the settings paint a picture of a people bound together by a common destiny. For example, one of the teenage girls from the opening of the film decides to commit suicide (like many others in Khoo's films). But her attempt to kill herself brings death to a destitute laborer instead. In these instances, Khoo illuminates the interconnectedness between strangers, how they influence and interfere in each other's lives, and how they affect each other's destiny. To overcome the pain of the past and the present, the film highlights the desire people have to be with those they love, and the hope they harbor of growing closer. *Be With Me* captures this desire of the heart and expresses the longings of Singaporean people today.

Eric Khoo's latest work is *My Magic* (2008), the story of an ex-magician who drowns his life in alcohol and comes to a reckoning after causing an accident. The focus is on repentance and forgiveness, which unfolds through the magician's attempt to repair his relationship with his son. Much like *Be With Me*, the newer film depicts the interconnectedness between people and how one person's tragedy and pain can have a lasting effect on the lives of others. Khoo shows that hope, which is required for healing and overcoming such wounds, is as profound as magic.

The lovelorn security guard finds solace in food.

Jackie wonders when Sam will contact her again.

Year and place of birth
1965   Singapore
—

Lives and works in
Singapore
—

Filmography
1990   *Barbie Digs Joe* (short)
1991   *August* (short)
1992   *Carcass* (short)
1993   *Symphony 92.4 Fm*
         (short)
1994   *Pain* (short)
1995   *Mee Pok Man*
1997   *12 Storeys (Shier Lou)*
2000   *Home Vdo* (short)
2005   *Be With Me*
2006   *No Day Off* (short)
2008   *My Magic*
—

Director's awards
Mee Pok Man
Singapore International
Film Festival
   (Special Mention –
   FIPRESCI, 1995)
Fukuoka Asian Film Festival
   (Special Jury Prize, 1996)
Pusan International Film Festival
   (Special Mention from the
   Jury – New Currents Award,
   Competition – Best New
   Asian Director, 1996)

12 Storeys
Hawaii International Film Festival
   (Golden Maile Award –
   Best Film, 1997)
Singapore International
Film Festival
   (UOB Young Cinema Award,
   NETPAC – FIPRESCI Critic's
   Prize, 1997)

My Magic
Fribourg International
Film Festival
   (Grand Prix – Regard d'Or,
   2009)
— —

Release date
2005
—

Country of release
Singapore
—

Language
English, Mandarin, Hokkien
—

Running time
90 min.
—

Genre
Drama, Romance
—

Producer
Brian Hong
—

Writers
Eric Khoo, Wong Kim Hoh
—

Cinematographer
Adrian Tan
—

Score
Kevin Mathews, Christine Sham
—

Key cast
Theresa Chan: Herself
Ezann Lee: Jackie
Samantha Tan: Sam
Seet Keng Yew: Security guard
Chiew Sung Ching: Father
Lawrence Yong: Son
Lynn Poh: Ann
—

Filming location
Singapore
—

Format
HD
—

Awards for *Be With Me*
Brussels International
Independent Film Festival
   (Best Director, 2005)
CJ Asian Independent
Film Festival
   (Audience Award, 2005)
Flanders International
Film Festival
   (Sabam Prize for
   Best Screenplay, 2005)
Stockholm International
Film Festival
   (FIPRESCI Jury Prizes –
   Best Film, Best
   Cinematography, 2005)

Tokyo International Film Festival
   (Special Mention, 2005)
Torino Film Festival
   (Best Director, CinemAvvenire
   Award – Best International
   Feature Film, Holden School
   Award for Best Screenplay –
   Special Mention, 2005)
Fantasporto – Oporto
International Film Festival
   (Directors' Week Award –
   Special Jury Prize, 2006)
Fribourg International
Film Festival
   (Jury Prize – Special Mention
   Ecumenical Jury Award,
   Don Quijote Prize – FICC Jury,
   2006)
Indianapolis International
Film Festival
   (The Best of East Asia Award,
   2006)
Mar del Plata International
Film Festival
   (Special Mention, 2006)
— —

Sam is troubled by her relationship with Jackie.

Theresa, though blind and deaf, cooks for herself.

Jackie reminisces about the good times she had with Sam.

At 14, I went deaf. Why, I don't know. One night blood and pus trickled down my cheek.

Both my mother and father didn't think much of it. My mother thought it was only a small boil which had burst open. The next morning, my hearing went. Mom was shocked. She shouted into my ears, but I couldn't make out what she was saying.

Theresa, at home, recounts the day she lost her sight and hearing.

Teenaged Aimie (Jiseon Kim), a newly arrived Korean immigrant, has fallen in love with her best and only friend, Tran (Taegu Andy Kang). She tries to express her feelings for him but is scared of losing their friendship. Their misunderstood affection for each other creates a delicate relationship that is challenged by the demands of living in a new country.

SO YONG KIM
IN BETWEEN DAYS

Tran tells Aimie she looks cool.

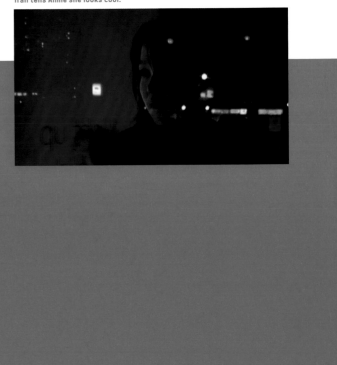

Aimie and Tran walk on the snow.

So Yong Kim was born in Pusan, South Korea, in 1968 and moved to Los Angeles in the 1980s. Her partner is filmmaker Bradley Rust Gray, who co-wrote and produced Kim's debut feature, *In Between Days* (2006). The two had previously lived together in Iceland, where Kim produced Gray's directorial debut, *Salt* (2003). These details are important because they help define Kim's aesthetic: both Korean and American, both personal and collaborative. There's even a hint of Reykjavik.

In Between Days is a portrait of Aimie, a Korean student living in an unnamed North American city. Part of the invisible nation of lonely urban migrants, Aimie drifts through a winter of dry classrooms and cold waits at the bus stop, until she meets a boy, Tran. Tran is everything she desires: cool, casual, and privy to teenage wisdom she can only guess at. She wants to get closer, but this is a boy destined to break a girl's heart.

Kim has said that the film was inspired both by her alienation as a young immigrant in Los Angeles and by the silence in her Korean family around matters of love and sex. As a result, the film is shaped by Aimie's inchoate and inexpressible desire. Remarkably for a debut feature, Kim finds a visual and aural language to express absences: unspoken urges, missed opportunities, all the questions and longings that regularly devastate teenage girls.

The film's title is taken from a song by The Cure. That alone immediately evokes an entire vocabulary of melancholy that Kim draws on with impressive fluency. Aimie is introduced walking through crunching snow, her head down, the hood of her parka up against the wind. Interludes of Aimie writing letters home to her father are set against still, exterior shots of the winter city, shot in 16 mm to contrast with the digital video used for the main story. We see her gazing at lingerie in a shop window, keeping her mother at bay, and responding to Tran's furtive sexual fumbles with explorations of her own body. All of these images serve to measure the distance between Aimie and the world around her. Kim establishes the girl's point of view by showing her standing apart, watchful.

Demonstrating surprising discipline for a first-time filmmaker, Kim does not rely on mournful indie-pop music to telegraph Aimie's inner state. That restraint allows the film to accrue the emotional intensity of Wong Kar-wai's romances, without the soundtrack. More precisely, *In Between Days* shows the influence of Jean-Pierre and Luc Dardenne. Under the admitted influence of their film *Rosetta* (1999), Kim keeps her camera close to her characters, stripping away teen-drama clichés in favor of attentive observation. A scene in which Aimie gives Tran a homemade tattoo is beautifully intimate. When the tattoo later refuses to heal, she snaps, "It's fine, you sissy." Aimie may be smitten, but her will is unbroken. Kim touches lightly on a timeless truth about love: how the helplessness of a romantic crush can mask a volcanic need to control the object of one's affection.

Writing in *The New York Times*, critic A. O. Scott termed Kim's approach "neo-neo realism," grouping her with peers in American independent cinema such as Kelly Reichardt, Lance Hammer, and Ramin Bahrani. One shared hallmark is an interest in social outsiders, along with the casting of "fictional characters most often played by nonactors from similar backgrounds." The underlying philosophy, Scott wrote, stands in opposition to Hollywood fantasy and raises the possibility that "engagement with the world as it is might reassert itself as an aesthetic strategy."

There's no doubt that Kim has absorbed the influence of practitioners of such realism, including the Dardennes, the Dogme 95 filmmakers, and her own contemporaries. But *In Between Days* cannot be contained within the scope of realism alone; the emotional intensity of the film derives just as much from melodrama and teen romance. Kim studied painting and made experimental films before shooting narrative features, evident in her ability to depict emotions that lie just beyond words. Her close camerawork is most powerful when exploring the face of Aimie. At rest, that face is round and impassive; at key moments, Kim's camera catches it as it transforms utterly into a smile.

In the end, Kim's aim is to find and sequence a succession of moments of a girl uprooted from home and unsure of her place in the city. In her writing, casting, locations, and shooting style, she chooses the tools of realism. But they are used to elicit not a clear, cerebral apprehension of Aimie's world, nor a political understanding of the plight of migrants, but a heightened emotional state. With a combination that may be equal parts Korea, Los Angeles, and Iceland, Kim works with precise rigor to suffuse her tale with the heart-bursting ache of first love.

Aimie sings karaoke by herself.

Year and place of birth
1968   Pusan, South Korea

—

Lives and works in
Brooklyn, N.Y., USA

—

Education
California Polytechnic State
    University, San Luis Obispo,
    USA
The School of the Art Institute
    of Chicago, Ill., USA

—

Filmography
2000   *Song from a Mother Frog*
          (short)
2002   *A Bunny Rabbit* (short)
2006   *In Between Days*
2008   *Treeless Mountain*

—

Director's awards
Treeless Mountain
Berlin International Film Festival
    (Prize of the Ecumenical Jury,
    2008)
Dubai International Film Festival
    (Muhr Award – Best Film,
    2008)
Pusan International Film Fetsival
    (NETPAC Award, 2008)
— —

Release date
2006

—

Country of release
USA

—

Language
Korean, English

—

Running time
83 min.

—

Genre
Drama

Producers
So Yong Kim, Bradley Rust Gray

—

Writers
So Yong Kim, Bradley Rust Gray

—

Cinematographer
Sarah Levy

—

Score
Asobi Seksu

—

Key cast
Jiseon Kim: Aimie
Taegu Andy Kang: Tran
Bokja Kim: Mom
Mike Park: Steve
Gina Kim: Michelle
Virginia Wu: Michelle's friend

—

Filming location
Toronto, Ont., Canada

—

Format
Digital, 16 mm

—

Awards for *In Between Days*
Berlin International Film Festival
    (FIPRESCI Prize, 2006)
Los Angeles Film Critics
Association
    (Independent/Experimental
    Film and Video Award, 2006)
Sundance Film Festival
    (Special Jury Prize –
    Dramatic, 2006)
Buenos Aires International
Independent Film Festival
    (Best Film, 2007)
— —

Aimie walks alone after Tran leaves.

Aimie listens to music after an argument with her mother.

Depressed over the news that Tran just wants to be friends.

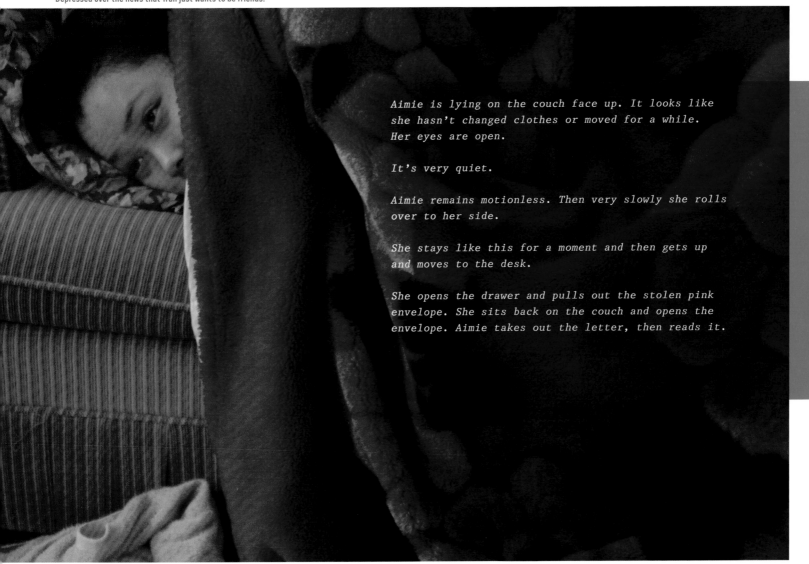

Aimie is lying on the couch face up. It looks like she hasn't changed clothes or moved for a while. Her eyes are open.

It's very quiet.

Aimie remains motionless. Then very slowly she rolls over to her side.

She stays like this for a moment and then gets up and moves to the desk.

She opens the drawer and pulls out the stolen pink envelope. She sits back on the couch and opens the envelope. Aimie takes out the letter, then reads it.

A new city, a new house—it could be a happy moment in a family's life. But Nina (Isabelle Menke) stands alienated in the half-empty space and leaves without telling anyone. She visits her brother at their parents' cottage, moves aimlessly through a surreal mountain landscape, and finds herself with an aging tennis star in a hotel. Nina's attempt to break out does not end in existential revolt but in a fleeting encounter between two people who no longer feel at home in their worlds. Like a sleepwalker, Nina returns, step by step, to her family.

ULRICH KOHLER
WINDOWS ON MONDAY

Frieder and Nina in the throes of an argument.

Rebelling against societal norms is a popular cinematic topos. There's a wealth of films featuring attractive young rebels without a cause, often attacking the conservatism of older generations in a haphazard and aimless manner. And there's one thing that the lead characters of these films have in common: we wouldn't expect them to do anything else.

The rebels that interest German director Ulrich Köhler don't follow this pattern. They revolt against what they've chosen for themselves, against an unnamed repression; they are their own enemies. For example, the young soldier in Köhler's *Bungalow* (2002) suddenly deserts from the army and holes up in his parents' empty house, having no alternative to the social order that he is fleeing from. This type of indiscriminate rebellion is more commonly found in literature and its internal monologues and reflections. Cinema, however, demands simplification, movement, tangible antagonisms. Audiences' sympathies lie with intentional rebels, young and wild. The phlegmatic heroes of Köhler's films are not attractive enough to gain such sympathies, they are not looking to create a presence; on the contrary, they strive to be invisible. The act of resistance here is not carried out by the protagonist but rather by the narrative itself, a resistance against cinematic norms.

Köhler's second feature, *Windows on Monday* (*Montag kommen die Fenster*, 2006), details a young doctor who breaks out of her family's provincial idyll. Nina has just moved with her husband, Frieder, and their daughter, Charlotte, from Berlin to Kassel, where the couple work in a hospital. In the first scene, Frieder brings Charlotte into the operating theater, much to the annoyance of Nina. Although tendernesses are exchanged in bed, the atmosphere is so frosty that viewers are grateful for an unexpected visit from Nina's brother Christoph, who has just left his girlfriend and hopes to get over his world-weariness out in the sticks.

The next day, Frieder frets about the expensive tiles he's laying in the hallway and plays with his daughter lovingly, while Nina dozes on the sofa. When Charlotte wakes her, a startled Nina pulls her daughter's long hair with a certain brutality. Later on, Nina goes to pick up Charlotte at Frieder's parents' house, but then gets back into the car and drives off. When Frieder calls her phone, she says, with complete lack of emotion, "I'm not coming back," and hangs up.

It's striking that Köhler introduces his protagonist with such little compassion; it's just as striking that this absence of empathy still manages to arouse the viewer's interest in someone whose amoral behavior remains a mystery.

The second part of the film is as unforgettable as it is unique. From a hut in the forest, where she was visiting her brother and his girlfriend, Nina sets out on her bike on an odyssey that leaves the realistic tone of the film's beginning far behind. She rises above withered treetops in a cable car until a gray concrete building block appears in the middle of the forest. She wanders through this isolated hotel like a ghost, straying through long corridors and utility rooms until she finds refuge in an empty room. Only one person there has eyes for her, someone who also seems to have come back from the dead: an aging professional tennis player there to play for the nouveau riche. At the end of the night, he knocks on the door, serves them champagne, and gets into bed with her. "I was paid to come here," she claims. "So was I. What a coincidence," he responds dryly. And later, "I'm a whore. You're not." You could imagine such a scene playing out in a late-80s Godard film.

Time stands still in this unreal place. Nina's flight is like a dream, although it's hard to say whether it's a good or bad one. When she awakens from it, there is snow on the ground in this fairy-tale forest. She meets her husband and daughter and acts as if turned to stone, refusing to say anything. It is only Frieder's furious question, "Do you actually find me boring?" that she counters with a clear, "Yes."

Now the film pulls out its second big surprise. Instead of continuing to follow Nina, the final section focuses on Frieder. On Monday, the new windows arrive. Frieder doesn't want them; they're not made from the right wood. The house, which is no longer a home, is protected from the cold only with makeshift plastic sheets. He looks for comfort in the arms of an ex-girlfriend, a form of protest so wretched that in retrospect Nina appears like a radiant heroine. Yet Köhler brings the couple back together in the same unexpected way that they split up, without any motive, unless you can call inertia a motive.

In *Windows on Monday*, Köhler develops the unique process he started with *Bungalow*. His is an ascetic kind of cinema that refuses any sort of simple psychological interpretation, maintaining a breathtaking balance between realism and dream.

Nina and her daughter, Charlotte, stoke the fire.

Year and place of birth
1969 Marburg, West Germany
—

Lives and works in
Berlin, Germany
—

Education
Ecole des Beaux Arts
     Quimper, France
University of Fine Arts
     Hamburg, Germany
—

Filmography
1996 *Epoxy* (short)
     (codirected by Nina
     Könnemann)
1997 *Starsky* (short)
1997 *Maria Tokyo* (short)
1998 *Palü* (short)
     (co-directed by Jochen
     Dehn)
1999 *Rakete* (short)
2002 *Bungalow*
2006 *Windows on Monday*
     (*Montag kommen die*
     ***Fenster*)**
—

Director's awards
Bungalow
Baden-Baden TV Film Festival
     (MFG Star, 2002)
Berlin & Beyond Festival
in San Francisco
     (Best First Feature Award,
     2002)
German Critics Award
     (Best First Feature, 2002)
Hessian Film Award
     (Feature Film, 2002)
Schwerin Art of Film Festival
     (Flying Ox Award, 2002)
Thessaloniki International
Film Festival
     (Silver Alexander, 2002)
— —

Release date
2006
—

Country of release
Germany
—

Language
German
—

Running time
88 min.
—

Genre
Drama
—

Producers
Katrin Schlösser, Frank Löprich
—

Writer
Ulrich Köhler
—

Cinematographer
Patrick Orth
—

Score
Martin Hossbach
—

Key cast
Isabelle Menke: Nina
Hans-Jochen Wagner: Frieder
Amber Bongard: Charlotte
Trystan Wyn Puetter: Christoph
Elisa Seydel: Nathalie
Ilie Nastase: David Ionesco
Ursula Renneke: Maria
—

Filming locations
Kassel, Germany
Braunlage, Germany
—

Format
35 mm
—

Awards for *Windows on Monday*
Hessian Film Award
     (Feature Film, 2006)
Ljubljana International
Film Festival
     (Best Film of the
     Perspectives Section,
     2007)
— —

David surprises Nina in her hotel room.

DAVID: You live in a country where people
don't know how to eat well, drink well, fuck
well and take tennis too serious...

Nina smirks.

DAVID: (*Smiling back*) I'm sorry, it's the truth.

*David takes his last sip of champagne. He wants
to stand up.*

NINA: Stop.

DAVID: I'm thirsty.

NINA: We have a deal.

DAVID: So what can I do?

Frieder and Nina wait in their camping car at their neighbor's funeral.

David is left behind by Nina.

The Alexandria Ceremonial Police Orchestra, an eight-man band, arrives in Israel from Egypt to play at an Arab cultural center. However, no one picks them up from the airport, and the band ends up lost in a small desert town where they are forced to spend the night. A local restaurant owner and her friends take them in, challenging everyone's ideas about Arab-Israeli relations.

ERAN KOLIRIN
THE BAND'S VISIT

The band arrives at the wrong destination.

How does a director build a bittersweet comedy on the back of an ongoing and relentless conflict? Israeli filmmaker Eran Kolirin, in the role of writer-director, does it with a tender heart, an absurd yet gentle sensibility, and with hardly a trace of overt politics. *The Band's Visit* (*Bikur Ha-Tizmoret*, 2007) is about the fictional Alexandria Ceremonial Police Orchestra, an Egyptian band visiting Israel to play at an Arab cultural center. But when no one shows up to meet them at the airport, they get lost and end up in the wrong place. Stranded with nowhere to stay in this small, desert town, they get help from Dina, an attractive local coffee-shop owner. But will the locals be able to provide them the welcome they need in a "hostile territory"?

Kolirin's deserted ghost town is far from heaven; it's more like a kind of purgatory. As Dina puts it, "There is no Arab culture, also no Israeli culture. Here there is no culture at all." But still, the place where this Egyptian band takes shelter functions as a safe haven. In one scene, Kolirin depicts the absurdity of the band's presence: all eight members, dressed in baby-blue uniforms—further emphasizing their olive skin and serious faces—carry the same suitcases and pass buildings that look nearly identical. The band members too appear to be identical. The only thing that distinguishes them is their different instruments, which raises the possibility that music may be the only thing that contradicts the monotony of life in this town.

The director subtly comments on the Arab-Israeli conflict by portraying the current situation as mostly a heightened "emotional state": as soon as someone is stripped of his or her political loyalties and prejudices, what remains is a sad and melancholic emotion that exists on both sides. The obligatory and short-lived intersection of the lives of the Egyptian musicians and the townsfolk is almost a fantastical wish come true. However, the equilibrium of drama and comedy manages to carry the film beyond a "let's live in harmony together" utopia. The tension between the Egyptians and their hosting families is apparent. Exchanged looks, long pauses, and strained interactions between the characters create moments both sad and funny. These comic touches are in the spirit of deadpan masters such as director Aki Kaurismäki, and create opportunities, however small, to shake up tension in the Middle East.

The musicians have to spend the night in town before catching the bus the following day. Played by the impeccable Ronit Elkabetz, Dina persuades coffee-shop regular Itzik (Rubi Moskovitz) to allow the musicians to stay with some of the townspeople. She herself takes home the fatherly and charismatic conductor, Tewfiq (the amazing Sasson Gabai), and the young womanizing trumpeter Haled, played by Saleh Bakri. Sparks fly between the Israeli Dina and the sad and distant Egyptian Tewfiq, who suffers a family tragedy from his past. While the film's common communication language is English, Dina tells Tewfiq: "Say something in Arabic. . . .Just to hear the music," emphasizing the traditional lack of effective communication between Israel and Egypt. Unfortunately, the film was disqualified from the Oscar race for Best Foreign Language Film because English was spoken for more than half of its duration.

Dina and Tewfiq merrily discover their common traits. For example, Dina tells him of her fondness for the legendary Egyptian singer Umm Kulthum and films with Egyptian actor Omar Sharif, and explains that Arab films are eagerly watched in Israel. The moody and introverted Tewfiq's defensive walls begin to crumble. Although he is cautious toward this beautiful woman, he mentions that music is the food of the human soul. However, when she makes a prejudiced remark about conservative Egyptian men with moustaches, the fragile balance is broken; Tewfiq shuts down and their relation is hindered from further development.

This is a film whose success rests on the subtle performances of its Arab and Israeli actors. Sasson, who sings in Arabic, is worth mentioning alone. When the band gathers the following day to perform, the viewer is left to deduce everything from his expressions alone: is the love song he sings dedicated to Dina, who was left behind? What do we make of how he looks at Haled? Is a relationship between Tewfiq and Dina still possible?

The storyline of *The Band's Visit* may not be radical, but the film never delves into clichés. Sarcasm replaces easy comedy, and melodrama is supplanted by the desires of ordinary people. By way of his characters, from both sides of the conflict, and his graceful handling of the subject matter, Kolirin manages to temporarily trespass borders in the Middle East—no small feat for a young filmmaker.

Tewfiq and Dina at Dina's restaurant.

Year and place of birth
1973   Holon, Israel

—

Lives and works in
Tel Aviv, Israel

—

Filmography
2004   *The Long Journey*
       (Ha'massa Ha'aroh)
2007   *The Band's Visit*
       (Bikur Ha-Tizmoret)

—

Director's awards
The Long Journey
Eilat International Film Festival
   (Best Feature, 2004)

— —

Release date
2007

—

Country of release
Israel

—

Language
Hebrew, Arabic, English

—

Running time
83 min.

—

Genre
Drama

—

Producers
Eilon Ratzkovsky, Ehud Bleiberg,
Yossi Uzrad, Koby Gal-Raday,
Guy Jacoel

—

Writer
Eran Kolirin

—

Cinematographer
Shai Goldman

—

Score
Habib Shehadeh Hanna

—

Key cast
Ronit Elkabetz: Dina
Sasson Gabai: Tewfiq
Saleh Bakri: Haled
Khalifa Natour: Simon
Shlomi Avraham: Papi
Rinat Matatov: Yula

—

Filming locations
Yeruham, Israel
Dimona, Israel

—

Format
35 mm

—

Awards for *The Band's Visit*
Athens International
Film Festival
   (City of Athens Best Director
   Award, 2007)
Awards of the Israeli
Film Academy
   (Best Actor, Best Actress,
   Best Costumes,
   Best Director, Best Film,
   Best Music, Best Screenplay,
   Best Supporting Actor, 2007)
Cannes International
Film Festival
   (Award of the Youth, FIPRESCI
   Prize, Un Certain Regard –
   Jury Coup de Coeur, 2007)
Copenhagen International
Film Festival
   (Audience Award, Jury
   Special Prize, 2007)
European Film Awards
   (European Discovery of the
   Year, European Film Award for
   Best Actor, 2007)
Jerusalem Film Festival
   (Best Actor, Best Actress,
   Wolgin Award for Best Israeli
   Feature, 2007)
Karlovy Vary International
Film Festival
   (NEPTAC Award, 2007)

Molodist International
Film Festival
   (Scythian Deer, 2007)
Montreal Festival of New Cinema
   (Feature Film Award, Louve
   d'Or, 2007)
Munich Film Festival
   (Audience Award, CineVision
   Award, 2007)
Sarajevo Film Festival
   (Audience Award, 2007)
Tokyo International Film Festival
   (Tokyo Grand Prix, 2007)
Valladolid International
Film Festival
   (Best New Director,
   Best Screenplay, 2007)
Warsaw International
Film Festival
   (Audience Award,
   Warsaw Award, 2007)
Cinemanila International
Film Festival
   (Lino Brocka Award, 2008)
Palm Springs International
Film Festival
   (Bridging the Borders Award,
   2008)

— —

Iris and Itzik host band members for a birthday dinner.

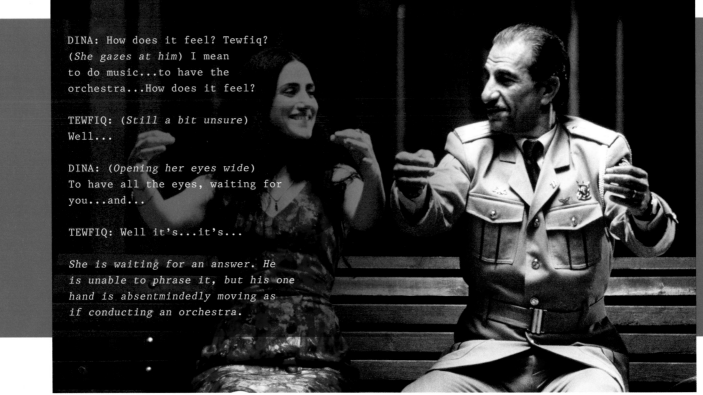

DINA: How does it feel? Tewfiq?
(She gazes at him) I mean
to do music...to have the
orchestra...How does it feel?

TEWFIQ: *(Still a bit unsure)*
Well...

DINA: *(Opening her eyes wide)*
To have all the eyes, waiting for
you...and...

TEWFIQ: Well it's...it's...

*She is waiting for an answer. He
is unable to phrase it, but his one
hand is absentmindedly moving as
if conducting an orchestra.*

Tewfiq shows Dina how to conduct.

Haled helps Papi make a move on Yula.

Tewfiq, Haled, and Dina arrive home late after a night out.

Isra (Israel Gómez Romero), the young gypsy boy who never sings again after his father's death, despite belonging to a tradition of flamenco singers, dreams of traveling far from the island on which he was born. Makiko (Makiko Matsumura), who comes to the island to learn more about traditional flamenco singing, hopes to understand the inexpressible emotions aroused by her father's illness. Although they don't know it yet, these two characters are about to learn what it means, and what it feels like, to grow up.

ISAKI LACUESTA
THE LEGEND OF TIME

Joji playfully tricks Isra.

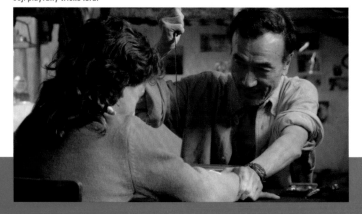

Isra plays in the salt mine with his friends.

Some of the most interesting and innovative work in contemporary Spanish cinema is emerging from Catalunya, one of the country's "autonomous regions." It has a number of dynamic film schools, including the Escola Superior de Cinema i Audiovisuals de Catalunya (ESCAC) and the Universitat Pompeu Fabra. And with support from the Centre de Cultura Contemporània de Barcelona (CCCB) and its exhibitions director, Jordi Balló, and from courageous producers like Luis Miñarro, Catalan cinema has increasingly been receiving more attention at festivals around the world.

One of its most promising directors is Isaki Lacuesta, part of the Catalan New Wave, a group currently leading a revival of Spanish cinema. At a very young age he started writing film reviews, music, and books, before picking up a camera. With extraordinary energy, he embarked on a film career that consisted of writing scripts, working as an editor and cameraman, teaching, and making lots of short films.

In 2002, he made *Cravan vs. Cravan*, his first full-length documentary, about Arthur Cravan, the legendary poet, boxer, and nephew of Oscar Wilde, who mysteriously disappeared in the Gulf of Mexico in 1918. He followed up in 2006 with *The Legend of Time* (*La leyenda del tiempo*), the title of which is taken from a 1979 album by the famous Andalucian flamenco singer Camarón de la Isla. *The Legend of Time* is made up of two superimposed stories about the celebrated singer, who died in 1992 at the age of forty-one. In the first one, "The Voice of Isra," a young Gypsy from San Fernando stops singing after his father's death. In the second, "The Voice of Makiko," a Japanese woman travels—somewhat naively—to Cádiz, hoping to learn to sing like the great master Camarón.

In the words of the distinguished Catalan writer Enrique Vila-Matas: "The two stories in the film are poetic and have a strange intensity; they subtly interweave to form a simple yet astonishing whole that breaks down the distinction between fiction and reality." And in the newspaper *El País* Teresa Cendrós wrote, "Isaki Lacuesta bursts through the boundary between fiction and reality and fiction, and makes a tender and moving, uncategorizable film in which, with perfect naturalness, he breaks all the rules of cinematographic language."

Lacuesta's films could be seen as "essays" in the sense that they represent an ongoing study of cinema, and, in this case, a reflection on memory and influence. The director, on the other hand, prefers the term "research," and says, "What research records is what exists between a beginning and an ending, without necessarily moving toward a specific goal. In that sense, I believe I have developed a kind of intermediary, tangential cinema. In *The Legend of Time* we took as our immediate starting point portraits of people and settings that fascinated me, and the experiences they had gone through until now, using their actual lives. . . . I'm not worried if anyone sees formal preoccupations in the film, or aspects that suggest an essay; that doesn't bother me, but I'd like those things to appear only on a second viewing, and the most concrete and immediate content—in other words, these people—to be seen first."

Lacuesta explores the boundaries of documentary in order to sidestep or cross them. In doing so, he is in the company of directors like Jean Renoir, Jean Vigo, and Roberto Rossellini in terms of their approach to the real, their need to search for a moment of truth to put before the camera. But Lacuesta is also something of an adventurer, for whom the journey of writing, shooting, and editing is a film in itself, in the style of Jean Rouch or Chris Marker. This is also a vision of cinema as a mutant art that is able to constantly transform and renew itself. So it's no surprise to find Lacuesta between films working on an art installation, preparing very detailed DVD bonus material, or corresponding—on film—with the Japanese director Naomi Kawase, for her film *In Between Days* (2009).

Lacuesta himself agrees: "I like the idea of a 'traveling' cinema in its most literal sense. Making a film is an excuse to visit places you would never otherwise have been allowed to go to, to meet very different people, and to live for a moment as if you were someone else, knowing that when you want, you can go home, no doubt a little bit changed."

In 2009, *The Condemned* (*Los condenados*), Lacuesta's third full-length and first "traditional" film, a thriller about memory and violence, shot mainly in Peru, won the International Critics' Prize at the San Sebastián International Film Festival.

Isra and Saray develop a flirtatious relationship.

Year and place of birth
1975 Gerona, Spain
—
Lives and works in
Barcelona, Spain
—
Education
Universitat Autònoma
    de Barcelona, Spain
Universitat Pompeu Fabra
    Barcelona, Spain
—
Filmography
2000 Caras vs. Caras (short)
2002 Cravan vs. Cravan
2004 Teoría de los cuerpos
        (short)
2006 The Legend of Time
        (La leyenda del tiempo)
2007 Las variaciones Marker
        (short)
2009 In Between Days
        (co-directed with
        Naomi Kawase) (short)
2009 The Condemned
        (Los Condenados)
—

Director's awards
Cravan vs Cravan
SITGES International
Fantastic Film Festival
of Catalonia
        (Best Film Gran Angular,
        Best New Director, 2002)
Festival de Cine de Vitoria
        (Best Film, 2002)
Opera Prima Festival de Cine
Ciudad de Tudela
        (Special Jury Prize, 2002)
Sant Jordi Awards
        (Best First Work, 2003)
— —

Release date
2006
—
Country of release
Spain
—
Language
Spanish, Japanese
—
Running time
109 min.
—
Genre
Drama
—
Producer
Paco Poch
—
Writer
Isaki Lacuesta
—
Cinematographer
Diego Dussuel
—

Score
Joan Albert Amargós
—
Key cast
Israel Gómez Romero: Isra
Francisco José Gómez Romero:
    Cheíto
Saray Gómez Romero: Saray
Makiko Matsumura: Makiko
Soichy Yukimune: Joji
—
Filming locations
San Fernando, Spain
Cádiz, Spain
Barbate, Spain
—
Format
HD
—

Awards for The Legend of Time
Alcances Film Festival
        (Best Film, Best Sound,
        2006)
Catalan Association of Film
Critics and Writers
        (Best Spanish Film, 2006)
CineLatino
        (Tübingen Public Award,
        2006)
Guayaquil International
Film Festival
        (Best Feature, Best Direction,
        Best Script, 2006)
Las Palmas International
Film Festival
        (Special Jury Award,
        Best Actor, 2006)
Nantes International
Film Festival
        (Special Jury Prize, Special
        Young Jury Prize, 2006)

San Sebastián International
Film Festival
        (Spanish Film Commission
        Prize, 2006)
Yerevan International
Film Festival
        (Silver Prize, 2006)
— —

A teacher talks with Cheíto and Isra about their relationship.

Joji and Isra go for a ride.

MAKIKO: I have to say goodbye.

JOJI: What?

MAKIKO: I've decided to go back to Japan.

JOJI: So you can see your father.

MAKIKO: Yes.

JOJI: You've finally made the decision. I didn't think it was good to be so far away from somone who is ill.

MAKIKO: It's true.

JOJI: As for the song...you can always sing at any time... but taking care of your father...you may not have another chance. When are you leaving?

Joji and Makiko talk on the beach.

In the midst of Pinochet's dictatorship in Chile, Raúl Peralta (Alfredo Castro), a man in his fifties, is obsessed with the idea of impersonating Tony Manero, John Travolta's character from *Saturday Night Fever* (1977). His urge to reproduce his idol's likeness, and his dream of being recognized as a successful showbiz star on national television, drive him to commit a series of crimes.

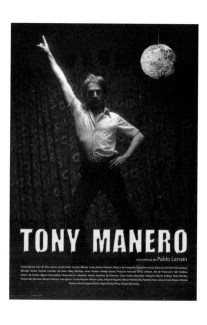

PABLO LARRAIN
TONY MANERO

Raúl, ready to perform his stage impersonation of Tony Manero.

Raúl reflects on the ways to live the fantasy life of his hero Tony Manero.

During a visit to Madrid's Reina Sofia museum, the young Chilean director Pablo Larraín came across a book entitled *Drink*, which contains a black-and-white photograph of a fifty-something man sitting in a chair wearing nothing but his underwear and his shoes, looking out of a window, with a gun in one hand and a cigarette in the other. Entranced by the image, Larraín bought the book and showed it to his friend, the actor Alfredo Castro, who immediately responded that the man in the picture looked like "a murderer . . . and also a dancer." From this seed grew the unusual plot of *Tony Manero*, a four-day fragment from the life of Raúl Peralta, a man who hopes to escape his environment by imitating Tony Manero, John Travolta's hip-swinging hero of John Badham's *Saturday Night Fever* (1977).

Larraín collaborated on the script with Castro and Mateo Iribarren, who had both appeared in Larraín's first feature, *Fuga* (2006). When the team discovered that *Saturday Night Fever* was released in Chile in 1978, they found the crucial context for their story in the early years of the dictatorial regime of Augusto Pinochet. As Larraín puts it, the release of Badham's film in Chile "pulled all the elements together. We had a conflict. We had a dramatic plot. And we had a context. . . . I wanted to show [. . .] how these two polar opposites create tension. The context was not just a background but was the floor on which everyone was standing."

At first glance, the plot suggests a comedy, an absurdist satire of a fantasist boogieing on a rotting wooden floor. Larraín's dancer, however, is far from a lovable loser. The film opens with shaky handheld camerawork tracking the distracted and nervous Raúl Peralta (played with powerful impassivity by Castro) outside a Chilean television studio where he is auditioning to appear on a program searching for Chile's best Tony Manero impersonator. Encountering Raúl in this setting, clutching Manero's trademark white suit like a comfort blanket, engages the emotions of the audience. It's hard not to feel touched by this man and his dreams of escape.

The film follows Raúl back to his lonely apartment via a visit to the cinema to watch *Saturday Night Fever* yet again. A tracking shot as he walks the street (still carrying his precious suit) echoes the opening sequence of Badham's picture—contrasting Travolta's cocky strut with Raúl's labored tread. From his apartment window he witnesses the mugging of an old lady (the themes of spying and eavesdropping are recurring motifs, all serving to underline the oppression of society by the military regime). Peralta runs to her aid and escorts her home, where she shows him her color television (a rare luxury afforded to her because she is a military widow). Up to this point, Larraín had masterfully elicited sympathetic feelings for Raúl—which makes it all the more shocking when Raúl casually punches the woman in the head. With the audience reeling from the first blow, Larraín moves the violence just out of frame as Raúl beats her to death, while Pinochet looks on from the television.

Larraín momentarily turns comic again as we encounter Raúl's dance troupe, a disparate group of amateurs performing in a ramshackle bar. However, a small misstep unleashes Raúl's rage and he begins to literally rip up the dance floor, anger and pent-up aggression seeping from every pore. The dance floor takes on a wider significance when it's revealed that Raúl wants to sell the stolen television in order to buy glass tiles to replace the rotting wooden planks in the bar. Raúl will stop at nothing to achieve this dream.

Larraín has commented in interviews that a misquote in the film's press notes talks about loss of identity. The director intended to express that the film was at heart about loss *and* identity. Raúl doesn't lose his identity, but he wants desperately to change it, to be Tony Manero. It's an obsession that forces audiences to examine the kind of environment that could produce this man. As part of his preparation, Larraín asked many people what they remembered of the time. "What they'd say was so imprecise and vague . . . Something is blurred, erased, like a bad dream. What I got from this research was not any particular idea of what happened in terms of facts, but a tone, an atmosphere . . . [a] combination of fear, sadness and strangeness—because they didn't know what was going to happen the next day." This sadness and uncertainty permeates the film, and Larraín purposefully allows some scenes to slide out of focus, while the constant wailing of passing sirens imply that the carabineros are never far away.

Tony Manero has been met with wide critical acclaim. It won the top prize at the Turin Film Festival, as well as the FIPRESCI Prize and the Best Actor Award for Alfredo Castro. The film was also Chile's submission to the 2009 Academy Awards for the Best Foreign Language Film category, cementing Larraín's reputation as a director to watch.

Cony sings on stage in a small bar located on the outskirts of Santiago.

Raúl seduces Pauli.

Year and place of birth
1976 Santiago, Chile
—

Lives and works in
Santiago, Chile
—

Education
**UNIACC University,
    Santiago, Chile**
—

Filmography
2006 *Fuga*
2008 *Tony Manero*
—

Director's awards
Fuga
**Trieste Festival of Latin
American Cinema
    (Audience Award –
    Best Film, Jury Prize –
    Best Performance, 2006)**
**Cartagena Film Festival
    (Best First Work, 2007)**
**Málaga Spanish Film Festival
    (Audience Award –
    Best Latin American Film,
    Best Latin American Actor,
    2007)**
— —

Release date
2008
—

Country of release
Chile
—

Language
Spanish
—

Running time
98 min.
—

Genre
Drama
—

Producer
Juan de Dios Larraín
—

Writers
**Pablo Larraín, Alfredo Castro,
Mateo Iribarren**
—

Cinematographer
Sergio Armstrong
—

Key cast
**Alfredo Castro: Raúl Peralta
Amparo Noguera: Cony
Héctor Morales: Goyo
Paola Lattus: Pauli
Elsa Poblete: Wilma**
—

Filming location
Santiago, Chile
—

Format
Super 16 mm
—

Awards for *Tony Manero*
**Festival Internacional del Nuevo
Cine Latinoamericano
    (Best Film, Best Actor,
    Distribution Award, 2008)**
**Latin Beat Film Festival
    (Best Actor, 2008)**
**Santiago Festival Internacional
de Cine
    (Best Film, Audience Award,
    2008)**
**Torino Film Festival
    (Best Film, Best Actor,
    FIPRESCI, 2008)**
**Viña del Mar Film Festival
    (Best Director, Special
    Jury Prize, 2008)**

**Warsaw International
Film Festival
    (Special Jury Prize, 2008)**
**Buenos Aires International
Independent Film Festival
    (FEISAL Award,
    Best Actor, 2009)**
**Cinema City – International
Film and New Media Festival
    (Grand Prix, 2009)**
**Cinemanila International
Film Festival
    (Vic Silayan Award for
    Best Actor, 2009)**
**International Film Festival
Rotterdam
    (Best Film – Association
    of Dutch Film Critics, 2009)**
**International Istanbul
Film Festival
    (Golden Tulip for
    Best Film, 2009)**
— —

Raúl dressed up for the nationally televised Tony Manero impersonating contest.

Raúl performs on the dance floor at the contest.

ENRIQUE: What's your name?

RAUL: Raúl Peralta Paredes O.

ENRIQUE: Very good. Like in the song: "Viejas paredes..."

RAUL: Yes.

ENRIQUE: Great. What do you do for a living?

RAUL: This.

ENRIQUE: You mean dancing? Great! Now with enthusiasm and energy! "I'm Tony Manero."

Raúl at the national television contest.

Liu Jiayin's sequel to *Oxhide* (*Niu pi*, 2004) centers around a family of three preparing dumplings for dinner. In nine real-time sequences, Liu Jiayin and her parents play themselves and show the delicate balance of a family struggling to make ends meet with limited resources. The family must consider the repercussions of their failing family business and come up with a strategy together.

LIU JIAYIN
OXHIDE II

The mother and father work together to prepare the dumplings.

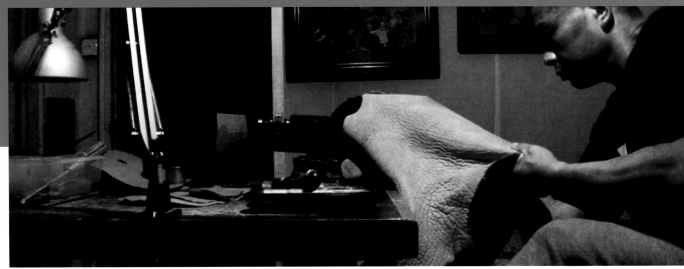

The father at work on his leather.

In just nine static shots, varying in length from five to twenty-one minutes, Liu Jiayin's *Oxhide II* (*Niupi er*, 2009) depicts a Beijing family of three making dumplings in real time. An honorable follow-up to the 2004 *Oxhide* (*Niu Pi*), the film presents even greater formal control and structural rigor. As in *Oxhide*, the parents and the child are in fact played by Liu's own parents and Liu herself. Despite resembling a modest, no-budget movie, *Oxhide II* is a groundbreaking work in Chinese independent cinema because of its experimental daring and originality.

The entire film was shot in Liu's own fifty-square-meter home. The narrow CinemaScope screen ratio not only has the effect of cutting off major parts of the family members' bodies (especially faces), but portrays the family through the eyes of Liu herself. *Oxhide II* was shot on HD, unlike *Oxhide* which was shot on DV, resulting in more brightly lit images and more saturated colors. Consequently, it has less a feel of a home movie and more of a conscious, intentional, experimental film form.

The family relationships and daily life portrayed in the film are real, but *Oxhide II* is not a documentary. Nine shots in sequence may sound straightforward, but Liu's use of close-ups and CinemaScope wide-screen in conjunction with off-screen dialogue is complex and unique. The low production values of the movie make its inventiveness stand out even more. Beneath the banal surface of the domestic scene of preparing dumplings, the anxiety, tension, comedy, and understanding within the family are evoked with subtlety and grace.

In the opening shot of the film, the father is working with a large piece of leather. Viewers may remember from *Oxhide* that the family earns a living from producing handmade leather bags. We first see the father in the right of the screen, his head going in and out of view, grappling with the piece of oxhide on his work table, adjusting the angle of a picture hanging on the wall, threading a needle, attending to each task with briskness and concentration. There is no dialogue, no music, and he remains the only figure on screen for twelve minutes before we hear the mother enter the apartment. The camera does not move; rather, the family members move about freely, entering and then re-entering the frame.

Eventually, some twenty minutes into the film, the father and mother begin to clear the work table, preparing their work station for dumpling-making. They rotate the table ninety degrees, leave the room, and thus the viewer's sight, and only then do the title credits appear on screen. The camera angle changes for the second time at this point, now appearing at an aerial view above the table, so that we can fully watch the mother's and father's hands at work, measuring flour, methodically mixing in water, sorting chives.

With this second film, Jiayin has set a harder problem for herself than the first, and solves it beautifully. Instead of creating a narrative structure out of different scenes taken from the family's daily life, she focuses on a single scene, a single task, conducted around a table. By breaking the scene up into nine shots she forms a visually geometrical structure that manages to be compelling and dynamic, even for a contemporary audience used to rapidly changing scenes and camera angles.

The first five shots of the film vary from one another by forty-five degrees and a change of camera angle. But the following three shots "violate" this system by changing the camera height instead of angle. For example, shot six stays at the table level, focusing on the hands of the father and daughter in close-up; shot seven rises to eye-level and captures the faces of the daughter and mother while in conversation; shot eight sinks to floor level and shows the pan and the stove, placed on the floor, boiling the dumplings. Only in shot nine, the final shot, does the camera move back to its original position of a frontal shot at table level.

This experimentation with form is beautifully enlivened by affectionate touches of humor, as seen in the conversations and interactions among the father, mother, and daughter. When Jiayin enters the scene she asks how she should chop the chives. Her father responds, "Each bit should be the same length as the width of the leaf." To which Jiayin playfully responds "How can you use chives as a reference for chopping chives?" The father concedes that this is a good point, then suggests "4 millimeters." The bickering between father and daughter deepens our vivid understanding of their relationship.

Liu shows a maturity far beyond her years in her understanding of family dynamics and the ways of the world, and she displays a sense of self-deprecatory humor in facing adversity. The result is as warm and engaging as *Oxhide*, and there is more yet to come: the filmmaker has already promised another installment.

The family fills the dumplings.

Year and place of birth
1981 Beijing, China
—
Lives and works in
Beijing, China
—
Education
Beijing Film Academy, China
—
Filmography
2002 *The Train* (short)
2004 *Oxhide* (Niu pi)
2009 *Oxhide II* (Niupi er)
—

Director's awards
Oxhide
Berlin International Film Festival
     (Caligari Film Award, FIPRESCI
     Prize, 2005)
Hong Kong International
Film Festival
     (Golden DV Award, 2005)
Vancouver International
Film Festival
     (Dragons and Tigers Award,
     2005)
— —

Release date
2009
—
Country of release
China
—
Language
Mandarin
—
Running time
132 min.
—
Genre
Drama

Producer
Liu Jiayin
—
Writer
Liu Jiayin
—
Cinematographer
Liu Jiayin
—

Key cast
Liu Zai Ping: Father
Jia Hui Fen: Mother
Liu Jiayin: Daughter
—
Filming location
Beijing, China
—
Format
HD
—

Awards for *Oxhide II*
Cinema Digital Seoul
     (Blue Chameleon Award,
     2009)
— —

The family compares the appearance of their dumplings.

FATHER: What if management doesn't renew the contract?
How should I explain the situation to everyone?

DAUGHTER: It's not a "what if" question.
It's almost a given.

MOTHER: Just tell them the contract came to an end.

FATHER: I don't think that will do.
A contract can always be renewed.

MOTHER: The rent is
too high.

FATHER: Can't say that
either. They will
know that the business
is bad.

The father discusses the family business with his wife and daughter.

The father asks the mother if the dumplings look like him.

As the family sits down to eat, the mother looks up at a mosquito.

In the meandering Yunnan Province in Southwest China, a traveling law court goes on a tour. Feng (Li Baotian) is a seasoned judge, Auntie Yang (Yang Yaning) a court clerk who's retiring because of a policy change, and Ah-Luo (Lu Yulai) a recent college graduate on his first tour of duty. They share a companion in an old horse, which carries all of their amenities. Ah-Luo later runs away with his bride, giving up the career he finds hopeless, and Auntie Yang retires early. Without the companion whom he secretly loves, Feng has to continue alone, feeling abandoned and desperate.

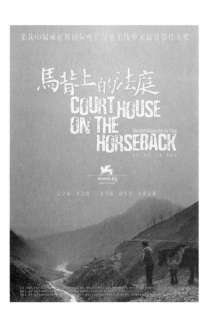

LIU JIE
COURTHOUSE ON
THE HORSEBACK

Angry farmers of the Pumi ethnic group carry the pig that destroyed their ancestral tomb.

Judge Feng and Ah-Luo have a dispute over whether to give an extra ten yuan to the farmer renting them his horse.

Cinematographer and producer Liu Jie's 2006 debut feature as a director is set in the mountainous rural province of Yunnan, in southwest China. An itinerant government judge, Feng, climbs the region's steep roads and paths on his annual circuit. Feng, an experienced and shy man in his fifties, is assisted by Yang, a woman of the Moso ethnic group who is now close to retirement. Ah-Luo, who is a brand-new graduate from law school, is from the Yi ethnic group.

The mountains of Yunnan are home to twelve different non-Han ethnic groups each with its own language and customs, and the trio relies on Yang and Feng's experience and knowledge of the languages. An old horse carries their luggage, their files, and, most importantly, the big, shiny, red-and-gold emblem of the People's Republic of China—the symbol of their official status and moreover of the State and the Law. Feng and Yang are veterans and old companions. But because the government wants to promote the advancement of ethnic minorities, Yang has to retire and train the young Ah-Luo.

From village to village the trio is confronted with various cases that raises issues of pragmatism versus legal code. The need to keep the peace and a good understanding of the human heart are often more useful and effective as guides than the letter of the law. In one village, a tomb has been devastated by someone's pigs. In another, someone steals the judges' horse and loses the national emblem. In still another, two sisters start a war over a pickle jar, and a poor in-law refuses to leave the house of a divorced woman, before they finally reconcile.

Ah-Luo is anxious to go back to his hometown to get married. But when Feng's behavior spoils his plans, he flees with his fiancée, thus facing the possibility of abandoning his career. Later, Yang retires to her Moso clan, and Feng has to go back to town alone. Neither Yang nor Feng finds the courage to admit that they have long been in love, and nothing but a bitter end awaits the two elders.

With a story that mixes humor and bitterness, humble situations and spectacular settings, Liu presents a changing China far from the roaring big cities and the terrible fates of migrant workers and lost country girls. He avoids the common tendency to portray ethnic minorities as exotic, a habit found in both Chinese cinema and Western documentary. At a quiet yet precise pace, he depicts the end of a generation who lived through China's most dramatic moments and managed to survive through pragmatism and a strong sense of loyalty.

Victims of an oppressive tradition that makes difficult any direct expression of one's feelings, Feng and Yang communicate through their work, using Ah-Luo as a kind of "common playground" for their emotions and thoughts. The court cases as well as the more intimate scenes recall the notion of distance that Bertolt Brecht developed in his theatrical work and theory: that the audience's emotions should never be aroused through calculated effects or devices, but rather through their involvement in the characters' actions, words, and struggle with fate.

Liu carefully cast his main characters and secondary parts, and through nuanced location work and a documentary-like style, he involves the real-life inhabitants of the villages. The result is a form of controlled improvisation. The villagers are free to reenact parts of their lives thanks to the admirably attentive camerawork, but always within Liu's insightfully situated frame (or, put another way, on his filmic stage). His first film is therefore also a first in Chinese cinema, by avoiding the exoticizing of so-called "minorities." The difficulty that Feng and Yang face in openly communicating with each other mirrors the sparse understanding that much of China's Han majority may have of their non-Han neighbors.

Liu has proclaimed Chen Kaige's 1984 film *Yellow Earth*, which takes place in a far-flung village, as a major influence on his decision to become a filmmaker. Set in the 1930's, Chen's story about rural villagers who speak their own dialect and practice their own mysterious rituals finds a kind of reversal in *Courthouse on the Horseback* (*Mabei shang de fating*, 2006). Ah-Luo sees himself as a "modern" young man, whose traditional roots are challenged by his desire to live by urban mores, while Feng and Yang try to preserve a broader sense of history.

Liu's second feature *Judge* (*Touxi*, 2009), is also set in a legal milieu. It shows his concern for not only the role—and the reach—of law in the affairs of men, but also the variations in people's behavior and thought as viewed from the historical perspective. Once again hewing close to Brecht's aim of a non-ideological viewpoint, Liu announces himself as one of the leading storytellers of China's history as it is lived.

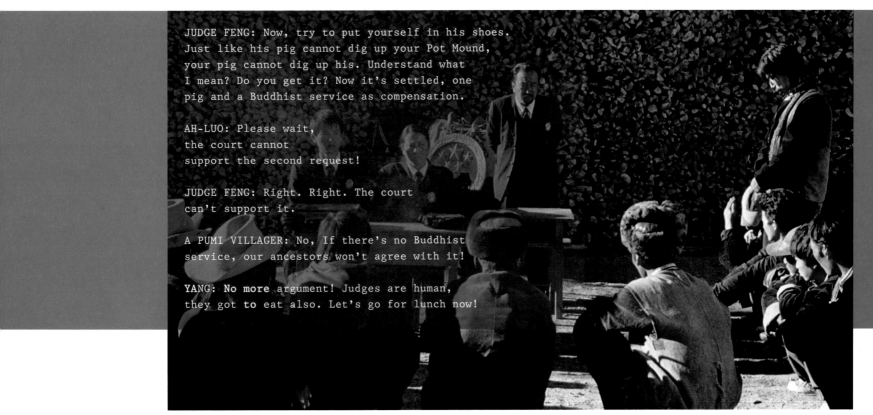

Judge Feng, Yang, and Ah-Luo hold court and reach a decision regarding the destroyed ancestral tomb.

Year and place of birth
1968 Tianjin, China
—

Lives and works in
Beijing, China
—

Education
Beijing Film Academy, China
—

Filmography
2006 *Courthouse on the*
Horseback
(Mabei shang de fating)
2009 *Judge*
(Touxi)
— —

Release date
2006
—

Country of release
China
—

Language
Mandarin, Moso, Pumi, Yi
—

Running time
105 min.
—

Genre
Drama
—

Producers
Liu Jie, Hsu Hsiao-ming
—

Writer
Wang Lifu
—

Cinematographer
Harrison Zhang
—

Score
Yang Xin
—

Key cast
Li Baotian: Judge Feng
Yang Yaning: Yang
Lu Yulai: Ah-Luo
—

Filming location
Yunnan, China
—

Format
35 mm
—

Awards for *Courthouse on*
the Horseback
Venice International Film Festival
(Premio Orizzonti, 2006)
— —

Judge Feng, Yang, and Ah-Luo, together with an old horse, walk toward the next village.

Judge Feng, Yang, and Ah-Luo seek help from a local leader after their horse is stolen.

A drunk Judge Feng advises the bride to be a good wife.

Judge Feng and Yang are reluctant to part from each other along the riverbank.

Set against the exquisite backdrop of the Qinghai-Tibetan Plateau, this is the tale of a group of brave locals who face death and starvation to save endangered antelope herds from a band of ruthless hunters. The film is inspired by the true story of illegal poaching in the region of Kekexili, the largest animal reserve in China. Ritai (Duo Buji), the patrol's leader, allows Beijing journalist Gayu (Zhang Lei) to tag along with the group in order to investigate the murder of a patrolman.

LU CHUAN
MOUNTAIN PATROL: KEKEXILI

The captain, Ritai, and his team, at a burial for one of the patrol's members.

Lu Chuan's *Mountain Patrol: Kekexili* (*Kekexili*, 2004) proved so popular with Chinese audiences that a mass campaign was launched to nominate it as China's entry for the Academy Award for Best Foreign Language Film in 2005. Despite wide support for the effort in the mainland press, Zhang Yimou's *House of Flying Daggers* (*Shi mian mai fu*, 2004) was selected.

Meaning "beautiful maidens" or "beautiful mountains" in Mongolian, Kekexili is an area of sprawling highlands that straddles Tibet and Qinghai Province, fifteen thousand feet above sea level. Over one million Tibetan antelope once grazed there peacefully, but illegal hunting for their pelts reduced their population to ten thousand by the mid-1980s. To combat the poachers, the local people formed a voluntary mountain patrol in 1993.

Kekexili is based on a true story and was shot in the same locations where the events took place. The film opens with the murder of a patrolman, which prompts Gayu, a Beijing journalist, to investigate. He is allowed to tag along on the patrol's next foray into the mountains by its leader Ritai. Through Gayu's eyes, we witness the infernal situations this bunch of hardened, idealistic men goes through during a ten-day pursuit of the poachers. The location shoot, lasting over one hundred days, was likewise a bitter ordeal for the crew, which weathered sickness, injuries, deserters, and even one accidental death.

Against a barren yet hauntingly magnificent landscape, the patrolmen brave frostbite, ferocious snowstorms, thin air, and treacherous quicksand. The poachers, who are better equipped, lie in ambush on the horizon. Meanwhile, Ritai and his troupe are short of men, guns, money, food, and gasoline. Gayu learns that they sometimes sell the pelts they confiscate, because it is the only way to finance their operation.

Lu's approach is a restrained but committed realism that avoids sensationalism or sentimentality, with powerful and visceral results. He takes full advantage of the beauty of the unspoiled wilderness and the brutality of post-poaching carnage: a field littered with bloody skinned carcasses, fed on by crows, and pelts with bullet holes, spread out to dry.

Lu has said that he drastically changed his script after spending three weeks with an actual mountain patrol. He cut out the action, drama, romance, and ethnic rituals, and focused instead on the meaning of faith and camaraderie in desperate situations, the essence of human existence when confronted with unforgiving nature, and the doomed sense of martyrdom in the face of death. When Ritai meets the poachers' ringleader, he is surrounded and shot dead matter-of-factly. For Lu, this was the only plausible treatment, rather than having Ritai strike a guns-blazing pose in a heroic death, as in popular legend.

The real-life Gayu's breaking of the story back in Beijing shook the nation. The Chinese government declared Kekexili a national nature preserve and established the Forest Public Security Bureau to protect it from poachers. As the film's closing titles report, the population of Tibetan antelopes climbed back to thirty thousand and continues to grow.

This "happy ending" showing a government responsive to injustices exposed by the press is doubtlessly pleasing to both Chinese censors and audiences. Yet the most brilliant conceit of the film lies in its depiction of an affinity between poachers and patrolmen: both share an existence in a no-man's-land unknown to the outside world. Lu found it hard to condemn the poachers, because they were mostly peasants left with few other options. The real culprits—international fur traders and consumers of antelope pelts, and a local government that fails to provide opportunities to the people—are left unaddressed.

The phenomenal enthusiasm that greeted *Kekexili* had a lot to do with the state of Chinese cinema at the time. With the domestic market growing fast and a Hollywood takeover feared, the need for a homegrown popular cinema was more urgent than ever. Following Ang Lee's *Crouching Tiger, Hidden Dragon* (*Wo hu cang long*, 2000), Zhang Yimou's blockbusters *Hero* (*Ying xiong*, 2002) and *House of Flying Daggers* were commercially successful but lacking in substance and national character. The formerly underground filmmaker Zhang Yuan made a few mainstream films, but none met with success. Meanwhile, independent filmmakers like Jia Zhangke gathered accolades in film festivals for works that could not be shown at home.

But Lu Chuan seems to have carved out a "third way" for aspiring young Chinese filmmakers, between commercial success with poor critical reception and critical acclaim without domestic release. *Kekexili* shows that it is possible to make films that are acceptable to Chinese censors and popular with audiences and critics both at home and abroad.

The patrol runs into the cold river in pursuit of poachers.

Liu Dong, on an anti-poaching patrol, sinks in quicksand.

Year and place of birth
1971   Kuitun, China
—
Lives and works in
Beijing, China
—
Education
University of International
   Relations, Beijing, China
Beijing Film Academy, China
—
Filmography
2001   *The Missing Gun*
         (Xun qiang)
2004   *Mountain Patrol: Kekexili*
         (Kekexili)
2009   *City of Life and Death*
         (Nanjing! Nanjing!)
—

Director's awards
The Missing Gun
Shanghai Film Critics Awards
   (Film of Merit, 2002)
—
City of Life and Death
San Sebastián International
Film Festival
   (Golden Seashell, Best
   Cinematography, 2009)
— —

Release date
2004
—
Country of release
China
—
Language
Mandarin, Tibetan
—
Running time
90 min.
—
Genre
Drama

Producers
Yang Du, Zhonglei Wang
—
Writer
Lu Chuan
—
Cinematographer
Cao Yu
—
Score
Zai Lao
—

Key cast
Duo Buji: Ritai
Zhang Lei: Gayu
Liang Qi: Liu Dong
Xueying Zhao: Leng Xue
—
Filming location
Kekexili, China
—
Format
35 mm
—

Awards for *Mountain Patrol: Kekexili*
Taipei Golden Horse Film Festival
   (Best Film, Best Director,
   Best Cinematography, Best
   Original Screenplay, 2004)
Tokyo International Film Festival
   (Special Jury Prize, 2004)
Berlin International Film Festival
   (Don Quixote Award –
   Special Mention, 2005)
Golden Rooster Awards
   (Best Film, Best Director,
   Best Music, Best Screenplay,
   Best Sound, 2005)
Huabiao Film Awards
   (Outstanding Director,
   Outstanding Film, 2005)
Shanghai Film Critics Award
   (Film of Merit, Best Director,
   2005)
Hong Kong Film Awards
   (Best Asian Film, 2006)
— —

Ritai arrests a poacher and asks about details of the crime.

RITAI: Zhanlin Ma, every time I catch you, you pay a fine. This time I am letting you go without a fine.

ZHANLIN MA: Really?

RITAI: Yes.

ZHANLIN MA: I can't make it back from here, I'm too old.

RITAI: I don't have food for you, I'm short of fuel too. I'm going after your boss. I can't take care of you.

ZHANLIN MA: I can't make it.

RITAI: Yes. You can. There are 200 kilometers to the Al Mountain. And 100 more to the Kunlun Pass. You can make it. If you can't make it then it's your fate. Good luck.

Ritai is eventually killed by poachers.

Ritai's daughter mourns the loss of her father.

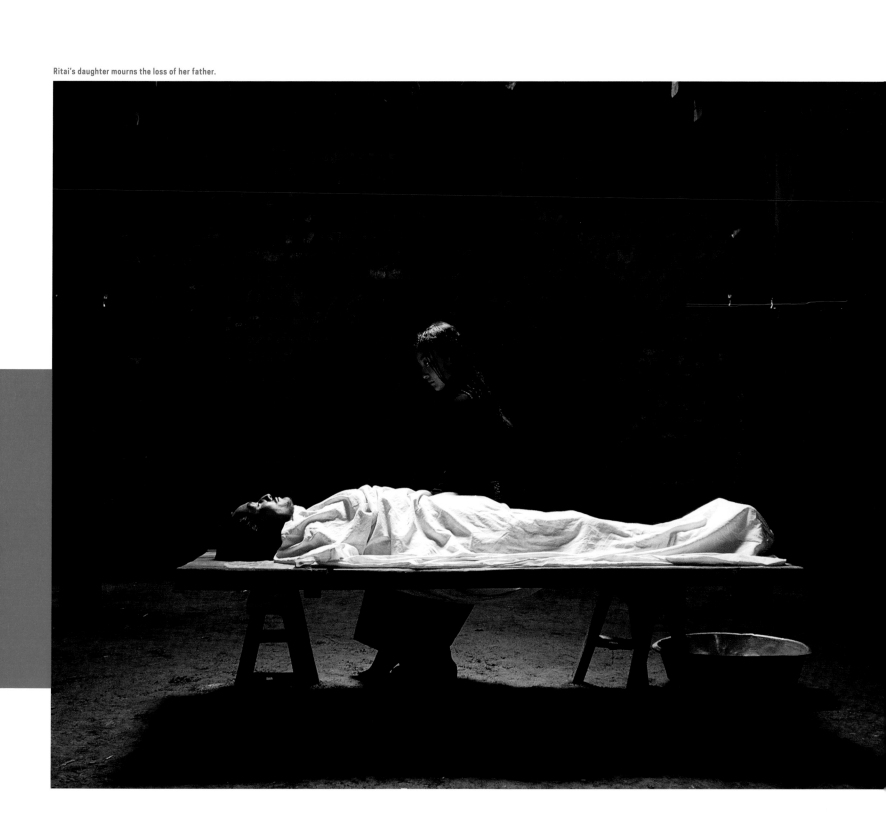

A woman is driving on the highway. She becomes distracted and runs into something. On the days following, she fails to recognize the feelings that used to bond her to the things and people around her. She just lets herself be taken by the events of her social life. One night she tells her husband that she may have killed someone on the highway. They go back to the road only to find a dead dog. Things return to normal and the bad moment seems to have passed, until news of a gruesome discovery comes back to haunt her.

LUCRECIA MARTEL
THE HEADLESS WOMAN

Verónica continues to drive after she hits something in the road.

Local kids and their dog run through a ditch before the storm.

On the eve of the new millennium, everyone seemed to be preoccupied with their own doomsday scenarios. As world cinema produced a downpour of tales depicting humanity trapped between post-Soviet disequilibrium and the borders of the New World, Lucrecia Martel—one of the key figures of New Argentine Cinema—arrived. In her first two features, *La ciénaga* (2001) and *The Holy Girl* (*La niña santa*, 2004), she created a mesmeric and ambiguous landscape, where nuanced gestures or background noises speak volumes. And like those films, *The Headless Woman* (*La mujer sin cabeza*, 2008) is set in her hometown of Salta, in the northern Argentinean province of the same name.

When *The Headless Woman* was first shown at Cannes in 2008, it divided the critics. On one side there were jeers and walkouts, while on the other it was hailed as a work of genius. Two years later, the film is still splitting audiences into two camps: those bemoaning it as plotless and vague, and those enraptured by the web of mystery and frustration spun by Martel.

The film begins with three boys of indigenous heritage playing with their dog in a storm drain. The boys toss casual insults as they run, crossing in and out of the frame. The film then cuts to a scene of middle-class ladies loading up their cars with dishes and numerous children. Verónica, a statuesque, brittle bottle blonde in the Hitchcock mold, drives away while a breezy pop tune plays on the radio. A ringing cell phone momentarily takes her attention away from the road. The car strikes something, causing Verónica to knock her head against the steering wheel.

Has she really hit something? Martel's camera stares relentlessly at Verónica's profile, refusing to turn back and see what she might have struck. This vantage point seen from the passenger's seat draws viewers in, making them complicit in the unfolding drama. Dazed from the jolt, Verónica reaches for her sunglasses in an attempt to regain her composure. Smoothing her hair, she drives away. She refuses to turn around, but a longshot through the car's rear window reveals what looks like the body of a dog in the road. As she drives away, small, sticky handprints catch the sunlight through the driver's window. Verónica slows the car and gets out seemingly in a daze as a torrential downpour engulfs her.

The essential thing here is doubt, and it stays afloat throughout. Her doubt takes on a form that completely disrupts her sense of reality and temporarily leaves her in a state of amnesia. Martel intends audiences to take an active part in Verónica's confusion. Close-ups of her face, changes in focus that blur the background, and off-screen sounds baffle viewers' perceptions. A feeling arises that incidents are taking place, which, though implied, aren't shown on-screen. We never see what goes on in her head, but instead, we watch, in a dreamy blur, her severed relationship with reality.

When Verónica is x-rayed at the hospital, the machine obscures her head, leaving her headless torso on-screen. This motif—Verónica's head leaving the frame, only her vulnerable torso in view—is repeated throughout the film. While undoutedly a metaphor for loss of control, stasis, and the immobility of

women in Verónica's situation, the film's title suggests a horror film or gothic tale, and indeed Verónica appears as a ghost in her own life, unable to engage with her surroundings.

Doubt spreads further when the body of an indigenous worker boy is found in the canal. Martel shoots Verónica's head in close-up as she anxiously reads the news. The boy, invisible and nameless to Verónica, now looms over her, a silent witness of her conscience. Eventually, when she can bear it no longer and admits to the possibility of a crime, the men around her try to cover it up, which reveals how a certain class sets its internal protection mechanism in motion to protect one of its own. Verónica, however, remains completely isolated and alienated: from her own memory, from the working and lower classes, and from her own family and patients who don't seem to notice she has become a ghost. Despite this ghostly element, *The Headless Woman* is closer to film noir (with Verónica dying her hair a darker color a clever reference to Kim Novak in *Vertigo* [1958]).

The Headless Woman is a film about a woman who becomes a passive observer of her own life. The isolated framing of shots would have pleased Antonioni, and Hitchcock would have revered its formalism, though Buñuel would have perhaps added a pinch of dark humor to its gothic takes on the bourgeoisie. Each new addition to Martel's body of work will no doubt be an unequaled cinematic experience, and will continue to secure her position as one of the most important talents in contemporary world cinema.

Verónica watches an old wedding video at Aunt Lala's house.

Year and place of birth
1966   Salta, Argentina
—

Lives and works in
Buenos Aires, Argentina
—

Education
Avellaneda Experimental,
   Argentina
National Experimentation
   Filmmaking School,
   Buenos Aires, Argentina
—

Filmography
1995   Dead King (Rey muerto)
         (short)
2001   La ciénaga
2004   The Holy Girl
         (La niña santa)
2007   The Headless Woman
         (La mujer sin cabeza)
—

Director's awards
Dead King
Havana Film Festival
   (Coral for Best Short Film,
   1995)

La ciénaga
Sundance Film Festival (NHK
   Filmmakers Award, 1999)
Berlin International Film Festival
   (Alfred Bauer Award, 2001)
Havana Film Festival
   (Best Director, Grand Coral,
   2001)
Toulouse Latin America
Film Festival
   (French Critics' Discovery
   Award, Grand Prix, 2001)
Uruguay International
Film Festival
   (First Work Award –
   Special Mention, 2001)
Argentine Film Critics
Association Awards
   (Silver Condor for Best
   First Film, 2002)

The Holy Girl
Cannes International
Film Festival
   (Nominated for Palme D'Or,
   2004)
Clarin Entertainment Awards
   (Best Director, 2004)
— —

Release date
2008
—

Country of release
Argentina
—

Language
Spanish
—

Running time
87 min.
—

Genre
Drama
—

Producers
Pedro Almodóvar, Agustín
Almodóvar, Esther García,
Verónica Cura, Enrique Piñeyro,
Lucrecia Martel, Marianne Slot,
Vieri Razzini, Cesare Petrillo,
Tilde Corsi
—

Writer
Lucrecia Martel
—

Cinematographer
Bárbara Alvarez
—

Score
Roberta Ainstein
—

Key cast
María Onetto: Verónica
Claudia Cantero: Josefina
Inés Efron: Candita
Daniel Genoud: Juan Manuel
Guillermo Arengo: Marcelo
César Bordón: Marcos
María Vaner: Aunt Lala
—

Filming location
Salta, Argentina
—

Format
35 mm
—

Awards for The Headless Woman
Cannes International
Film Festival
   (Nominated for Palme D'Or,
   2008)
Lima Latin American Film Festival
   (Critics' Award, 2008)
Rio de Janeiro International
Film Festival
   (FIPRESCI Prize, 2008)
Argentine Film Critics
Association Awards
   (Silver Condor for Best
   Director, Best Screenplay,
   Best Original Picture, 2009)
— —

LALA: (Off screen) Don't look at him.

Verónica approaches to be able to hear better.

LALA: (Off screen) Don't look at them and they'll
leave... The house is full...there is this huge
dark black woman. It's horrid.

From the corner of her eye, Verónica looks
at the boy who is making the wheel roll slowly
towards the door.

LALA: (Off screen) Don't look at him, he's leaving...
don't look at him, don't look at him...I would have
preferred something modern. You move and something
creaks. They are horrors.

Aunt Lala talks about the ghosts in her house.

Aunt Lala's room fills with visitors who come to take care of her.

Verónica reads in the newspaper that a dead body was found on the road.

Set in the 1890s against the backdrop of the brewing revolution between the Philippines and Spain is a collection of silent-cinema-inspired tales revolving around an "indio," the common man during the colonial times. The film reveals different situations of a people previously excluded from historical considerations and how their circumstances revolve around birth, war, and death.

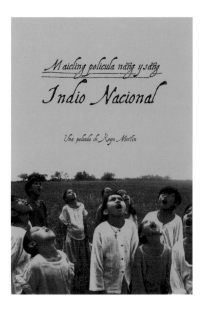

RAYA MARTIN
A SHORT FILM ABOUT
THE INDIO NACIONAL

Native children witness the eclipse.

The bellringer opens the doors to the church.

Things are stirring in the Philippines. The overall annual figure for national film production has steadily fallen, but independent "auteur" cinema is thriving. Since 2000, newcomers have been making their mark at the big international festivals, with a host of films that display a kind of modern radicalism that confronts the country's history and politics head-on.

Among the many new Filipino directors, Raya Martin stands out for his youth, prolific output, and, above all, his wildly ambitious artistic and cinematographic projects. Martin, born in Manila in 1984, studied cinema before becoming a scriptwriter, journalist, and film critic. Since 2005, he's made eight feature films. He even undertook a commissioned film, the curious *Manila* (2009), co-directed with Adolfo Alix, Jr., that pays homage to two modern Filipino classics, Lino Brocka's *Jaguar* (1979) and Ishmael Bernal's *Manila by Night* (1980).

Martin's films invent forms that are totally innovative yet appropriate to a project that is, to say the least, unique and extremely ambitious. The subject of all Martin's films is the Philippines and its history. Repeatedly colonized, first by Spain, then Japan, then the United States, the country has no film archives to speak of. It is truly a subject nation because even the traces of its struggles and rebellions have been expunged. All its silent films have been lost or destroyed for want of serious attention to conservation and archiving. That is the underlying concern of Martin's films, and his approach has a very precise aim: to invoke the past in order to build the present, to rescue a history from oblivion. Martin's films are often silent, or contain very little dialogue, and express an absolute belief in the evocative power of images. All of them, in different ways, aim to reconstruct memories by inventing false visions of the past via manipulated image and sound used to create the impression that one is watching the projection of film reels found on the shelves of a hypothetical cinémathèque.

A Short Film About the Indio Nacional (or the Prolonged Sorrow of Filipinos) (*Maicling pelicula nañg ysañg Indio Nacional*, 2005) is Martin's first feature film. A year previously, he made a very successful documentary, *The Island at the End of the World*, in an ethnographic style similar to that of Jean Rouch and Johan van der Keuken. With his second film, Martin had established the foundations of a body of vibrant work that also made extreme demands.

A Short Film About the Indio Nacional is a reinvention of a historical and biographical tragedy. Set in the 1890s, it is a distant evocation of the bloody emancipation of the Philippines from Spanish domination seen through the fate of three characters whose lives are utterly changed by revolution. Like Martin's subsequent films, it is made up of heterogeneous narrative and visual material, full of abrupt breaks and cuts, and organized in distinct sections. The film begins on a summer night, in a hut, where a woman is unable to sleep. She wakes her husband, sleeping beside her, and orders him to tell her a story. The husband relates an allegorical fable about the destiny of the Philippines—specifically the revolt of the Katipunan against Spanish occupiers, in 1896—told as the meeting between an old man and a child. This introduction gives the film the feeling of a waking dream, or a nighttime hallucination. Martin's films aren't history lessons, they're reveries about history, in which fact is sometimes mixed with legend.

The remainder of the film recounts the life of a man, with title cards, a repetitive musical score, and sublime black-and-white images that seem to come from a distant past, whereas in fact they are the work of today, by a twenty-one-year-old young man. The film is certainly no hoax, or a self-conscious parody of silent cinema, in the manner of some postmodern directors.

Martin's use of the sound and visual quality of old films continued in *Independencia* (2009), which re-creates in great detail the style of films shot in studios during the American occupation in the early twentieth century. But this project is not limited to 35 mm films, or to images that have a heritage value. In other films, Martin has handled more mundane visuals with the same subtlety. His conceptual framework applies equally to home movies, amateur video productions, and the photography of soap operas with which the collective imagination of the Philippines is saturated.

Although Martin's objective is to restore visual images to a country that has lost them, there is no preaching in his films—the medium of cinema is itself the message. There's an element of idealism in his insanely ambitious venture, but also great lucidity. His films try to fill a gap, but they can only provide an imaginative substitute. They constitute an epic, the great cinematic story of a country and a people, but rather than militant action, its dominant quality is melancholy nostalgia for a lost world.

More children gather to watch the eclipse.

Year and place of birth
1984 Manila, Philippines
—

Lives and works in
Manila, Philippines
—

Education
**College of Mass Communication,
University of the Philippines,
Diliman, Philippines**

Filmography
2004 *The Visit (Bakasyon)*
(short)
2005 *The Island at the End*
of the World (Ang Isla sa
Dulo ng Mundo/No Pongso
Do Tedted No Mondo)
2005 *A Short Film About the*
Indio Nacional (or the
Prolonged Sorrow
of Filipinos) (Maicling
pelicula nañg ysañg
Indio Nacional [O Ang
Mahabang Kalungkutan
ng Katagalugan])
2006 *Life Projections (short)*
2007 *Long Live Philippine*
Cinema! (short)
2007 *Track Projections (short)*
2007 *Autohystoria*
2008 *Possible Lovers*
2008 *Now Showing*
2008 *Next Attraction*
2009 *Manila (co-directed with*
Adolfo Alix, Jr.)
2009 *Independencia*
—

Director's awards
The Visit
Cinemanila International
Film Festival
(Ishmael Bernal Award for
Young Cinema, 2004)

*The Island at the End
of the World*
.MOV International Digital
Film Festival
(Best Documentary, 2005)

Autohystoria
Cinemanila International
Film Festival
(Best Director,
Best Picture, 2007)
Marseille Festival
of Documentary Film
(Special Mention, 2007)

Next Attraction
Cinemanila International
Film Festival
(Grand Jury Prize, 2008)

Independencia
Bangkok International
Film Festival
(Best Southeast Asian Film,
NETPAC Award, 2009)
Valdivia International Film
Festival
(Special Jury Prize,
Critics' Award, 2009)
— —

Release date
2005
—

Country of release
Philippines
—

Language
Filipino
—

Running time
96 min.
—

Genre
Experimental Historical Drama
—

Producers
Raya Martin, Arleen Cuevas
—

Writer
Raya Martin
—

Cinematographer
Maisa Demetillo
—

Score
Khavn
—

Key cast
Bodjie Pascua: Man
Suzette Velasco: Woman
Lemuel Galman: Indio kid
Mark Joshua Maclang: Indio boy
Russell Ongkeko: Indio man
—

Filming location
Bulacan, Philippines
—

Format
DV, 35 mm
—

Awards for *A Short Film About
the Indio Nacional*
**Pesaro International
Film Festival**
(Best Film, 2006)
— —

The friar scolds the lowly bellringer.

Santo Niño and the bellringer engage in a duel.

The young man becomes ill.

Title card: Beautiful Native
Women Arguing

The statue seems...

...real.

Can it be performing a miracle?

The statue moves!

A statue comes alive in the church.

Tom McCarthy's second film in the role of director centers around the story of Walter Vale (Richard Jenkins), a dispirited college professor mourning the death of his wife. When Walter meets Tarek (Haaz Sleiman), a Syrian musician, and his girlfriend Zainab (Danai Gurira), unknowingly subletting his New York City apartment illegally, his world starts to change. Tarek begins teaching Walter how to play the drums, lessons that lead to a kind of joy Walter hasn't experienced for a long time. An unlikely friendship develops between the two men and strengthens further when Tarek is later detained by immigration officials.

TOM MCCARTHY
THE VISITOR

Tarek gives Walter his first drum lesson.

Tarek practices his drum and sees Walter walk in.

As the millennium approached, American cinema turned inward. Its concerns were parochial, its landscapes composed of interior worlds. The events of 9/11 rudely shattered this withdrawal, and filmmakers responded accordingly. They began to open up, either by exploring Iraq and terrorism in detail or by taking a closer look at realities at home.

Tom McCarthy's two films are emblematic of this dynamic. Both works deal with repressed men in retreat from the world. In *The Station Agent* (2003), Finbar, a dwarf, re-settles in a small town where he has inherited a semi-abandoned train depot. Initially skeptical of everyone he meets, he is a tightly wound, self-contained bundle of a man. But his efforts to remain disengaged prove short-lived, and eventually Finbar loosens up. He rejoins people, and thereby life.

In many respects *The Station Agent* is a rough sketch for McCarthy's more complex, subtle, and rewarding second film, *The Visitor* (2007). Walter Vale, the protagonist, is a middle-aged university professor based in Connecticut. Withdrawn and strained, Walter behaves as if angry at something. In encounters with a tardy student and with his piano teacher, he shows no sympathy. He appears to be disconnected from his own life; little seems to register, or matter.

All this changes abruptly when Walter reluctantly travels to New York to deliver a lecture. Entering his Manhattan apartment after several months' absence, Walter discovers, to his shock, a young couple living there. The interlopers have rented in good faith from an unscrupulous third party. They also happen to be Syrian and Senegalese, and their background provides McCarthy with a platform to explore issues of immediate relevance to the America of 2006.

Walter confronts the Other not as a vague notion of something far away across an ocean, but on his very doorstep. And, inevitably, these foreigners prove to be human: charming, vulnerable, open. The outgoing Tarek, a musician, soon engages Walter's musical interest with his drumming. Earlier in the film Walter is shown laboriously plinking away at a piano. His withdrawal gradually proves to be related: he is in mourning for his wife, a well-known pianist who has recently passed away. But now that the world comes knocking, he welcomes it.

Tarek and his girlfriend, Zainab, are both illegal immigrants, yet they have carved out a little space for themselves in America. Tarek joyously plays his drums in parks and bars; Zainab makes some money by selling her handcrafted jewelry. Their indomitable spirit, especially Tarek's buoyant energy, melts Walter's circumspect nature. He starts to hang out with them, takes up the drums, removes his jacket and tie, and opens up.

Their unexpected presence in his apartment is the first shock to Walter's equilibrium. The second comes with Tarek's arrest, which Walter witnesses. His friend is incarcerated for the most minor of misdemeanors. It is in fact a misunderstanding, but for an "illegal" like Tarek, life is anything but fair. Walter's involvement sends him on a journey through places he has never seen. Detention centers and immigration lawyers occupy his days. America, his country, assumes different hues and dimensions. His Connecticut university suddenly seems irrelevant to what is going on in the rest of the world.

The third surprise of the film comes with the arrival of Tarek's mother, who seeks news of her son. Mouna is an elegant, attractive woman, also Syrian. Like Walter, she has lost her spouse. Her husband was imprisoned for his writings—something well beyond Walter's experience. In her presence Walter blooms, and the film flirts with a novel set of possibilities.

McCarthy, thankfully, resists clichés, resolving his film in a manner closer to reality and refusing to pander to the audience. Tarek is deported. Mouna leaves for Syria to be there for him. Zainab is abandoned. By the end, Walter is alone, as he was at the beginning of the film. But he is a changed man. The final shot of him, blissfully drumming on a subway platform, is partly an homage to Tarek and partly a recognition that Walter has learnt something from another culture—and from a Syrian, purportedly an enemy of his country.

McCarthy never lets his political agenda overwhelm the film. No politicians are ever mentioned, no current event cited. His style is effortless and unadorned; he concentrates on the ordinary people in front of his camera—people who live very different realities all in the same city. New York in 2006 is a place that McCarthy believes cannot ignore the multitude of ethnicities and religions within its precincts. Much is to be learned by opening up to the world. As America watches its borders, clamps down on immigration, and increases domestic surveillance, *The Visitor* shows another way.

Tarek and Walter grab a quick bite to eat before going to the drum circle.

Year and place of birth
1966   Summit, N.J., USA
—

Lives and works in
New York, N.Y., USA
—

Education
Boston College, Mass., USA
Yale School of Drama,
**   New Haven, Conn., USA**
—

Filmography
2003   The Station Agent
2007   The Visitor
—

Director's awards
The Station Agent
Marrakech International
Film Festival
**   (Special Jury Award, 2003)**

Mexico City International
Contemporary Film Festival
**   (Audience Award, 2003)**
San Sebastián International
Film Festival
**   (SIGNIS Award, Special Prize**
**   of the Jury, 2003)**
Sundance Film Festival
**   (Audience Award, Waldo Salt**
**   Screenwriting Award, 2003)**
Bristish Academy of Film
and Television Arts
**   (Best Original Screenplay,**
**   2004)**
Independent Spirit Awards
**   (Best First Screenplay, John**
**   Cassavetes Award, 2004)**
**   — —**

Release date
2008
—

Country of release
USA
—

Language
English
—

Running time
104 min.
—

Genre
Drama

Producers
Mary Jane Skalski,
Michael London, Omar Amanat,
Jeff Skoll, Ricky Strauss
—

Writer
Tom McCarthy
—

Cinematographer
Oliver Bokelberg
—

Score
Jan A.P Kaczmarek
—

Key cast
Richard Jenkins: Prof. Walter Vale
Haaz Sleiman: Tarek Khalil
Danai Gurira: Zainab
Hiam Abbass: Mouna Khalil
—

Filming location
New York, N.Y., USA
—

Format
35 mm
—

Awards for The Visitor
Brisbane International
Film Festival
**   (Interfaith Award, 2008)**
Method Fest
**   (Best Actor, Best Director,**
**   Best Supporting Actress,**
**   2008)**
Moscow International
Film Festival
**   (Silver St. George, 2008)**
National Board of Review, USA
**   (Spotlight Award, 2008)**
—

San Diego Film Critics
Society Awards
**   (Best Original Screenplay,**
**   2008)**
Satellite Awards
**   (Best Actor in a Motion**
**   Picture Drama, Best Original**
**   Screenplay, 2008)**
Deauville Film Festival
**   (Grand Special Prize, 2009)**
Independent Spirit Awards
**   (Best Director, 2009)**
St. Louis International
Film Festival
**   (Best Music, 2009)**
**   — —**

Walter and Tarek stand in front of the drum circle
in Central Park.

TAREK: What do you think?

Walter sizes it up and makes his assessment.

WALTER: I think I'll just watch.

TAREK: Come on, Walter. It's easy. You just wait
until you feel it. Let's go.

Tarek joins the drum circle. Walter lingers.
Walter is on the edge of the drum circle, waiting
to "feel it." Tarek is next to him playing away.
Tarek looks at Walter and nods. Finally Walter starts
to play. Slowly at first, but then he starts to
really commit. Tarek encourages him with a smile.

Tarek and Walter watch the other drummers before joining them.

Walter enjoys his first drumming circle, as Tarek looks on.

Walter and Mouna go to meet Zainab at her jewelry stand.

Zainab and Mouna discuss Tarek's situation.

The film follows life in the Maze Prison in Northern Ireland, with an interpretation of the highly emotive events surrounding the 1981 IRA hunger strike led by Bobby Sands (Michael Fassbender). With an epic eye for detail, the film provides a timely exploration of what happens when body and mind are pushed to the utmost limit.

STEVE MCQUEEN
HUNGER

Raymond takes a tea break in Maze Prison.

Big-boned and physically imposing, Steve McQueen has played with a capacity for unspoken menace since his 1993 film installation, *Bear*. A black man in a mostly white Western art world, McQueen's identity brings its own noise to most encounters. But even more than his body, it is the aggression in his work that is daunting. In installations dating back over a decade and a half, and now in his remarkable feature-length debut, *Hunger* (2008), McQueen pushes the boundaries of film narrative, imposes harsh discipline on his materials, and confronts the viewer with images of suffering that sometimes provoke strong reactions. At one screening of *Hunger* at the Toronto International Film Festival, a woman fainted.

Building on his oeuvre in the art world, which emphasized the stolid persistence of the body, McQueen portrays Irish hunger striker Bobby Sands as the embodiment of palpable, physical sacrifice. In its first moments, *Hunger* initiates a kind of dialogue of menace. Over a black screen, a percussive metallic noise rises on the soundtrack and suddenly cuts to a louder volume; a woman, shown in close-up, moves rhythmically in time. Although the scene is never explained, the reference is to the Irish Troubles: women once banged trash-can lids against the pavement to warn of British soldiers approaching. This overture ends abruptly in silence and establishes a structure of radical contrasts: bold shifts in sound dynamics, composition, and volume that create a mood of constant dissonance and unease.

In the film's first act, a man soaks his bruised hands in a sink full of water, gets dressed, and eats breakfast, all without speaking. Upon leaving his home, he looks both down the road and under his car before he starts the engine. He is Ray Lohan, a guard at the Maze—the cellblock where Sands and others are imprisoned—and he is being watchful against the threat of assassination. He is shown soaking his hands a second time before the film makes clear just how he gets his bruises: by slamming his fists into the faces of prisoners. This first section continues without any real dialogue, other than joking among guards and a voiceover excerpt from a speech by Prime Minister Margaret Thatcher about denying the prisoners any political status. Like most of the film's narrative strokes, her speech is stark and isolated.

The pattern of sharp contrasts can be found both within scenes and in the greater structure of the film as a whole. The largely silent opening section establishes the routine of life in the prison, first from the guards' perspective and then from that of the prisoners. The camera lingers on scenes of discomfiting physicality: maggots crawling around a man asleep on a cell floor, body cavities used to smuggle contraband into and out of the prison, a wet kiss in the visiting room that exchanges something forbidden, and, of course, the excrement smeared in protest on the cell walls. The lack of dialogue allows bodily sounds to predominate, creating an almost claustrophobic intimacy. This intimacy is simultaneously both shattered and heightened by the film's next section, in which guards brutalize the prisoners' bodies.

The sound and kinetic energy of the abuse sequences is followed by an initially quiet scene: Lohan visits his immobile mother in a retirement home. But the moment ends in a quick jolt of violence that presages not an escalation of action but the film's most audacious scene. In a wide-ranging conversation that lasts for twenty-two minutes (including one sixteen-minute shot), Sands talks with Father Moran, a priest visiting the prison. They begin with banter but soon progress to questions of theology and political philosophy that surround Sands's decision to starve himself to death. The scene compresses all of the film's verbalized ideas even as its duration extends beyond the limits of conventional narrative filmmaking.

In addition to the contrasts between dialogue and silence, guards and prisoners, intimacy and politics, *Hunger* also progressively changes its thematic focus. It moves from the mind, to the body and the violence it endures, and from there to the transcendence of the spirit. Its parallels are not simply to free-floating Christian tradition, however; the film recalls the rigor of perhaps cinema's greatest exploration of Christian sacrifice, Carl Theodor Dreyer's *The Passion of Joan of Arc* (1928).

Consistent with McQueen's work as a visual artist, *Hunger* pursues the persistence of the flesh as an act of the spirit, until it can persist no more. The final act confronts the viewer with disturbing images of Sands's suffering, emaciated body. In McQueen's work, the very look of things transmits violence and demands responsibility. It requires close attention to its formal precision, endurance of its sometimes extreme images, and engagement with rhythmic patterns that close like a tightening fist.

Bobby and Father Dominic Moran meet prior to the hunger strike.

Year and place of birth
1969 London, UK
—

Lives and works in
Amsterdam, Netherlands
—

Filmography
2008 Hunger
— —

Release date
2008
—

Country of release
UK
—

Language
English
—

Running time
96 min.
—

Genre
Drama
—

Producers
**Laura Hastings-Smith,
Robin Gutch**
—

Writers
Enda Walsh, Steve McQueen
—

Cinematographer
Sean Bobbitt
—

Score
David Holmes, Leo Abrahams
—

Key cast
**Michael Fassbender:
  Bobby Sands
Liam Cunningham:
  Father Dominic Moran
Liam McMahon: Gerry Campbell
Stuart Graham: Raymond Lohan
Laine Megaw: Raymond's Wife
Brian Milligan: Davey Gillen**
—

Filming location
Belfast, Ireland
—

Format
35 mm
—

Awards for Hunger
**Britannique de Dinard
Film Festival**
  (Heartbeat Award, 2008)
**British Academy of Film
and Television Arts Awards**
  (Carl Foreman Award, 2008)
British Independent Film Awards
  (Douglas Hickox Award,
  Best Actor, Best Technical
  Achievement, 2008)
**Cannes International
Film Festival**
  (Caméra D'Or, FIPRESCI Prize,
  2008)
**Chicago International
Film Festival**
  (Gold Hugo for Best Film,
  Silver Hugo for Best Actor,
  2008)

Jerusalem Film Festival
  (In the Spirit of Freedom
  Award, 2008)
**Ljubljana International
Film Festival**
  (Kingfisher Award, 2008)
**San Sebastián International
Film Festival**
  (Special Mention, 2008)
Stockholm Film Festival
  (Best First Film, Best Actor,
  2008)
Sydney Film Festival
  (Sydney Film Prize, 2008)
**Toronto International
Film Festival**
  (Diesel Discovery Award,
  2008)
Venice Film Festival
  (Gucci Group Award, 2008)
— —

FATHER DOMINIC MORAN: And what does your heart say Bobby?

BOBBY: I thought you had me all figured out...

FATHER DOMINIC MORAN: What's it saying tell me!?

BOBBY: (Calmly) My life means everything to me. Freedom means everything. You're seeing me as a sectarian nut, right? Seeing my beliefs as some poison or something or other. I know you don't mean to mock me Dominic so I'll let all that pass. This is one of these times when we've come to a pause Dominic. It's a time to keep your beliefs pure. You call it sectarian...I call it faith.

Bobby explains his beliefs to Father Dominic Moran.

William, a hospital orderly, in Maze Prison Hospital.

A flashback to twelve-year-old Bobby.

Iliac (Coco Martin) is a twenty-year-old who works in a massage parlor that caters to a gay clientele, and where sex is part of the package. One day, Iliac's first customer is a homosexual romance novelist, and his current girlfriend, a bartender who works in Japan, asserts her sexual dominance over him. While back home, his estranged father dies, and as Iliac makes the trip to the province he is faced with the reality of decay, love, life, and survival—all within the context of performing of one's duty.

BRILLANTE MENDOZA
THE MASSEUR

Iliac (left) with the other masseurs.

At times, the masseurs don't have customers for hours.

Including *The Masseur* (*Masahista*, 2005), Brillante Mendoza has made nine movies in five years, rapidly joining the front ranks of the Philippines' burgeoning independent cinema. With the controversial *Kinatay* (2009), he became the first Filipino to win the Best Director Award at Cannes. Perhaps Mendoza, who previously worked as a production designer in advertising and started shooting features at age forty-five, is making up for lost time.

The energy demonstrated by his prodigious output is part and parcel of the movies themselves. Rooting his work in the culture and rhythms of his native country, Mendoza plunges us into the bustle and intimacy of daily life—both its quotidian details and its life-changing dramas. In *Foster Child* (2007), a mother in a hectic Manila hovel takes care of her toddler for one final day before relinquishing him to his new American parents at a sleek hotel. *Serbis* (2008) takes place in a family-run skin-flick movie house, where the cruising camera tracks casual hook-ups and intergenerational arguments. Multiple storylines set among the frantic and the desperate in a sewer-lined slum vie for our attention in *Slingshot* (*Tirador*, 2007).

Often drawing on personal experience, Mendoza does not choose his stories for shock value. A candid, sympathetic engagement marks his work, which shows people, places, and experiences that many audiences are not used to seeing on screen. *The Masseur*, his first feature, is no different: Iliac, the polite young man at the center of the action, works in a massage parlor attending to the sexual needs of its all-male clients. When Iliac's promiscuous father dies, he is called back to his hometown to aid with funeral arrangements, and the experience triggers fresh and complicated feelings about life and love.

Mendoza's intuitive feel extends to the film's flashback structure, which moves between the funeral trip and the days preceding news of the father's death. Iliac's time at work exists in a vivid yet mundane present tense, while the funeral trip has the dreamy aspect of many such major life events—like a memory much meditated upon and overshadowed by the feeling of the moment. The film repeatedly juxtaposes the body of Iliac's dead father, stretched out on a slab to be dressed, and the clients at the massage parlor, lying on tables in tiny rooms awaiting lotion. While some say the plot of the film resembles that of *Macho Dancer* (1986) by seminal Filipino director Lino Brocka, these juxtapositions and Iliac's internal struggles also evoke the early films of the British filmmaker Terence Davies.

The comparison between massage customer and corpse sets sensuality and mortality side by side, but it arises out of Iliac's reflections, not directorial imposition. Sexuality in Mendoza's films is part of the continuum of human experience, though of course matters are especially open at a massage parlor. Iliac and the other masseurs stand in array for prospective clients to browse, while the manager trumpets their assets. Thin walls let in the grunts, sighs, and moans from one room to the next, as Iliac playfully chats with a repeat customer who turns out to be a novelist.

Beyond the earthiness, some of the most lyrical moments in Mendoza's work occur in *The Masseur*. In the opening sequence, trees strung with lights flash by as the camera tracks down a street at night. When the body of Iliac's father is being prepared for presentation, the new clothes chosen for the occasion are ripped to fit more easily, and the tearing sound drives home the finality of his death and his break with the living. The director has become widely associated with handheld camerawork, but *The Masseur* has a slightly more composed style, nowhere near as frenetic as the seemingly constant churn of motion (and emotion) in *Slingshot*, or the documentary gaze of *Foster Child*.

This might be because Mendoza began *The Masseur* as a director for hire, supposedly with the stipulation that the film's title be retained for its appeal. But Mendoza takes Iliac's character seriously, and accepts without judgment the young man's mix of subservience, moxie, and confusion. The father's death provides him with the opportunity to grow in new ways, and, by the end, Iliac proclaims a new appreciation for his father's love and intends to follow his heart the next time he falls for someone. While this may seem a kind of happy ending, it equally reflects the boy's sense of hope and his naïveté.

Ultimately, *The Masseur* captures a classic turning point in many coming-of-age tales: the death of a parent leading to reflection upon present and past relationships, and a fresh self-reckoning. This time it happens to a twenty-year-old in a massage parlor, but Mendoza's talent is to render the specifics of the milieu without making a fuss, and more importantly, without losing sight of his characters' emotional experiences. For these reasons, Mendoza is a director to watch—provided he doesn't wear himself out.

ILIAC: Sir, let's take this off. Just relax, Sir.

ALFRED/MARINA HIDALGO: Where did you learn to do massage?

ILIAC: From my grandfather, Sir.

ALFRED/MARINA HIDALGO: Did **your** grandfather also work **in a joint** like this?

ILIAC: No, Sir. He was some kind of a chiropractor, fixing sprains and fractures. I don't know if he hooked up with his patients.

Iliac massages romance novel writer Alfredo/Marina, his regular customer.

Year and place of birth
1960　San Fernando, Philippines
—
Lives and works in
Manila, Philippines
—
Education
University of Santo Tomas,
**　Manila, Philippines**
—
Filmography
2005　The Masseur (Masahista)
2006　Summer Heat (Kaleldo)
2006　The Teacher (Manoro)
2007　Foster Child
2007　Slingshot (Tirador)
2008　Serbis
2009　Kinatay
2009　Lola
—

Director's awards
Foster Child
Gawad Urian Awards
**　(Best Director, 2007)**

Slingshot
Singapore International
Film Festival
**　(Best Director, 2008)**

Serbis
Gawad Urian Awards
**　(Best Director, 2008)**

Kinatay
Cannes International
Film Festival
**　(Best Director, 2009)**
Sitges International Film Festival
**　(Best Director, 2009)**
— —

Release date
2005
—
Country of release
Philippines
—
Language
Tagalog, Pampango
—
Running time
80 min.
—
Genre
Drama
—

Producer
Ihman Esturco
—
Writer
Boots Agbayani Pastor
—
Cinematographers
Timmy Jimenez, Monchie Redoble
—
Score
Jerrold Tarog
—

Key cast
Coco Martin: Iliac
Jaclyn Jose: Naty
Alan Paule: Alfred/Marina Hidalgo
Katherine Luna: Tessa

Filming locations
Mandaluyong City, Philippines
San Fernando, Philippines
—
Format
Mini DV
—

Awards for *The Masseur*
Locarno International Film
Festival
**　(Golden Leopard, 2005)**
Pasado Awards
**　(Best Film, Best Film for**
**　Using Local Dialect, 2005)**
Young Critics' Circle
**　(Best Film, Best Performer,**
**　Best Director, 2005)**
Brisbane International
Film Festival
**　(Interfaith Award, 2006)**
Turin Gay and Lesbian
Film Festival
**　(Audience Award, 2006)**
— —

Iliac with his mom Naty and siblings at his father's funeral.

The masseurs are interrupted when a coworker has an allergic reaction to baby powder.

Iliac and Alfredo/Marina after the massage.

Otilia (Anamaria Marinca) and Gabita (Laura Vasiliu) share the same room in a student dormitory. They are colleagues at the university in a small town in Romania, during the last years under Communism. Otilia rents a room in a cheap hotel. In the afternoon, they meet a certain Mr. Bebe (Vlad Ivanov). Gabita is pregnant, abortion is illegal, and neither of them have gone through something like this before.

CRISTIAN MUNGIU
4 MONTHS, 3 WEEKS AND 2 DAYS

Otilia and Mr. Bebe check into the cheap hotel.

With only a handful of shorts and one feature to his name, Cristian Mungiu leapt to international fame and attention with *4 Months, 3 Weeks and 2 Days* (*4 luni, 3 saptamâni si 2 zile*, 2007), a crystalline dissection of pre-glasnost Romania. Made one year after Florian Henckel von Donnersmarck's equally damning period piece *The Lives of Others* (*Das Leben der anderen*, 2006), *4 Months, 3 Weeks and 2 Days* turns a similar microscope on its story, with a grey, muted tone and wintry feel. Mungiu's film chronicles the harrowing experience of abortion, a commonplace occurrence in Eastern Europe but at the time illegal and therefore highly dangerous. The Romanian filmmaker is determined to reveal the ugly underside of his society's past and uncover its bitter truths and stories. By touching on the issue of abortion, he touches directly or indirectly on the lives of many ordinary Romanians.

4 Months, 3 Weeks and 2 Days focuses on three characters, transpires in three locations, and is composed of three distinct acts. This structure yields a certain intensity, which is accentuated by Mungiu's camerawork. Working with modest tools and a small budget, Mungiu finds great freedom within the limitations. He embeds the film's damning vision of his society in a highly sophisticated visual scheme based on stasis and movement.

Both these qualities are present from the earliest moments. A long, static, and claustrophobic opening shot introduces a twenty-three-year-old student, Gabita, whose inability to take action we immediately sense. Her world is restricted, a function of the frame. When her friend Otilia enters the picture, she brings a larger sense of what lies outside the box. Otilia negotiates the exterior world, and she is portrayed as a restless woman in motion; the camera trails after her numerous voyages throughout the film. Through this dialectic of the still and the moving shot, Mungiu visually suggests his thesis: a people and a society torn between entrapment and escape.

Gabita is pregnant and needs an abortion; Otilia will help her obtain it. The villain of *4 Months, 3 Weeks and 2 Days* is the abortionist, a certain Mr. Bebe. He is businesslike, ultimately unfeeling, and unsympathetic, but in this situation he has power, and the film is very much about who has power and how it is used. Gabita and Otilia need things: a hotel room, favors, consideration, and of course someone who can conduct an abortion. Mungiu effortlessly captures the shape that the necessary negotiations take.

The encounter with the abortionist fills the entire central section of *4 Months, 3 Weeks and 2 Days*. It is shot as a miniature set piece, skillfully exploiting the setting of the hotel room. Gabita, a victim, lies on the bed. Sitting on chairs that flank a small table at the foot of the bed are Mr. Bebe and Otilia, who negotiate the terms of the abortion. The scene crackles with suspense and anticipation, and Mungiu emphasizes its peculiar formality by filming entirely in squared-off shots. The denouement of the scene is shocking and humiliating: Otilia must have sex with Mr. Bebe to cover the full price of the abortion.

The genius of the film is how Mungiu proceeds to confound our expectations. Once the procedure has been completed and the odious Mr. Bebe has left the premises, most of the final act is spent with Otilia as she visits the third location in the film: the ordinary apartment of her boyfriend's parents, where his mother is celebrating her birthday. If the preceding scenes with Mr. Bebe shock with their blunt, ruthless honesty, here we find their opposite: a typical, boozy family gathering that does not allow for much truth-telling. Otilia, grappling with what she has just been through, puts on a good face for public consumption, in a kind of social lie. Her boyfriend senses something is wrong, but Mungiu provides no moment where confidences are shared.

As we move from the brutal reality of power politics to its aftermath, the concealment of the truth, Mungiu plays again with our expectations. Until this moment, the force of the film has been in its use of words. But when Otilia returns to the hotel to check up on Gabita, we come face to face with the most shocking image the filmmaker will employ: the aborted fetus. It is a complex moment. Having invested all our emotional sympathy with the two women, we are suddenly confronted with the fact of an abortion. The scene is incomparably haunting, and Mungiu does not allow our gaze to wander.

Played out within the Aristotelian dramatic confines of a single day, *4 Months, 3 Weeks and 2 Days* shows Mungiu giving voice to an entire generation of women who, as is made apparent in the final scene of the film, prefer not to talk about the horrors they have undergone. In this disturbing reclamation of history, Mungiu reveals himself to be a social documentarian of uncommon sensitivity.

Mr. Bebe explains the fee for his abortion service to Otilia and Gabita.

Year and place of birth
1968   Iasi, Romania

—

Lives and works in
Bucharest, Romania

—

Education
University of Iasi, Romania
Bucharest Theatre and
    Film Academy, Romania

—

Filmography
2002   *Occident*
2005   *Lost and Found*
    ("Turkey Girl")
2007   *4 months, 3 weeks*
    and 2 days (4 luni,
    3 saptamini si 2 zile)
2009   *Tales from the Golden*
    Age (Amintiri din Epoca
    de Aur) **(co-directed**
    with Ioana Uricaru,
    Hanno Höfer, Răzvan
    Mărculescu, and
    Constantin Popescu)

—

Director's awards
Occident
Cannes International
Film Festival
    (Quinzaine des Réalisateurs –
    Special Mention, 2002)
Leeds Film Festival
    (Best New Director, 2002)
Mediterranean Film Festival
    (Nova Prix, 2002)
Rennes Film Festival
    (Jury Award, 2002)
Sofia International Film Festival
    (FIPRESCI Award, 2002)
Thessaloniki International
Film Festival
    (Audience Award, 2002)
Transilvania International
Film Festival
    (Best Film, 2002)
Annonay International
Film Festival of First Films
    (Jury Prize, 2003)
Mons International Love
Film Festival
    (Grand Prix, 2003)

— —

Release date
2007

—

Country of release
Italy

—

Language
Romanian

—

Running time
115 min.

—

Genre
Drama

—

Producers
Cristian Mungiu, Oleg Mutu

—

Writer
Cristian Mungiu

—

Cinematographer
Oleg Mutu

—

Key cast
Anamaria Marinca: Otilia
Laura Vasiliu: Gabita
Vlad Ivanov: Mr. Bebe
Alex Potocean: Adi

—

Filming locations
Bucharest, Romania
Ploiesti, Romania

—

Format
35 mm

Awards for *4 months, 3 weeks*
and 2 Days
Cannes International
Film Festival
    (Palme d'Or, FIPRESCI Award,
    2007)
Chicago Film Critics Awards
    (Best Foreign Language Film,
    2007)
European Film Academy
    (Best European Film,
    Best European Director,
    2007)
Flemish Film Critics Association
    (Best Film of the Year, 2007)
Los Angeles Film Critics
Association
    (Best Foreign Language Film,
    Best Supporting Actor, 2007)
San Sebastián International
Film Festival
    (FIPRESCI Grand Prix –
    Best Film of the Year, 2007)
Toronto Film Critics Association
    (Best Foreign Language Film,
    2007)

— —

Gabita waits in the bathroom.

Otilia stares at the bathroom wall after agreeing to Mr. Bebe's conditions.

Otilia meets her boyfriend at his mother's birthday party.

INT. HOTEL ROOM, BATHROOM - EVENING

Otilia opens the door and enters. A rumpled blood-stained sheet is in the bath tub. Otilia then stares at the floor, her face free of expression. The strip light flickers. Otilia takes a towel from the rail and wraps it round her hand. She crouches down. A fetus has been laid out on a towel on the floor. Its tiny white bones are protruding from its limbs like fish bones. It is lying on its side. Otilia examines it closely. The telephone in the room rings. Otilia gives a start, hesitates a moment, then stands up.

Gabita asks Otilia to dispose of the body.

Lieutenant Neagu (Adi Carauleanu) and his armored unit are ordered to patrol Bucharest's suburbs while radio and TV broadcasts air vague reports of "terrorist" attacks on the national television station by anti-Ceauşescu forces. Conscript Costi (Paul Ipate) believes that it is every Romanian's duty, after so many years under dictatorship, to battle Ceauşescu supporters, irrespective of orders. Despite Neagu's threats, Costi heads to the station to fight for the revolution. During this night of madness, soldiers receive orders from poets and actors via television, radios transmit garbled signals, arms are distributed to civilians, and gypsies are arrested as Arab terrorists.

RADU MUNTEAN
THE PAPER WILL BE BLUE

The lieutenant points his gun at Costi and commands him not to desert.

Costi chooses to fight for the revolution.

Of all the countries involved in the revolutions of 1989, Romania has developed one of the most interesting "auteur" cinemas. An entire New Wave of young directors established themselves on the international scene in the 2000s: in 2005 Cristi Puiu won the Un Certain Regard prize at Cannes for *The Death of Mr. Lazarescu*, Corneliu Porumboiu was awarded the Caméra d'Or in 2006 for his very funny *12:08 East of Bucharest*, and Cristian Mungiu won the Palme d'Or in 2007 for the chilling *4 Months, 3 Weeks and 2 Days*.

Less known but perhaps more interesting than some of his colleagues is Radu Muntean. He was born in 1971, and after studying at Bucharest's Theatre and Film Academy, he in quick succession made a number of shorts and documentaries, including *Life is Elsewhere* (1996), which was awarded a prize in Locarno's video section. With over 400 commercials to his name, he made his first feature film, *The Rage* (*Furia*, 2002), and followed with the *The Paper Will Be Blue* (*Hîrtia va fi albastră*, 2006), which was presented in competition at the Locarno International Film Festival. He then made *Boogie* (2008), and is currently working on his next feature, *Tuesday, After Christmas*.

In December 1989, revolution broke out in Romania. On the twenty-first, residents were urged to come out in support of the dictator, Nicolae Ceauşescu, whose power had been weakened by the growing opposition, but he was shouted down and the army fired on the crowd. This marked the beginning of the uprising in Bucharest. The following day, a state of emergency was proclaimed throughout Romania. After violent confrontations, demonstrators and the army began to fraternize and Ceauşescu ceded power to the National Salvation Front. Although the army threw its weight behind the NSF, some troops in Bucharest carried on fighting through the evening of December 23. The film begins in the early hours, when an armored car stops at a roadblock and two men in uniform get out to smoke a cigarette. The men inside the vehicle have difficulty establishing communication with those guarding the roadblock, and in a tense moment, the guards open fire, killing all the passengers, unsure if they are on their side or not. There follows a flashback to the night before the death of these men. Driving through the city, confined to the inner shell of their vehicle, not knowing whether they should be supporting or fighting the "terrorists" who appear to have stormed the national television studios, they exchange their points of view on the revolution that is overtaking them.

In a stifling atmosphere in which popular excitement, confusion, and indiscriminate violence are mixed together, *The Paper Will Be Blue* presents scenes of astonishing realism. Muntean constructs a reflection on the hopes and disappointments of this popular insurrection. Almost twenty years after the events themselves, he returns, like several other Romanian filmmakers, to the crucial moment when their country was radically transformed.

The film is based on an actual event: members of two armed units of the Ministry of the Interior did indeed accidentally kill each other. As Muntean says, "In the days that followed the departure of Ceauşescu, neither the Romanian people nor the army could identify the enemy, and 'accidents' of this kind caused the death of over a thousand people." At the same time, the film is not a documentary that tries to record a historical event accurately: "My aim was to re-create the emotions of those days through the eyes of ordinary people."

Rather than use the kind of revolution images shown on television, many of which he considers untruthful, Muntean instead tried to offer a fairer version of the events, turning them, as he says, into a "tragicomedy": "This film is not a documentary with a historical perspective, but attempts to re-create the feelings of ordinary people who took part in the events it relates. It's the story of an entire generation's loss of innocence, and of the popular uprising that brought out the best and worst in human nature: the sense of solidarity as well as the selfishness and malice that had built up over decades of frustration. During that first night of freedom, the armed forces received orders broadcast on television by poets and actors. People were called upon to protect the national television station from invisible enemies, garbled messages were sent by walkie-talkie, weapons were handed out to civilians, and Gypsies were arrested the same way Arab 'terrorists' are today. It's a story about the loss of innocence suffered by a whole generation whose emotions swung from fear to excitement to simple disappointment . . . Alongside the great solidarity that came out of that chaos, we witnessed unspeakable abuse, selfishness, and pure nastiness, the products of decades of frustration, fear of the system, and violation of the most basic human rights."

Costi ignores orders and passes large crowds to get to the TV station.

Year and place of birth
1971   Bucharest, Romania
—

Lives and works in
Bucharest, Romania
—

Education
**Bucharest Theatre and Film
    Academy, Romania**
—

Filmography
1994   *Ea* (short)
**1996   *Tragica poveste de
    dragoste a celor doi*
    (short)**
1996   *Life is Elsewhere* (short)
2002   *The Rage* (*Furia*)
**2006   *The Paper Will Be Blue*
    (*Hîrtia va fi albastră*)**
2008   *Boogie*
—

Director's awards
*Tragica poveste de dragoste a
celor doi*
**Continesti Film Festival
    (1st Prize, 1996)**

Life is Elsewhere
**Locarno International Film
    Festival
        (Special Award Video Art
        Section, 1996)**

Boogie
**Hamptons International
    Film Festival
        (Best Screenplay, 2008)
Pali'c Film Festival
        (Special Mention, 2008)
— —**

Release date
2006
—

Country of release
Romania
—

Language
Romanian
—

Running time
96 min.
—

Genre
Drama
—

Producer
Dragos Vîlcu
—

Writers
**Alex Baciu, Radu Muntean,
Răzvan Rădulescu**
—

Cinematographer
Tudor Lucaciu
—

Key cast
**Paul Ipate: Costi
Adi Carauleanu: Lt. Neagu
Dragoş Bucur: Dragos
Tudor Aron Istodor: Bobo
Alexandru Potocean: Vasile
Andi Vasluianu: Aurel
Dana Dogaru: Mrs. Andronescu
Ion Săpdaru: Craciun
Mimi Brănescu: Lt. Deleanu
Alexandru Georgescu:
    Lt. Voinescu**
—

Filming location
Bucharest, Romania
—

Format
16 mm
—

Awards for *The Paper Will Be Blue*
**Antalya Golden Orange
Film Festival
    (Golden Orange for Best
    Foreign Language Film, 2006)
Balkan Black Box
    (Golden Black Box, 2006)
Cottbus Film Festival of East
European Cinema
    (Special Prize for
    Best Director, 2006)
Marrakech International
Film Festival
    (Special Jury Award, 2006)
Namur International Festival
of French-Speaking Film
    (Jury Special Prize, 2006)
Sarajevo Film Festival
    (CICAE Award, Special
    Mention, 2006)**

Gopos Awards
**   (Gopos Award for Best Sound,
    2007)
Las Palmas International
Film Festival
    (Best Young Director, 2007)**
—

Costi takes the subway to the TV station.

In the confusion, Costi and Aurel are arrested as terrorists.

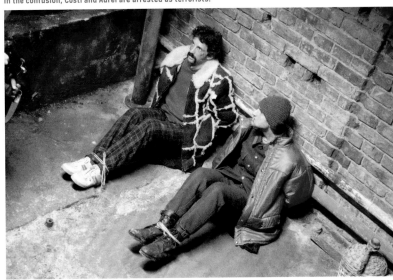

Instantly, at Costi's nod, the two get up by the window and shoot simultaneously towards the truck. Their bullets hit the wheels and the cab of the truck. A car comes speeding from the right, and briefly shines its headlights on the tree by the truck. The car then slows down and its sidelights are turned off. For 2-3 seconds, as long as the lights are on, Costi and Aurel see a soldier with a wounded shoulder being helped by another soldier to get into the Dacia. The car speeds off to the left and vanishes in the dark of the night.

Costi and Aurel shoot against suspected terrorists.

Set in Guanajuato, Mexico, the story revolves around Román (Juan Pablo de Santiago) and Maru (Maria Deschamps), two troubled teenagers who attempt an impossible rebellion against the adult world. They run away to a place where they don't have to answer to anyone. There they discover their sexuality and an intense new life as a couple that both unites and confuses them. The young fugitives eventually jeopardize the security of their hiding place and test the limits of their newfound paradise by returning to the real world, where wounds are real and actions have consequences.

GERARDO NARANJO
I'M GONNA EXPLODE

Román and Maru think about the possibility of having sex.

Román and Maru escape from school after the shooting.

The third feature by Mexican filmmaker Gerardo Naranjo is a fresh, dreamy addition to the canon of young-lovers-on-the-run movies, but Román and Maru, the heroes of *I'm Gonna Explode* (*Voy a explotar*, 2008), are not your typical fugitives. For one thing, the two teenagers don't run very far, at least at first: they spend half the movie camped out on the roof of Román's house. While his congressman father waits and wonders downstairs with his wife and others, the runaways listen to music, laze about, and fitfully flirt. The wild-haired Román may have wrought havoc in school waving a gun, but their stolen freedom resembles nothing so much as summer vacation.

Naranjo ensconces us in the world of these two young soulmates, who are brought together after Román attempted to hang himself at the school talent show, and Maru was the only one who clapped. If Román's rebellious streak suggests a darker undercurrent to their innocence, it may come from the voice of experience: growing up in a small town, the director too ran away from home (and even hid on the roof). His choice of career would also mark a kind of escape, as the Mexican native moved on from university cineclubs to study at the American Film Institute. Naranjo, a cinephile clearly enamored of Godard's *Breathless* (1960) and *Pierrot le Fou* (1965), provides an update to the pioneering New Waver's doomed romanticism. These youngsters need to master their own moods before conquering the world.

Naranjo is far from the first Mexican filmmaker to set off sparks in recent years. In addition to festival favorites such as Fernando Eimbcke (*Lake Tahoe*, 2008), the well-established trio of Guillermo del Toro (*Pan's Labyrinth*, 2006), Alejandro González Iñárritu (*21 Grams*, 2003), and Alfonso Cuarón (*Y tu mamá también*, 2001) have garnered both critical interest and studio deals. *Drama/Mex* (2006), Naranjo's second feature but his first to get attention, was inevitably compared to the interwoven storylines of Iñárritu's films and the free sexuality of Cuarón's debut. Set in the little-seen underbelly of Acapulco, it featured three grimy tales of love and theft, shot with a handheld camera and rife with scenes of conflict.

But it was with the touching intimacy and restless energy of *I'm Gonna Explode* that Naranjo came into his own, finding perfect subjects for his kinetic style. Maru is all too happy to tag along with the impetuous Román, and after continued hide-and-seek with their families, the two eventually go to a quinceañera party for a local resident's daughter, where Román starts a fight. The next day, they wake up in the middle of a field; anything seems possible with this boy, whom Maru nicknames Romántico. Or as she puts it in a letter to a friend, Román "exists, but I also made him up." Naranjo captures an affecting sense of possibility and romantic projection, and his actors, Juan Pablo de Santiago and Maria Deschamps, seem at ease on screen, whether hiding in the red glare of their translucent tent or staggering about the field in partywear. Yet Naranjo's handheld camerawork, tightly trained on their fresh faces, fills the wide screen with a reminder of how young they still are.

Though *I'm Gonna Explode* does not attempt to hammer home a political message, Naranjo does lace the story with reminders of reality, past and present. Class inequality, as is often the case in Mexican cinema, has a way of rearing its head. The political position and wealth of Román's father has shielded the teen from repercussions for past provocations; this time, his name is kept out of news reports, and the police are told that the matter will be handled "in house." Maru, however, comes from a poorer background, and her loving mother's first reaction to Román's cynical parents is anger: this kind of attitude, she says, is why their country is mired in corruption.

Naranjo doesn't hold up Román and Maru as examples of some liberated consciousness. When the two seek refuge with a family friend who protested with Román's father back in their university days, the ex-radical gives them shelter but lambasts Román for his recklessness. The filmmaker may exult stylistically in these two outcast specimens of a new generation, matching their freedom of movement with lively visuals scored to music by French New Wave fixture Georges Delerue and songs by Interpol and Bright Eyes. But as Román and Maru's days away from the real world wear on, there's a sense that something must break.

A girl and a gun: so went Godard's infamous recipe for making a movie. The gun part eventually catches up with this young couple, unpredictably but no less tragically. To the very end, however, Naranjo demonstrates an affection for the spirit of his young characters. It's this ability that distinguishes Naranjo as one of his generation's most promising chroniclers— a filmmaker as energetic as his young subjects, and just as eager to make something happen.

Román listens to a public service announcement about Maru.

Year and place of birth
1977   Salamanca, Mexico
—

Lives and works in
Mexico City, Mexico
—

Education
**American Film Institute,
    Los Angeles, Calif., USA**
—

Filmography
2000   *Perro negro* (short)
**2002   *The Last Attack
    of the Beast* (short)**
2004   *Malachance*
2006   *Drama/Mex*
**2008   *I'm Gonna Explode
    (Voy a explotar)***
—

Release date
2008
—

Country of release
Mexico
—

Language
Spanish
—

Running time
106 min.
—

Genre
Drama
—

Producers
**Pablo Cruz, Hunter Gray,
Alain de la Mata, Gerardo Naranjo**
—

Writer
Gerardo Naranjo
—

Cinematographer
Tobias Datum
—

Score
Georges Delerue
—

Key cast
**Maria Deschamps: Maru
Juan Pablo de Santiago: Román
Daniel Giménez Cacho: Eugenio
Martha Claudia Moreno: Helena
Rebecca Jones: Eva**
—

Filming location
Guanajuato, Mexico
—

Format
35 mm
—

Awards for *Voy a explotar*
**Thessaloniki Film Festival
    (FIPRESCI Prize –
    International Competition,
    2008)
Guadalajara Mexican
Film Festival
    (MEZCAL Award,
    Mayahuel Award for
    Best Cinematography,
    Press Award, 2009)**
— —

Killing time on the roof.

Román and Maru rush to their hideout when the adults arrive.

Maru tries on a dress that belonged to Román's mother.

INT. CAMPING TENT. NIGHT.

The tent makes the light look orange. Román unpacks
their things. Maru is already in the makeshift bed,
covered with blankets, watching Román.

ROMAN: Shit it's cold. How are you?

Maru smiles and shrugs her shoulders.

MARU: A little cold. But all right.

Román stops what he's doing, crawls into bed and
lies down beside Maru.

They are both excited. They roll over and look
at a big poster of Morrissey stuck to the ceiling
with masking tape. They look at each other.

Román and Maru hide in a tent with their new dog Marrani.

Against the tumultuous backdrop of Iran's 1953 CIA-backed coup d'état, the destinies of four women converge in a beautiful orchard, where they find independence, solace, and companionship. Acclaimed photographer Shirin Neshat makes her directorial debut with this incisive and sumptuously filmed reflection on the pivotal moment in history that directly led to the Islamic Revolution and the Iran we know today.

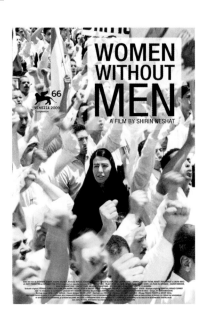

SHIRIN NESHAT
WOMEN WITHOUT MEN

Munis leaps off the roof to free herself from her traditional brother.

"In Iran," Shirin Neshat told an interviewer about a decade ago, "women are quite powerful, unlike their clichéd image. What I try to convey through my work is that power, which is quite candid." In Neshat's provocatively titled feature-film debut, *Women Without Men* (*Zanan-e bedun-e mardan*, 2009), that power does indeed emerge in the solidarity of several women in a 1953 Iran rocked by political upheaval, and yet the forces of repression prove just as devastatingly persistent.

In the Iran of recent memory, one could say it was ever thus, and arguably we would not have Neshat's artistic contributions otherwise. Born to a Westernized family, she was sent to the United States to study art and eventually settled in as an exile in New York, yet it was a disappointing return visit to her much-changed home country in 1990 that spurred her to make art in earnest. Her *Women of Allah* series of photographs (1993-97), depicting militant Muslim women, was soon followed by split-screen video installations. *Rapture* (1999) won her an award at the Venice Biennale and international acclaim. Throughout her female-centered work, she employed bold contrasts to capture crosscurrents of liberation and repression, song and silence, desire and concealment, Islam and Western attitudes.

Women Without Men builds upon an array of individual installations that were ultimately exhibited under the same title. All draw inspiration from the book also of the same name by Iranian author Shahrnush Parsipur, a work of magic realism that has been banned in Iran since the 1990s. Set in the run-up to the U.S.-triggered coup, Neshat's film interpretation is at once sumptuously produced and stringent in its themes as it brings together the stories of four women from different classes and stations in life. *Women Without Men* bears some of the hallmarks of her vivid installation work, but also stands on its own feet as a drama tracking the trajectories and interior lives of its affecting characters.

Munis, whom we meet first, lives with a brother who harangues her about suitors and the shame of becoming an old maid (at 30!), but she is more interested in radio reports of political unrest. Her friend Faezeh likes Munis's brother, but after being assaulted in the street, she bears a burden of shame. Zarin is an anorexic prostitute who says nothing and one day begins to scrub herself raw at a public bath. Finally, Fakhri is an middle-aged upper-class woman who would seem to be at a comfortable point in life, but she decides to leave her insufferable military-man husband to move in artistic circles.

Neshat has said she learned much about filmmaking while making an earlier incarnation of Zarin's story, *Zarin* (2005), and *Women Without Men* gave her the opportunity to develop characters over a broader canvas. Yet she does not abandon her use of potent symbolism and arresting images with mystical and visceral impact. As part of her new life, Fakhri buys a house in a walled garden ringed by trees, and this dreamlike locale becomes a sanctuary. Different paths of serendipity rather than clear cause and effect seems to lead the others there, and the camera lingers on a serene stream that leads into the compound.

It is a physical place, yes, but it is also an allegorical place of the mind, heart, and spirit (though not one where all problems are solved).

Part of what helped Neshat rise to prominence in the art world was her use of binaries, both thematically and visually through opposed screens. *Women Without Men* is of course a feature film that is projected according to convention, but it demonstrates Neshat's ability to find tensions through character arcs and moments with an éclat that transcends drama. The film opens, for example, with the image of a veiled figure atop a ledge, which at first resembles an abstract arrangement of shapes more than a woman about to embark on a suicidal leap. Less abstract but no less mesmerizing are Zarin's bathhouse scenes; even Zarin herself, with her unnervingly emaciated and pale body, resembles a ghost, an embodiment of self-negation and the desire to be anywhere but here. (That she says nothing over the course of the film recalls Neshat's earlier work with speech and silence.)

Bringing to bear the force of a talent honed in other visual arts, Neshat is a force to be reckoned with in the world of cinema, and she has already earned another award (also in Venice, as it turns out). *Women Without Men* traces Iranian political history in different ways than she has done before, but it continues the bracing engagement with ideology that is characteristic of her strongest work. Neshat bookends the film with an aestheticized suicidal leap, and it is at once a poetic and highly potent political statement, suggesting all that can be found within the power of will.

Zarin sits before a mirror on a dresser, plucking her eyebrows. Music from the reception room can be heard through the walls.

MADAM PARI: Zarin! Your client is waiting! Hurry, get yourself downstairs! Hey Zarin.

Zarin ignores the Madam and continues with her makeup.

Zarin finally walks out of her bedroom and onto the balcony. She hangs over the railing, looking down at the scene. We hear the sound of music and other commotion in the reception area.

MADAM PARI: Zarin, your client is waiting for you in Mahin's room! Hurry up!

Zarin waits for her next customer in the brothel.

Year and place of birth
1957   Qazvin, Iran
—

Lives and works in
Berlin, Germany
New York, N.Y., USA
—

Education
University of California,
**   Berkeley, USA**
—

Filmography
2009   Women Without Men
**   (Zanan-e bedun-e**
**   mardan)**
— —

Release date
2010
—

Country of release
Greece
—

Language
Farsi
—

Running time
99 min.
—

Producers
Susanne Marian,
Martin Gschlacht, Philippe Bober
—

Writers
Shirin Neshat, Shoja Azari
—

Cinematographer
Martin Gschlacht
—

Score
Ryuichi Sakamoto

Key cast
Pegah Ferydoni: Faezeh
Arita Shahrzad: Fakhri
Shabnam Tolouei: Munis
Orsi Tóth: Zarin
—

Filming locations
Casablanca, Morocco
Marrakesh, Morocco
—

Format
Super 35 mm Cinemascope
—

Awards for Women Without Men
Hessischer Filmpreis
**   (Cinema for Peace Special**
**   Award, 2009)**
Venice International Film Festival
**   (Silver Lion, Prix La Navicella,**
**   Prix Unicef, 2009)**
— —

Women and children in the bath house.

The army invades Farokh Legha's party.

Faezeh returns to Tehran after the death of Zarin and the fall of the party.

The people who live near the border of Inner Mongolia and Mongolia never care about the changes in their lives, but still their lives are changing unnoticeably. A common white ping-pong ball floats down in the creek and comes to a stop in front of Bilike (Hurichabilike), a Mongolian boy. Having never seen a ping-pong ball, Bilike and his friends believe the ball to have magical powers. They embark on a journey to Beijing in an attempt to return the ball to what they believe to be its home.

NING HAO
MONGOLIAN PING PONG

Bilike finds a ping-pong ball in the river.

Bilike and his family pose for photos in front of a big screen of Beijing.

Ning Hao's best-known movie, *Crazy Stone* (*Fengkuang de shitou*, 2006), was a box-office hit, a low-budget black comedy that earned him the moniker "the Chinese Quentin Tarantino." His most recent release, *Crazy Racer* (*Fengkuang de saiche*, 2009), was even more successful, and made him a mainstay of Chinese cinema. But before Ning became famous for labyrinthine Guy Ritchie–style tales enlivened by earthy slang, he made two independent films, *Incense* (*Xiang huo*, 2003) and *Mongolian Ping Pong* (*Lü Cao Di*, 2005). Neither was commercially released in China, but both reaped great acclaim on the international festival circuit.

Mongolian Ping Pong showcases Ning Hao's ingenuity and comedic talent. The premise grew out of a request from his former teacher at the Beijing Film Academy: tell a story using three specific elements— a farming village, children, and a ping-pong ball. Ning set the movie in the grasslands of Inner Mongolia, where one day a small white ball comes bobbing along in a stream. It stops in front of Bilike, a boy from a nomadic family, and a charming tale ensues.

Bilike and his two friends, none of whom have ever seen a ping-pong ball, are led to believe by his grandma that they have found a glowing pearl from the gods, and they spend a night waiting futilely for it to light up. A projectionist who has come to the grasslands to show films tells them that the object is called a ping-pong ball, but offers no further explanation. Later, the father of Bilike's friend Dawa wins a television, but the reception is too poor for them to watch a broadcast of a ping-pong game, though they hear the commentator remark that the "ping-pong ball is the ball of our nation." Full of excitement, the three fearless boys hop onto their horses and motorcycle and begin a long trek to Beijing to return the ball, without telling their parents.

Ning often speaks of his fondness for the unpretentious people who live on the steppes, for their nomadic life and their feeling that "all under the sky is my home." The film strings together snatches of daily life; his camera generally records from middle and long distances, silently observing with spectacular results. In one scene, Bilike gets drunk one night and passes out in the grassland. The next morning, when his mother comes to knock some sense into him, he asks why his father, a drunkard, is always let off the hook. His father is so ashamed that he disappears into the family's yurt. The entire sequence is filmed in one extreme long shot with a static camera, as if reflecting the point of view of the other two boys, who delightedly watch from a distance. The serene tone suits the rhythm of life far away from urban civilization. The three child actors, who use the regional dialect, had no prior acting experience, but under Ning Hao's careful guidance, their distinct personalities, innate goodness, and determination emerge easily and admirably. Their scenes are often shot in long takes, without the crutch of cutaway shots.

Mongolian Ping Pong is an anomaly among Chinese independent productions. A children's film with characters who belong to a minority, it managed to skirt the ire of the censors (although the Chinese title was changed to the bland *The Green Grassland*).

In addition to the patriotism in the idea of returning "the ball of our nation," Ning subtly touches upon a number of other themes. The movie opens with a photographic backdrop of Tiananmen Square, but the camera then pans right to show the green grassland behind it, underscoring the gap between the Mongolian steppes and Beijing. Yet life on the steppes is not wholly pristine. With the incursion of Western materialism, Bilike's father is so taken by the picture of a windmill in a copy of *Elle* magazine that he trades in his sheep for bricks to build a new house. Likewise, Dawa's father wants to watch television so badly that he fashions his own antenna out of scrap metal. *Mongolian Ping Pong* also dwells on the degradation of the environment: the boys, convinced that the nearby lake is polluted, decide not to draw any water before embarking for Beijing. For the girls in the story, getting an education in Inner Mongolia remains a problem. Bilike's sister, Wurina, does not get the opportunity to go to school at all. Her only chance to make something of her life is to join a song-and-dance troupe.

The absence of exoticism and stereotypes in *Mongolian Ping Pong* is especially noteworthy. Both respectful and self-respecting, it is full of humor and wisdom. Even the most mundane events in the everyday life depicted are imbued with a strong poetical sense. But nothing demonstrates Ning's self-confidence better than his decision never to show an actual ping-pong game. Near the end, Bilike goes to school in the city. As he pushes open the door, the sound of countless ping-pong balls bouncing is audible. Then, abruptly, the film comes to a magical stop.

Bilike asks his grandma whether the ping-pong ball is from the gods.

Year and place of birth
1977   Shanxi, China
—

Lives and works in
Beijing, China
—

Education
**Taiyuan Film School,
    Shanxi, China
Beijing Normal University, China
Beijing Film Academy, China**
—

Filmography
2001   *Thursday, Wednesday*
      (short)
2003   *Incense (Xiang huo)*
2005   *Mongolian Ping Pong*
      (*Lü cao di*)
2006   *Crazy Stone*
      (*Fengkuang de shitou*)

2009   *Crazy Racer*
      (*Fengkuang de saiche*)
2010   *No Man's Land*
      (*Wu ren qu*)
—

Director's awards
Thursday, Wednesday
**Beijing Student Film Festival
   (Best Director, 2001)**

Crazy Stone
   (*Fengkuang de shitou*)
**Beijing Student Film Festival
   (Best Director, 2007)
Huabiao Film Awards
   (Outstanding New Director,
   2007)**
— —

Release date
2005
—

Country of release
China
—

Language
Mongolian
—

Running time
105 min.
—

Genre
Drama
—

Producers
He Bu, Lu Bin
—

Writer
Ning Hao
—

Cinematographer
Du Jie
—

Score
Wuhe
—

Key cast
**Hurichabilike: Bilike
Geliban: Erguotou
Dawa: Dawa
Yidexinnaribu: Bilike's Father
Badema: Bilike's Mother
Wurina: Bilike's Sister
Dugema: Bilike's Grandmother**
—

Filming location
Xilinguolemeng, Inner Mongolia
—

Format
35 mm
—

Awards for *Mongolian Ping Pong*
**Shanghai International
Film Festival
   (Asian New Talent Award,
   2005)
Vallodolid International
Film Festival
   (Best Director of
   Photography, 2005)**
— —

Bilike spends the night waiting for his ping-pong ball to light up.

Bilike looks out at the praying altar as he plays games with his friends.

Bilike wrestles with another boy.

The local people watch a film in a mobile cinema offered by the government.

After his girlfriend breaks up with him, Hyuk-jin (Sam-dong Song) hangs out at a bar with friends. Totally drunk, they make plans to travel to Jeongseon, a small town in Gangwon Province, to console Hyuk-jin's broken heart. The next day, Hyuk-jin gets on the bus, but upon arrival finds out he is the only one who made it to the destination. He calls up his friends, but they don't want to join him because of their terrible hangovers.

NOH YOUNG-SEOK
DAYTIME DRINKING

HYUK-JIN: (*On the phone*) What am I supposed to do there?

KI-SANG: Just relax. It would be refreshing. Give it a try. You won't regret it. Go enjoy the barbecue and booze. I'll join you soon.

HYUK-JIN: When are you coming?

KI-SANG: I'm a little busy, so...the day after tomorrow?

HYUK-JIN: Are you telling me to stay here till the day after tomorrow?

KI-SANG: Why not? That place is great! I bet you'll change your mind.

HYUK-JIN: Forget it.

Hyuk-jin rests on his way to find the guest house.

Noh Young-seok had hoped to pursue a career in music, but was unsuccessful in obtaining a place at the Korean conservatory. Not giving up on the idea of making a living in the arts, he went to Seoul National University, majored in ceramics (an art form known to be one of Korea's richest traditions), and graduated in 2003. It was then he caught the cinema bug. In 2004 he began writing screenplays, none of which was sold. He decided to shoot one himself, as an independent, with very little money at his disposal–a $10,000 loan from his mother, in fact.

Because of his extremely tight budget, Noh Young-seok made *Daytime Drinking* (*Naj sul*, 2008) with a very small crew, and took on the cinematography, editing, music, costumes, and sets himself. In his own words, "I shot the film mainly outdoors, using natural light. To keep the size of the crew down, I asked the actors to go straight home after each scene. In addition to that, before I started shooting I did a lot of location scouting in the province of Gangwon, where the film is set, and that way I was able to negotiate favorable rates when I shot the interior scenes."

Hyuk-jin, a rather reserved young man whose girlfriend has just left him, suffers from a broken heart. While getting drunk with friends on soju, a Korean liquor made from rice or sweet potatoes, Ki-sang, hoping to drag his friend out of his sluggish state, suggests they take off and visit his brother's house by the sea. Hyuk-jin, who's been spending his days looking at photos of his ex-girlfriend, feels forced to accept, and the friends agree to meet at the vacation spot the following day.

But when Hyuk-jin arrives, he waits in vain, because nobody else shows up. His friends have forgotten to come–and he won't see them again for quite some time. Feeling lost in a hostile and unfamiliar place, where all the shops are closed and he can't even find the guesthouse where he and his friends were supposed to stay, the unfortunate traveler falls into even deeper despair.

This is the starting point for a journey whose destination changes periodically; the people Hyuk-jin meets in the course of his wanderings spark an awareness of his life, his friendships, and his naïveté. Tossed about and unable to make decisions he can stick to, the young man perpetually allows himself to be seduced by the hope of enjoying new pleasures. With soju, whiskey, and some more exotic beverages, his journey turns into a huge drinking session; at first he accepts it wholeheartedly, but eventually tires of it. Unable to cure the dizziness caused by too much alcohol, and having lost faith in everyone around him, his only wish is to go home. But will he be able to resume his old life after such an experience?

Daytime Drinking was voted the year's best Korean film at the Jeonju International Film Festival and received an honorable mention at the Locarno International Film Festival. It's both a comic road movie, built around a series of increasingly absurd misunderstandings, and a portrait of young middle-class people with nothing to do. They search for meaningful and lasting emotional experiences, but are all at sea in a society freed from dictatorship barely a generation ago.

In the words of Noh Young-seok, "The plot of *Daytime Drinking* is made and unmade by people who meet, then separate, and drink during the time they spend together. A journey makes you drift. If you travel alone and meet somebody, that's even better. Could I make a journey like that? Could other people do it? The film's plot came out of those questions. There's an old Korean proverb that says if you drink in the daytime, you won't recognize your parents in the evening. And anyway, the effects of alcohol are greater if you drink during the day than during the night. The more you drink, the more you act by instinct. At that moment, something will happen, inevitably."

Based on the director's own (also sometimes boozy) experiences, *Daytime Drinking* is impressive for its finely judged performances, its careful description of waiting, editing tricks that distort time, and the clever economy of its dialogue. It succeeds in putting the best elements of comedy in the service of a very acidic depiction of contemporary Korean society, and more broadly, of a young generation that, like the film's main character, have little idea of where they are or where they're going, unable to see a reason for living or a direction to follow, in the stream of events that is their existence.

Noh Young-seok is already working on his next feature film, which, though also a black comedy, will be very different from the first one. It's certainly something to look forward to.

Hyuk-jin eats a hot cup of noodles on the beach.

Lan-hee asks Hyuk-jin to take a picture of her.

Year and place of birth
1976   Seoul, South Korea
—

Lives and works in
Seoul, South Korea
—

Education
**Seoul National University,
    South Korea**
—

Filmography
**2008   Daytime Drinking
    (Naj sul)**
— —

Release date
2009
—

Country of release
South Korea
—

Language
Korean
—

Running time
116 min.
—

Genre
Drama, Comedy

Producer
Noh Young-seok
—

Writer
Noh Young-seok
—

Cinematographer
Noh Young-seok
—

Score
Noh Young-seok
—

Key cast
**Sam-dong Song: Hyuk-jin
Sang-yeop Yuk: Ki-sang
Kang-Hee Kim: Girl next door
Seung-joon Tak: Boy next door
Lan-hee Lee: Lan-hee
Woon-seop Shin: Truck driver
Seung-yeon Lee: Senior**
—

Filming locations
**Jeongseon City, South Korea
Gangneung City, South Korea**
—

Format
HD
—

Awards for Daytime Drinking
**Jeonju International
Film Festival
    (JJ-Star Award, Audience
    Critics Award, 2008)**
— —

Hyuk-jin drinks on the beach with his next-door neighbors.

Hyuk-jin drinks with a truck driver.

A woman Hyuk-jin meets in the bus station tells him where she is headed.

Hyuk-jin, Ki-sang, and Ki-sang's friend drink together near the river.

The lives of six inhabitants of Soviet-era tower blocks are united by feelings of loneliness. Mati (Rain Tolk), a writer, spends his time spying on his ex-wife and unsuccessfully approaching other women. Augusti (Sulevi Peltola), a barber, lives a drab existence as a bachelor and befriends a little girl, only to be accused of pedophilia. Laura (Maarja Jakobson), a single mom, watches sappy soap operas and pushes away men's advances. Maurer (Juhan Ulfsak), an architect, ponders the well-being of humanity, but forgets his own wife (Tiina Tauraite), who in turn looks for solace in the coatroom attendant, Theo (Taavi Eelmaa).

VEIKO ÕUNPUU
AUTUMN BALL

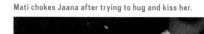
Mati chokes Jaana after trying to hug and kiss her.

Mati stands on the balcony prior to confronting his wife.

Toward the end of *Autumn Ball* (*Sügisball*, 2007), a moody doorman at a nightclub/restaurant drags out a drunken patron and, upon learning that he writes "relationship comedies," beats him to a bloody pulp. The moment is probably the most macabre bit of black comedy in Veiko Õunpuu's funny-sad feature debut, but it's representative of the simultaneously bleak and ridiculous humor in its stories. A stoic architect, a nervous divorced mother, a creepy barber—nobody in this slice of Tallinn, Estonia, seems very happy, about the past, the present, or the future.

Is it possible to be excited and a little apprehensive about a promising filmmaker? Õunpuu's visually stunning film pulls no punches in its portraits of desperate souls; the laughter can curdle into pity, sadness, and (as with the beating) even horror—and back—without much warning. In the first fifteen minutes, we watch a suicidal writer nearly strangling his wife when she tries to leave him, then a pretentious architect's wife asking her husband why they live in a drab housing complex, and finally, a chunky guy in a bellhop uniform grooving to "Beat It" by Michael Jackson.

Getting a handle on the film's shifting tales, which do not link up neatly, can be a challenge, but a common strand is an anxiety about how best to lead one's life, or at least how to maintain hope. Should the architect give up the pretensions to humility he claims by living where he and his wife do? Can the writer pull himself together, or should we even care when he pathetically and incompetently stalks his ex and drunkenly harasses other women? And do either of these concerns seem important alongside the pitiful factory-worker mother whose preteen daughter has attracted the eye of a middle-aged barber? Each character seems poised at a tipping point, though Õunpuu also seems intent on finding the pratfall in their topple into the abyss.

Before making movies, Õunpuu floated between various jobs (carpet sales, advertising) and studies (painting, semiotics), and he seems to have developed a writerly skepticism about a lot of things. The nattily dressed creative types in the film are suffused with anxieties about compromising ideals; the bookish doorman has a lot of sex but gets little satisfaction (or respect) from his partners. The slightly farcical deadpan that hovers over many scenes has the tendency to put everyone on the same level. Õunpuu, who comes across as self-deprecating and enthusiastic in interviews, has suggested as much about his philosophy on the characters: "The quality of our existence is not conditioned by our social status and position in the hierarchies of the world." His latest film, *The Temptation of St. Tony* (2010), which had its U.S. premiere at the Sundance Film Festival, centers on a much-praised middle manager facing a moral and existential crisis.

Autumn Ball was adapted from the book by another Estonian, the writer and theater director Mati Unt, whose work also yielded the source for Õunpuu's short, *Empty* (*Tühirand*, 2006). The characters' uncertainty about their station and identity comes to reflect the growing pains of the country at large, as it deals with independence since the dissolution of the Soviet Union. But Õunpuu's mordant humor applies here too: in one cheeky scene, the doorman picks up an academic at a conference that purports to be about "Baltic consciousness." Some have compared Õunpuu's comedy to that of the Finnish filmmaker Aki Kaurismäki, but the unpredictability of its events also bears comparison to the surreal Russian meltdown rendered in Ilya Khrzhanovsky's *4* (2005).

Working with his usual cinematographer, Mart Taniel, Õunpuu intersperses the tragicomic scenes with glacially beautiful long shots of the city. Some dramatic moments run hypnotically with music instead of sound, drawing especially on the apocalyptic esoterica of Canadian band Godspeed You! Black Emperor. And Õunpuu always has an eye for a particularly vivid detail in the background: a poster for the movie *Love Streams* (1984) in the writer's apartment, a depressing row of empty jars at the doorman's bachelor pad, or simply a TV playing *The Thorn Birds* that sends the young mother into tears.

Tucked in at the end of the credits, Õunpuu dedicates his film to "all the men with gentle heart and weak liver who stand alone in the night in underwear." With this final gesture, the filmmaker declares himself to be on the side of the sufferers, and not a mordant puppeteer looking down on his odd playthings. When the architect's wife sleeps with the doorman, but flees when he mentions his plans for a career in waste management, his baffled and hurt reaction is simple and true: "What just happened?" In the films to come, we can rely on Õunpuu to confront what does happen when cracks open up in our little worlds.

After being attacked, Jaana sits alone while Mati takes some pills in the kitchen.

Year and place of birth
1972   Saaremaa, Estonia
—

Lives and works in
Tallinn, Estonia
—

Education
Estonian Institute of Humanities,
   University of Tallinn, Estonia
Estonian Academy of Arts,
   Tallinn, Estonia
—

Filmography
2006   Empty (Tühirand) (short)
2007   Autumn Ball (Sügisball)
2009   The Temptation of
   St. Tony (Püha Tõnu
   kiusamine)
—

Director's awards
Empty
Estonian Film Critics' Award
   (Best Feature, 2006)
National Festival of
Estonian Film
   (Best Film, 2006)
Tallinn Black Nights Film Festival
   (Best Estonian Film, 2006)
European Talent Award
   (2007)
— —

Release date
2007
—

Country of release
Estonia
—

Language
Estonian
—

Running time
123 min.
—

Genre
Drama
—

Producer
Katrin Kissa
—

Writer
Veiko Õunpuu
—

Cinematographer
Mart Taniel
—

Score
Ulo Krigul
—

Key cast
Rain Tolk: Mati
Taavi Eelmaa: Theo
Juhan Ulfsak: Maurer
Sulevi Peltola: Augusti Kaski
Tiina Tauraite: Maurer's wife
Maarja Jakobson: Laura
Mirtel Pohla: Jaana
—

Filming location
Tallinn, Estonia
—

Format
35 mm
—

Awards for Autumn Ball
Bratislava International
Film Festival
   (Best Director, 2007)
Estonian Film Critics' Award
   (Best Estonian Film, 2007)
European Film Festival Estoril
   (Special Jury Prize, 2007)
Festival d'Angers Premiers Plans
   (Best Original Music, 2007)

Marrakech International
Film Festival
   (Golden Star, Grand Prix,
   2007)
Tallinn Black Nights Film Festival
   (Special Jury Prize, Best
   Actress, Best Estonian Film,
   FICC Award, 2007)
Thessaloniki International
Film Festival
   (Best Director, 2007)
Venice International Film Festival
   (Venice Horizons Award,
   Orizzonti Prize, 2007)
Cinema Jove – Valencia
International Film Festival
   (Golden Moon of Valencia,
   2008)
— —

Mati sees Jaana in his dream.

Mati on his way to spy on Jaana.

Theo takes a smoking break while attending the coatroom.

Ulvi rushes across the desolate field. Theo runs after her.

THEO: Please wait! Wait!

Ulvi lets him stop her.

THEO: What just happened?

ULVI: Nothing happened. I just have to go.

THEO: But I thought...we had something. Don't say you didn't feel it.

ULVI: Yes, I felt it.

Ulvi quickly kisses Theo before walking away.

Amongst the daily commuter mania, the lives and dreams of three young men working in the gridlock on Istanbul's Bosphorus Bridge unknowingly intersect. Fikret (Fikret Portakal) sells roses illegally and strives for a regular job, Murat (Murat Tokgöz) is a lonely traffic policeman who uses the Internet to find dating opportunities, and Umut (Umut Ilker) is a taxi driver searching for a better apartment in order to satisfy his wife's cravings. The men who were the inspiration for the story appear as themselves enabling a realistic glimpse of Turkish urban life.

ASLI ÖZGE
MEN ON THE BRIDGE

Murat chats with a girl on the Internet while his roommate Serkan mocks him.

Fikret tries to sell flowers to drivers stuck in traffic on the Bosphorus Bridge.

Imagine a city divided by a wide expanse of sea, by the diversity of its historical heritage, and by economic and cultural imbalances. A "cradle of civilizations," boasting unrivaled beauty—owing largely to its preserved geographical features—and home to civilizations and religions long past. Istanbul surely suffices to fulfill a Westerner's orientalist fantasies, with the common faulty perception of itself being a Western city—a misinterpretation that it carries as a burden. And then imagine a film that plays on this pseudo self-image of a megalopolis that has its eyes turned to the West while seated in the East. Asli Özge's *Men on the Bridge* (*Köprüdekiler*, 2009) is set on the Bosphorus Bridge, built on the stretch of water that divides the city into two symbolically diverse, contradicting parts: Europe and Asia.

The bridge, which joins two parts of the city, and two continents that have since millennia represented opposing forces, is the focus of Özge's film. One of its main characters, a symbol as large as life—indeed, representative of life—the bridge is a microcosm of Istanbul, a megacity that has set its diverse communities as far apart from one another as possible. Three representatives of these communities, three spines of an urban backbone, are represented in the film.

Fikret is a style-conscious seventeen-year-old who sells roses illegally on the bridge. Raised on the streets and without education, he hopes for a better life. Umut, twenty-eight, drives a shared taxi, passing Fikret on the bridge nearly every day. He is newly married and his wife, Cemile, desires the lifestyle she sees on television. Umut wants to fulfill her wishes, and

they visit real estate agents in search of a better apartment. Despite what his name suggests ("umut" means hope in Turkish), he is distracted, uninspired, and unhappy in his marriage. Murat is a twenty-four-year-old traffic policeman who was recently transferred from a small town to the big city. Squeezed between millions of cars, Murat feels alone. He spends his evenings at home searching for a girlfriend online.

All three characters live in the suburbs of Istanbul and come to work in the city's center, the main vein, the throbbing pulse. The strangers intersect during rush hour along with millions of other Istanbulites. Their dreams are vibrant, fragile, and vivid, unlike the faces of anonymous drivers passing by, honking their way across the bridge. Basically, the bridge is a passage, a sort of purgatory and symbol of the path that leads from the East to the West. Fikret, Murat, and Umut are somehow trapped on the bridge, in this purgatory, and it actually doesn't matter whether they are crossing to the European or the Asian side. As long as they remain on the bridge, their dreams cannot be realized.

Özge had at first intended to make a documentary that by following these three characters would reveal her multilayered hometown of Istanbul. (She currently divides her time between the city and Berlin, which, interestingly, like Istanbul, was at one time split between East and West.) However, after extensive research in Istanbul starting in 2006, she was so intrigued by her original subjects that she decided to instead write a screenplay based on the lives of these three men. And thus *Men on the*

Bridge became a fiction feature in which the real-life characters—Fikret, Umut, and Murat—starred as themselves in their original environments. The film's working title of Rush Hour was aptly changed to *Men on the Bridge* right before its world premiere at the Istanbul International Film Festival, where it won the prize for the Best Turkish Film of the Year in the National Competition.

The originality of *Men on the Bridge* doesn't lie in its plot, or in the fact that it uses nonprofessional actors. Its power comes mainly from its unique strength of observation, no doubt originating from the perspective of the director—who, as a young, dynamic woman, had chosen the path of a documentarian. With a sense of immediacy, Özge searches the traces of grace still found in Istanbul following a sprawling history. The film is all too real—so real that it forms a blurry bond between fact and fiction, like its protagonists, and like the bridge itself. The three colliding stories reflect the anxieties, contradictions, and hopes of their heroes, which are typical of a new, globalized world. Fikret, Murat, and Umut aspire for more than they're handed—the comings and goings of the many vehicles that pass over the bridge, traveling from one continent to the other, represents this as well. The characters aim beyond local boundaries.

Men on the Bridge is a fresh look at Turkish urban life that employs an unprecedented technical and narrative structure in Turkish cinema. Asli Özge is certainly a director to watch, whether she's making documentaries or fiction films.

After visiting a real estate agent, Umut and his wife Cemile realize they can't afford a better apartment.

Year and place of birth
1975   Istanbul, Turkey
—

Lives and works in
Istanbul, Turkey
Berlin, Germany
—

Education
Marmara University,
    Istanbul, Turkey
—

Filmography
2000   *Capital C* (short)
2003   *Little Bit of April*
        (*Ein bisschen April*)
2005   *Hespero's Apprentices*
2009   *Men on the Bridge*
        (*Köprüdekiler*)
—

Director's awards
Capital C
Ankara International Film
Festival
    (Best Short Fiction Film
    Award, 2000)
Antalya Golden Orange Film
Festival
    (Best Dramatic Video Award,
    2000)
Istanbul International Short
Film Festival
    (Best Short Fiction Film
    Award, 2001)

Little Bit of April
Junior Chamber
International Turkey
    (TOYP Cultural Achievement
    Award, 2002)
— —

Release date
2010
—

Country of release
Turkey
—

Language
Turkish
—

Running time
87 min.
—

Genre
Drama
—

Producers
Fabian Massah, Asli Özge
—

Writer
Aslı Özge
—

Cinematographer
Emre Erkmen
—

Key cast
Fikret Portakal: Fikret
Murat Tokgöz: Murat
Umut Ilker: Umut
Cemile Ilker: Cemile
—

Filming location
Istanbul, Turkey
—

Format
HD

Awards for *Men on the Bridge*
Adana Golden Boll International
Film Festival
    (Best Film, National
    Competition, 2009)
Istanbul International Film
Festival
    (Best Turkish Film, National
    Competition, 2009)
London Turkish
Film Festival
    (Golden Wings Digital
    Distribution Award, 2009)
— —

Umut and Cemile watch fireworks over the Bosphorus on Turkey's national holiday.

Fikret walks along the street and sees a job offer in a display window.

After a lonely stroll on his day off, Murat reflects by the water and calls his mother.

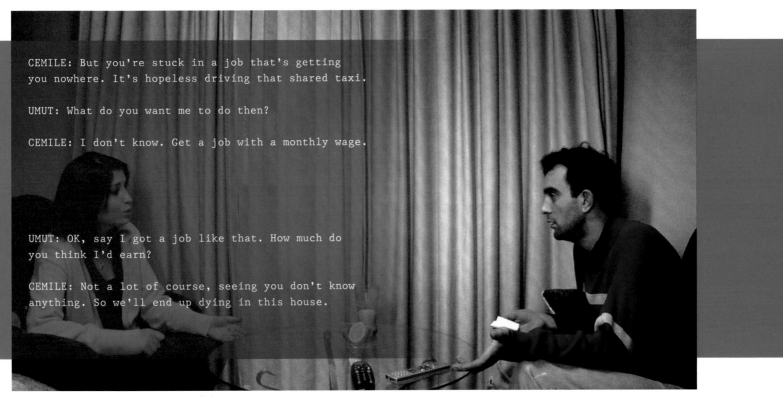

CEMILE: But you're stuck in a job that's getting you nowhere. It's hopeless driving that shared taxi.

UMUT: What do you want me to do then?

CEMILE: I don't know. Get a job with a monthly wage.

UMUT: OK, say I got a job like that. How much do you think I'd earn?

CEMILE: Not a lot of course, seeing you don't know anything. So we'll end up dying in this house.

Umut and Cemile argue about money.

This film follows three stories—those of a grandfather, father, and son—linked together by recurring motifs. The dim grandfather, an orderly during World War II, lives in his bizarre fantasies. The father seeks success as a top athlete in the postwar Soviet era. The grandson, a meek, small-boned taxidermist, yearns for something greater: immortality. He wants to create the most perfect work of art of all time by stuffing his own torso. Historical fact and surrealism become intertwined in this film, based in part on the stories of Hungarian writer Lajos Parti Nagy.

GYORGY PALFI
TAXIDERMIA

LIEUTENANT: Morosgoványi!

VENDEL: Yes, Lieutenant!

LIEUTENANT: What day is today, Morosgoványi?

VENDEL: Saturday, Lieutenant.

LIEUTENANT: Second Saturday.

VENDEL: Bathing Saturday, Lieutenant.

LIEUTENANT: What does a batman do on bathing Saturday?

VENDEL: I humbly report the batman is obliged to set up the tube in a kitchen heated up for the purpose, to render it stable on four...or six sides, then to fill it up with boiling water of the right temperature from the cauldron...

Lieutenant gives orders to Vendel.

György Pálfi burst onto the international scene with his first feature-length film, *Hukkle*, in 2002. *Hukkle* introduced the director's surreal outlook on life with its hyperdetailed focus on the weird daily rituals of a remote Hungarian village. This quirky, silent comedy received great critical acclaim on the film festival circuit and led to his bigger-budget second feature, *Taxidermia* (2006). Pálfi was drawn to the stories of Hungarian writer Lajos Parti Nagy, because he felt they shared the same vision of the world: a strange mixture of realism and mysterious, magical elements. *Taxidermia* weaves two different short stories by Parti Nagy into a single narrative with additions from the director himself. Pálfi is clearly aiming to push the boundaries of taste in contemporary cinema, and there are few taboos that are left unbroken in his second feature.

The story is split into three narratives with each protagonist fathering the next. The three men are united by the habits of self-flagellation and obsessive behavior, which ultimately lead to their humiliation and sense of failure. The description may seem bleak, but the elements of the story are bound together with idiosyncratic humor and compelling visual techniques, some of which take the form of grotesque body horror.

The first generation of this degenerative family is Morosgoványi Vendel, a witless army orderly serving a family in World War II. Vendel is consumed with the urge for sexual intimacy, and every aspect of his daily life becomes a lustful outlet for his depravity. The two younger women of the household are the main focus of his desires, and he spies on them at every

opportunity. In one scene, he lubricates and penetrates a knothole in the wood shed while watching the girls have a snowball fight. He is humorously denied sexual gratification when a rooster pecks his penis. Vendel is permitted one final taste of intimacy when he has sex with Irma, the officer's wife, who also craves the warmth of another human being. The pleasure comes at a price: he is executed by his commanding officer, Orëg, and the child is born with a pig's tail.

Vendel's son is adopted by Orëg and named Balatony Kálmán, which leads to a new story arc following Kálmán's life as a Soviet international speed-eater. Where Vendel obsessed over sexual intimacy, Kálmán is immersed in the world of eating competitions. As with the painful sexual experiences of his father, Kálmán's gluttony becomes a form of self-punishment. He is forced to gorge himself at competitions and in training, repeatedly vomiting the contents so that he can continue.

The third and final narrative of the film is the tale of Kálmán's offspring, Balatony Lajoska, a taxidermist. Small and thin, Lajoska is the physical opposite of his father. Kálmán figures in the story, but he is now hideously obese and homebound, in a clear parody of Monty Python's Mr. Creosote (from *The Meaning of Life*, 1983). He perishes when his own overfed cats start eating him alive, and his son can only react to these horrific events through his own obsession, taxidermy. Lajoska stuffs the body of his dead father and then proceeds to stuff his own as well, while he is still alive. This ingenious process is shot in hideous detail, featuring many close-ups

of internal organs and the slicing of flesh. The scenes are graphic and abhorrent but also strangely compelling in their detail. Lajoska contrives a machine that will ultimately decapitate him and remove his unstuffed arm to produce a grotesque taxidermic parody of both Michelangelo's *David* and the *Venus de Milo*. At the conclusion of the film, we see that the literati herald the act as great art, and that Lajoska and his father have achieved a kind of immortality.

Pálfi weaves these three tales together expertly with a strong thematic narrative and beautiful technical virtuosity. Long crane shots contrast with extreme close-ups to simultaneously distance us from the characters and underline the intensely personal nature of the three stories. With a larger budget for this production, Pálfi was able to attempt complex maneuvers such as a stunning 360-degree tracking shot around a wooden bath that encompasses all aspects of Vendel's life in one seamless movement. Not only does Pálfi seem indebted to Monty Python for the obese Kálmán, but many of his surrealist elements are reminiscent of Terry Gilliam's oeuvre. *Taxidermia* has a hyperreal sense of grotesque detail, and yet the characterization of each protagonist firmly grounds the film in the real world.

Pálfi is clearly not a director who can be pigeon-holed. His first feature was a silent comedy, his second a bizarre surreal landscape, and his new film, *I Am Not Your Friend* (*Nem vagyok a barátod*, 2009), rejects stylized visuals for an improvised emotional tour de force. The only sure thing to expect from György Pálfi's next project is that it will be unexpected.

Speed eating at the Eastern Bloc Contest.

Kálmán's trainer times the speed of his champion.

Year and place of birth
1974   Budapest, Hungary
—
Lives and works in
Budapest, Hungary
—
Education
**Theatre and Film Academy,
    Budapest, Hungary**
—
Filmography
**1993   Break & Csekk II (short)
1997   A hal (short)
1997   The Fish – Ichthys (short)
1999   Round and Round (short)
1999   Devil's Knot, The 7th
    Room in the Knock Knock
    (short)
2002   Hukkle
2003   A Bus Came...
    ("ShaMan and Ikarus")
2006   Taxidermia
2008   Poker Ace and People's
    Best Friend (short)
2009   I Am Not Your Friend
    (Nem vagyok a barátod)**
—
Director's awards
Hukkle
**European Film Awards
    (European Discovery
    of the Year, 2002)
Film Festival Cottbus
    (Audience Award, FIPRESCI
    Prize, First Work Award
    of the Student Jury, Special
    Prize for an Outstanding
    Artistic Contribution, 2002)**

**Hungarian Film Week
    (Best Debut Film,
    Gene Moskowitz Critics
    Award, 2002)
Molodist International
Film Festival
    (Festival Diploma –
    Best Full-Length Feature
    Film, 2002)
San Sebastián International
Film Festival
    (Special Mention –
    Best New Director, 2002)
Sante Fe Film Festival
    (Luminaria for
    Best Feature, 2002)
Cleveland International
Film Festival
    (Best Eastern European
    Film, 2003)
Hong Kong International
Film Festival
    (Golden Firebird Award, 2003)
Hungarian Film Critics Awards
    (László B. Nagy Award, 2003)
Sochi International Film Festival
    (Golden Rose, 2003)
Titanic International
Film Festival
    (Audience Award, 2003)
Torun Young European
Film Festival
    (Main Prize, 2003)**
— —

Release date
2006
—
Country of release
Hungary
—
Language
Hungarian
—
Running time
90 min.
—
Genre
Drama
—
Producers
**Alexander Dumreicher-
Ivanceanu, Emilie Georges,
Gabriele Kranzelbinder,
Alexandre Mallet-Guy**
—
Writers
György Pálfi, Zsófi Ruttkay
—

Cinematographer
Gergely Pohárnok
—
Score
Amon Tobin
—
Key cast
**Csaba Czene:
    Morosgoványi Vendel
Gergely Trócsányi:
    Balatony Kálmán
Piroska Molnár: Hadnagyné
Adél Stanczel: Aczél Gizi
Marc Bischoff: Balatony Lajoska
Gábor Máté: Öreg
    Balatony Kálmán
Zoltán Koppány: Miszlényi Béla
Géza Hegedüs D.:
    Dr. Regőczy Andor**
—
Filming locations
**Budapest, Hungary
Vienna, Austria**
—
Format
35 mm

Awards for *Taxidermia*
**Antalya Golden Orange
Film Festival
    (Eurasia Film Festival
    Award – Best Director, 2006)
Brussels European Film Festival
    (Iris Award for Best Film,
    2006)
Film Festival Cottbus
    (Don Quijote Award, 2006)
Hungarian Film Critics Awards
    (Best Actor, Best Director,
    Best Supporting Actress,
    2006)
Hungarian Film Week
    (Best Supporting Actor,
    Best Supporting Actress,
    Gene Moskowitz Critics
    Award, Grand Prize, 2006)
Mexico City International
Contemporary Film Festival
    (FICCO Prize for
    Best Director, 2006)
Tallinn Black Nights Film Festival
    (Estonian Film Critics
    Award, 2006)**

Transilvania International
Film Festival
    (Best Director, 2006)
Fantasporto
    **(Audience Jury Award,
    2007)**
— —

Gizi and Kálmán enjoy their holiday at Lake Balaton.

Lajoska polishes the bear's nails.

The love life of karaoke waitress Shirley (Tao Hong) and her boyfriend Ken (Daniel Wu) is stable until the day Ken's ex-girlfriend, Ching (Gillian Chung), comes to see her. After their breakup, Ken had posted an erotic picture online that cost Ching her job. Immediately realizing that she too could head down the same track, Shirley joins forces with Ching to infiltrate Ken's home and retrieve her nude photos as well. Ching and Shirley soon grow supportive of each other, and a unique friendship develops between them.

HO-CHEUNG PANG
BEYOND OUR KEN

Ching cries at the supermarket after her breakup with Ken.

Shirley takes a birthday cake to the VIP room.

You might say that Hong Kong's Ho-Cheung Pang is one of the most loquacious directors of our time. Pang's greatest enjoyment in his films is to comment upon the situations his characters face by extensively quoting and reworking motifs from film history.

Beyond Our Ken (*Gung ju fuk sau gei*, 2004) explores the dramatic revenge that Ching, a woman with a broken heart, carries out against her ex-boyfriend Ken. Ching meets Shirley, Ken's current girlfriend, and they develop a friendship that allows them to share their honest feelings about Ken—a situation that brings the two women into the delicate territory of psychological tension and contradiction. Ching finds it difficult to forget Ken even as she criticizes him, while Shirley finds it difficult to leave Ken even though she knows about his sordid past. Pang incessantly comments on this peculiar situation throughout his film. Though revenge lends shape to the story, the goal of the narrative is actually to expose and explore the familiar desires of city dwellers over the course of various dramatic developments.

This layered style of storytelling is a recurring feature of Pang's work. For instance, *Men Suddenly in Black* (*Daai cheung foo*, 2003) opens with the declaration that it is "based on an actual event that took place in 2002," but simply viewing the film reveals this statement as untrue. The "actual event" is a ridiculous situation in which four married men connive to have affairs while their wives are away. As soon as their significant others leave for the airport, the four men carefully prepare everything necessary for their mission: cash, condoms, prepaid mobile phones, and a car with a driver. However, the women soon sniff out their scheme and immediately pursue their men. The ensuing action challenges our ingrained perceptions of masculinity and femininity, and here too Pang chooses vengeance as his theme while at the same time departing from convention in his execution.

Men Suddenly in Black reinterprets styles that are staples of Hong Kong genres such as film noir and martial arts. For instance, the image of Eric Tsang burning incense for the success of an extramarital affair recalls his performance as Triad boss Hon Sam, who burnt incense in the crime-thriller *Infernal Affairs* (*Mou gaan dou*, 2002). Later, Pang stages a scene in which the men are confronted by private detectives as a shoot-out, with their cameras as the guns.

Much as *Men Suddenly in Black* reworks crime films, *Beyond Our Ken* recapitulates motifs from familiar genres, in this case an assortment of melodramatic styles. The characters' tears and rage echo the formulaic acting patterns of typical Hong Kong films. Yet instead of downplaying these similarities, Pang quotes their analogues in film history. He reveals that his characters are indeed living self-conscious, cinematic lives, and that Hong Kong is the embodiment of a film set. This is what distinguishes Pang from his fellow filmmakers. He is not afraid to show that he has a firm handle on his sources as he aggressively parodies and quotes varied genres, while peppering the film with his own stylistic twists.

Pang's films are also of great import as explorations of Hong Kong film history and as opportunities for historical reflection. He references living directors such as John Woo, Wong Kar-wai, and Andrew Lau Wai-keung, as well as martial arts classics from the past. His works may seem like simple comedies, and while he does reference Stephen Chow, a pillar of the genre in Hong Kong, Pang avoids being pigeonholed into one type of humor by tapping into black comedy and satire.

Like other Hong Kong filmmakers, Pang turns out his films rapidly. Yet his work is not merely about speed and comic wit. One of Pang's most distinctive characteristics is the ability to deconstruct Hong Kong film while caricaturing the extent to which formulaic conventions have come to dominate the industry in recent years. This is also Pang's way of reengaging with Hong Kong's history. For instance, *Exodus* (*Cheut ai kup gei*, 2007) is set in 1996, the year before the transfer of sovereignty to China. The main character quits his job as a cop and plans a move to Tokyo with his wife, but whether he will be able to achieve this dream before 1997 is unknown. The film is therefore structured as a mystery that evokes the apprehensive mood that preceded the transfer.

For Pang, quoting and referencing the history and film of Hong Kong is a process of remembering the past and an introspective means of understanding where contemporary feelings of unease are rooted. Thus, the humor he throws at us is tinged with bitterness, and his films suggest a sense that something is missing. However, this feigned lack is what allows us the space to interpret our own histories and perspectives, and precisely what makes Ho-Cheung Pang the leading filmmaker in Hong Kong today.

Ken and Shirley kiss on the staircase.

Year and place of birth
1973, Hong Kong
—
Lives and works in
Hong Kong
—
Filmography
2001   *You Shoot, I Shoot*
       (Maai hung paak yan)
2003   *Men Suddenly In Black*
       (Daai cheung foo)
2004   *Beyond Our Ken*
       (Gung ju fuk sau gei)
2005   *A.V.*
2006   *Isabella*
       (Yi sa bui lai)
2007   *Exodus*
       (Cheut ai kup gei)
2007   *Trivial Matters*
       (Por see yee)
—
Director's awards
You Shoot, I Shoot
Hong Kong Golden Bauhinia
Film Awards
   (Best Screenplay, 2002)
Hong Kong Film Awards
   (Best Debut Director Award,
   2007)

Men Suddenly In Black
Hong Kong Film Critics'
Association
   (Top 10 Chinese Movies,
   2003)
Hong Kong Film Awards
   (Best New Director, 2004)
Hong Kong Film Critics Society
   (Film of Merit, 2004)

A.V.
Hong Kong Golden Bauhinia
Film Awards
   (Top 10 Chinese Movies,
   2006)

Isabella
World Film Festival of Bangkok
   (Best Feature Film, 2006)
Oporto International
Film Festival
   (Best Film Orient Express
   Award, 2007)

Exodus
Hong Kong Golden Bauhinia
Film Awards
   (Best Creative Awards, 2007)
— —

Release date
2004
—
Country of release
Hong Kong
—
Language
Cantonese, Mandarin
—
Running time
98 min.
—
Genre
Drama
—
Producer
Catherine Hun
—

Writers
**Ho-Cheung Pang,
Wong Wing Sze**
—
Cinematographer
Charlie Lam
—
Score
Alan Wong, Janet Yung
—

Key cast
**Gillian Chung: Chan Wai Ching
Tao Hong: Shirley
Daniel Wu: Ken
Jim Chim: Shirley's ex-boyfriend**
—
Filming location
Hong Kong
—
Format
35 mm

Awards for *Beyond Our Ken*
Hong Kong Golden Bauhinia
Film Awards
   (Top 10 Chinese Movies,
   Best Screenplay, 2005)
— —

Ching thinks about stealing Ken's key in the cinema.

Ching rides a motorcycle across town.

CHING: Dad says I was a scumbag magnet since I was little. He thinks all my boyfriends are scumbags. So I never dare introduce them to my parents.

Ching and Shirley listen to music and discuss their lives.

In Sarah Polley's mesmerizing adaption of an Alice Munro short story, we get to know the aging couple Fiona (Julie Christie) and Grant (Gordon Pinsent), struggling to come to terms with the newfound realization that Fiona is developing Alzheimer's disease. The decision to move Fiona into a nursing home tests the couple's bond, particularly during the first thirty days, when the facility has a no-visitors' policy. Grant must learn to come to terms with Fiona's new relationships in the nursing home and the gradual but widening distance between the two of them.

SARAH POLLEY
AWAY FROM HER

Fiona and Grant, cross-country skiing near their home.

Sarah Polley was born into acting . . . but I feel that she was born to direct. That's not to say she isn't one of the finest actors of her generation—she is. Rather, it's a commentary on her complete understanding of the art of film. Her acting choices have always been about the art, not the commerce. Thus, we can take those choices as a means to work with certain esteemed directors, like David Cronenberg, Atom Egoyan, and Hal Hartley, to witness their technique firsthand. Polley is as renowned for her intelligence as she is for her remarkable talent. A problem with the intelligent person as a performer is that he or she is not ultimately in control of the medium. But whereas actors are a piece of the puzzle, directors put it together.

Her coming-out effort as a director was a short called *Don't Think Twice* (1999), a stubbornly antagonistic look at infidelity and the dark nature of man. Her second short, *I Shout Love* (2001), was more refined and truly showed off her gift for directing. It's a compelling, occasionally wrenching drama about a woman who convinces her reluctant soon-to-be-ex-boyfriend to reenact on video significant moments of their relationship. It's a brave and mature depiction of the histrionics of emotional desperation, and the acumen Polley exhibited handling these themes made it even clearer that she was destined for great things as a director. However, it was just the tip of the iceberg of her directing prowess, which would be fully unleashed with her feature debut, *Away from Her* (2006).

The film is based on Alice Munro's "The Bear Came Over the Mountain," a powerfully moving and insightful short story pitched from the point of view of a bereaved husband facing the onset of Alzheimer's in his wife. There are many pitfalls that could accompany making a film about someone with Alzheimer's. It could easily become manipulative in a way that belittles the intricacies of the situation, but Polley delicately paints the little moments and actions that can say so much more than the monumental ones.

The film begins with Fiona, played by Julie Christie, and her retired husband Grant, played by Gordon Pinsent, washing the dishes together. Grant hands her a frying pan, and he just looks on silently as she puts it in the freezer. Polley reveals that Grant's love for his wife blinds him to the inevitable and that it will be up to Fiona to check herself into the hospital. Before she does, Polley leads us in that direction, subtly conveying Fiona's inner struggles. When she can't remember how to ask her dinner guests if they would like some more wine, she pauses and instead says she feels like she's disappearing. This is a complex notion, yet Polley figures out ways to represent it visually. In one scene, Fiona is cross-country skiing and forgets her way home. She finds herself alone in the woods, which Polley captures with a beautiful, haunting overhead shot that looks down at Fiona lying there consumed by the white snow that symbolizes her fading memories.

It is remarkable that a film with such heart-wrenching pain is also so filled with humor. When Fiona leaves a disquieting doctor's visit and sees a baby cutely sitting on its mothers lap, she says, "What an ugly baby." Another brilliant stroke of humor comes when Fiona reads through medical texts about all of the hardships that spouses deal with in caring for a loved one with Alzheimer's and says, "Sounds like a regular marriage."

Another thing that distinguishes the film is Polley's decision to make Fiona the strong one. It would have been easier and more obvious for her to be the victim and Grant the heroic one. One of the few times Fiona's resolve cracks is in the devastating scene in which she is first admitted to the hospital and tells Grant that she would like to make love, but then asks him to leave because if he makes her time there more difficult she might cry so hard she'll never stop. Julie Christie in the role of Fiona conveys all of the complexities involved in "disappearing." Her eyes express the inner turmoil buried beneath layers of strength, brought on by trying to remember the past—and the comfort that comes from not trying.

Perhaps Polley's smartest choice came in casting such magnificent actors. Gordon Pinsent's Grant is gruff and bearish on the outside yet fragile and confused on the inside. Julie Christie's Fiona is gorgeous and exquisitely blank. Throughout her career there was always something remote and vaguely chilly about her beauty—and never has that chill been used so effectively as by Polley.

Polley's final stamp of maturity in her direction comes at the end of the film. While it would have been easy to fade out on a down note, she instead shows Fiona and Grant dancing, followed by a shot of a young Fiona when she still had the "spark of life." That spark is something that Polley has to the extreme, and whether in front of or behind the camera, she uses it to enlighten anyone lucky enough to see her graceful work.

Fiona stumbles for a word over dinner with friends.

Year and place of birth
1979 Toronto, Ont., Canada

Lives and works in
Toronto, Ont., Canada
—

Filmography
1999 *Incoherence* (short)
1999 *The Best Day of My Life*
      (short)
2000 *Don't Think Twice* (short)
2001 *I Shout Love* (short)
2006 *Away from Her*
—

Director's awards
I Shout Love
Genie Awards
   (Best Adapted Screenplay,
   2003)
— —

Release date
2007
—

Country of release
USA
—

Language
English
—

Running time
110 min.
—

Genre
Drama
—

Producers
Daniel Iron, Jennifer Weiss,
Simone Urdl
—

Writer
Sarah Polley
—

Cinematographer
Luc Montpellier
—

Score
Neil Young
—

Key cast
Gordon Pinsent: Grant Anderson
Julie Christie: Fiona Anderson
Stacey LaBerge: Young Fiona
Olympia Dukakis: Marian
Deanna Dezmari: Veronica
Grace Lynn Kung: Nurse Betty
Michael Murphy: Aubrey
—

Filming locations
Kitchener, Ont., Canada
Hamilton, Ont., Canada
Lake of Bays, Ont., Canada
Paris, Ont., Canada
Toronto Film Studios, Ont.,
   Canada
—

Format
35 mm
—

Awards for *Away from Her*
Directors Guild of Canada
   (DGC Craft Award Direction,
   Best Picture Editing,
   DGC Team Award, 2007)
New York Film Critics
Circle Awards
   (Best Actress,
   Best First Film, 2007)
Phoenix Film Critics
Society Awards
   (Best Performance by
   an Actress in a Leading
   Role, Breakthrough
   Behind the Camera, 2007)
Sedona International
Film Festival
   (Excellence in Filmmaking,
   2007)
Writers Guild of Canada
   (WGC Award Feature Film,
   2007)
Chlotrudis Awards
   (Best Adapted Screenplay,
   2008)

Genie Awards
   (Claude Jutra Award,
   Best Achievement
   in Direction, Best Motion
   Picture, Best Performance
   by an Actor in a Leading
   Role, Best Performance
   by an Actress in a Leading
   Role, Best Performance by
   an Actress in a Supporting
   Role, Best Adapted
   Screenplay, 2008)
Golden Globes
   (Best Performance by an
   Actress in a Motion Picture
   Drama, 2008)
Screen Actors Guild Awards
   (Outstanding Performance
   by a Female Actor in
   a Leading Role, 2008)
— —

Fiona comforts Grant about her move.

Grant drops by to bring Fiona some books and finds her spending time with Aubrey.

Cristi (Dragos Bucur) is a policeman who refuses to arrest a young man who offers hashish to two of his schoolmates. In Romania, even offering drugs is punished severely by the law, but Cristi believes that the law will change. He does not want to bear the burden of a young man's fate, one whom he considers merely irresponsible. To Cristi's boss (Vlad Ivanov), however, the word conscience has a totally different meaning.

CORNELIU PORUMBOIU
POLICE, ADJECTIVE

Cristi outside Alex's home, on a stakeout.

Alex, Victor, and Doina smoke in the schoolyard.

Corneliu Porumboiu has been described as the herald of a new wave of Romanian cinema. His first feature, *12:08 East of Bucharest* (*A fost sau n-a fost?*, 2006), won the Camera d'Or at the Cannes Film Festival, and with fellow Romanian directors Cristian Mungiu and Cristi Puiu, he has become part of a golden age for Eastern European film. The title *12:08 East of Bucharest* refers to the exact time that Romanian dictator Nicolae Ceaușescu fled his country after the revolution in 1989. Porumboiu sets his films in a post-revolution landscape where the morals and perceptions of society are constantly called into question. In his first feature, Porumboiu questions the notion of revolution, the changes it brought about in his country, and the very definition of the word. In his second film, *Police, Adjective* (*Politist, adj.*, 2009), the director seeks to define conscience and the ways in which it affects our behavior in everyday life.

Cristi is a young detective working in contemporary Romania who suffers a crisis of conscience when he is assigned to tail a teenager, Victor, suspected of dealing drugs. The act of following and the daily routine of this officer become tremendously important as we follow him from moment to moment, often in real time. Large swaths of the film are composed of wordless scenes in which Cristi watches and trails Victor through a bleak urban landscape. These sequences soon arouse our boredom, but we remain connected to the protagonist through a shared mundanity. There is no accompanying soundtrack, and the colors of the film are muted and unexciting. Porumboiu maintains a neutral stance with simple shots and angles; these keep the viewer at a distance from the action and reveal the absurdity of the activity.

Cristi concludes that Victor is guilty of nothing more than sharing hashish with his peers and decides there is no need to prosecute the teenager and ruin his life. These feelings come into direct conflict with the laws he is employed to uphold; possession of marijuana is an offense in Romania punishable by up to seven years in prison. In written reports and meetings with his superiors, Cristi tries to explain the actions of the irresponsible teenager, but his appeals are ignored. He brings up the more relaxed drug policies prevalent in the rest of Europe, drawing attention to the differences between their dysfunctional post-communist society and its political neighbors. Cristi is sure that Romania will relax its laws soon and that prosecution for this offense is unfair to Victor.

The key issues raised by the film are brought to a climax when the young detective proposes to the police captain that they drop the charges. The suggestion leads to a dialectic debate about the nature of conscience. The police captain makes Cristi look up the word, as well as "law" and "moral," in a dictionary to prove that the concept of moral law is meaningless and that the personal feelings of the individual have no bearing on the practice of the police. The conclusion that individuality leads to chaos reminds us that the communist heritage of this country is still having effects in the present day. Cristi's desire to change the strictures of the world around him groups him with the aspirational younger generation that desires reform. The police captain represents the older, more authoritative order, and his simple logic proves to be irrefutable. The entire scene is shot from one unmoving camera angle, focusing the viewer on the content of this all-important argument.

Dragos Bucur was cast as Cristi while the second version of the script was being drafted, and the rest of the actors were cast around him. The long sequences chronicling his professional duties could be oppressive, but subtle humor and a captivating performance from Bucur draws us into the life of the young policeman. Though his existence is depicted as melancholic, we can't help but be amused at the content of his daily life and the characters that surround him, especially the bumbling Nelu (humorously played by Ion Stoica). Ivanov's appearance as the police captain is brief, but it is a commanding performance that focuses the film on the engaging debate on language that gives the film its title.

Police, Adjective is an intensely personal commentary on the director's nation. Porumboiu asked those close to him to help him define the concept of conscience before writing the screenplay, and he shot the film in his hometown of Vaslui. At a time when Romania is struggling to define itself, the film is a subtle and effective commentary on the relationship between the individual and the state. *Police, Adjective* won the Un Certain Regard Jury Prize at Cannes and only gathered more accolades as it toured the festival circuit. Porumboiu is quickly establishing himself as a new master among Romanian filmmakers with his first two witty, insightful productions.

Cristi verifies Doina's last name on the mailbox.

Year and place of birth
1975   Vaslui, Romania
—

Lives and works in
Bucharest, Romania
—

Education
National University of Drama
    and Film, Bucharest, Romania
—

Filmography
2003   *A Trip to the City*
    (*Calatorie la oras*) (short)
2003   *Liviu's Dream*
    (*Visul lui Liviu*) (short)
2006   *12:08 East of Bucharest*
    (*A fost sau n-a fost?*)
2009   *Police, Adjective*
    (*Politist, adj.*)
—

Director's awards
A Trip to the City
CineMAiubit International
Student Film Festival
    (Best Script, Critic's Award,
    2003)
Cannes International Film
Festival
    (Second Prize –
    Cinefondation Award, 2004)
Montpellier Mediterranean
Film Festival
    (Best Short Film, 2004)

Liviu's Dream (*Visul lui Liviu*)
Transilvania International
Film Festival
    (Best Romanian Film, 2004)

12:08 East of Bucharest
Bobbio Film Festival
    (Gobbo d'Oro, 2006)
Cannes International
Film Festival
    (Camera d'Or, Label Europa
    Cinemas, 2006)
Cinessonne European
Film Festival
    (Jury Award, Prix
    Emergence, Student
    Jury Award, 2006)
Copenhagen International
Film Festival
    (Golden Swan for Best Film,
    Best Screenplay, 2006)
Film Festival Cottbus
    (Special Prize for
    an Outstanding Artistic
    Contribution, 2006)
International Eurasia
Film Festival
    (Audience Award, 2006)
Molodist International
Film Festival
    (Grand Prix, 2006)
Siena International Film Festival
    (Audience Award, 2006)
Transilvania International
Film Festival
    (Audience Award, Best
    Romanian Film, Transilvania
    Trophy for Best Film, 2006)
Gopo Awards
    (Best Film, Best Director,
    2007)
— —

Release date
2009
—

Country of release
Romania
—

Language
Romanian
—

Running time
115 min.
—

Genre
Drama
—

Producer
Marcela Ursu
—

Writer
Corneliu Porumboiu
—

Cinematographer
Marius Panduru
—

Key cast
Dragos Bucur: Cristi
Vlad Ivanov: Anghelache
Irina Saulescu: Anca
Ion Stoica: Nelu
—

Filming locations
Bucharest, Romania
Vaslui, Romania
—

Format
35 mm
—

Awards for *Police, Adjective*
Barcelona Independent
Film Festival
    (L'Alternativa – Best Fiction
    Feature, 2009)
Cannes International
Film Festival
    (Un Certain Regard Prize,
    Jury Prize, 2009)
EntreVues Belfort International
Film Festival
    (Feature Film Award, 2009)
Filmfest Hamburg
    (Foreign Press Award, 2009)
Transilvania International
Film Festival
    (Transilvania Trophy for
    Best Film, 2006)
— —

Cristi leaves the passport office.

Cristi and Anca discuss Romanian grammar over dinner.

Cristi plays foot tennis.

ANGHELACHE: Fine. So far so good. Now read just
the passage about qualms of conscience.

CRISTI: Qualms of conscience—remorse, regret.
To have a clean conscience: to be sure of not having
transgressed moral law or the laws of the state.
Against moral law or the laws of the state. Yes?

ANGHELACHE: Yes.

CRISTI: Fine...

ANGHELACHE: So now I have to ask
you, if you don't **arrest** Victor,
won't you have qualms **of** conscience
for defying the **law?**

CRISTI: No.

Cristi and Nelu, in Captain Anghelache's office, look up the definitions of conscience, law, moral, and police.

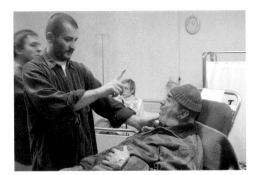

Mr. Lazarescu (Ion Fiscuteanu), age sixty-three, lives in an apartment with his three cats. His wife died eight years ago, and his daughter has moved to Canada. One Saturday evening Mr. Lazarescu does not feel too well, so he calls for an ambulance and is taken to a hospital. What looks to be a mere formality at the hospital— admitting and monitoring an old man who has been throwing up and complains of a headache— turns into a nightmare. As the night progresses and his health deteriorates, Lazarescu is driven around Bucharest accompanied by a paramedic, who looks for a hospital that will accept the patient.

CRISTI PUIU
THE DEATH OF MR. LAZARESCU

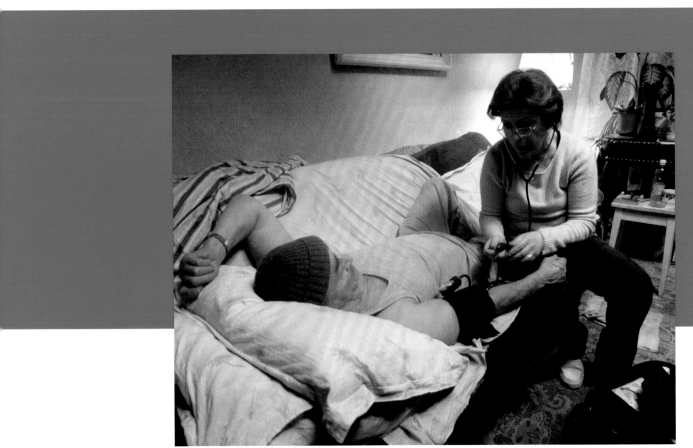

Mioara, a paramedic, consults with Mr. Lazarescu.

In Cristi Puiu's debut, *Stuff and Dough* (*Marfa si banii*, 2001), a young man's delivery of a package from one place to another is turned into a powerful lesson on the confinement of the human body. The film is a meditation on claustrophobia as a product of both the harsh conditions in which we live and our emotional reactions as we try to survive in a world gone numb. But it is also a tightly constructed tale of suspense, combining influences as disparate as Abbas Kiarostami and the early work of Steven Spielberg. This unlikely combination of styles allows Puiu to capture the dark humor in his characters' most pathetic moments.

The subject of Puiu's second film, *The Death of Mr. Lazarescu* (*Moartea domnului Lazarescu*, 2005), is of a piece with his debut. It traces the final night in the life of a sixty-three-year-old man, who feels a slight pain in his stomach during Saturday dinner and ends up dying after a lengthy pilgrimage from hospital to hospital. This time, Puiu does not focus on the journey itself; Bucharest's sickly suburbs stream past like ghost towns. Instead, he dwells on the process by which Lazarescu's body is turned into a thing, not unlike the package that is transported in *Stuff and Dough*.

The human body takes center stage in *The Death of Mr. Lazarescu*, much as it has preoccupied philosophers in recent decades, from Michel Foucault and Alain Badiou to Gilles Deleuze and Félix Guattari. What's remarkable about Puiu's attention to the body is the way in which Lazarescu is progressively objectified before our very eyes. Early on, Lazarescu is able to speak with his doctors and nurses as they interrogate him about his health. But as the night goes on, the questions and medical procedures are repeated to the point of absurdity. (It's as if he were Josef K. from Kafka's *The Trial*, only in a hospital clinic.) As Lazarescu slowly turns into an object, his voice becomes inaudible. Puiu's depiction of the human body is a far cry from the lithe figures in many films of the 1960s or the naked bodies of 1970s counterculture, nor is it the mutating sort seen in the work of David Cronenberg. In *The Death of Mr. Lazarescu*, the body is no longer a body at all, but it is also incapable of becoming something else. Neither metaphor nor allegory, it is purely a thing.

The sudden illness that overtakes Lazarescu is a rude interruption of his life, one that ultimately destroys him. But there is little suspense in Puiu's depiction of the descent; the movie's very title leaves little doubt as to the fate of its main character. That obscene question ("Is he going to die?") is answered right away, leaving us with another, more relevant one: how will it happen? Puiu chooses to focus on the time between the first intimations of death and its ultimate arrival—i.e., the medicated period of waiting to die that we are not supposed to know about. Dying, he reveals, is merely a series of repetitions and transitions.

Lazarescu's journey—first as a person, then as a thing—is not a traditional odyssey, driven by plot. Nor can it be understood merely as a single night narrated in real time, during which the story unfolds at the same pace as what we see on the screen, while kind but helpless characters appear at his deathbed. Instead, Lazarescu's journey consists of his body's ceaseless transit from one hospital room to the next, even when he can no longer move by his own volition. He is a passenger, gazing at the world passing by. But he is also like a single, faltering cell increasingly powerless within the great body that surrounds him: society itself.

Puiu does not intend for Lazarescu's sickness to be a window on the Romanian health-care system. His character's ordeal is rather an indictment of the platitudes and generalities with which we mask capitalism's savage nature. Above all, it is a critique of the way capitalism reduces people to things and renders society profoundly inhuman. Repeated interactions, endlessly delayed answers, and a total absence of responsibility make for a world in which Lazarescu's increasingly shapeless body is just another link in a chain. This is Puiu's version of "body politics": our bodies' movements—that is to say, our lives—are determined not by our own decisions, desires, or hard work, but by the political and economic system to which we belong. Puiu is unmistakably a critic of contemporary life, which is perhaps why one astute observer likened him to Balzac.

The Death of Mr. Lazarescu combines almost all of the great challenges of contemporary film: a blurring between fiction and reality; a plotline that unfolds in real time; a subtle political dimension; a bleak tone that oscillates between harsh realism and irony; and a limited point of view that ultimately disperses into multiple perspectives (as Lazarescu nears death). Yet all of these qualities are secondary to the director's critique of the human body. Puiu's camera is a scalpel that dissects our social fabric as only truly lasting cinema can.

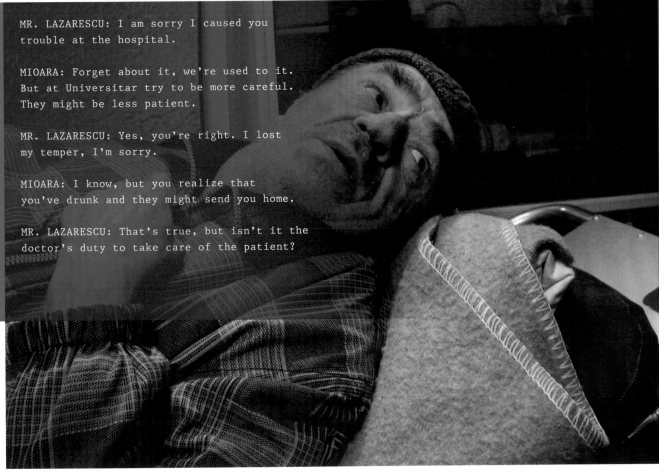

MR. LAZARESCU: I am sorry I caused you trouble at the hospital.

MIOARA: Forget about it, we're used to it. But at Universitar try to be more careful. They might be less patient.

MR. LAZARESCU: Yes, you're right. I lost my temper, I'm sorry.

MIOARA: I know, but you realize that you've drunk and they might send you home.

MR. LAZARESCU: That's true, but isn't it the doctor's duty to take care of the patient?

Mr. Lazarescu travels to another hospital in the ambulance.

Year and place of birth
1967 Bucharest, Romania

—

Lives and works in
Bucharest, Romania

—

Education
**Ecole Supérieure d'Art Visuel,
    Geneva, Switzerland**

—

Filmography
1995 *Before Breakfast*
    (short)
2001 *Stuff and Dough*
    (*Marfa si banii*)
2004 *Cigarettes and Coffee*
    (*Un cartus de Kent si un
    pachet de cafea*) (short)
2005 *The Death of Mr.
    Lazarescu* (*Moartea
    domnului Lazarescu*)
2008 *An Attempt to Rediscover
    Bucharest*

—

Director's awards
Stuff and Dough
Film Festival Cottbus
    (Special Jury Award, Findling
    Award, 2001)
Thessaloniki Film Festival
    (FIPRESCI Award for
    International Competition,
    2001)
**Angers European First
Film Festival**
    (PROCIREP Award, 2002)
**Buenos Aires International
Independent Film Festival**
    (Abasto Award, 2002)

Coffee and Cigarettes
Berlin International Film Festival
    (Golden Berlin Bear Award
    for Best Short Film, PRIX UIP
    Berlin Award for European
    Short Film, 2004)
**Buenos Aires International
Independent Film Festival**
    (Short Film Award, 2004)
Zagreb Film Festival
    (Golden Bib Award, 2004)
— —

Release date
2005

—

Country of release
Romania

—

Language
Romanian

—

Running time
153 min.

—

Genre
Drama

—

Producer
Mandragora

—

Writers
Cristi Puiu, Razvan Radulescu

—

Cinematographer
Oleg Mutu

—

Key cast
Ion Fiscuteanu:
    Remus Dante Lazarescu
Luminita Gheorghiu:
    Mioara Avram
Adrian Titieni:
    Dr. Dragos Popescu
Rodica Lazar: Dr. Laura Serban
Doru Ana: Sandu Sterian
Monica Barladeanu: Mariana
Alina Berzunteanu: Dr. Zamfir
Mimi Branescu: Dr. Mirica
Mihai Bratila: Dr. Breslasu
Mirela Cioaba: Marioara
Dana Dogaru: Mihaela Sterian

—

Filming location
Bucharest, Romania

—

Format
35 mm

—

Awards for *The Death of
Mr. Lazarescu*
**Bratislava International
Film Festival**
    (Prize of the Ecumenical
    Jury – Special Mention,
    Special Jury Prize – Award
    of the Student Jury, Special
    Mention Award – Special
    Mention of the Jury, 2005)
**Cannes International
Film Festival**
    (Un Certain Regard
    Award, 2005)
**Chicago International
Film Festival**
    (Silver Hugo, 2005)
**Copenhagen International
Film Festival**
    (The Golden Swan Award
    for Best Actor, Grand
    Jury Special Prize, 2005)
Motovun Film Festival
    (Amnesty International
    Award, Propeller of Motovun
    Award, 2005)
**Namur International Festival
of Francophone Film**
    (Golden Bayard for Best Film,
    Golden Bayard for Best
    Actress, Special Mention –
    Best First Film, 2005)

**Norwegian International
Film Festival**
    (Norwegian Film Critics
    Award, 2005)
**Reykjavik International
Film Festival**
    (The Discovery of the Year
    Award, 2005)
**Transilvania International
Film Festival**
    (Audience Award,
    Best Direction, Best Actor,
    Best Actress, Best Romanian
    Film, FIPRESCI Prize, 2005)
**Los Angeles Film Critics
Association Awards**
    (Best Supporting Actress,
    2006)
**Mexico City International
Contemporary Film Festival**
    (The Best Film, 2006)
**Palm Springs International
Film Festival**
    (FIPRESCI Prize –
    Best Actor, 2006)
San Francisco Film Critics Circle
    (Special Citation, 2006)
Trieste Film Festival
    (Prize Trieste, 2006)
— —

Mioara and Mr. Lazarescu wait to be helped at the hospital.

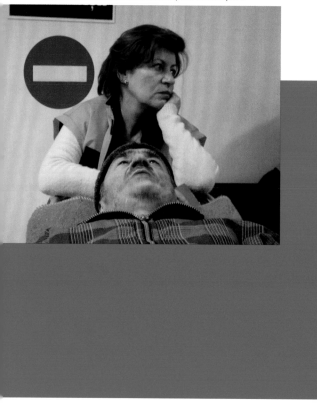

Dr. Filip consults with Mr. Lazarescu.

Mr. Lazarescu and Mioara at the x-ray machine.

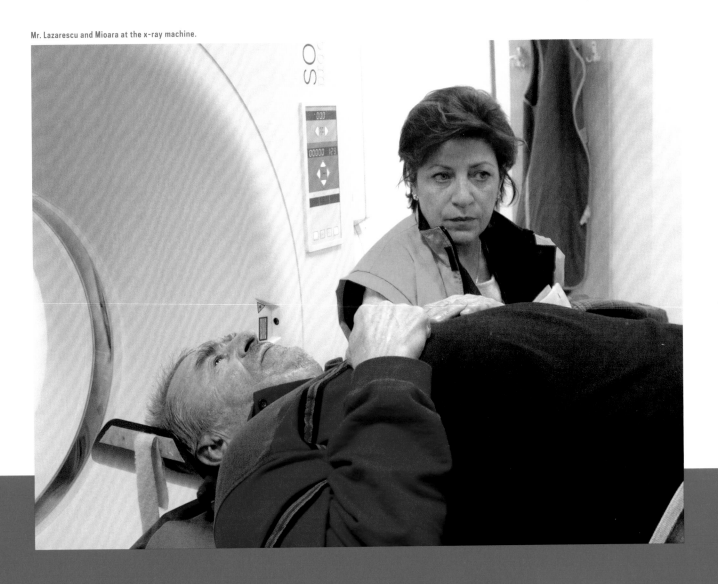

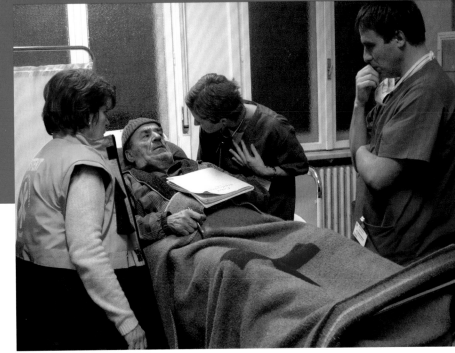

Under the supervision of Dr. Mirica, the young resident consults with Mr. Lazarescu.

This interpretation of Herman Melville's classic, *Moby-Dick*, begins in the United States in 1840. Ahab (Virgil Leclaire)—a young orphaned boy and an avid bible reader—runs away from a cruel aunt and uncle. Who could imagine that this boy, living in a hunting hut, lost in the middle of the woods, would one day become the commanding captain of a whaling ship? Nevertheless, Ahab (Denis Lavant) grows up and seizes the ocean, where he meets a dazzling white whale called Moby-Dick.

PHILIPPE RAMOS
CAPTAIN AHAB

Louise about to kiss the young Ahab.

The young Ahab finds an old bible in his father's lodge and reads about the death of King Ahab.

Philippe Ramos, who was born in Southwestern France, has had a somewhat atypical career as a filmmaker. He was a huge fan of comic strips, and since the day a biology teacher introduced him to Super 8 he hasn't stopped shooting films. He started out making animated and narrative shorts, before moving on to longer, increasingly professional ones. His first two full-length films, *Noah's Ark* (*L'arche de Noé*, 2000) and *Farewell Homeland* (*Adieu pays*, 2003), were shown at festivals all over the world. In 2004, he made a short, *Captain Ahab* (*Capitaine Achab*), about the character from Herman Melville's *Moby-Dick*. This film was the springboard for his third feature, which was entered in competition, and won the Silver Leopard for Best Director, at the Locarno International Film Festival.

In *Captain Ahab* (*Capitaine Achab*, 2007), five characters, whose paths have crossed with the Captain's, narrate in voiceover different stages of Ahab's eventful, ultimately tragic life. The story begins in the mid-nineteenth century in the northeastern United States. The young orphan Ahab is being raised by his aunt, a severe, pious woman married to a dandy who is quick to whip the boy as punishment. Ahab bravely flees this prison in the dead of night, making it appear that he has died. Free of family attachments, he discovers his passion for the sea, and after being taken in briefly by a minister of religion, enrolls in naval training school. He becomes a captain, living by and for the sea, and embarks on an endless struggle with a mysterious white whale called Moby-Dick.

As Ramos explains, "It was never a matter of adapting *Moby-Dick*. I started out from a character in the novel, Captain Ahab, for whom I created a life. Of the five sections of the film, four are pure invention, and only the fifth, entitled 'Starbuck,' coincides more or less directly with Melville's book. Given the cosmic dimension that runs through the novel, my approach has been via the private and personal. *Moby-Dick* depicts a deity—the white sperm whale—while my film is the portrait of a seaman, Ahab. The [original] title of the book [was] *Moby-Dick or the Whale*; my film could be called *Captain Ahab or the Man*. It was very much the man I was interested in, and there's a big difference. The scene showing the leviathan on the ocean is highly symbolic of this decision: it's not the whale that's enormous but the captain! In short, I could say I approached the book in a very simple way: one day, I made Ahab sit down in front of me, I took out my brushes and drew a face on my canvas . . . A whole life was recorded in that face."

Ramos recounts Ahab's life like a showman, presenting images from five different stages and points of view: "My first thought was to recount an entire life story, from birth to death, rather than just a passage in this captain's history, as is the case in *Moby-Dick*. The film's opening shot is a close-up of the mother's genitals, which seems to be saying, 'This is where it all begins,' and the closing one is of the sky, saying, 'This is where it all ends.' Between these two shots, more than forty years of life unfold."

Ramos was also the film's art director, and he re-created the mythical world of nineteenth-century

America using pieces of comparable countryside that he found in France and Sweden, as well as minimal sets and costumes. In this form of stylization he rediscovered a cinema that brings to mind the heyday of silent movies and the work of D. W. Griffith. As far as the performances are concerned, his remarkable cast (Dominique Blanc, Jacques Bonnaffé, Jean-François Stévenin, Carlo Brandt, and Philippe Katerine) is dominated by the impressive figure of Captain Ahab, played by Leos Carax's favorite actor, Denis Lavant.

As a counterpoint to the film's visuals, Ramos assembled a varied, highly original musical score that alternates between Fauré's *Requiem* and contemporary British pop. "I believe that as a genre the 'history film' needs updating in many places, especially in terms of the music," says Ramos. "For example, I've always been deeply impressed by Pasolini's decision to put Louis Armstrong over the scene of the Three Wise Men, in his *Gospel According to St Matthew* [1964]."

Using this spare yet very accessible form, the director suggests several traditions at once: a literary dimension that evokes great novelists like Victor Hugo and American adventure movies of the 1950s. There's even a nod in the direction of Indiana Jones. In his totally original combination of re-readings of literature and fiction, and especially of Hollywood, Ramos presents us with a cinema that is decidedly modern, bold, and tremendously appealing.

AHAB: Don't move, mister!

JIM LARSSON: You're a bit jumpy, ship's boy!

AHAB: I know who you are...Jim Larsson... I've seen your head on a wanted poster.

JIM LARSSON: My head? What price did they put on it?

AHAB: 800 dollars.

Jim whistles through his teeth. He is proud of himself.

Ahab runs into two strange vagabonds.

Year and place of birth
1966   Vienne, France
—
Lives and works in
Paris, France
—
Filmography
1993   *Les îles désertes* (short)
1995   *Vers le Silence* (short)
1996   *Ici-bas* (short)
1999   *Noah's Ark*
**   (*L'arche de Noé*)**
2002   *Farewell Homeland*
**   (*Adieu Pays*)**
2004   *Captain Ahab*
**   (*Capitaine Achab*) (short)**
2007   *Captain Ahab*
**   (*Capitaine Achab*)**
—

Director's awards
Ici-bas
Grenoble Short Film Festival
**   (Prix Canal +, 1997)**

Noah's Ark
Pantin Festival Côté Court
**   (Press Jury Prize, 1999)**

Captain Ahab (short)
Pantin Festival Côté Court
**   (Press Jury Prize, 2003)**
Paris Festival du Film Court
**   (Press Jury Prize, 2003)**

Farewell Homeland
Douai First Film Festival
**   (Professional Jury Prize,**
**   2003)**
— —

Release date
2007
—
Country of release
France
—
Language
French
—
Running time
100 min.
—
Genre
Drama
—

Producer
Florence Borelly
—
Writer
Philippe Ramos
—
Cinematographer
Laurent Desmet
—
Score
Olivier Bombarda
—

Key cast
Denis Lavant: Ahab
Jean-François Stévenin:
**   Ahab's father**
Virgil Leclaire: Ahab as a Child
Jean-Paul Bonnaire: Pastor
Handé Kodja: Louise
Bernard Blancan: Will Adams
Mona Heftre: Rose
Philippe Katerine: Henry
Carlo Brandt: Mulligan
Dominique Blanc: Anna
Lou Castel: Dr. Hogganbeck
Jacques Bonnaffé: Starbuck
—
Filming locations
Orust, Sweden
Region of Centre, France
Region of Rhône Alpes, France
—

Format
35 mm
—
Awards for *Captain Ahab*
Locarno International
Film Festival
**   (Silver Leopard for**
**   Best Director, FIPRESCI**
**   Prize, 2007)**
— —

Ahab, captain at the naval academy of Nantucket.

After an accident at sea, Ahab is accommodated by the beautiful widow, Anna.

Anna looks for the captain at the harbor.

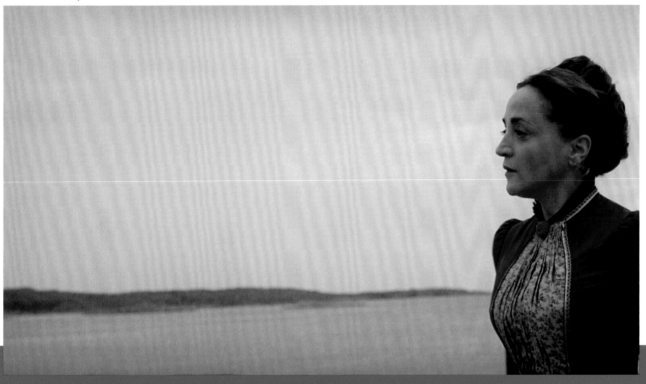

The mariners sing "The Drunken Sailor" while leaving Nantucket harbor.

Kurt (Will Oldham) and Mark (Daniel London), old friends, reunite for a camping trip in the Cascade Mountains east of Portland, Oregon. For Mark, the weekend outing offers respite from the pressures of his imminent fatherhood. For Kurt, it is part of a long series of carefree adventures. As the hours progress and the landscape evolves, the twin seekers move through a range of subtle emotions, enacting a pilgrimage of mutual confusion, sudden insight, and recurring intimations of spiritual battle. When they arrive at their final destination, a hot spring in a forest, they must either confront their divergent paths or transcend their growing tensions.

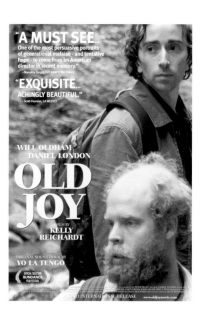

KELLY REICHARDT
OLD JOY

Kurt and Mark stock up on groceries and firewood for the trip.

The basic premise of *Old Joy* (2005) is not especially original: two friends reunite to go camping for a weekend. Kurt is a washed-up hippie, one step away from becoming homeless, who explains everything away with a single sentence: "The universe is falling, man." Mark, meanwhile, has a car, a dog, and a pregnant girlfriend—the trappings of a life of conformity. Their ephemeral reunion is bittersweet. It's partly an escape from civilization and a brief return to the "old joy" of more youthful times. But the trip also confronts the duo with the dreams of theirs that never come true. This peculiar relationship with the past emerges as the film's greatest strength.

The past may be a primary concern for Kurt and Mark, but not for director Kelly Reichardt. What makes her film both powerful and true to the current moment is that she does not attempt to return to the past: Kurt and Mark do not simply regress to their earlier ways, like the protagonists in John Cassavetes' film *Husbands* (1970), in which three adults flee their obligations and rediscover happiness by acting young again. Instead, *Old Joy* asks what we should do with our past and with all the culture we have lived and acquired over the years. What to do with the United States, a country that no longer makes sense and never will again? And what do we do with the cinema that it has produced?

Although Kurt and Mark appear eager to recover their past, they unmistakably live in the here and now. That is because for Reichardt, nostalgia poses little danger; the past should never be allowed to come back to life. But despite its power, the past can

be cherry-picked for ways to understand the present. Thus Reichardt reuses elements from old movie genres but strips them of their context and metaphorical weight. Her first feature, *River of Grass* (1994), is a clever parody of fugitive films. *Wendy and Lucy* (2008) touches on the tradition of road movies, yet Wendy cannot even get her car started. And if the two protagonists in *Old Joy* bear some resemblance to the heroes in a Western, the film's complete lack of adventure turns the comparison on its head.

As in all of Reichardt's movies, the characters in *Old Joy* are actively trying to imagine and construct a world in which to live. Their urge to visit or invent such worlds spurs their travels and guides their searches. These travels, however, are aimless; they end almost before they've begun. It's as if the director was trying to explode the traditional dramatic notion that journeys beget transformation (or perhaps just to prove how little interest she has in the classics). If there is no voyage from point A to point B, there is no transformation.

In *Old Joy*, it is only logical that the trip turns out to be more of a gesture than a call to action; for Kurt and Mark, introspection is what's important, not impulse. Reichardt's great challenge—and her great achievement—is to convey this introspection without words, dialogue, or lengthy explanations. Thoughts and emotions flow between the characters and their surroundings via their senses, especially touch and sight. The result is that the forest affects Kurt and Mark in the same way that it affects the audience: it washes over us like a flood.

If dialogue is kept simple in *Old Joy*, so too is the sense of time. This is no surprise, since Reichardt also edited the movie. Time is neither condensed nor drawn out; it unfolds so naturally and without artifice that the audience does not notice its passing. Nor does Reichardt use ellipses like a magic wand to speed along the film. Simply put, nothing happens during the night Kurt and Mark spend together. The director allows time to run its course rather than manipulating it in one way or the other.

As for genre, Reichardt takes only isolated bits and pieces: a dash of travel story here, a hint of melodrama there, and an occasional dose of disorderly comedy. Yet this thoroughly modern mixed approach does not make her movies feel cynical. The opposite is true: they become reservoirs of aesthetic resistance to the morbid, homogenizing repetition of film genres. In doing so, Reichardt asks why a movie cannot be just a movie. Why must it be fixed to a particular time, place, and genre in film history?

In lieu of adhering to a specific genre, each of Reichardt's movies employs a particular tone or emotional timbre: the irony of *River of Grass*, the contemplation of *Old Joy*, and the sadness of *Wendy and Lucy*. Each has a different take on the world it captures, a world that is ultimately too real, harsh, and inhumane for Reichardt's liking. What makes *Old Joy* such a modern film is its attempt to rediscover the humane in a world—a cinema, a country, an age—in which humanity seems to be a relic of the past. In this sense Kurt and Mark are heroes not only of the past, but of the present as well.

Mark sits by the fire.

Year and place of birth
1964   Miami, Fla., USA
—

Lives and works in
Queens, N.Y., USA
—

Education
**School of the Museum
    of Fine Arts, Boston,
    Mass., USA**
—

Filmography
1994   *River of Grass*
1999   *Ode* (short)
2002   *Then A Year* (short)
2004   *Travis* (short)
2005   *Old Joy*
2008   *Wendy and Lucy*
— —

Release date
2006
—

Country of release
USA
—

Language
English
—

Running time
76 min.
—

Genre
Drama
—

Producers
**Neil Kopp, Lars Knudsen,
Anish Savjani, Jay Van Hoy**
—

Writers
Jon Raymond, Kelly Reichardt
—

Cinematographer
Pete Sillen
—

Score
Yo La Tengo

Key cast
Will Oldham: Kurt
Daniel London: Mark
Tanya Smith: Tanya
—

Filming location
Portland, Ore., USA
—

Format
Super 16 mm
—

Awards for *Old Joy*
**International Film Festival
Rotterdam
    (Tiger Award, 2006)**
**Sarasota Film Festival
    (Narrative Feature Award,
    2006)**
— —

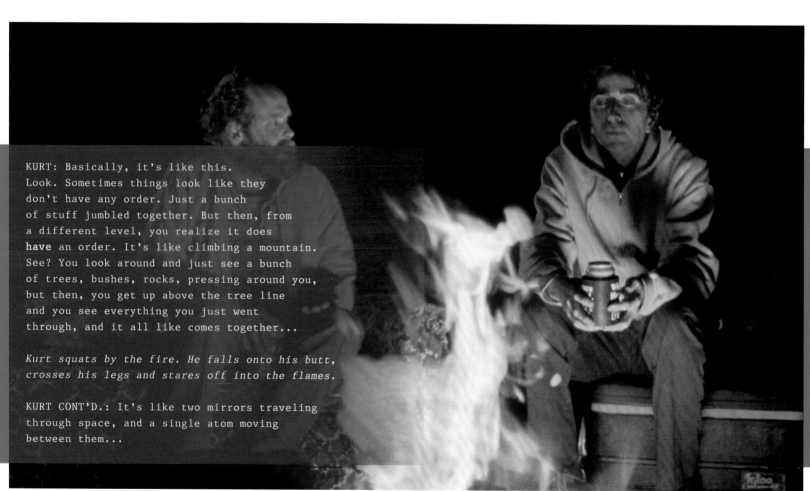

KURT: Basically, it's like this.
Look. Sometimes things look like they
don't have any order. Just a bunch
of stuff jumbled together. But then, from
a different level, you realize it does
have an order. It's like climbing a mountain.
See? You look around and just see a bunch
of trees, bushes, rocks, pressing around you,
but then, you get up above the tree line
and you see everything you just went
through, and it all like comes together...

*Kurt squats by the fire. He falls onto his butt,
crosses his legs and stares off into the flames.*

KURT CONT'D.: It's like two mirrors traveling
through space, and a single atom moving
between them...

Kurt and Mark try to re-connect.

Packing up in the morning.

Over breakfast, Kurt tries to convince Mark that they're not lost.

Mark and Kurt arrive at the hot springs.

Johan (Corneliu Wall) and his family live in the north of Mexico. Against the laws of his faith and traditional beliefs, Johan—a married man—falls in love with another woman, thus facing an internal dilemma: whether to betray his wife, the woman he once loved, and disrupt the apparent stability of the community, or whether to sacrifice his true love and future happiness.

CARLOS REYGADAS
SILENT LIGHT

Marianne and Johan look at each other lovingly on top of the hill.

The sun rises over the Mennonite farm in Mexico.

Carlos Reygadas burst upon the scene in 2003 with the precocious *Japón*. The darkly subversive *Battle in Heaven* (*Batalla en el cielo*) followed three years later, but Reygadas blossomed into a significant voice with the startling and strange *Silent Light* (*Stellet Licht*, 2007). Part of a recent resurgence of Mexican cinema–which includes directors Alejandro González Iñárritu, Alfonso Cuarón, and Guillermo del Toro–the equally original Reygadas arrived with a fully developed filmic personality in place. One could never tell that he was originally educated as a lawyer and never formally trained as a filmmaker.

Shot with minimal resources, *Japón* has an authoritative, highly composed style that takes full advantage of the wide CinemaScope frame. Using nonactors, Reygadas effortlessly immerses us in a singular universe, following a painter who journeys to a remote part of the country with the intent of committing suicide. What ensues is a languid portrait of a man who reconnects with himself amidst the beauty of the landscape and finds solace in the wisdom of an elderly woman.

Japón was compared to the works of Andrei Tarkovsky, partly because of its deliberate pacing and style, but Reygadas elicits a host of other connections. Certainly the transcendent cinema that critic and filmmaker Paul Schrader identified in the oeuvres of Robert Bresson and Carl Theodor Dreyer hovers over all of Reygadas's films (and especially *Silent Light*). *Battle in Heaven*, a controversial mix of sexual and class-based politics, teases out his concerns further but suffers from more overtly stated intentions.

The film explores the ties that bind an overweight, middle-aged chauffeur and a beautiful young woman (who happens to be the daughter of his employer and who has *Belle de jour*–style sexual proclivities). But Reygadas wraps everything in an expansive view of what ails Mexico, making prominent use of the national flag. Despite its bravado and evident craft, he seemed to lose touch temporarily with the mystical, visionary power that fuels *Japón*.

Silent Light is very much a return to the terrain of his debut. Physically, it takes place in the country-side, and psychically, it centers upon a man grappling with his ghosts and demons–a key theme in Reygadas's universe. Set in a rural Mennonite community in Mexico, the film is an arresting introduction to places we did not know existed. Reygadas transports us into a timeless world, initially disorienting, that could be anywhere.

He brilliantly reinforces this effect both in his use of sound, image, and language, and in how he deploys his actors. *Silent Light* famously opens with a magnificent shot of the sparkling nighttime sky gradually turning into dawn, and ends on this same shot in reverse: dusk turning into night. The shots last approximately seven minutes, and ambient sounds of animals and insects gloriously animate the soundtrack. We are immediately forced to pay close attention to the world Reygadas will portray; the effect is pantheistic, but the opening also implies an entrance into a kind of Eden. The subsequent scenes–a Mennonite family at prayer over the breakfast table, a clock loudly ticking on the wall–reinforce this sense of otherness and

timelessness, as does the language, an archaic German dialect called Plautdietsch.

Where are we, we might well ask? We rapidly discover that if we are in Eden, it is definitely not Paradise. Johan, husband and father, is undergoing a spiritual crisis. He is having an affair with another woman. It is not a secret to his friends or to his wife, Esther. Johan's love for his mistress, Marianne, is deep and troubling.

Reygadas's long, languid shots consistently affirm a sense of order: through nature (the regular milking of cows) and through man (family rituals such as meals, the washing of hair, the massaging of feet; clocks that significantly tick away). But Johan's transgressive love flies in the face of the structure and harmony of marriage, family, and societal mores. It is disruptive and is ultimately depicted as a destructive force. In a most extraordinary scene–after Johan and Esther have been grappling with their conflicting emotions while driving through a looming storm–Esther angrily leaves the car, sobs by a tree in the woods, collapses, and dies.

In the long mourning sequence that follows, Reygadas transcends everything that has brought the film to this point. It is too trite to call what follows a moment of magic realism. The scenes present something far more profound, a moment of transcendent power and redemption (and yet possibly a hallucination). Anger and tears, death and grief–dark, divisive emotions–are replaced almost magically (and arbitrarily, as is a poet's prerogative) by a positive, bonding sense of resurrection, life, affirmation, and forgiveness.

One of Johan and Esther's daughters, bathing in the spring water with the family.

Year and place of birth
1971   Mexico City, Mexico
—
Lives and works in
Mexico City, Mexico
—
Education
**Escuela Libre de Derecho,
   Mexico City, Mexico**
—
Filmography
2002   *Japón*
**2005   *Battle in Heaven*
         (*Batalla en el cielo*)**
**2007   *Silent Light*
         (*Stellet Licht*)**
—
Director's awards
Japón
**Bratislava International
Film Festival
   (Best Film, 2002)**
**Cannes International
Film Festival
   (Caméra d'Or –
   Special Mention, 2002)**
**Cuenca Film Festival
   (Best Film, 2002)**

**Edinburgh International
Film Festival
   (New Director's Award, 2002)**
**La Havana International
Film Festival
   (Best First Film, 2002)**
**Thessaloniki International
Film Festival
   (Best Director, 2002)**
**Guadalajara International
Film Festival
   (Best Script, 2003)**
**The Mexican Academy
of Film Arts and Sciences
   (Best First Film,
   Best Script, 2004)**

Battle in Heaven
**Festivalissimo
   (Best Film, 2005)**
**Lima Latin American Film Festival
   (Best Film, 2005)**
**Rio de Janeiro Film Festival
   (Best Latin American Film,
   2005)**
— —

Release date
2007
—
Country of release
Mexico
—
Language
Plautdietsch
—
Running time
132 min.
—
Genre
Drama
—

Producers
**Jaime Romandia,
Carlos Reygadas**
—
Writer
Carlos Reygadas
—
Cinematographer
Alexis Zabe
—
Key cast
**Cornelio Wall: Johan
Miriam Toews: Esther
Maria Pankratz: Marianne
Peter Wall: Father**
—

Filming location
Chihuahua, Mexico
—
Format
35 mm
—
Awards for *Silent Light*
**Bergen International
Film Festival
   (Best Foreign Film, 2007)**
**Cannes International
Film Festival
   (Jury Award, 2007)**
**Chicago International
Film Festival
   (Golden Hugo for Best Film,
   2007)**
**Huelva Ibero-American
Film Festival
   (Golden Colon for
   Best Script, 2007)**
**La Havana International
Film Festival
   (Coral for Best Film, Best
   Sound, Best Cinematography,
   2007)**

**Lima Latin American Film Festival
   (Best Film, Critic's Award,
   Best Cinematography, 2007)**
**São Paulo International
Film Festival
   (FIPRESCI Prize, 2007)**
**Stockholm International
Film Festival
   (Best Script, 2007)**
**Cine Ceará – Fortaleza
Ibero-American Film Festival
   (Best Director, Best
   Cinematography, Best Sound,
   Critic's Award, 2008)**
**The Mexican Academy of
Film Arts and Sciences
   (Best Cinematography,
   Best Supporting Actress,
   Best Script, Best Director,
   Best Film, 2008)**
**Sydney Film Festival
   (Special Mention Best Film,
   2008)**
— —

Johan carries Esther back to his car in the rain.

A doctor looks out the window while consoling Johan.

The family attends a wake.

FATHER: Johan, she's in peace now.

JOHAN: Now, everything's broken, dad.

FATHER: The enemy is implacable...

JOHAN: It's not the devil or anyone else...It's me.

FATHER: Johan...Johan...You **are** nothing in the face **of this**, Johan. It was all written **beforehand**.

Johan's father tells Johan that the death is not his fault.

Beto (Nolberto Coria) is the caretaker of a now empty house in Mexico City, where he worked as a domestic helper ten years earlier. He leads a life of solitude, one that could seem suffocating to some, but for him provides a safe and stable environment. Yet he has developed a pathological fear of the outside world, to the extent that some of his only contacts are the lady of the house (Tesalia Huerta) and Lupe (Nancy Orozco), a friend and lover. Upon learning that the house has been sold, Beto is confronted with either having to get out or finding a way to remain in his safety zone.

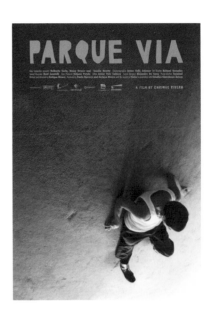

ENRIQUE RIVERO
PARQUE VIA

Beto whistles as he irons his shirts.

Beto looks at the possible buyers for the house.

Enrique Rivero was born to Mexican parents in Madrid in 1976. He trained to be an industrial engineer and worked at a bank in the United States for a year before pursuing a career in the cinema. After studying film in Madrid, he was hired as a production assistant on José Luis Padilla's *El silencio* (2002), and made two shorts, *Nidra* (2004) and *Schhht!* (2005). *Schhht!* is about a man's inability to conform to the world he lives in, forcing him to become someone he's not. Rivero then worked as first assistant director on Pedro Aguilera's *La Influencia* (2007), which served as his passport into a new Mexican radical cinema movement alongside directors like Carlos Reygadas—who made *Japón* (2002), *Battle in Heaven* (Batalla en el cielo, 2005), and *Silent Light* (Stellet licht, 2007)—and Amat Escalante, who made *Sangre* (2005).

These two filmmakers have been strong advocates for Mexican directors being given the opportunity to remake movies in their country, with their own financial resources. Dividing his time between Spain and Mexico, Rivero made his first feature film, *Parque vía*, in 2008. It went on to win the Golden Leopard at the Locarno International Film Festival before securing international distribution.

Beto, an old "Indian," is the caretaker of a luxurious mansion in Mexico, where he's lived for over forty years—thirty in the company of its owner and ten alone, waiting for it to be sold. He is a recluse, with his solitude disrupted only by his female boss, who comes by to inspect Beto's maintenance work; Lupe, a prostitute, whom he pays once a week for a little company; and the occasional visit from a potential buyer. Beto has cut himself off from bustling Mexico City, an overcrowded, stressful place, where even a simple visit to the market now seems like a real chore. Television is his only window to the outside world, even if the news is always the same: bloody demonstrations, sordid murders, and ghastly wars.

One day, the owner informs Beto that the house has been sold and he will have to leave. Despite his former employer's efforts to help him find a new job, he fears he will be unable to work elsewhere, because he's gotten so used to being alone. How he ultimately responds to the news is unexpected, perhaps provoked by the violence he sees on TV.

The bond between the owner of the house and the old employee in *Parque vía* illustrates modern Mexico's social inequalities: the gulf between rich and poor, between whites and the country's indigenous population. And the poverty of a single man represents the poverty of an entire population forced to take on the least desirable jobs. The film, which combines aspects of fact and fiction, is based on the life of Nolberto Coria, who, as Beto, plays a version of himself.

Rivero says, "It's important to film the beauty of the real world. In order to do that, we used 16 mm. This format creates an image that is similar to what you see in documentaries, and that helps us identify with the character." He presents his protagonist within carefully framed long shots, and in scenes that are repeated several times, which function to lock him into his social framework. And benefiting by amateur actors who agreed to act out what could be chapters from their own lives, Rivero confronts us with a very powerful message.

In the director's words: "This film's greatest point of interest is the fact that in certain respects the story is a true one. Beto exists and this is how he lives. He has always worked for a family and it's possible he'll end his days that way. But the thing that interests me most about these characters—the owner's family and Beto—is their relationship: they come from contrasted worlds and yet they're together for almost their whole lives. They like and respect one another without ever crossing the line that clearly marks their class differences. My way of presenting that is unprejudiced; I'm objective and nonjudgmental, like an onlooker. My aim is to show this character, Beto, and his every-day life, as well as his habits and influences, like, for example, Mexico's endemic culture of terror, transmitted by TV news programs like *Primer Impacto* and newspapers like *Esto* and *Alarma*. The story told in this film could be seen as a news item from one of those papers."

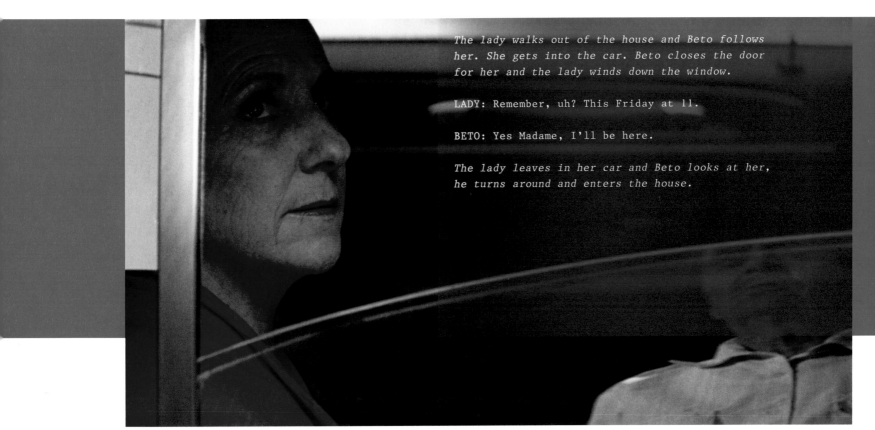

The owner provides instructions to Beto.

Year and place of birth
1976   Madrid, Spain
—

Lives and works in
Madrid, Spain
—

Education
**Universidad Anáhuac,
    Huixquilucan, Mexico**
—

Filmography
2004   Nidra (short)
2005   Schhht! (short)
2008   Parque vía
— —

Release date
2008
—

Country of release
Mexico
—

Language
Spanish
—

Running time
86 min.
—

Genre
Drama
—

Producers
Paola Herrera, Enrique Rivero
—

Writer
Enrique Rivero
—

Cinematographer
Arnau Valls Colomer
—

Score
Alejandro de Icaza
—

Key cast
**Nolberto Coria: Beto
Nancy Orozco: Lupe
Tesalia Huerta: The owner**
—

Filming location
Mexico City, Mexico
—

Format
Super 16 mm
—

Awards for Parque vía
**Havana Festival of New Latin
American Cinema
    (Grand Coral – First Work,
    2008)
Huelva Latin American
Film Festival
    (Best New Director, 2008)
Locarno International
Film Festival
    (FIPRESCI Award,
    Golden Leopard, 2008)**

**Mexico City International
Contemporary Film Festival
    (Audience Award, Best Latin-
    American Film, 2008)
Miami International Film Festival
    (Best Director, 2008)
The 3 Continents Festival
    (Best Actor, Golden
    Montgolfière, 2008)
Valdivia International
Film Festival
    (Audience Award,
    Best Director, 2008)
Göteburg International
Film Festival
    (Ingmar Bergman
    International Debut
    Award, 2009)**
— —

The last conversation between the owner and Beto.

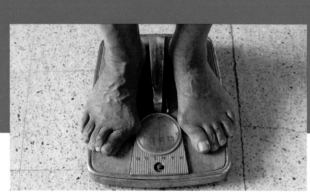

Every day Beto checks his weight.

As a daily routine Beto cleans up the windows.

Lupe arrives at the house.

Beto faces a picture of Jesus and prays for a change or a miracle.

Pedro (João Carreira) and Rui (Nuno Gil) had been lovers for a year when Pedro gets into a brutal car accident and dies in Rui's arms. All alone, Rui feels hopeless and lost, with no taste for living. Pedro's neighbor Odete (Ana Cristina de Oliveira), a roller-skating supermarket employee, insists on getting pregnant, which causes her lover, Alberto (Carloto Cotta), to run away. Her dream of having a baby becomes an obsession, and although she didn't really know Pedro and Rui, she inserts herself into their lives.

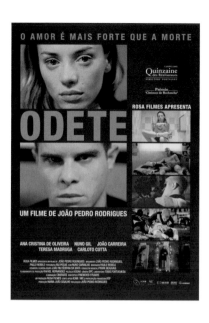

JOAO PEDRO RODRIGUES
TWO DRIFTERS

At Pedro's burial, Odete jumps into his grave.

Rui kisses Pedro minutes before the car accident.

Portugal is a country of cinema—and a cinema exclusively of artists. It has its influential figures and its poètes maudits, but it also has its new breed of incredibly talented young directors, including Miguel Gomes, João Nicolau, and a number of others. From that generation, João Pedro Rodrigues is a maverick who has quickly established a very personal homoerotic world, full of fantasy and spirits, as the title of his first feature, *O Fantasma* (2000), suggests.

Rodrigues was born in Lisbon in 1966. He studied biology, then cinema, before serving as assistant director or assistant editor on several films. *O Fantasma* had a huge international impact and became a cult item among a particular community of both gay and straight movie buffs constantly on the lookout for radical, uncompromising cinema. His second film, *Two Drifters* (*Odete*, 2005), again explores the territories of passion, obsession, and transgression. This time, the sensual, vaguely androgynous body of a gorgeous young woman adds a new dimension of "otherness" to Rodrigues's gay films. This intrusion of the feminine into a male world is precisely the subject of *Two Drifters*, which illustrates the flow of desire between life and death, and between the sexes, culminating in a confusion of sexual identity. Rodrigues goes even further by devoting his third film, the splendid, funereal *To Die Like a Man* (*Morrer como um homem*, 2009), to the melodramatic suffering of a transsexual, unhappy in love and in his body.

Rodrigues's films are "trans" in two senses of the word—transgender in the sexual context and "trans-genre" in cinematic terms. In fact, Rodrigues makes a heterogeneous range of references. He oscillates between quasi-Bressonian rigor, the flamboyant lyricism of Douglas Sirk's melodramas, the pared-down fantasy of Jacques Tourneur, and the operatic baroqueness of Werner Schroeter. *Two Drifters* is, in fact, the story of a journey toward the absolute.

Odete is a beautiful young girl, working in a Lisbon supermarket. She glides down the aisles on roller skates, and is in love with Alberto, a security guard at the store. She wants to have his child, but Alberto refuses and leaves her. At the same moment, Pedro and Rui, two boys in love, are separated by death. On the evening of their anniversary, Pedro is killed in a car accident, minutes after their last kiss.

Odete and Pedro had lived in the same building. She goes to his wake and meets Rui, who is over-whelmed by grief. This is where the destinies of Rui and Odete, and of Pedro, merge: Odete inserts herself into Pedro and Rui's grieving families, like a necrophilic foreign body. In a kind of hysterical trance, she declares she is pregnant by Pedro. Between fits of vomiting and exhaustion, she spends her time at the young man's grave, provoking anger in Rui and skeptical tenderness from Pedro's mother. Finding refuge in the cemetery, and then in the actual bedroom of her made-up lover, she takes on Pedro's appearance in order to get closer to Rui.

The film's last shot, shocking as it is, makes complete sense. Through images, it actualizes a slow process of vampirization and the raising of specters. In a strange simulacrum of sexual intercourse, in which the woman takes the place of the man, in the voyeuristic presence of the deceased, the three lovers are symbolically united.

Two Drifters belongs to a particular tradition of melodramatic fantasy in which love triumphs over death, couples make love from beyond the grave, beyond the boundaries between dream and reality, life and death. *The Ghost and Mrs. Muir* (1947), *Peter Ibbetson* (1935), and *Portrait of Jennie* (1948) all come to mind. The shadow of *Vertigo* (1958) also hovers over the entire film with an atmosphere of morbid fetishism.

Odete is haunted by Pedro, and the film is haunted by Hollywood. "Moon River," the two lovers' favorite song, was originally sung by Audrey Hepburn in *Breakfast at Tiffany's* (1961), and appears in several versions on *Two Drifters'* soundtrack. Rodrigues is not the first director to test the aesthetic codes of Hollywood films of the 1950s and 1960s against a contemporary reality. Before him, Rainer Werner Fassbinder had made daring transpositions of Douglas Sirk's melodramas to drab 1970s Germany.

In *Two Drifters*, Rodrigues drives his passion for cinema to the furthest limit, almost in a form of osmosis with his heroine's obsession with motherhood. This passion is expressed in the extravagant screenplay, which draws on fantasy and magic rather than on psychology and psychoanalysis. It is a night wind that lifts the drapes at the window of Odete's basement apartment and penetrates her with Pedro's spirit. In the space of one sublime shot, realism slides toward a parallel dimension, Portugal ceases to be the country of the film, and we enter a larger-than-life universe that belongs only to the cinema of João Pedro Rodrigues.

Odete takes a pregnancy test.

Year and place of birth
1966   Lisbon, Portugal
—

Lives and works in
Lisbon, Portugal
—

Education
Lisbon Film School, Portugal
—

Filmography
1997   *Happy Birthday!*
      (Parabéns!) (short)
1998   *Trip to the Expo*
      (Viagem à Expo) (Part I)
1999   *This is My House*
      (Esta é a minha casa)
      (Part II)
2000   *O Fantasma*
2005   *Two Drifters (Odete)*
2007   *China, China* (short)
2009   *To Die Like a Man*
      (Morrer como um homem)
—

Director's awards
Happy Birthday!
Venice International Film Festival
      (Special Mention of the Jury,
      1997)

O Fantasma
EntreVues Belfort International
Film Festival
      (Best Foreign Feature
      Film, 2000)
The New Festival
      (Best Feature Film, 2001)

China, China
EntreVues Belfort International
Film Festival
      (Best Short Film, Audience
      Award, 2007)

To Die Like a Man
Cannes International
Film Festival
      (Un Certain Regard, 2009)
— —

Release date
2005
—

Country of release
Portugal
—

Language
Portuguese
—

Running time
101 min.
—

Genre
Drama
—

Producer
Maria João Sigalho
—

Writers
João Pedro Rodrigues,
Paulo Rebelo
—

Cinematographer
Rui Poças
—

Score
Olivier Bombarda
—

Key cast
Ana Cristina de Oliveira: Odete
Nuno Gil: Rui
João Carreira: Pedro
Teresa Madruga: Teresa
Carloto Cotta: Alberto
—

Filming location
Lisbon, Portugal
—

Format
35 mm
—

Awards for *Two Drifters*
Bogota Film Festival
      (Círculo Precolombino de
      Bronze for Best Film, 2005)
Cannes International Film
Festival – Directors' Fortnight
      (Special Mention Cinémas
      de Recherche, 2005)
EntreVues Belfort International
Film Festival
      (Janine Bazin Award for
      Best Acting, 2005)
Caminhos do Cinema Portugues
Film Festival
      (Special Mention of the Jury,
      2006)
Cineport Festival
      (Best Supporting Actress,
      2006)
Milan International Lesbian and
Gay Film Festival
      (Special Mention of the Jury,
      2006)
— —

Odete is kneeling on the grave, her back to the tombstone, and has just lit, with a lighter, several candles she has displayed all around the grave. They have different sizes and shapes and she has found them in various graves and inside tombs. She looks at the lit candles. She warms her hands to the candles' heat. She lies down, her head against the tombstone. She looks at the sky with a lost look. She closes her eyes. Her body, absolutely still, lies on the marble, among the candles, seeming to be dead.

Odete sleeps over Pedro's grave.

Rui watches *Breakfast at Tiffany's* on TV.

Odete looks out the window of Pedro's old bedroom.

Set in rural South Korea and the Philippines, this is a film about intersecting lives, environmental degradation, and spirituality. Ji-young Jang (Kim Sun-Young), a transgender amateur sculptor, is a gypsy-like loner who lives a very isolated life. Dressed as a man, with her breasts strapped down, she visits the Philippines and returns with a new bride, Rain (Phuong Thi Bich Nga), who later discovers she has married a biological woman. Meanwhile, Loi-Tan (Jung Du-won), a recently fired restaurant worker, goes in search of what he believes to be his real family, a quest that leads him to Rain.

GYEONG-TAE ROH
LAND OF SCARECROWS

The scarecrows over the field begin to fall due to pollution.

Three characters cross paths in *Land of Scarecrows* (*Heosuabideuleui ddang*, 2008), the second feature film by Korean director Gyeong-Tae Roh. The central figure is Ji-young Jang, an amateur installation artist who earns a living by washing dead bodies at a mortuary. As a transgender person, Ji-young lives as a woman but continues to deal with her past as a man named Ji-seok. Years ago, Ji-seok adopted a boy named Loi-Tan, whom he gave up by simply sending him away. Later, Loi-Tan embarks on a search for his long-lost father, only to find that Ji-young is now a woman and has given up life as a gay man.

Ji-young gets pulled into joining a group of Korean men from the countryside who are on a mission to find brides in the Philippines. There she meets Rain, a Filipina who wants to live the Korean dream, and the two get married. Rain follows Ji-young back to Korea, and upon learning that her new husband is a woman, she falls into deep confusion and emotional turmoil. She leaves Ji-young and wanders the foreign land like a ghost, until she encounters Loi-Tan and falls in love with him. Rain and Loi-Tan eventually decide to return to the Philippines, but agree that they should see Ji-young one last time.

With his first film, *The Last Dining Table* (*Majimak babsang*, 2006), Gyeong-Tae Roh began unfolding his narratives by following each character's life in fragments rather than adhering to a linear plot. The relationships between different characters become apparent only after a considerable amount of time has passed. Their lives seem to move slowly, restricted within their own fragments of time and space, as if tied down. In this respect, the title of *Land of Scarecrows* reflects Roh's cinematic worldview. The encounters between the people in the film—the transgender Ji-young, her estranged adopted son, and Rain, the confused bride-to-be—all fail to become enriching experiences, and instead confirm and heighten a looming sense of isolation.

Bleak visuals and chilly sound are key to Roh's style, and these features also determine the rhythm in his films. The fantastic scenarios, which involve people of diverse racial backgrounds, transpire in desolate settings, but the fantasy does not provide viewers any comfort or pleasure. The isolation of the three characters in *Land of Scarecrows* gives the impression that they have left their physical bodies on earth while their souls dance at the edges of the screen. When their fluctuating, coiled-up emotions are rendered like this, the bleakness of Roh's style creates a world that feels larger than life.

This stylized way of portraying characters made it easier for Roh's debut feature to receive a release in France early on. *Land of Scarecrows* takes everything one step further. Roh uses the empty images of these isolated individuals to tap into environmental issues, as well as the social problems arising from the diasporas of the modern world. With his poetic visuals, Roh suggests the continual decay of civilization and depicts the void within each character. Feelings of confusion and exclusion are rife throughout the film. Ji-young struggles with her identity, unable to determine whether she wants to be a man or a woman. She believes she is a man inside and brings Rain to Korea with the intention of marriage, but at the same time she hopes to become pregnant. The other two characters bear heavy emotional burdens as well. Loi-Tan faces racial discrimination in Korean society, and Rain wanders the streets after discovering that Ji-young is a woman.

The confusion depicted relates not only to one nation, but to modern society as a whole. Just as the environment has been polluted, so have our minds been contaminated. The questions posed by the Koreans seeking brides in the Philippines are a clear reminder of this fact. After making the women line up, the men ask questions such as "Have you ever been married?" or "Do you have any diseases?" The scene underlines the conditioning of today's society, in which material goods take precedence over spiritual or mental wellness, and the body becomes a commodity that can be bought. Their questions, Roh suggests, epitomize the diseased state of the human mind and heart.

The frequent images drawn from traditional Korean shamanism in the film reflect Roh's attempt to bridge what cannot be understood through logic or science, and also serve as an invitation to journey to a new world. However, none of this leads to a clear conclusion or solution. In the second half of the movie, Rain cultivates hope in her heart as she holds a small pebble and says, "When a flower buds from this small stone, they say your wish will come true." A full interpretation of Rain's words must wait to be revealed in the director's future films.

Ji-young Jang copes with loneliness by making art in her small house.

Loi-Tan separates trash in a landfill.

Year and place of birth
1972   Masan, South Korea
—

Lives and works in
Hong-Seong, South Korea
—

Education
**Korea Advanced Institute
of Science and Technology,
   Daejeon, South Korea
Columbia College, Chicago,
   Ill., USA
San Francisco Art Institute,
   Calif., USA**
—

Filmography
**2005   *Reincarnation* (short)
2005   *Father and Son* (short)
2006   *The Last Dining Table*
        (*Majimak babsang*)
2008   *Land of Scarecrows*
        (*Heosuabideuleui ddang*)**
— —

Release date
2008
—

Country of release
South Korea
—

Language
Korean, Tagalog
—

Running time
93 min.
—

Genre
Drama, Experimental
—

Producer
Gyeong-Tae Roh
—

Writer
Gyeong-Tae Roh
—

Cinematographer
Choi Jung-soon
—

Score
Jaesin Lee
—

Key cast
**Kim Sun-Young: Ji-young Jang
Phuong Thi Bich Nga: Rain
Jung Du-won: Loi-Tan**
—

Filming locations
**Hong-Seong, South Korea
Cebu City, Philippines**
—

Format
Super 16 mm
—

Awards for *Land of Scarecrows*
**Pusan International Film Festival
   (New Currents Award, 2008)
Seoul Independent Film Festival
   (Kodak Award, 2008)**
— —

JI-YOUNG JANG: *With a touch
of thin blue remained*

*when holding a sunset
in the sky*

*I hear a sound gently coming
round a long way*

over my shaking hand.

I am still on the road

Fluttering on the autumn beach

*like a tail flag on the pole,
still I stay on the road.*

Ji-young Jang sings in a gay bar.

Rain wanders alone after running away from her husband, Ji-young.

Simon Wolberg (François Damiens) can make an amazing speech on American soul music to astounded schoolkids and can get his eighteen-year-old daughter to swear that she will never, ever leave home. He is the mayor of a small provincial town who meddles in the private lives of his fellow citizens. He's madly in love with his wife, Marianne (Valérie Benguigui), but is also an invasive father and a provocative son driven by his obsession with his family. It causes him to scrutinize their bonds, putting their strength and fragility to the test.

AXELLE ROPERT
THE WOLBERG FAMILY

François and Simon break a bottle of champagne to conclude the speech on a jazz singer.

Marianne smiles at her son Benjamin as they cook together.

"Nothing endures but a secret violence that overwhelms all things." This quotation from Lucretius ends the most beautiful French film of 2009 by a first-time director. Axelle Ropert's *The Wolberg Family* (*La famille Wolberg*) is overwhelming and full of secrets but, above all, has a heartrending sweetness. Simon Wolberg (François Damiens) is the mayor of a small provincial town. He's passionate about his job and devoted to his family, whom he smothers with love.

Simon adores his wife, Marianne. Out of boredom or pique, she has an affair with a young local man. Simon knows about it and makes it a point of honor to confront his rival. There's also the arrival of his wife's brother, Alexandre, a bohemian artist who disrupts the even tenor of Simon's life and position of authority with his children. His son, Benjamin, worships Alexandre, and his daughter, Delphine, wants to move in with her boyfriend. And there's a darker secret running through the film: Simon has cancer and only a short time to live, but can't bring himself to tell his family.

What legacy has "classic" cinema left today? This is a question few contemporary viewers, obsessed with novelty, ask themselves, but to which certain directors respond by making films that transcend passing fashion. Ropert, a regular attendee at the Cinémathèque and out-of-the-way Paris movie theaters, is a newcomer to directing, but she has a track record as a scriptwriter. She penned Bozon's *L'amitié*, 1998, *Mods*, 2002, and *La France*, 2007, some of the most original and exciting ventures by a young French filmmaker in recent years.

The Wolberg Family avoids the clichés that many avid movie-buff directors fall into. It contains no obtrusive references to cinema history and no clumsy acts of homage. Instead, there's an unspoken sense of heritage, and of loyalty to certain directors (Jean-Claude Biette, Paul Vecchiali, Jacques Tourneur, Vincente Minnelli) in its form as well as its subject: the family. With Ropert's film, it is not a matter of falling back into a conservative or nostalgic position but of imagining the family as a little theater of the most elemental passions: love, betrayal, jealousy, loyalty, fear of separation and death. There's the family and there's the world, but the family is also a world, made somewhat stifling by the quiet hysteria of a father who loves his wife and children too much. *The Wolberg Family* is haunted by Nicholas Ray's *Bigger Than Life* (1956) in a way that is as subtle as it is profound.

Ropert's film combines intelligence and passion in equal parts. A sensitive reworking of the family melodrama, it is stylized and antinaturalist, demonstrating a confident grasp of dialogue and a great skill in handling actors. Ropert's filmmaking is elegant and discreet, with dialogue that is carefully written, almost literary, in contrast to the type of realism found in many French films that tries to present itself as natural speech.

A filmmaker's ability also reveals itself in the way he or she selects and directs actors. Ropert imaginatively and deliberately casts against type by giving leading dramatic roles to comedic actors, like Damiens and Benguigui. It is a personal triumph for Damiens, who is able, like the best American actors, to express several contradictory emotions through a simple expression, gesture, or movement of the body, with a calculated awkwardness and imagination that can easily tip over into tragedy.

The actors add dimensions of physicality, warmth, and occasional lunacy that prevent the film from being a simple exercise in style or a cerebral construction. The walls of the Wolbergs' bedroom are covered in photos of African-American singers, and the soundtrack is punctuated by 1960s soul music. Simon's Jewishness defines him as an outsider, despite his strong sense of integration. The same could be said about the film, which creates a slight feeling of disconnection from reality. The director's style is closer to 1950s Hollywood than French neo-naturalism.

Is *The Wolberg Family* then the most "American" French film since those of Jacques Becker? Without imitating the superficial features of English-language cinema, it captures its essence. Ropert's traditional direction style and Céline Bozon's cinematography, at once sober and stylized, seem almost to challenge contemporary cinema, in which "auteur" films have to display external signs of originality to be taken seriously by critics and festival directors. Here there are no interminable silences, no flight from meaning, or smug formalism. Ropert has produced a paean to clarity, and has embarked on a search for new ways of telling a story. She sees experimentation as a dead end, and classicism as an obvious choice and a form of resistance. It's an unusual but admirable path to choose in a world where so-called independent or art cinema tends to be plagued by uniformity.

Simon and his father celebrate an anniversary at the grave of Simon's mother.

Year and place of birth
1972   Paris, France
—

Lives and works in
Paris, France
—

Education
University of Paris III, France
—

Filmography
2005   *Purple Star*
        (*Etoile violette*) (short)
2009   *The Wolberg Family*
        (*La famille Wolberg*)
— —

Release date
2009
—

Country of release
France
—

Language
French
—

Running time
80 min.
—

Genre
Drama
—

Producer
David Thion
—

Writer
Axelle Ropert
—

Cinematographer
Céline Bozon
—

Key cast
François Damiens:
        Simon Wolberg
Valérie Benguigui:
        Marianne Wolberg
Léopoldine Serre:
        Delphine Wolberg
Valentin Vigourt:
        Benjamin Wolberg
Serge Bozon: Alexandre
Joceyln Quivrin: The blonde-
        haired man
—

Filming locations
Mourenx, France
Villeneuve-la-Guyard, France
—

Format
35 mm, CinemaScope
— —

Simon has a fight with the man his wife is seeing.

SIMON: What I hate about you blonds is your perpetual poise. Your obsession with poise. This elegance in every situation, in snow, rain or a storm. Your impeccable hair...Your ironic quips...That shitty irony. You lose.

THE BLOND-HAIRED MAN: Poise or Marianne?

SIMON: Marianne. You don't even exist, you're so blond, you look like a china cherub. Genderless. You're like a chick with your yellow hair. I bet you stink of eggshell.

THE BLOND-HAIRED MAN: Your wife has beautiful breasts.

SIMON: Her breasts don't remember you.

THE BLOND-HAIRED MAN: My hands do.

Marianne explains to her son that the problem in his parents' relationship isn't his fault.

This is the story of Ken and Lili, of Carol and Wayne, of Mike, Cindy, and Sterling. The film covers four years of their lives and their lives write the script of those years. They reside in the vast desert of Southern California, 190 miles southeast of Los Angeles. Its inhabitants are those who have sensed the fault lines running through their culture and now play out this understanding below sea level, where all the debris, physical and mental, of our times comes to rest. The place may look like the apocalypse, but it feels like home.

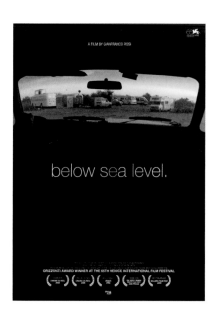

GIANFRANCO ROSI
BELOW SEA LEVEL

Ken plays ball with his dog, Corky.

Sterling and Cindy fill her water tank together.

One hundred ninety miles southeast of Los Angeles and one hundred twenty feet below sea level, on an abandoned army base next to an Air Force bombing range, lies the sprawl of Slab City—an immense camp of caravans, tents, mobile homes, dilapidated buses, pick-up trucks, and a few shacks. This is the home of social misfits with no water or electricity supply, no police, no government. They did not come in search of another world; they are not pioneers in the American tradition, nor even 1960s–style pursuers of a better life. They are those pushed away from "normal" society. Solitude lies at the end of their journeys. Their tents and cars, and the desert where heat and wind rage, have become the harsh sanctuary of lives broken by sickness, failure, lack of work, or psychological fragility.

We know them only by their first names: Lili, "The Doctor," who lost everything when her son was taken from her; Wayne ("Insane Wayne"), who looks like a bushy-mustached outlaw out of a 19th-century daguerreotype and is introduced threatening to go postal with a shotgun; Ken, who accumulates a mess of unfinished boats and cars; Mike, a man in grief; "Bulletproof" Carol, whose son died in her arms after taking a bullet meant for her; and Cindy, a Vietnam veteran with a family who has chosen to go off and live life as a woman. Each missing surname echoes with a personal history but also conceals it by its absence. But a few photographs, an anecdote, a cell phone, a song or a few drinks too many are enough to bring back the past and the pain.

Gianfranco Rosi starts with his subjects' morning rituals before easing, imperceptibly, into the longer, slacker rhythms of their lives, of where to go from here, and whom and how to love. Mike is somebody's dad in the world he left behind, but his daughter does not return his phone calls. He spends his nights composing a ballad about Slab City, an expression of the desert and of the destiny of these unusual inhabitants. The song becomes the thread that guides the story from character to character through their attempts to change, or to escape and re-enter the world. Cindy opens a beauty parlor in her truck; Lili and Ken try to build a relationship; Mike and the man who delivers water scatter the ashes of a deceased friend in the desert wind. Wayne and "Bulletproof" engage in a sex session that reveals both their sweetness and thirst for love.

In the light of hot summers and windy winters, Rosi (who spent months living in a truck near his characters-to-be) gives cinematically palpable meaning to the word "empathy." His admirable work with camera and sound, which he handled solo, gives the viewer a specific "place" from which to watch and listen without feeling intrusive or embarrassed. Through his careful approach and a great sense of framing and position, Rosi brings the audience close to him, becoming part of the conversations and part of a complex yet always respectful relationship. *Below Sea Level* (2008) does the opposite of what television typically does: observation is never an obscene process akin to watching wildlife; conversation and complicity take the place of interviews; time and space, silences and hesitations, are part of the characters' language; and editing is never a matter of selecting the most "significant" or "useful" moments. This is how Cindy, Lili, Mike, and the others slowly become part of viewers' lives—that 100-minute stretch of life we are offered to share with them.

Eventually, Ken leaves the camp, and Lili wishes him well. Cindy once more hopes for a man to love, and Mike's song slowly comes to completion:

> *We live way out there below sea level*
> *We never could get on society's track*
> *But we like it here and we ain't coming back*

In 1993, Rosi shot the one-hour-long documentary *Boatman* while traveling on the Ganges, listening to his guide's stories and chronicling the life-and-death events that occur on the banks of the sacred river. With *Below Sea Level*, he goes deeper into the capacities of documentary filmmaking to create filmic universes and characters that are in no way inferior to fiction features. In his hands, the image of Slab City undergoes a reversal. It is not a world alien to ours, not a planet populated by freaks and hobos. It is, instead, the ultimate image of our own world and the image of its ending—when everyone is left alone, in a vast garbage dump in the middle of the desert, as military airplanes pass overhead.

And so *Below Sea Level* may be added to the list of movies that depict the apocalypse of mankind, and the efforts to rebuild the world. But this is also how documentary cinema becomes a poetic way of knowing more about others and ourselves, and envisioning how much the present contains our past and future.

Ken talks about Slab City.

Ken relaxes on his hammock.

Year and place of birth
1964   Asmara, Eritrea
—

Lives and works in
New York, N.Y., USA
Rome, Italy
—

Education
New York University Film, Tisch
  School of the Arts, USA
—

Filmography
1985   *Car Wash* (short)
1985   *Coney Island* (short)
1986   *Roosevelt Island* (short)
1987   *Vaudeville* (short)
1993   *Boatman*
2000   *Afterwords*
2008   *Below Sea Level*
—

Director's awards
Boatman
Hawaii International Film Festival
  (Best Documentary, 1994)
— —

Release date
2008
—

Country of release
Italy
—

Language
English
—

Running time
115 min.
—

Genre
Documentary
—

Producer
Gianfranco Rosi
—

Writer
Gianfranco Rosi
—

Cinematographer
Gianfranco Rosi
—

Score
Mike Brigh
—

Key cast
Sterling: Himself
Ken: Himself
Lili: Herself
Mike Brigh: Himself
"Bulletproof" Carol: Herself
Cindy: Herself
Insane Wayne: Himself
—

Filming location
Slab City, Calif., USA
—

Format
35 mm
—

Awards for *Below Sea Level*
Cinéma du Réel International
Documentary Film Festival
  (Jury's Award, Student's
  Award, 2008)
Venice Film Festival
  (Orizzonti Award, Doc/It
  Award, Lancia Award, Venice
  Horizons Documentary Award,
  2008)
One World International
Human Rights Documentary
Film Festival
  (Grand Jury Prize, 2009)
— —

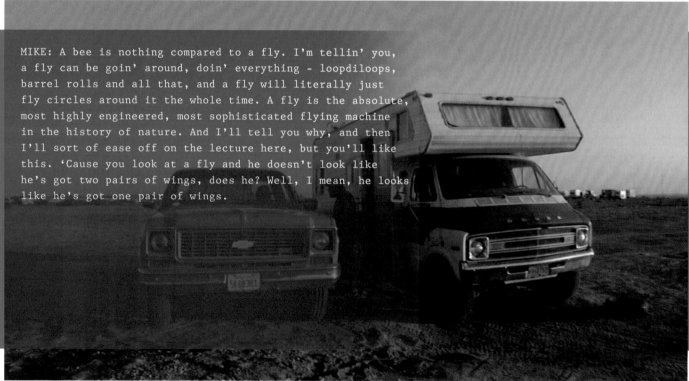

MIKE: A bee is nothing compared to a fly. I'm tellin' you,
a fly can be goin' around, doin' everything - loopdiloops,
barrel rolls and all that, and a fly will literally just
fly circles around it the whole time. A fly is the absolute,
most highly engineered, most sophisticated flying machine
in the history of nature. And I'll tell you why, and then
I'll sort of ease off on the lecture here, but you'll like
this. 'Cause you look at a fly and he doesn't look like
he's got two pairs of wings, does he? Well, I mean, he looks
like he's got one pair of wings.

Mike gives Sterling a lecture on flies.

Sterling plays golf while filling a water tank.

Cindy combs her new wig.

Lili, the newest resident of Slab City, sits inside her shelter.

A brutal assault changes the life of Marieke (Rifka Lodeizen). She leaves her familiar city rhythms for the solitude of a dilapidated house in an empty countryside. Her irrational fears on the frozen farm are a constant struggle. As spring's orchestra begins, her curiosity for new things that cover the cold rot of winter pull her out of the suffocating interior of her mind. Slowly she accepts the help of John (Wim Opbrouck), her neighbor, but as the seasons change so does she.

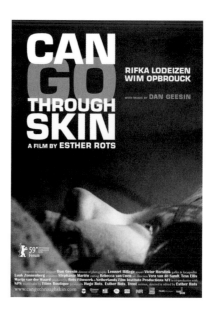

ESTHER ROTS
CAN GO THROUGH SKIN

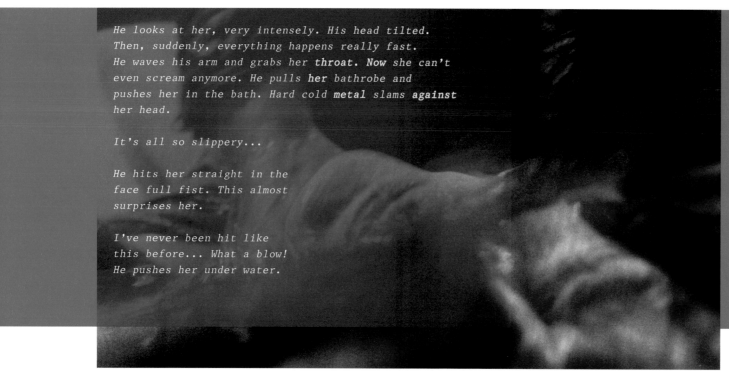

He looks at her, very intensely. His head tilted. Then, suddenly, everything happens really fast. He waves his arm and grabs her **throat**. **Now** she can't even scream anymore. He pulls **her** bathrobe and pushes her in the bath. Hard cold **metal** slams **against** her head.

It's all so slippery...

He hits her straight in the face full fist. This almost surprises her.

I've never been hit like this before... What a blow! He pushes her under water.

Marieke's attacker submerges her face under water in the bathtub.

"All of my films toy with similar ideas: the tremendous and intense difference between knowing and feeling; the conscious and the subconscious; reality and the way in which we experience everyday life as if on autopilot; interpretation and fact—and how these are remembered afterward. I find such processes deeply fascinating: the wonderful logic of the subconscious." Dutch director Esther Rots has already proven with her short films that she is capable of translating this fascination into an extraordinary cinematic language. With her first feature, *Can Go Through Skin* (*Kan door huid heen*, 2009), she exhibits that her talent for story and images extends above and beyond capturing fleeting moments within constrained running times.

Marieke, a self-confident and fun-loving young woman from Amsterdam, is left by her boyfriend. While trying to stop feeling down, with a little help from alcohol and defiance, fate strikes a second time. Marieke is brutally attacked inside her own flat, managing to escape only with the help of a friend. Shortly afterward, she decides to drop everything and move to the country. Neither the inhospitable winter weather nor the bleakness of her new dilapidated home is particularly conducive to any sense of security. Perhaps they mirror Marieke's emotional state, because however hard she tries to leave everything behind and forget what's happened to her, she's constantly reminded that you can't just decide not to be a victim.

Instead, she is consumed wholly by the emotional chaos brought on by her misfortunes, experiencing feelings of fear, shame, and helplessness. The house where Marieke seeks to seal herself off from the world becomes one with her internal state. Before becoming the film's title, "can go through skin" referred to, as lead actress Rifka Lodeizen explains, a part in the script where Marieke injures herself while carrying out renovations on the house. It's also possible to interpret the words as bringing Marieke's internal struggles, torments, and contradictions to the surface. In order to achieve this, Marieke's perspective is taken on in a radical way. Not only does she appear in every single scene but the (largely handheld) camera also often gets incredibly close to her, almost appearing to be seeing through her eyes. But Rots's interest in the wonderful logic of the unconscious doesn't end here. She is also able to dissolve the traditional hierarchy between real and imagined events.

Among all the different types of media, cinema is perhaps the best suited to not only address the human psyche but also to imitate it. And if seemingly disparate elements are placed next to one another so that they are viewed in the same way, and the appropriate way of reading them is not indicated by cinematic devices such as fades or alienation effects, the challenge to the viewer can be highly enriching. Marieke's revenge fantasies, in which she keeps the man who assaulted her prisoner and torments him, are presented with the same level of reality as the court proceedings that allowed her attacker to get away with a relatively lenient punishment. And as Marieke slowly opens up to her down-to-earth neighbor John (Wim Opbrouck) and begins a relationship with him, she also starts making contact with other victims of violence on the Internet and forges revenge plans.

By the end of the film, the only thing that's clear is that Marieke can no longer be the same person as before. And how the film tells her story leaves a great deal of leeway regarding who she will now become. That the narrative is conceived in a deliberately ambiguous manner makes it all the more striking.

Rots doesn't approach Marieke's soul as a surgeon or a psychotherapist. She is first and foremost an artist, capable of employing the means at her disposal in an assured way. Part of this process involves taking on many key duties herself. In addition to writing and directing the film, Rots was also responsible for editing and producing it. This was the only way for her to retain the freedom necessary for her particular artistic approach, one that can be described as highly intuitive. Even after shooting had begun, Rots continued to rewrite and rework the story; she therefore chose to hire a small crew suited to working under such conditions. Sound designer Dan Gees further amplifies the feeling that viewers are experiencing events intensively and from Marieke's perspective. Encompassing silence, noise, and songs composed especially for the film, the soundtrack heightens the story—and sometimes even tells a different version of the events we are seeing.

One could consider the casting of Lodeizen as a genuine stroke of luck, but it was certainly no fluke that brought Rots and the outstanding actress together. Perhaps it should instead be assumed that this collaboration can be best attributed to Rots's artistic determination, precise imaginative power, and intuitive approach, which make her work so enthralling.

Standing in the empty field, Marieke contemplates her new home.

Marieke hides in a dilapidated country house.

Year and place of birth
1972   Groenlo, Netherlands
—
Lives and works in
Amsterdam, Netherlands
—
Education
School of Fine Arts, Arnhem,
Netherlands
—
Filmography
2002   *Play with Me*
(*Speel met me*) (short)
2003   *I sprout* (*Ik ontspruit*)
(short)
2005   *Dialogue exercise no.*
1: City (*Dialoogoefening*
no. 1: Stad*) (short)
2009   *Can Go Through Skin*
(*Kan door huid heen*)
—
Director's awards
Play with Me
InterFilm: International Short
Film Festival Berlin
(Best Cinematography,
2002)

Zinebi Film Festival
(Silver Mikeldi for Fiction,
2002)
Filmfest Dresden: International
Short Film Festival
(3rd Prize Best Short Film
International Competition,
2003)
Granada Film Festival
(Best Experimental Film,
2003)
Houston International
Film Festival
(Silver Remi, 2003)

Dialogue exercise no. 1: City
NPS
(Best Short Film, 2005)
Netherlands Film Festival
(Golden Calf Best Short Film,
2005)
— —

Release date
2009
—
Country of release
Netherlands
—
Language
Dutch
—
Running time
94 min.
—
Genre
Psychological drama
—

Producers
Trent, Hugo Rots, Esther Rots
—
Writer
Esther Rots
—
Cinematographer
Lennert Hillege
—
Score
Dan Geesin
—

Key cast
Rifka Lodeizen: Marieke
Wim Opbrouck: John
Chris Borowski: Pizzaman
—
Filming locations
St. Margriete, Belgium
Rotterdam, Netherlands
Amsterdam, Netherlands
—
Format
Super 16 mm
—

Awards for *Can Go Through Skin*
Calgary International
Film Festival
(Special Mention New Voices
in Fiction, 2009)
Netherlands Film Festival
(Golden Calf Best Editing,
Golden Calf Jury Award,
Golden Calf Best Actress,
2009)
Transilvania International
Film Festival
(FIPRESCI Award, 2009)
— —

Marieke meets other victims on the Web.

John kisses Marieke's pregnant belly and whispers to the baby.

John tries to calm Marieke in the shower.

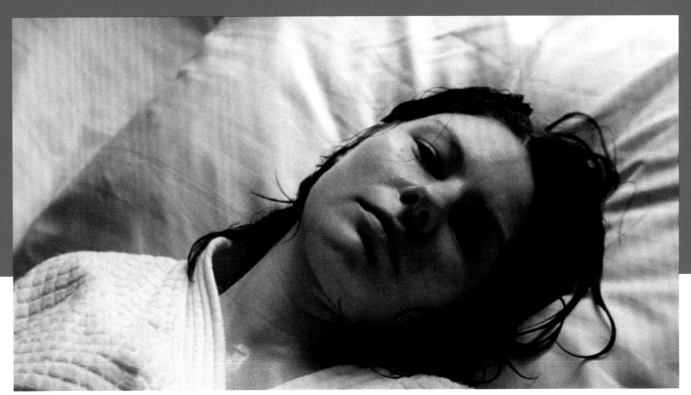

Marieke lies in bed after her frantic episode.

Pod (Mahasmut Bunyaraksh) is a migrant worker from the countryside who moves to Bangkok and drifts from job to job: sardine-factory worker, security guard, and eventually taxi driver. He meets Jin (Sanftong Ket-U-Tong), a maid who has her nose perpetually buried in a mysterious white book written in a foreign language that she dreams of someday understanding. Pod is smitten. But then Jin becomes obsessed with a hippie Westerner and the environmental movement. Pod eventually becomes well-known because he is the only guy in Bangkok without a tail.

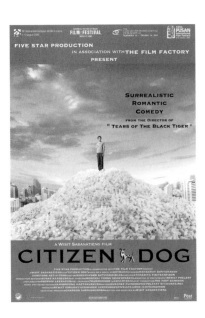

WISIT SASANATIENG
CITIZEN DOG

Pod leaves his hometown to find work in the city.

Wisit Sasanatieng excels at capturing the essence of contemporary Thailand on film. His second feature, *Citizen Dog* (*Mah nakorn*, 2004), showcases the country's many facets by portraying the life and times of Pod, a naïve village boy who moves to Bangkok. Pod is unswayed by his grandmother's warnings that he will grow a tail if he goes, and he begins work in an assembly-line job in the city.

In Bangkok, he befriends Yhod at the factory and falls in love with a quirky but unapproachable girl named Jin. He also meets Kong, a zombie motorcyclist, and Tik, who suffers from memory loss. Driving around, he gives lifts to Nawng Ma'am, a girl who looks no older than eight but claims to be twenty-two; her best friend is a talking, chain-smoking teddy bear. The bizarre bunch is reminiscent of the characters from *The Wizard of Oz* (1939), and they represent different caricatured visions of reality in Thailand.

As the title *Citizen Dog* suggests, these unique individuals are marginalized for their unusual qualities, which are manifested in compulsive behavior. For example, Jin is obsessed with cleaning, and Tik is fixated on licking. All of the characters fashion their own surreal worlds out of their outsider status. Jin believes that a mysterious white book that fell from the sky is the key to her destiny. She falls in love with a hippie referred to as Peter; later she thinks he has died at an environmental demonstration she watches on TV. Tik has lost all his memories aside from his name and cannot even recall his destination after taking a cab. And Muay, Yhod's girlfriend, leaves for China in the belief that she is the daughter of a Chinese emperor.

These scattered experiences, tinged with absurdity, reflect characters who are open to the many possibilities and meanings that life presents. Each character represents a highly individual way of maintaining identity amidst the fast-paced modernization of Thailand, where the nation and its people have largely shed their traditional identity. For instance, the white book that Jin thought to be sacred turns out to be gay pornography, and she comes to realize that the object of her love is not Peter. She confronts the truth behind her beliefs, and the disillusionment leads her in a new direction that represents a new and self-aware Thailand.

Sasanatieng successfully weaves these types of threads into a tapestry of colorful desires and kitschy sensibilities that together amount to pure Bangkok. The characters find harmony in this disjointed world through the shared understanding that every city dweller must endure loneliness when pursuing a dream. By muddling what is real and what is dreamlike, Sasanatieng creates a film that feels like many different dreams coming together as one.

The shabby spaces that Pod and Jin occupy in Bangkok are stateless and incoherent places with their own autonomous identity. Sasanatieng uses eye-popping colors and surreal sets to illustrate the harsh and unpleasant reality of Bangkok, underlining the artificiality and reality that coexist in urban life. The director has said that the film expresses "Thai-ness," but its true charm lies in revealing the boundary between what is considered Thai and what is excluded and marginalized. The pretty images placed on the borderline are offered up as consolation to all Bangkok inhabitants exhausted by the burdens of life in the city.

Under scrutiny, the disparate stories of *Citizen Dog* appear straightforward. Amid the exhaustion of physical labor, Pod and Jin experience the range of romantic travails through misunderstandings, quarrels, and separation, and eventually fall in love. The multiple voices of supporting characters lend the film a certain ebullience, balance the narrative arc, and flesh out character psychology. However, the true power of *Citizen Dog* is a visual language that stands apart from the story, superimposing the characters upon their settings instead of forcing them to blend in. They all live in the same city but form varied and autonomous universes that are entirely their own.

In the second half of the film, Sasanatieng fills the screen with a striking image: an enormous mountain of plastic bottles. Inspired by Peter's death, Jin has built the pile in an effort to recycle and save the environment; the heap of trash in turn becomes a popular spot for couples on dates. Pod, upon returning from a trip back home, observes the changes in Bangkok but is able to accept things as they are. He sings, "All I see is waste and garbage . . . but in the midst of it I also see stars." The paradox of the film lies here, as the mountain of waste is a place where new perspectives emerge, where one may contemplate the true meaning and importance of the stars. *Citizen Dog* shows that it is impossible to hide our tails or our plastic waste, and that we should instead coexist with that waste, transform it, and recognize that, without it, we would be unable to see beauty.

Pod tries to find his lost finger and hears the canned fish talking to him.

Year and place of birth
1964   Bangkok, Thailand
—
Lives and works in
Bangkok, Thailand
—
Education
Silpakorn University,
    Bangkok, Thailand
—
Filmography
2000   *Tears of the Black Tiger*
       (Fah talai jone)
2004   *Citizen Dog (Mah nakorn)*
2006   *The Unseeable*
       (Pen choo kab pee)
2009   *Sawasdee Bangkok*
       ("Sightseeing")
—

Director's awards
Tears of the Black Tiger
Vancouver International
Film Festival
    (Dragons & Tigers Award,
    2000)
Cannes International
Film Festival
    (Un Certain Regard, 2001)

The Unseeable
Fantasia Film Festival
    (Best Asian Film – Bronze
    Prize, Most Groundbreaking
    Film – Silver Prize, 2006)
Thailand Ministry of Culture
    (Silpathorn Award
    for Filmmaking, 2006)
— —

Release date
2004
—
Country of release
Thailand
—
Language
Thai
—
Running time
99 min.
—
Genre
Comedy
—

Producers
Aphiradee Iamphungphorn,
Kiatkamon Iamphungporn,
Rewat Vorarat
—
Writer
Wisit Sasanatieng
—
Cinematographer
Rewat Prelert
—
Score
Amornpong Maetakunvudh
—

Key cast
Mahasmut Bunyaraksh: Pod
Sanftong Ket-U-Tong: Jin
Sawatwong Palakawong
    Na Ayuthaya: Yhod
Nattha Wattanapaiboon: Kong
Ruenkam San-In: Grandmother
Pakapat Bunsomtom: Tik
Pattareeya Sanittwate:
    Baby Mam
—
Filming location
Bangkok, Thailand
—
Format
35 mm
—

Awards for *Citizen Dog*
Thailand National Film
Association Awards
    (Best Visual Effects, 2005)
Deauville American Film Festival
    (International Critics Prize,
    2006)
Yubari International Fantastic
Film Festival
    (Minami Toshiko Prize, 2006)
— —

Pod and Jin ride the elevator together.

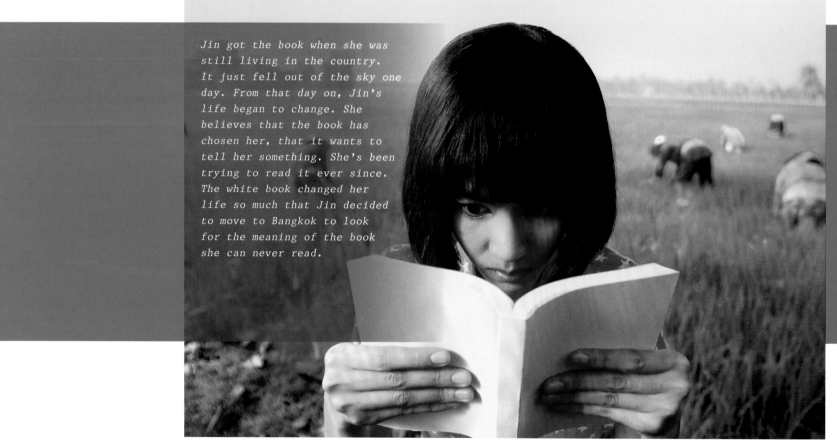

Jin got the book when she was still living in the country. It just fell out of the sky one day. From that day on, Jin's life began to change. She believes that the book has chosen her, that it wants to tell her something. She's been trying to read it ever since. The white book changed her life so much that Jin decided to move to Bangkok to look for the meaning of the book she can never read.

Jin tries hard to read the white book.

Pod, at his house, tries to figure out what to do with his life.

Pod searches for Jin on the mountain of plastic bottles that she has been collecting.

In an unspecified African country, commander Johnny Mad Dog (Christopher Minie) and his Small Boy Unit advance on a decrepit capital city. Trapped inside the kill zone is his opposite: an ambitious student named Laokolé (Daisy Victoria Vandy), who tries to flee with her little brother and legless father. Armed with AK-47s, wired on coke, and spurred on by grown-up General Never Die (Joseph Duo), the child death dealers kill and rape everything in their path. As they finally enter the city, nothing escapes their obliterating tactics. What will be the outcome of the unavoidable meeting between Johnny and Laokolé?

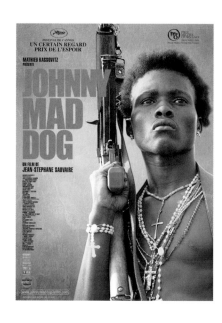

JEAN-STEPHANE SAUVAIRE
JOHNNY MAD DOG

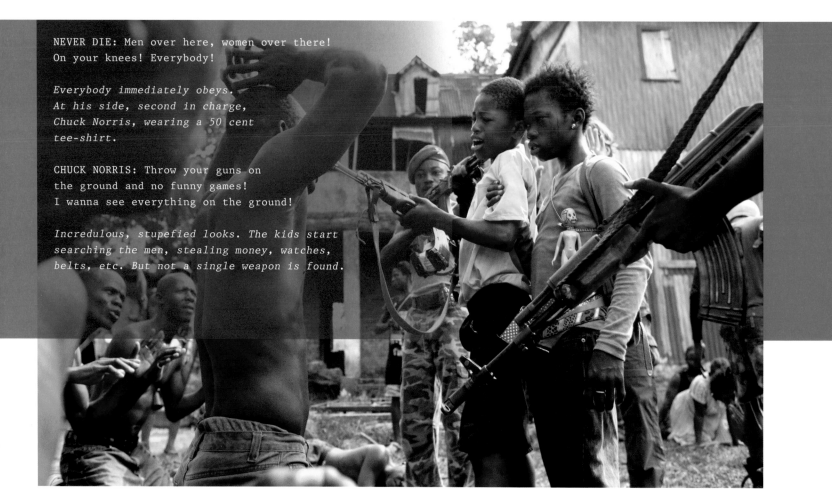

NEVER DIE: Men over here, women over there!
On your knees! Everybody!

Everybody immediately obeys.
At his side, second in charge,
Chuck Norris, wearing a 50 cent
tee-shirt.

CHUCK NORRIS: Throw your guns on
the ground and no funny games!
I wanna see everything on the ground!

Incredulous, stupefied looks. The kids start
searching the men, stealing money, watches,
belts, etc. But not a single weapon is found.

The Small Boy Unit attacks the village.

The scope and ambition of first features can often be quite modest. Filmmakers are known to focus on the familiar, cutting their teeth on personal stories about growing up or falling in love. Jean-Stéphane Sauvaire remarkably obliterates this notion with *Johnny Mad Dog* (2008), a masterpiece that ambitiously tackles significant and extremely difficult subject matter. I urge everyone to see it . . . but brace yourselves.

Fiction based on horrifying fact, this film adaptation of Emmanuel Dongala's harrowing novel portrays the atrocities of an ongoing civil war in an unnamed African nation from the vantage point of child soldiers. It could have come across as manipulative and two-dimensional at best or completely offensive at worst. However, in the capable hands of writer/director Sauvaire, it is instead a sublime exploration of humanity that delves the depths of the apocalyptic world we're invited to witness. He prepared for the film by moving to Liberia for one year, immersing himself in the region and its people featured in the story. But don't be mistaken, this isn't one of those vérité slice-of-life dramas in which a Westerner travels to a foreign land and lets the camera quietly "document" the lives of its inhabitants. Rather, it's a spectacularly stylized war film, for which he cast real-life child soldiers and allowed them to speak their own words in order to fully embody their characters. The film scorches the sensibilities of even the most jaded viewer, while raising the question: can evil be forgiven?

Fifteen-year-old Johnny Mad Dog heads a platoon of soldiers who are younger than he is. They're armed to the teeth, dressed in a variety of bizarre outfits (odd headgear, angel wings, a wedding dress), and have adopted names such as No Good Advice, Captain Dust to Dust, and Chicken Hair. Charged with overtaking a city in an attempt to unseat the government, Johnny leads this band of killers on a murderous rampage toward their destination.

Johnny Mad Dog pulses with atmosphere and authority, thanks in large part to a cast that brings the weight of experience to the screen and unleashes some of the bravest and most riveting performances I have ever seen. We tag along with them as they travel from block to block, destroying anything that crosses their path. And while we are aware that much of what they do, including rape and murder, is wrong, we also catch glimpses of their facial expressions that mask ravaged innocence, and help us to see that they are tragic pawns in a hellacious game of senseless war.

Johnny Mad Dog feels more truthful than a documentary and a million times more visceral than a news report. It explicitly conveys what the war is really like, and tears up expectations by depicting real kids beyond the headlines. It's even more devastating to try to understand their world than to simply condemn it.

Representing youth on the other, more clear-headed side of the insanity is Laokolé, the character we can most easily sympathize with. She lives with her younger brother and disabled father and dreams of a better life—until Johnny's hurricane of destruction comes her way. The film splits its time between the soldiers and Laokolé, who, with her brother, wanders through the ravaged city, searching for medical attention for their wheelbarrow-bound father. The incredible scene in which Johnny and Laokolé first meet face to face is intense in a Hitchcockian way, as the band of young, fearsome soldiers make their way down the street where Laokolé and her brother are hiding. But during the encounter, Johnny actually has mercy and spares them their lives, which adds an unexpected layer of hope. When the two meet for a second time toward the end of the film, we are again exposed to Johnny's humanity. It seems he previously believed that violence and barking orders made him an adult, but is recognizing his place as a cog in the wheel, a victim of war instead of a hero.

Sauvaire grasps the gravity of his film's issues, yet serves them in a hyper-stylish, almost surreal package that exhibits a true visionary at work. Beautifully conceived, the film's fluid camera movements and engaging stylistics bring color, depth, and immediacy to almost every scene. Audiences feel like they're part of the action, right in the middle of a war-torn place where a bullet can claim the life of anyone at any time. Perhaps no other movie in recent memory has been driven so fully, and so powerfully, by its direction and cinematography. The stark beauty of the world, even in destruction, is an incredible sight. Yet Sauvaire constantly reminds us of the insanity with brutal images that challenge us not to look away. It's not just a film, it's a warning. Presenting true-to-life experience in place of classic narrative structure, *Johnny Mad Dog* is a gripping, poetic, disturbing, provocative, thrilling, and terrifyingly primitive experience that screams "this is what filmmaking is all about!" with every frame.

Johnny Mad Dog and No Good Advice about to attack a TV station.

Barry and the Small Boy Unit sit together at the base.

Year and place of birth
1968   Paris, France
—

Lives and works in
Paris, France
—

Filmography
2000   *The Mule (La mule)*
          (short)
2001   *A Dios* (short)
2004   *Carlitos Medellin*
2005   *Matalo!* (short)
2008   *Johnny Mad Dog*
—

Director's awards
The Mule (La mule)
Avignon Film Festival
          (Best Short Film, 2000)
Festival Cinéma d'Alès
          (Jury Award, 2000)
Rencontres Cinématographiques
d'Istres
          (Starfix Award, 2000)

A Dios
Festival du Court Métrage
en Plein Air de Grenoble
          (Canal+ Award, 2001)
Festival L'Avis de Château
          (Jury Award, 2001)
Jeunes Filmvideo
          (Jury Award, 2001)
Aspen Shortsfest
          (Best Short Film –
          Documentary, 2002)
New York Exposition
of Short Film and Video
          (Jury Award, 2002)
Olympia Film Festival
          (Jury Award, 2002)

Carlitos Medellin
Human Rights Watch
International Film Festival
          (Best Film for Children's
          Rights, 2004)
— —

Release date
2008
—

Country of release
France
—

Language
English
—

Running time
93 min.
—

Genre
Drama
—

Producers
Mathieu Kassovitz,
Benoît Jaubert
—

Writers
Jean-Stéphane Sauvaire,
Jacques Fieschi
—

Cinematographer
Marc Koninckx
—

Score
Jackson Tennessee Fourgeaud
—

Key cast
Christopher Minie:
          Johnny Mad Dog
Daisy Victoria Vandy: Laokolé
Dagbeh Tweh: No Good Advice
Barry Chernoh: Small Devil
Mohammed Sesay: Butterfly
Leo Boyeneh Kote: Pussy Cat
Prince Kotie: Young Major
Nathaniel J. Kapeyou:
          Nasty Plastic
Eric Cole: Chicken Hair
Joseph Duo: Never Die

Filming location
Monrovia, Liberia
—

Format
HD

Awards for *Johnny Mad Dog*
Cannes International
Film Festival
          (Prize of Hope, 2008)
Deauville American Film Festival
          (Michel d'Ornano Award for
          Best First French Film, 2008)
Filmfest Hamburg
          (Neue Sentimental Film
          Hamburg Young Talent Award,
          2008)
The International Film Festival
of Contemporary Cinema
2morrow
          (Best Film, 2008)
Stockholm International
Film Festival
          (Best Directing Debut, 2008)
Festival du Film de Compiègne
          (Audience Award, 2008)
Festival du Premier Film
Francophone
          (Lumière d'Or, 2009)
Skip City International
D-Cinema Festival
          (Best Director, 2009)
— —

No Good Advice smokes under the bridge as he waits for the next mission.

Johnny Mad Dog and Lovelita stand by the fire as the other soldiers celebrate a successful mission.

The Small Boy Unit attack on the bridge.

A young American Jewish man (Elijah Wood) begins an exhausting search, aided by a naïve Ukrainian translator (Eugene Hutz), to find the righteous gentile woman who saved his grandfather when his small Ukrainian village (along with most of the populace) was obliterated during the Nazi invasion of Russia in 1941.

LIEV SCHREIBER
EVERYTHING IS ILLUMINATED

Jonathan examines his grandfather's memento.

Upon it release in 2001, Jonathan Safran Foer's novel *Everything Is Illuminated* was one of the most praised debuts in some time. It seemed improbable, if not impossible, that a movie could be made from the precocious author's dazzling metafiction about an American Jew investigating his heritage. But the actor Liev Schreiber has never been one to shy away from challenges, and indeed was himself something of a wunderkind in his ascent as an acclaimed actor on stage and screen. For the graduate of the Yale School of Drama, Shakespeare was an early specialty, including a turn as Hamlet, while the American independent film scene of the 1990s allowed him to craft engaging, intimately rendered characters in such movies as *Big Night* (1996), *Walking and Talking* (1996), and *The Daytrippers* (1997). He has since maintained an impressive and varied résumé combining highly respected theater work with a variety of screen roles in pictures of all budgets.

Candid and verbally nimble, casual and nebbishy but able to tap a darker side, Schreiber turned out to be a perfect match as the interpreter of Foer's material. As adapted by Schreiber for the screen, the story follows a young American, Jonathan, as he travels to the Ukraine in search of information relating to a friend of his grandparents, with the help of a rap-obsessed local guide, Alex, and Alex's crotchety grandfather. As for so many American Jews, the specter of the Holocaust is a force to be reckoned with, and as Jonathan makes a series of discoveries, Schreiber deftly navigates the film through a range of tonal shifts.

The film displays a complex sensitivity that comes from a clear personal investment in the material. Raised on New York's Lower East Side by an artistic mother, Schreiber was working on his own screenplay about his Ukrainian grandfather before reading Foer's novel and being impressed by its lively, affecting treatment of similar issues of diaspora, memory, and identity. In preparation for the movie, he even made a similar journey through the Ukraine searching for his grandfather's village. The bespectacled Jonathan, a writer, is dubbed "the collector" for storing every imaginable kind of memento from family members in plastic baggies, tacked on to the wall in his room as if an obsessive museum display. The ironies of such an existence are not lost on Schreiber, who crafts the first half of the film as a road movie based around a comical culture clash between Jonathan, Alex, and Alex's grandfather. Jonathan, dressed in boring 1950s jacket and tie, seeks to capture the past and obsessively preserve its memory; Alex dresses in tracksuits, fancies himself a ladies' man, and unself-consciously loves a peculiar retro vein of American pop culture.

As Schreiber has put it, in this equation, "the American becomes the alien. What we do is find ourselves through the foreigner." But Schreiber recognizes that finding ourselves involves the mingled hope and fear of just what might come to light. When Jonathan finally meets an old woman who is the sister of someone from his grandparents' past, it is at first a wondrous experience; she lives in a field of beautiful sunflowers that suggest a heavenly bounty of goodness, and she, too, is a collector. (Images such as this are one

way in which the film preserves the omitted magic-realist sections of the book set in the village Jonathan seeks.) But as it becomes clear the village no longer exists, the history that emerges is horrible: in flashback, Schreiber shows Nazis executing a group of Jews, and Alex's grandfather escapes death by playing dead. Later, the old man, who professes to be blind as if in total denial, deals with his own personal torment in a tragic way.

As an actor with a wide range of experience, Schreiber is especially aware of the importance of casting and the resulting dynamics. In the role of Jonathan, Elijah Wood (best known as the wide-eyed Hobbit hero of the *Lord of the Rings* trilogy) adds a layer of innocence that underpins the bookish character's saga of discovery. Meanwhile, Alex the guide is played by Eugene Hutz, a musician of Ukrainian Gypsy heritage, with good-humored brio. This is a movie that within the first five minutes shows Jonathan at a graveyard, and Alex break dancing on a disco-lit dance floor. Through their misadventures in the Ukrainian countryside, Schreiber achieves a multilayered approach to the often difficult-to-dramatize, grave history of the Holocaust and its survivors.

What results, between Schreiber's film and the Foer source material, is a profound fusion of cross-generational responses to a deeply complex legacy. By film's end, Schreiber has taken viewers on a journey spanning the sentiment in the opening voiceover ("The past should remain past") and the hard-won wisdom of the ending: "Everything is illuminated in the light of the past."

ALEX: He says he does not eat any meat.

GRANDFATHER: (*Baffled*) Not even sausage?! What is wrong with him?

ALEX: What is wrong with you?

JONATHAN: Nothing, I just don't...

There is a crash and some shouting from behind the kitchen doors. Everyone freezes.

Jonathan's first meal in the Ukraine with his guides, Alex and the grandfather.

Year and place of birth
1967 San Francisco, Calif., USA
—

Lives and works in
New York, N.Y., USA
—

Education
**Yale University, New Haven,
    Conn., USA**
—

Filmography
2005 Everything Is Illuminated
— —

Release date
2005
—

Country of release
USA
—

Language
English, Russian, Ukrainian
—

Running time
106 min.
—

Genre
Drama
—

Producers
Peter Saraf, Marc Turtletaub
—

Writer
Liev Schreiber
—

Cinematographer
Matthew Libatique
—

Score
Paul Cantelon
—

Key cast
Elijah Wood:
    Jonathan Safran Foer
Eugene Hutz: Alex
Jonathan Safran Foer:
    Leaf Blower

Jana Hrabetova:
    Jonathan's Grandmother
Stephen Samudovsky:
    Jonathan's Grandfather
Ljubomir Dezera: Young Jonathan
Oleksandr Choroshko:
    Alexander Perchov, Father
Gil Kazimirov: Igor
Zuzana Hodkova: Alex's Mother
Laryssa Lauret: Lista
—

Filming locations
Hradčany, Czech Republic
Prague, Czech Republic
Odessa, Ukraine
—

Format
35 mm
—

Awards for *Everything Is
Illuminated*
**Bratislava International
Film Festival**
    (Audience Award, FIPRESCI
    Prize, 2005)
**National Board of Review
of Motion Pictures**
    (Special Recognition for
    Excellence in Filmmaking,
    2005)
**São Paulo International
Film Festival**
    (International Jury Award
    for Best Screenplay, 2005)
Venice Film Festival
    (Biografilm Award, Laterna
    Magica Prize, 2005)
— —

Alex approaches Lista's house.

Lista recognizes Jonathan.

The group arrives at Trachimbrod.

Director Albert Serra adapts Miguel de Cervantes's novel about Don Quixote (Lluís Carbó) and Sancho Panza (Lluís Serrat). The two men canter off, directionless, in search of adventures. On the way, their discussions tackle spiritual, chivalrous, and practical matters, and their friendship deepens.

ALBERT SERRA
HONOR OF THE KNIGHTS

Don Quixote watches Sancho care for his armor.

Why have so many filmmakers failed to turn *Don Quixote* into cinema? One of the freest and boldest answers to the question comes from the filmmaker Albert Serra. The relationship between his film, *Honor of the Knights* (*Honor de cavalleria*, 2006), and the novel by Miguel de Cervantes is perhaps best understood in terms of the book itself: Serra is determined not to share in the same madness that Quixote famously brought on by reading too many chivalric romances. On the contrary, the filmmaker believes that making a movie out of the book does not entail translating words into images and sounds. He has intuitively discovered that the main secret to dealing with literary material is to forget by remembering.

The power of *Honor of the Knights*, not just as a modern film but also as a decisive landmark in contemporary cinema, lies in a crucial realization by the filmmaker: just as Cervantes's novel signaled the end of classicism, so must the book itself be over-hauled. Making the movie is not a matter of following the original source, because no text has pathways that can be read like a map. A text must instead be skirted around, shattered, and thought about. Serra focuses on this periphery; he knows the risk involved in trying to "do" *Don Quixote*, because it has already been done. What is subversive about Serra's approach is that he sets about unmaking the novel in order to reconstruct it in another way. He knows that it can only serve as a springboard for meditation.

What many critics saw as a zeal for gratuitous destruction in fact constitutes Serra's method of appropriating the novel. In this film, Don Quixote doesn't tilt at windmills or even pursue a fleeting love. Instead, over the course of very long scenes, we see Sancho cleaning and assembling his master's armor, Quixote and his squire wandering aimlessly in nondescript open spaces, or the two of them bathing naked in a river (one of the most authentic and beautiful moments that cinema has produced in recent years). The uneasy reactions to the film by the guardians of Cervantes's text can be attributed to Serra's refusal to seek cinematic equivalents for the novel's words. He is not interested in what can be salvaged from the novel, in keeping afloat a ship on the verge of sinking. Instead, Serra seeks to create a film that serves as a distant memory of the novel, like a dream.

Honor of the Knights is not a film in which the action is more important than the characters. In fact, the opposite is true, because for Serra, nothing exists beyond Quixote and Sancho. What action there is lacks the imperative for spectacle that so-called great cinema still preaches to a deaf audience. All we see are a few very minor, banal occurrences in a natural space apparently unaffected by the passing of time. It is this ordinariness that, almost imperceptibly, draws us in, while also prompting conversation between the two main characters. This dialogue proves to be really more of a monologue by Quixote, although his words could hardly be described as beautiful language; Serra is not interested in preserving the essential poetic function that they serve in the source text. Quixote's lines here consist of merely orders, moaning, or

circular questions repeated obsessively, crazily, as if Serra imagines the pair as (per)versions of Abbott and Costello doing a brutally farcical version of *Don Quixote* in Catalan.

The use of Catalan is Serra's final blow in his demolition of the Quixote myth, which is stripped not only of beautiful words but also of the very language that triggered its consecration as the pinnacle of Spanish literature. Hollywood and its clumsy disciples may still believe that cinema is literature by other means and may define the transition from literature to film with a word more appropriate to psychiatric medicine—adaptation. But Serra believes that this is the wrong path to follow, and making a version of *Don Quixote* in Catalan is his ultimate act of defiance. The director treats the text without respect, conscious that cinema must appropriate literature and not be its servant. He challenges literature by sweeping aside all its conventions, in a manner befitting any avant-garde artist worthy of the name.

Don Quixote asks Sancho to decide which path to take.

Year and place of birth
1975 Banyoles, Spain
—

Lives and works in
Barcelona, Spain
—

Education
Universitat de Barcelona, Spain
—

Filmography
2003 *Crespià, the Film*
Not the Village
2006 *Honor of the Knights*
(Honor de cavalleria)
2008 *Birdsong*
(El cant dels ocells)
—

Director's awards
Birdsong
Gaudí Awards
(Best Director, 2009)
— —

Release date
2006
—

Country of release
Spain
—

Language
Catalan
—

Running time
110 min.
—

Genre
Drama
—

Producers
Albert Serra, Montse Triola
—

Writers
Albert Serra,
Miguel de Cervantes
—

Cinematographer
Christophe Farnarier,
Eduard Grau
—

Score
Ferran Font

Key cast
Lluís Carbó: Don Quixote
Lluís Serrat: Sancho
Albert Pla: A knight

Filming locations
Alt Empordà, Spain
Pla de l'Estany, Spain
Garrotxa, Spain
—

Format
35 mm
—

Awards for *Honor of the Knights*
Barcelona Film Awards
(Best Film in Catalan
Language, Best New Director,
2006)
Entre Vues Belfort International
Film Festival
(Janine Bazin Award –
Best Actors, Gran Prix –
Best Film, 2006)
Torino International Festival
of Young Cinema
(Lancia Award –
Best Film, Special Jury –
Best Actors, 2006)
Viennale
(FIPRESCI Prize, 2006)
Cuenca International
Film Festival
(Best Actor, Best
Cinematography, 2007)
Split International Festival
of New Film
(Special Award of the Jury,
2007)
— —

Don Quixote in a mystical trance searches for God.

The two walk and wait for adventures.

Don Quixote thinks he hears music coming from the top of the tree.

DON QUIXOTE: As you know...we've had a lot of adventures...
we've won through...but I still feel sad. It is a sad
path...life, very sad. Because bad people exist. God shows
me the path of death. He says to me: 'Quixote, come.'
I am exhausted, Sancho...but you will follow my path.
I know that God has called me...and I feel so exhausted
that I feel death. But I have faith in you. God has
told us...that you will continue the work we have begun.
You, Sancho, have been sent by God.

Don Quixote feels death is near and asks Sancho to follow his path.

This comic-book adaptation is set in an alternate 1985 America in which costumed superheroes are part of the fabric of everyday society, and the "Doomsday Clock"—which charts the tension between the United States and the Soviet Union— is permanently set at five to midnight. When a former colleague is murdered, the washed-up vigilante Rorschach (Jackie Earle Haley) sets out to uncover a plot to kill all past and present superheroes. As he reconnects with his former crime-fighting legion, Rorschach glimpses a wide-ranging and disturbing conspiracy with links to their past and with potential catastrophic consequences for the future.

ZACK SNYDER
WATCHMEN

Dr. Manhattan intervenes in the Vietnam War at the request of President Richard Nixon.

The Comedian, Silk Spectre II, Dr. Manhattan, Ozymandias, Nite Owl II, and Rorschach pose for a picture.

It's a rare filmmaker today who simultaneously creates and critiques visual images, makes viewers both dream and think, and engages the collective imagination while crafting his own unique vision. That is Zack Snyder's manifesto for cinema.

Born in Green Bay, Wisconsin, Snyder moved to London, where he became one of the most respected commercial directors of his generation. His first film was a remake of George A. Romero's 1978 horror masterpiece *Dawn of the Dead*. Despite mistrust among Romero's fans, Snyder exhibited a natural talent for horror movies, respectful but also able to adapt to the modern demands of the genre. The film succeeds because he takes it seriously; it never falls into parody but presents with great virtuosity the despair of a world facing apocalypse.

Snyder's second film, *300* (2006), adapted from Frank Miller and Lynn Varley's graphic novel, deals with the famous Battle of Thermopylae, using a profusion of digital effects that transform the actors into animated figures inhabiting virtual settings. Once again, Snyder demonstrated a certain taste for blood, yet the slightly off-putting values of the comic perhaps left admirers of his previous film somewhat skeptical.

Snyder's third feature, *Watchmen* (2009), confirmed his visual talents, which flowered thanks to richer, more political material. The film is a live-action telling of Alan Moore and Dave Gibbons's comic-book series, which for decades had been considered impossible to adapt. *Watchmen* appeared during a rise in Hollywood's trend for comic-book and superhero adaptations; with its violence, darkness,

and political dimension, *Watchmen* stands out among them. Using spectacular visual effects, the film problematizes the myth of the superhero, a human being with a double identity, neurotic and full of misgivings about his heroic deeds. Despite an element of kitsch, mainly in the costumes, the film is closer to M. Night Shyamalan's *Unbreakable* (2000) than Sam Raimi's *Spider-Man* (2002).

It has to be said that the *Watchmen* comic, which addresses heroism and "alternate histories," is among the most original and ambitious of its kind. It takes place in 1985, in an alternate America where the Vietnam War has been won and Richard Nixon is still president. Watergate never happened and Nixon has returned to office in every election since 1968, prolonging the Cold War and making nuclear conflict with the Soviet Union an imminent threat. Against this background of heightened tension, the film relates the adventures of a group of superheroes in semi-retirement, whose actions have been decisive in U.S. history and politics over the past forty years.

Moving at a magisterial pace, the film switches back and forth in time, chopping up the chronological development of the plot. It begins with the assassination of the Comedian, one of the retired Watchmen, then follows with the credit sequence, over Bob Dylan's "The Times They Are a-Changin'," depicting vignettes of a parallel U.S. history from 1940 to 1980, in which the Watchmen's interventions have changed the face of the world. Those who come to the film knowing nothing about the original comic gradually discover the many plot layers, which span two generations and

include several time-shifts. The main narrative and subplot intersect, and one particular shot and piece of dialogue make it clear that the Comedian, a mercenary on Nixon's payroll, murdered JFK and later the journalists Bob Woodward and Carl Bernstein, thus averting the Watergate scandal.

Snyder shuffles imagery of twentieth-century culture and counterculture and draws on cinema, music, television, and comics as a vast reservoir of ideas and memories; this mass of references belongs to a visual context similar to that of Pop art. When the subject is nuclear war between the two blocs, Snyder sifts through cinema's back catalog and reproduces the famous control room in Stanley Kubrick's *Dr. Strangelove* (1964), with a Nixon look-alike replacing Peter Sellers. In *Watchmen*, Snyder has carried off a brilliant piece of recycling.

Snyder's film is a visionary fresco, composed of superb images that surprise even the most blasé viewer. He's an inspired director, one who can make an almost three-hour work, bursting with special effects, without sacrificing the complexity of the screenplay or the psychology of the characters. On the contrary, the film is fascinating as much for its intelligence as for its beauty. Snyder also handles time—the crux of the film—with masterful skill, using digressions, slow motion, and freeze-frames to capture its comic-book origins and heighten moments of action or sensory intensity. It not often nowadays that a Hollywood film dazzles and astonishes in quite this way.

As Ozymandias stands beside him, the Comedian declares that it is a joke to try and save the world.

Year and place of birth
1966 Green Bay, Wis., USA
—

Lives and works in
Pasadena, Calif., USA
—

Education
Art Center College of Design,
 Pasadena, Calif., USA
Heatherley's School of Fine Art,
 London, UK
—

Filmography
2004 *Dawn of the Dead*
2006 *300*
2009 *Watchmen*
—

Director's awards
300
The Academy of Science Fiction,
 Fantasy & Horror Films
 (Saturn Award for Best
 Director, 2007)
Hollywood Film Festival
 (Hollywood Movie of the Year,
 2007)
— —

Release date
2009
—

Country of release
USA
—

Language
English
—

Running time
186 min.
—

Genre
Action, Thriller
—

Producers
Lawrence Gordon, Lloyd Levin,
Deborah Snyder
—

Writers
David Hayter, Alex Tse
—

Cinematographer
Larry Fong
—

Score
Tyler Bates
—

Key cast
Malin Akerman:
 Laurie Juspeczyk/Silk
 Spectre II
Billy Crudup:
 Jon Osterman/ Dr. Manhattan
Matthew Goode:
 Adrian Veidt/Ozymandias
Jackie Earle Haley:
 Walter Kovacs/Rorschach
Jeffrey Dean Morgan:
 Edward Blake/The Comedian
Patrick Wilson:
 Dan Dreiberg/Nite Owl II

Filming locations
Vancouver, B.C., Canada
Burnaby, B.C., Canada
New York, N.Y., USA
—

Format
35 mm
—

Awards for *Watchmen*
BMI Film and Television Awards
 (BMI Film Music Award, 2009)
— —

Nite Owl II is haunted by fears of Armageddon as he embraces Silk Spectre II.

RORSCHACH (*Voice-over*): I heard a joke once. Man goes to a doctor, says he's depressed. Life seems harsh and cruel. Says he feels all alone in a threatening world. Doctor says treatment is simple. The great clown Pagliacci is in town. Go see him. **That** should pick you up. Man bursts into tears. "**But** doctor," he says. "I am Pagliacci." **Good** joke. Everybody laughs. Roll on snare **drum**. Curtains.

Rorschach visits Edward Blake's grave and recalls an old joke.

Silk Spectre II in the burning tenement building.

Maximo (Nathan Lopez) is a feminine preteen boy cared for and loved by his widowed father and two older brothers, who are all petty criminals. Maxi cooks, cleans, sews, and supports his family, and his squalid slum environment is brightened by improvised fashion parades and playing with other kids. Maxi's life takes a drastic turn when he falls in love with his new neighbor, Victor (J.R. Valentin), a young, good-looking cop, who eventually angers the family by encouraging Max to aspire to a better life.

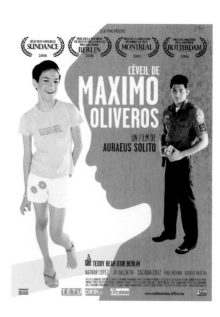

AURAEUS SOLITO
THE BLOSSOMING OF
MAXIMO OLIVEROS

Bog teases Janet, the prostitute.

A pioneering Filipino entry in Sundance's World Cinema Competition, Auraeus Solito's *The Blossoming of Maximo Oliveros* (*Ang pagdadalaga ni Maximo Oliveros*, 2005) was one of the first movies to raise Western awareness of the country's burgeoning cinema. And it remains one of the most distinctive. Many Filipino movies that see festival play abroad are set in the slums, but few are focused on an indomitably sweet spirit like that of Maximo Oliveros, or "Maxi," as his family and friends call him.

Within the first fifteen minutes of the film, Maxi, a joyfully flamboyant gay preteen played by Nathan Lopez, sashays down the alleys of his neighborhood, cooks for his family, and puts on a hilarious Miss Universe pageant with two friends. He is loved by his father and brothers, and his shy smile, pastel outfits, and flower barrette project a carefree sense on sometimes dilapidated surroundings. The movie opens with a shot of a plastic bag floating in stagnant water, but under Maxi's influence, even details like that acquire a lyrical beauty—a baby in tiny tub, two women politely arguing over trash, a crazed-looking man hammering away at a piano as kids look on.

When a hunky new policeman, Victor, takes up his beat in the neighborhood, it's love at first sight for Maxi, though Victor sees himself as a paternal figure. Conflict looms because Maxi's tight-knit family makes money from running numbers and hawking black-market gear. Solito's film develops as a coming-of-age story, tracing the contours of Maxi's tender crush and the tensions posed by clashing loyalties. Because of his sweet disposition, the boy politely makes excuses for his family's occupation as well as for Victor's attempts at cracking down on their illegal activity. He calls his brothers and Victor alike "kuya" (older sibling).

Maximo Oliveros is Solito's feature debut, but his penchant for warm stories and his eye for playful color were already on display. Later that same year, Solito explored sexual coming-of-age in greater depth within a milieu reflecting his own deep ties to his tribal roots in *Tuli*, the rural tale of the daughter of the village circumciser who is in love with another girl. Perhaps because of the frank and affectionate treatment of sexuality, both *Tuli* and Solito's later film *Boy* (2009) faced censorship at home and abroad, respectively. With *Maximo Oliveros*, Solito had already achieved his goal of directing a "progressive gay film," but his tender touch makes the controversy seem irrelevant: drawing on his own memories of growing up gay in Manila, the filmmaker and the superbly-cast newcomer Lopez imbue the film with heart and sincerity.

Solito's story takes on a melodramatic shape, as one of Maxi's brothers is suspected of murder, but the director takes care not to vilify either the police or Maxi's family. Maxi cooks, sews, and launders for his father and brothers, but they always appreciate it and show him affection. And even though his father pressures him to stop spending time with Victor, he doesn't become enraged with the boy. Victor, who looks so upstanding, ultimately finds himself needling his infatuated little friend into tattling on his family, and later on, with the arrival of a brutal new police chief, makes moral compromises in the line of duty that cause Maxi to reevaluate their bond. Perhaps fittingly, two of the movie's most vivid settings are Maxi's charmingly cluttered home (with the dinner table pushed to the wall) and the spacious, spare lobby of the police station where Victor works (and endures the teasing of his colleagues for his frequent visitor).

Solito even introduces a mild, unobtrusive religious element into his depiction of Maxi. When Victor is beaten up in retaliation for his scrutiny of the family's affairs, Maxi ministers to his wounds in his bedroom, while Victor is virtually unconscious. Although his devotion stems from his infatuation, there is still something almost spiritually selfless about it, and the story's themes of loyalty and betrayal complicate traditional divisions of right and wrong. As a filmmaker, Solito seems to have found the point where melodrama, meaning, and more down-to-earth emotion become effortlessly superimposed. It's reflected in his visual schemes, which will often position members of the family in an evocative arrangement (of joy, of grief, of day-to-day domestic order) and then let the scene unfold naturally.

Making a soundtrack out of old-fashioned classics, dance oddities, and acoustic guitar, Solito has made a film that rolls along with ease and at the same time shades in bits of exposition, such as the father's shame over not making enough money in his previous career as a factory worker. The film ends with both tragedy and a new vision of the nuclear family, as Maxi goes off to school for the first time after years of housework. In this brave boy, Solito has created the first of many finely drawn and vivacious portraits he will bring to screen.

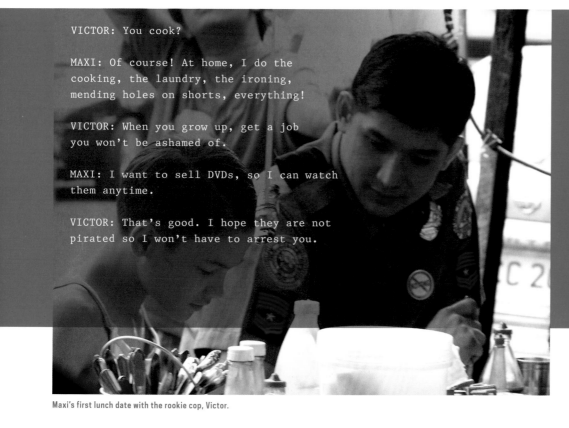

Maxi's first lunch date with the rookie cop, Victor.

Maxi is upset over his conversation with Victor about bad people.

Year and place of birth
1969   Manila, Philippines
—
Lives and works in
Sampaloc, Manila, and Palawan, Philippines
—
Education
Theater Arts, University of the Philippines, Quezon City, Philippines
—
Filmography
1995   *The Brief Lifespan of Fire, Act 2 Scene 2: Suring and the Kuk-ok (Ang Maikling Buhay ng Apoy, Act 2 Scene 2: Suring at ang Kuk-ok)* (short)
1998   *Black Nuisance (Impeng Negro)* (short)
2002   *Sacred Ritual of Truth (Basal Banar)*
2005   *The Blossoming of Maximo Oliveros (Ang pagdadalaga ni Maximo Oliveros)*
2005   *Tuli*
2007   *Philippine Science (Pisay)*
2009   *Boy*
—
Director's awards
The Brief Lifespan of Fire
Cultural Center of the Philippines Awards
   (Best Experimental Short Film, 1995)

Black Nuisance
Cultural Center of the Philippines Awards
   (Best Short Feature, 1998)

Sacred Ritual of Truth
Eksperimento Film Festival
   (Best Feature Film, 2005)
Montreal First People's Film Festival
   (Best Feature Documentary, 2005)

Tuli
Cinemanila International Film Festival
   (Best Digital Feature Film, Best Director, 2005)
Berlin International Film Festival
   (NETPAC Jury Prize, 2007)
Outfest: The Los Angeles Gay and Lesbian Film Festival
   (Best International Feature Film, 2007)

Philippine Science
Cinemalaya Philippine Independent Film Festival
   (Best Director, Audience Prize, 2007)
Golden Screen Awards
   (Best Picture, Best Director, Best Screenplay, 2008)
Vesoul International Festival of Asian Cinema
   (Special Jury Prize, Audience Prize, 2008)
— —

Release date
2005
—
Country of release
Philippines
—
Language
Filipino
—
Running time
100 min.
—
Genre
Drama
—

Producer
Raymond Lee
—
Writer
Michiko Yamamoto
—
Cinematographer
Nap Jamir
—
Score
Pepe Smith
—
Key cast
Nathan Lopez: Maxi
J.R. Valentin: Victor
Soliman Cruz: Paco
Neil Ryan Sese: Boy
Ping Medina: Bogs
—

Filming location
Manila, Philippines
—
Format
Mini DV
—
Awards for *The Blossoming of Maximo Oliveros*
Asian Festival of First Films
   (Best Film, 2005)
Cinemalaya Philippine Independent Film Festival
   (Special Jury Prize, Best Production Design, Special Mention for Best Actor, 2005)
Gawad Urian Awards
   (Best Picture, 2006)
Glitter Awards
   (Best International Festival Feature, 2006)
imagineNative Film + Media Arts Festival
   (Best Feature Film, 2005)
Montreal World Film Festival
   (Golden Zenith Award for Best First Fiction Feature Film, 2005)

Berlin International Film Festival
   (Teddy Award for Best Feature Film, Kinderfest International Jury Prize, Kinderfest Special Mention Children's Jury, 2006)
International Film Festival Rotterdam
   (Best Asian Film NETPAC, 2006)
Las Palmas International Film Festival
   (Best Film, Best Actor, Audience Prize, 2006)
Star Awards
   (Best Digital Film, Best Director, Best Actor, 2006)
Torino Gay & Lesbian Film Festival
   (Best Feature Film, 2006)
— —

Maxi sees his crush, the policeman Victor.

Paco, the patriarch and petty thief leader, discovers that his eldest son, Boy, killed a student for a cell phone.

Boy runs after Maxi, his younger brother, because he knows the truth about the murder.

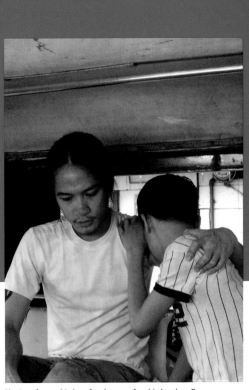

Maxi confesses his love for the cop after his brother, Bogs, reads his letter.

Kitagawa (Hiromasa Hirosue) suffers from a panic disorder and, unable to keep his job, begins to secretly frequent the seminars of a religious cult. His girlfriend, Shizu (Akie Namiki), makes every effort to bring him back to normalcy. But Kitagawa's illness cannot be cured, and he refuses to abandon the cult. Meanwhile, Shizu is forced to quit her own job when her company relocates, and her frustration escalates as she is unable to find a new job. All of these things take a toll on the couple's relationship, and their separation eventually becomes inevitable.

IZUMI TAKAHASHI
THE SOUP, ONE MORNING

Shizu listens to music after leaving the apartment.

Kitagawa is preparing to go out when Shizu demands to know where.

For the last thirty years, the PIA Film Festival in Japan has been a launching pad for Japanese independent filmmakers. *The Soup, One Morning* (*Aru asa, soup wa*, 2004), winner of its Grand Prize in 2004, signaled the arrival of a filmmaking duo of exceptional talent. The director, Izumi Takahashi, was catapulted to immediate fame, while the lead actor, Hiromasa Hirosue, who had worked with Takahashi closely on many shorter projects, was subsequently able to direct his own first feature, *The Lost Hum* (*Hanauta dorobo*, 2005). With the help of PIA's scholarship program, Hirosue then shot *Fourteen* (*Ju-yon-sai*, 2006) with a professional crew a year later. Hirosue acted in all three films; Takahashi wrote the screenplays.

Kitagawa, the main character in *The Soup, One Morning*, suffers from panic attacks. Sitting idle at home, he refuses medical help and is drawn to a religious cult. Shizu, his girlfriend, tries in vain to turn him around. Punctuated by the title cards of months ranging from October to April, which mark the passage of time from fall to spring, the film follows a clearly delineated structure that chronicles the disintegration of their relationship with harrowing precision and sensitivity.

The Soup, One Morning is a typical zero-budget independent production. There are only two main actors, both nonprofessional, and all the indoor scenes were shot in Hirosue's apartment. The actors doubled as the crew, and when not on camera, each would assist by holding the microphone just out of sight. Shooting was done with a DV camera owned by Takahashi. But rather than being cramped by such meager resources, a talented director like Takahashi can always turn them to his advantage.

Takahashi overcomes his limited shooting locations by creatively reworking shots and using voiceover, as in Kitagawa's first visit to the doctor. (With a close-up of some barbed wire, he is even able to turn the hospital into a symbol of war.) During the visit, Shizu is shown waiting behind the door, enveloped in darkness; a nearby window is blocked on the outside by dark, dry branches. Takahashi uses a similar window shot later when Shizo picks up medicine for Kitagawa, utilizing the same off-screen approach to dialogue. The shot returns once more in the final chapter, April: the view is the same, but now it is vacant of any human presence.

Takahashi takes full advantage of the flexibility offered by the DV camera without being bound by any of its limitations. When Shizu discovers that four hundred thousand yen is missing from their bank account, Kitagawa explains that the new yellow sofa contains amniotic fluid that will turn their karma around. The two get into an intense argument, and then a scuffle. All of this is captured with close-up handheld camerawork, but not in an obtrusive way. The insertion of static shots that periodically survey the scene from above gives the scene a distinct rhythm. When their friend Nishino comes to visit, however, Takahashi directs the camera at fixed spots in the living room and the kitchen instead of following the movement of the actors. As people move in and out of range, what we can't see happening off screen serves to create tension and suspense. The final showdown between the couple makes resourceful use of the bathroom: one stands inside, the other outside, the two separated by a ventilation window. The situation approaches the absurd as Shizu tries to whack Kitagawa with a stick and he holds onto it. The sequence goes on for three minutes, but Takahashi shoots it in a single, long, handheld take.

The most memorable moments in *The Soup, One Morning* are the two breakfast scenes that bracket the film, echoing each other while gesturing to the title. They are shot with a fixed camera setup. In the first breakfast, the two of them sit at opposite ends of the table, lit by refracted sunlight from the window; at this point, they are capable of carrying on a normal conversation. But during the concluding breakfast, the background wall is covered in shadow, and the black frame of a sliding door seems to separate the couple into two different worlds. Shizu is bathed in the sunlight and the shadows of leaves coming from outside, while Kitagawa is covered in dark and gloom. Shizu is struck by a sense of déjà vu and poignantly recalls the days when the two vacationed in Atami. The typhoon had struck, and everything was closed down. "Why don't we leave?" she asked then. "The weather will get better," Kitagawa replied, because he could see the sunlight filtering through the thick clouds.

The moment passes, and we return to the present. Dressed up to attend a cult gathering, Kitagawa graciously stands up and moves away, only to turn back and say, "I really thought it'd work out." He goes out of the camera's view again, and Shizu ends the scene with a heartrending remark: "We're strangers, after all."

Shizu laughs with Kitagawa about his eccentricity.

Year and place of birth
1973 Konosu, Japan
—

Lives and works in
Tokyo, Japan
—

Filmography
2004 The Soup, One Morning
(Aru asa, soup wa)
2007 What the Heart Craves
(Musunde hiraite)
— —

Release date
2005
—

Country of release
Japan
—

Language
Japanese
—

Running time
90 min.
—

Genre
Drama
—

Producer
Izumi Takahashi
—

Writer
Izumi Takahashi
—

Cinematographer
Izumi Takahashi
—

Score
Akie Namiki
—

Key cast
Hiromasa Hirosue: Kitagawa
Akie Namiki: Shizu
Izumi Takahashi: Cult member
Kazunari Kakihara: Doctor
—

Filming location
Tokyo, Japan
—

Format
MiniDV
—

Awards for The Soup, One Morning
PIA Film Festival
(Grand Prize, Technical
Achievement Award, 2004)
Vancouver International
Film Festival
(Dragons & Tigers Award for
Young East Asian Cinema,
2004)
Alba International Film Festival
(Albacinema Award for Best
Film, 2005)
Directors Guild of Japan
(New Directors Award, 2005)
Hong Kong International
Film Festival
(Golden DV Award, 2005)
— —

Kitagawa draws many eyes on his arm with a magic marker.

Shizu sees the train go by with "normal" people commuting to work.

Kitagawa starts to leave and Shizu bursts into tears.

SHIZU: It's not good for you.

KITAGAWA: How do you know? You've never been.

SHIZUKO: I know. I just do.

KITAGAWA: Because you hate it. That's the only reason.

SHIZU: Normal religions **don't** sell Karmic sofas.

KITAGAWA: What's normal? Christianity, Islam, and Buddhism? You don't mind them? **I'm free** to believe what I wish.

SHIZU: But we live **together**.

KITAGAWA: Does that mean **we** have to think the same way? We're strangers.

Kitagawa and Shizu discuss their religious differences.

For more than ten years a "slow war" has been going on in Algeria: a war without battlefields but with more than 100,000 people killed. It is this wilderness that Zina (Samira Kaddour) and Kamel (Rachid Amrani)—a young couple, bewildered and merry, gloomy and undisturbed—want to traverse one last time, before leaving for somewhere else.

TARIQ TEGUIA
ROME RATHER THAN YOU

Zina has a coffee on the balcony of her apartment.

A young man in a green sports jersey simulates an execution.

Tariq Teguia's feature-length debut, *Rome Rather Than You* (*Roma wa la n'touma*, 2006), and his follow-up, *Inland* (*Gabbla*, 2008), are full of breathtaking compositions of desolate streets and desert landscapes. The Algerian director's stories of people searching for meaning are a vital addition to world cinema, mixing the existential and political.

Teguia studied philosophy and arts. He teaches art history at a university in Algiers and works as a photographer; prior to his features, he also directed some amazing short films. He often cites the influence of the photographer Robert Frank on his work and expresses the desire to bridge the artificial boundaries between the plastic arts, philosophy, photography, documentary, and fiction film.

The setting of *Rome Rather Than You* is Algiers and its suburb La Madrague. Algeria has recently emerged from a ten-year civil war in the 1990s that cast a shadow on an entire generation. Twenty-four-year-old Zina, a doctor's assistant, lives with her old-fashioned parents in the city and trades affectionately barbed flirtations with her boyfriend, Kamel. Indefinitely between jobs, he is chasing after a man named Bosco, a fixer for those seeking to emigrate to Europe. One day he persuades her to leave work early, promising a trip to the beach, with a stop for some business along the way in the industrial dockside neighborhood of La Madrague.

The journey quickly becomes the destination, as Kamel, fast and loose, stops to ask around for Bosco, leaving Zina fuming in the car. Construction projects and garages line the streets; the beach does turn out to be gorgeous, though, even if it's in the middle of nowhere. Earning comparisons to Jean-Luc Godard, Teguia depicts their restless, desultory search with playful shifts between still compositions, ebullient handheld camerawork, and walking tracking shots, while the banter between the young couple has the cool yet bitter swing of the characters in Godard's *Band of Outsiders* (*Bande à part*, 1964). Zina is first seen reading a book by black American expat-to-Paris Chester Himes; Kafka and Rimbaud come up; title cards present provocative thoughts.

Equally important to the effect of the film is the gorgeous cinematography, especially at night, and the subtly musical sense of rhythm. These two qualities fold us into the lived experience of Zina, Kamel, and Algiers itself. Teguia's extraordinary editing scheme regularly slips in haunting landscapes that are not clearly related to the couple's journey, and boldly cuts between stillness (Kamel and Zina on a beach) and movement (a view from a train, a car). Music is also key: Ornette Coleman, Cheb Azzedine, Archie Shepp.

Yet as aesthetically pleasing as all this may sound, *Rome Rather Than You* takes place over the course of a day and night when Kamel is trying to change his life and to escape this world, preferably with Zina. This is not an easy task in the politically fraught climate of contemporary Algiers. Teguia abruptly stops the couple's wanderings (now joined by a friend) with a tense scene in a café captured in one continuous shot. Three cops in plain clothes, led by a viciously cynical chief, harangue them about everything from the ages on their papers to soccer-team loyalties. The purpose is intimidation, the generational anger is close to the surface, and the right answers, it is clear, do not exist. The night ends in jail, and then a stay, since it is past state curfew, with friends (one of whom seems to be a dissident journalist). Teguia shoots the tail end of their wretched night bathed in the red-haze light of sodium-vapor lamps. It is nighttime in Algiers.

Kamel and Zina eventually arrive at a half-abandoned building where Bosco is supposed to be running his passport operation. They find a passport, but they also discover what appears to be Bosco's body, in a tub—as if the threat of violence lurking underneath the café scene could not be avoided after all. Earlier, Teguia took the time to portray dockside goings-on at night, tracking three figures as they crept alongside ship containers that look expressionistically huge. Speaking to the camera, one of them expresses his desire to leave the country and seek a better life. With the appearance of this ordinary, unexplained bit character, the predicament of Kamel and Zina that we had been following is now shown from a fresh angle, and with the charismatic couple's grisly discovery, the difficulty of realizing such a dream is made painfully clear.

Thus fiction is embedded in documentary poetry, as the result of what the director calls "an attention to what lies around, a concern for sudden appearances." Far from producing ready-made fiction, and always prepared to change the script according to reality during the shoot, Teguia achieves a stunningly beautiful and sensitive portrayal of souls in crisis and fully deserves recognition as a filmmaker to watch.

Zina walks through the street before running into Kamel.

Year and place of birth
1966   Algiers, Algeria
—

Lives and works in
Algiers, Algeria
Paris, France
—

Education
Université Paris 1
    Panthéon-Sorbonne, France
Université Paris 8 Vincennes
    Saint-Denis, France
—

Filmography
1992   Kech' mouvemen
       (short) (co-directed with
       Yacine Taguia)
1996   The Dog (Le Chien) (short)
1998   Ferrailles d'attente
       (short)
2002   The Fence (Haçla) (short)
2006   Rome Rather Than You
       (Roma wa la n'touma)
2008   Inland (Gabbla)
—

Director's awards
The Fence
Marrakech International
Film Festival
    (Special Jury Award, 2003)

Inland
Venice International Film Festival
    (FIPRESCI Award
    for Best Film, 2008)
Jeonju International
Film Festival
    (Special Jury Prize, 2009)
— —

Release date
2006
—

Country of release
France
—

Language
Arabic
—

Running time
111 min.
—

Genre
Drama
—

Producers
Yacine Teguia, Tariq Teguia,
Cati Couteau, Helge Albers
—

Writer
Tariq Teguia
—

Cinematographers
Nasser Medjkane,
Hacène Aït Kaci
—

Score
El Hachemi L'Kerfaoui Tchamba
—

Key cast
Rachid Amrani: Kamel
Samira Kaddour: Zina
Ahmed Benaïssa: Policeman
Kader Affak: Malek
Rabie Azzabi:
    Young man in green tracksuit
Lali Maloufi: Merzak
Fethi Ghares:
    Young man in work overalls
Moustapha Benchaïb: Mahmoud
Khaddra Boudedhane:
    Zina's mother
—

Filming location
Algiers, Algeria
—

Format
35 mm

Awards for Rome Rather Than You
Thessaloniki International
Film Festival
    (Everyday Life:
    Transcendence or
    Reconciliation Award, 2006)
EntreVues Belfort International
Film Festival
    (Jury Prize Award,
    Best Actress and Actor
    Awards, 2007)
Fribourg International
Film Festival
    (Jury Prize Award, 2007)
— —

The mysterious young man in green at work.

Zina looks away as Kamel dreams of leaving Algiers.

ZINA: You'd go and leave all this?

KAMEL: Marseille's calling!
Marseille...kingdom of France...
we're not finished with them.
Spain. Alicante. It's been a while,
but we still dream. Naples...the
cousins. America, where there is
a just king under whom no one will
know persecution. Australia...
Australia...

ZINA: To do what? There's only sheep
and kangaroos there!

Kamel tells Zina he wants to hear her breath, the breath of a living girl.

They look out at a sea they may never cross.

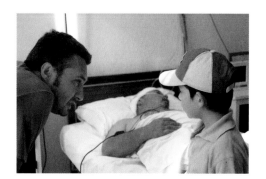

Mustafa (Osman Inan) is a hard-working and ambitious agricultural merchant who is cold and austere toward his family. One day he has a brain hemorrhage on a business trip and falls into a coma. His wife, Güler (Ayten Tökün), is convinced her husband was having an affair. Mustafa's brother, Hasan (Taner Birsel), who chose to live a life of solitude after a divorce and has always been an outsider to his relatives, now finds himself involved with his brother's family. Hasan is faced with the mystery of his brother's mistress and the money he lost during his potentially fatal trip.

SEYFI TEOMAN
SUMMER BOOK

Ali walks to school.

It's no surprise that a new generation of directors— pioneers of a renaissance in Turkish cinema—have been revisiting rural areas. Because now is the time to confront the consequences of deficient modernization efforts in Turkey, following a rapid urbanization in the 1980s. Traditionally there's been an escape of artists from the country to the city, but lately the return of directors to the countryside has enabled them to question issues of "ruralness." Beginning with Nuri Bilge Ceylan's *Clouds of May* (*Mayis sikintisi*, 1999), filmmakers continue to address this not as a social phenomenon but as a personal dilemma. This dilemma can roughly be stated as a person or character feeling "neither here nor there," a kind of rural anxiety that expresses the ambiguity of the new millennium.

In this context, *Summer Book* (*Tatil kitabi*, 2008), by young director Seyfi Teoman, is a new link in the chain of "rural films." It follows a family in the Southern Anatolian seaside town of Silifke over one summer. There is no central character, although the events are mainly told from the point of view of Ali, a ten-year-old boy. His family members include a repressive and authoritarian father who makes a living as a merchant; an older brother who wants out of the military school he is attending; an uncle who left for the big city to follow his dreams, only to return in defeat; and a homemaker mother who suffers from her husband's potential infidelities. Rural life is still presented as quiet and calm, but *Summer Book* neither romanticizes the rural town nor makes it a symbol of a dead end. Rather, *Summer Book* depicts

human contradictions in a setting that it perceives as a microcosm of the rest of the world.

Renowned for his short films, Teoman opens his debut feature with kids in blue uniforms joyfully pouring out of classrooms as they start their summer holidays. This flawless scene sets the groundwork for the director to question the idea of "holiday," and forms a contrast with his later observation that "rural is the incarnation of growing up." Following the warning of a teacher—don't be lazy, do your homework—Ali's summer reading is snatched away by bullying classmates, thus severing his bonds with school but designating the summer months to come as his "education of life." Dramatic events take place over the course of the film, but Teoman prefers not to reveal them on screen. For instance, the brain hemorrhage that Ali's father suffers, which shakes up the status quo of the family and causes crucial transformations in their lives, is not shown, but the reactions of the characters are observed instead.

One of the most fundamental issues of the film is the requirement to sustain social roles. Ali's older brother cannot leave the military academy because of the hefty reparations he would have to pay, and therefore cannot change or rebel against his father's plans for him. It seems as if everyone would be pursuing their dreams if not for the father. However, the characters who try to disrupt the order are mere reflections of conformism. The circle closes when the uncle, who previously appeared sympathetic to the family because he objected to his brother, ends up assuming his throne. The status quo is indeed a vicious

circle. At the end of the film, Ali returns to school when summer is over, thus completing that idea.

Ali's father forcing him to sell chewing gum on the street; his brother's inability to pay his way out of his military academy; the wife's conviction that her husband is cheating on her; and the mysterious vacations of their father, who mentions a certain sum of money that needs to be found, add an illicit dimension to the film.

It's in the details—the ordinary moments of life, which here reflect inspiration from Kiarostami and Antonioni—where Teoman searches for meaning. Promotional announcements made on public loud-speakers of the municipality, the ruffling sound that the worker women make as they pack lemons, Ali's mother desperately beating wool in the backyard: The film successfully defines the flow of time and the rhythm of the small town as a gear that eternally turns the same way. The tradesmen who sit in front of their stores looking at the passersby represent the standstill of the permanent citizens, while the youth, dreaming about life in the city, represent the possibility of escape. Consequentially, as the events that unfold during the summer demonstrate, people change but their roles remain the same.

Although *Summer Book* is somewhat didactic, it achieves a great deal using no music and very little dialogue. Teoman defines "rural anxiety" as the order of the family, small town, country, and, finally, the world, and in effect anticipates possible subjects for future films.

Veysel glances at a woman.

Year and place of birth
1977   Kayseri, Turkey
—

Lives and works in
Istanbul, Turkey
—

Education
Bogazici University,
**   Istanbul, Turkey**
Polish National Film School,
**   Lodz, Poland**
—

Filmography
2004   Apartment (Apartman)
2008   Summer Book
**   (Tatil kitabi)**
2010   Bizim Buyuk
**   Caresizligimiz**
**   (Our Grand Despair)**
— —

Release date
2008
—

Country of release
Turkey
—

Language
Turkish
—

Running time
92 min.
—

Genre
Family Drama
—

Producers
Yamaç Okur, Nadir Öperli
—

Writer
Seyfi Teoman
—

Cinematographer
Arnau Valls Colomer
—

Key cast
Taner Birsel: Hasan
Tayfun Günay: Ali
Harun Özüağ: Veysel
Ayten Tökün: Güler
Osman Inan: Mustafa
—

Filming locations
Silifke, Turkey
Urgup, Turkey
—

Format
35 mm
—

Awards for Summer Book
Artfilm International
Film Festival
**   (Best Film Award, 2008)**
European Film Festival Palic
**   (FIPRESCI Special**
**   Mention, 2008)**

Istanbul International
Film Festival
**   (Best Film Award, FIPRESCI**
**   Award in National**
**   Competition, 2008)**
Montreal World Film Festival
**   (Bronze Zenith – First**
**   Feature Films Competition,**
**   2008)**
Taormina International
Film Festival
**   (Special Jury Prize, 2008)**
— —

Hasan and Veysel drink beer next to the river.

Ali decides to cut off part of his hair.

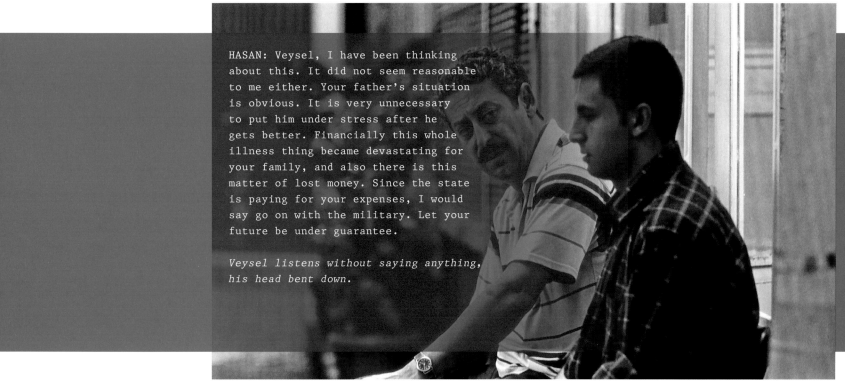

HASAN: Veysel, I have been thinking about this. It did not seem reasonable to me either. Your father's situation is obvious. It is very unnecessary to put him under stress after he gets better. Financially this whole illness thing became devastating for your family, and also there is this matter of lost money. Since the state is paying for your expenses, I would say go on with the military. Let your future be under guarantee.

Veysel listens without saying anything, his head bent down.

Hasan and Veysel sit in front of the butcher shop.

Since 1980, German institutions have been sending teenagers to the south of Portugal as part of several experimental projects of social re-education. Katrin (Sylta Fee Wegmann) comes to Alentejo within this context. She does not establish a relationship with her environment, a situation heightened by the harshness of the landscape and the void of a socially barren region. Katrin, Julia (Alice Dwyer), and Pedro (Luís Guerra) form an enclave in a no-man's land—a physical and mental desert.

HUGO VIEIRA DA SILVA
BODY RICE

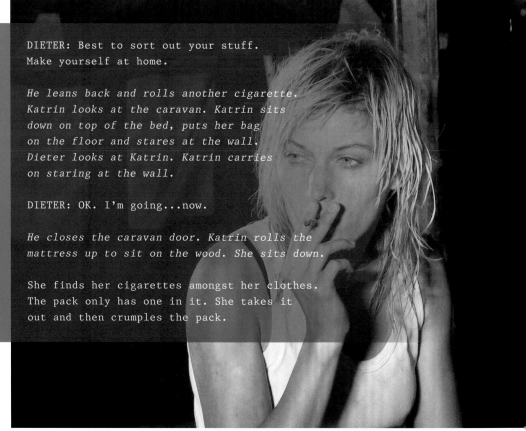

DIETER: Best to sort out your stuff.
Make yourself at home.

He leans back and rolls another cigarette.
Katrin looks at the caravan. Katrin sits
down on top of the bed, puts her bag
on the floor and stares at the wall.
Dieter looks at Katrin. Katrin carries
on staring at the wall.

DIETER: OK. I'm going...now.

He closes the caravan door. Katrin rolls the
mattress up to sit on the wood. She sits down.

She finds her cigarettes amongst her clothes.
The pack only has one in it. She takes it
out and then crumples the pack.

Katrin smokes a cigarette in the caravan.

Katrin rests outside of a home upon arriving in Alentejo.

Hugo Vieira da Silva was born in 1974 in Porto, where he studied law before enrolling at Lisbon's Escola Superior de Teatro e Cinema. In 2001, he made the documentary, *Grupo Puzzle* (2001), about a leading 1970s Portuguese artists' collective.

Body Rice (2006), Vieira da Silva's first fictional feature film, produced by Paulo Branco, was entered in competition at the 2006 Locarno International Film Festival, and worldwide distribution followed. In 2009 he was invited by Cannes' L'Atelier program to complete his new film, *Red Cross* (2009), whose subject is the taboo surrounding death.

He then moved to Berlin, a city he's drawn to because of his interest in contemporary dance, the visual arts, photography, and poetry. And, above all, this young director is interested in offering the public different kinds of stories than those being told every day. As he says, "I want to make problems, to provoke questions, and not to provide solutions. Otherwise, we'd be forever saying the same thing."

For *Body Rice*, Vieira da Silva took his inspiration from a world he had been curious about for a long time: the "social rehabilitation" centers run by German agencies in Portugal. Making the film was a way for somebody wearing the two hats of ethnologist-documentarian and image-thief to address the theme of adolescence head-on, without pulling any punches.

Katrin, a young German offender, has been sent to one of these rehab programs in Portugal. Dragging her feelings of alienation across the dry plains of Alentejo, she meets Julia, who has also been placed by social workers, and Pedro, who lives in the region and is as lost and marginalized as Katrin is. The confrontations these youngsters seek are constantly thwarted and the bonds they form are inevitably destroyed, because they cannot break free from their feelings of lethargy and isolation.

The training program does nothing to change the nihilism and selfishness of Katrin's existence. The more she wanders through the countryside surrounding the barrack-like center, the more lost and removed from reality she becomes. She has no enthusiasm, no hope, no particular desire, except, perhaps, to go back to Germany, or to concentrate on her situation and the people around her long enough to serve as a momentary distraction before falling back into the blackness.

Body Rice is like a jigsaw puzzle in the sense that it features many pieces that look like they can be assembled in countless ways, but, as always, comes together in the end. The film's pieces (re)compose themselves from the moments of brute emotion that punctuate it, and the bursts of music that make up its multilayered, harrowing, mind-blowing soundtrack.

The film's ashy, washed-out images signify the feeling of flatness and indifference that marks the everyday lives of these young people—a lost generation, heirs of the "no future" of the 1980s. *Body Rice* rests on a risky but extremely original strategy, focusing on moments of contemplation and waiting, on what is unsaid. This intense, engrossing, "reading between the lines" allows us to enter the world of these characters, bringing us very close to their disenchantment, echoed in the dryness of the setting. Their existence, always on the verge of eruption, extreme violence, or even death, forms the heart of a film that is constantly on razor's edge, a tragic vision of the contemporary world.

"My characters are shadows," says Vieira da Silva. "We'll never get to know everything about them, in the same way that we never get to know everything about anyone. I wanted to film their bodies peripherally—their surfaces and their skin. Formally, I did exactly the same thing: events are suggested rather than made explicit. I am interested most in what is not shown . . . An idea took shape when I first worked with some of these young people: nothing would come to a clear end, all would be fragmented, and my (our) job would be to continually build, reconstruct, and lose everything anew . . . These feelings invade and infect the film; the sensation of fullness or love is not achievable . . . An action is started, halted, and forgotten, like a silent, irreversible catastrophe that slowly develops like a disease. And it's this development that becomes the film's sole subject, which in order to be observed calls for a suspension of time."

A rave party in Alentejo, Portugal.

Year and place of birth
1974   Porto, Portugal

—

Lives and works in
Berlin, Germany

—

Education
Catholic University, Porto,
**   Portugal**
Escola Superior de Teatro e
**   Cinema, Lisbon, Portugal**

—

Filmography
2001   Grupo Puzzle
2002   Confesso
**   (Albuquerque Mendes)**
2006   Body Rice
2009   Red Cross

— —

Release date
2006

—

Country of release
Portugal

—

Language
German, Portuguese

—

Running time
120 min.

—

Genre
Drama

—

Producer
Paulo Branco

—

Writer
Hugo Vieira da Silva

—

Cinematographer
Paulo Ares

—

Score
Joey Beltram, X-mal
Deutschland, Joy Division,
Einstürzende Neubauten,
Kosmonautentrau

—

Key cast
Sylta Fee Wegmann: Katrin
Alice Dwyer: Julia
André Hennicke: Dieter
Julika Jenkins: Anja
Pedro Hestnes: Joaquim
Luis Guerra: Pedro

—

Filming location
Alentejo, Portugal

—

Format
Super 16 mm

—

Awards for Body Rice
Locarno International
Film Festival
**   (Special Mention, 2006)**
Buenos Aires International
Independent Film Festival
**   (Best Director, 2007)**
Cine Ceará National
Cinema Festival
**   (Best Cinematography,**
**   Best Sound, 2007)**
Mexico City International
Contemporary Film Festival
**   (Best Director, 2007)**

— —

Dieter's corpse is found in the dam.

Julia and Katrin rest after leaving home and wandering without purpose.

Lily (Loren Horsley) is an awkward, lonely waitress. Jarrod (Jemaine Clement) is a self-obsessed candlemaker. When Jarrod returns to his hometown on a mission of revenge, a love-struck Lily follows him. Jarrod needs someone to have a bit of faith in him; Lily needs someone to love. It's not the perfect match, but it may be one worth fighting for.

TAIKA WAITITI
EAGLE VS SHARK

Jarrod breaks up with Lily.

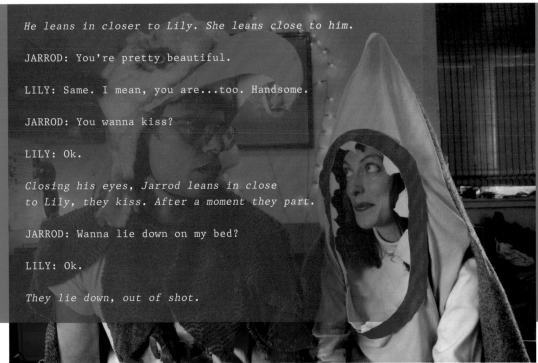

He leans in closer to Lily. She leans close to him.

JARROD: You're pretty beautiful.

LILY: Same. I mean, you are...too. Handsome.

JARROD: You wanna kiss?

LILY: Ok.

Closing his eyes, Jarrod leans in close to Lily, they kiss. After a moment they part.

JARROD: Wanna lie down on my bed?

LILY: Ok.

They lie down, out of shot.

Lily and Jarrod meet at a costume party.

In the past few decades, New Zealand has placed itself firmly on the cinematic map for housing a huge talent pool of filmmakers. While most people are familiar with Peter Jackson, and perhaps fewer with Jane Campion, many of the most innovative and interesting works the country gives birth to sadly never make it much further than the film-festival circuit. Even after winning some sixteen Oscars (yes, eleven for Jackson's *Lord of the Rings* [2001–3] trilogy), it's still not that easy to catch up with the fine work being produced there. That, however, is changing very quickly.

In 2004, I was taken with Taika Waititi, a new filmmaker whose short film would soon be met with much well-deserved global fanfare. His Oscar-nominated *Two Cars, One Night* (2004) focused on a boy and a girl who meet in a parking lot outside a pub while their caretakers presumably have a drink inside. They start off teasing each other before breaking down their own insecurities and connecting in the most sweetly simple yet profound way possible. The film featured a real sense of style made possible by Waititi's mastery of black and white, and struck a chord with the kid in all of us. As a result, people were quick to take notice.

Waititi's follow-up short, *Tama tu* (2005), was about a group of Maori soldiers waiting in a destroyed edifice as a battle quickly approaches. Using no dialogue, Waititi proved he could use visuals to drive a story—one that favored character over plot and combined drama with some very funny moments. It's an engaging piece of work that scored an Honorable Mention prize at the 2005 Sundance Film Festival,

a number of film-festival prizes after that, and opened a door for Waititi to explore feature filmmaking.

With that goal in mind, Waititi entered the Sundance Screenwriters and Directors Lab. With much support from Bird Runningwater, Associate Director of the Sundance Native American and Indigenous Program (Waititi is of Te Whanau-a-Apanui descent), he put together what would later become *Eagle vs Shark* (2007), a positively peculiar comedy that introduced the rather brilliant actress Loren Horsley to American audiences, and helped Jemaine Clement rise from a respected but relatively unknown singer-comedian to the international star of HBO's *Flight of the Conchords*.

Eagle vs Shark centers on a very awkward but quite lovable girl, Lily. She falls in love with Jarrod, who by all accounts and purposes becomes quite the Mr. Wrong. Lily and Jarrod begin a relationship whose potential quickly ebbs because of Jarrod's lack of sincerity and true compassion for Lily, his seemingly misfit family, and his mindless plot to seek vengeance on his childhood bully. You can only imagine where it goes from there.

A tonally absurd piece that generates laughs from beginning to end, *Eagle vs Shark* exhibits what Waititi does best: allow somewhat ridiculous characters to connect with audiences. This sense of connection works so well because of the combination of smart writing (tipping to the bizarre yet never going too far) and endearing performances (conveying humor that comes across as familiarly uncomfortable rather than completely unrealistic). Waititi understands the fine

line where too much absurdity can sacrifice a level of heart and earnestness, and in effect, instead of making us laugh *at* the antics of Lily and Jarrod, we laugh *with* them. Pulling off this kind of balance would be a real challenge for any filmmaker, and first-timer Waititi lives up to it with great skill.

It's nearly impossible to label *Eagle vs Shark* a romantic comedy without incorporating quote marks. This can be attested to the story's transcendence of the genre's usual "girl meets boy" trappings. And that's not to say the film doesn't contain elements of the romantic-comedy formula—it very much does—but even for all its outrageous moments, the film maintains a captivating level of depth that is missing from most others produced under the same limiting genre classifications. Factor in Waititi's skillful eye and expertise behind the lens—the entire film is complemented by a striking, colorful vision that employs cinematography, animated sequences, costume, and design to their fullest—and it's no wonder that the film found a distributor in Miramax and performed to an international audience ready for an anomalous take on love and relationships.

There's no doubt that Waititi's best work is still ahead—and with the success of *Eagle vs Shark*, that is saying a lot. Also blessed with the skill to perform (Waititi had a small role in *Eagle vs Shark* as well as on *Flight of the Conchords*), Taika is a true triple-threat to the business. He's someone who knows both comedy and drama, visual style and characterization, and will inevitably master the mainstream audience as he keeps his indie integrity very much in check.

Lily runs, but goes nowhere, on the mousewheel.

Lily plays guitar and becomes the life of the party.

Year and place of birth
1975   Wellington, New Zealand
—
Lives and works in
Auckland, New Zealand
—
Education
**Victoria University of Wellington,
New Zealand**
—
Filmography
2002   *John & Pogo* (short)
**2004   *Two Cars, One Night*
(short)**
2005   *Tama tu* (short)
2007   *Eagle vs Shark*
2010   *Boy*
—
Director's awards
Two Cars, One Night
**AFI Fest
(Short Award, 2004)**
**Hamburg International
Short Film Festival
(Hamburg Short Film
Award, 2004)**

**Oberhausen International
Short Film Festival
(Award of the Theatre
Owners, 2004)**
**Seattle International
Film Festival
(Best Short – Live Action,
2004)**

Tama tu
**Berlin International Film Festival
(Panorama Special Jury Short
Film Award, 2005)**
**Indianapolis International
Film Festival
(Best Short, 2005)**
**Palm Springs International
Short Fest
(Best Live Action Over 15
Minutes, 2005)**
**Stockholm Film Festival
(Best Short Film, 2005)**
— —

Release date
2007
—
Country of release
New Zealand
—
Language
English
—
Running time
93 min.
—
Genre
Comedy
—

Producers
Ainsley Gardiner, Cliff Curtis
—
Writer
Taika Waititi
—
Cinematographer
Adam Clark
—
Score
The Phoenix Foundation
—

Key cast
Loren Horsley: Lily
Jemaine Clement: Jarrod
Joel Tobeck: Damon
Brian Sergent: Jonah
Craig Hall: Doug
Rachel House: Nancy
Morag Hills: Vinny
Bernard Stewart: Zane
Taika Waititi: Gordon
—
Filming location
Wellington, New Zealand
—
Format
35 mm
—

Awards for *Eagle vs Shark*
**Newport Beach Film Festival
(Outstanding Achievement
in Filmmaking – Comedy,
2007)**
**Newport International
Film Festival
(Best Actress, Best Narrative
Feature, 2007)**
**U.S. Comedy Arts Festival
(Film Discovery Jury Award –
Best Screenplay, 2007)**
**New Zealand Film and TV Awards
(Achievement in Directing
in Film, 2008)**
— —

Jarrod is beaten up by his high school nemesis.

Lily and Jarrod lie side by side and watch the sunset together.

Jule (Julia Jentsch) is a waitress who can't make ends meet. She moves in with her boyfriend Peter (Stipe Erceg) and his friend Jan (Daniel Brühl), two young men united by their passion to change the world. While Peter is away on vacation, feelings between Jan and Jule intensify. Jan and Jule impulsively break into the home of Hardenberg (Burghart Klaussner), a well-to-do stranger, but their growing passion has made them careless. When they're forced to return the following night to retrieve a forgotten cell phone, Hardenberg surprises them. After calling Peter for help, the trio decide to kidnap Hardenberg and hide in the mountains.

Jan sits in the park.

HANS WEINGARTNER
THE EDUKATORS

Police aggressively stop protestors in Berlin.

A happy, nuclear family returns from vacation to discover that their home has been occupied in their absence. What appears to be a simple burglary takes a sinister turn when the owners discover their designer furniture piled high like a bonfire heap in the center of the room. Discomfited, the family immediately search for their most valued objects: the stereo and a set of military figurines (which have suffered the indignity of being rehoused in a toilet bowl). Nothing has been taken, but the intruders have left an ominous note: "Your days of plenty are numbered."

So opens the playfully revolutionary *The Edukators* (*Die fetten Jahre sind vorbei*, 2004), the second feature-length film from Hans Weingartner. Popular with audiences around the world, it garnered a Palme d'Or nomination at Cannes in 2004. At least one reason for its success is undoubtedly the film's sense of humor and Weingartner's lightness of touch when dealing with issues such as anticapitalist sentiment, greed, terrorism, and rampant consumerism. For although the plot includes trespassing and kidnapping, *The Edukators* is punctuated with fresh air, bright sunlight, and childlike optimism.

The movie centers on the exploits of three young idealists: Jan, Peter, and Jule. Peter and Jan share a squat in central Berlin. Jan is a complex and brooding character who, unlike the more garrulous Peter, eschews smoking cannabis because it "dulls a young person's revolutionary spirit." He is played with grumpy charm by Daniel Brühl (fresh from Wolfgang Becker's *Good Bye Lenin!*, 2003), while Peter is portrayed by the lupine Stipe Erceg. Together they

are "the Edukators," and under the cover of night they break into the homes of the wealthy. The pair rearrange furniture and other objects in an effort to freak out the pampered owners. Weingartner's film stresses that the goal of the break-ins is not financial gain, but a form of poetic terrorism, designed to unsettle the wealthy and make them aware of their excesses. One variant of the notes they leave behind reads simply, "You have too much money." In a comic moment, Weingartner reveals that the less militant Peter is not above sharing the wealth by pocketing the occasional Rolex.

In an example of the film's almost Situationist plotting, Peter goes on a trip to Barcelona, and moody Jan is dispatched to assist Peter's girlfriend, Jule, with packing up the apartment she's about to be evicted from. With a warm nod toward Truffaut's *Jules and Jim* (1962), Jule and Jan grow closer. Jule reveals that she owes almost one hundred thousand euros after a car accident with a Mercedes driver a few years ago. Jule's lack of insurance and her partial culpability for the accident are not lost on the audience, but Jan is immediately appalled that one person's life can be so damaged by another for whom the car and the amount of money mean nothing. The scenario echoes the plight of the sweatshop workers on whose behalf Jule is seen protesting earlier in the film.

When Jan reveals to Jule the secret nighttime hobby he shares with Peter, she is at first shocked, but quickly realizes that the man to whom she owes the money is on their list. She begs Jan to carry out a break-in, daring him to do "something really extreme." When they go ahead with it, the pair escape undetected, but

on the pretext of a missing cell phone, the film brings the couple back to the house, where they are found by the returning homeowner, Hardenberg. Trapped now in a far more serious situation, the pair call Peter, kidnap Hardenberg, and flee to the mountains to decide what to do.

It is there, in the picturesque Tirol, that Weingartner's film spreads its wings. The script throughout gives voice to the disillusionment and disappointment felt by today's youth over the abandoned ideals of their parents' generation, but with the addition of Hardenberg, these divergent sentiments are made flesh. Hardenberg reveals that he too was once a radical, but is now comfortably ensconced in bourgeois conservatism, implying that a lean to the right is unavoidable as one matures. Over beers and a joint, however, Hardenberg starts to enjoy the company of his captors, and at one point even covers for them by referring to Jan as his son.

Weingartner's lingering shots of the lush countryside reinforce the suggestion that Hardenberg is growing and even learning a lesson from his youthful captors. Yet he is not a simple character: he takes pleasure in reminiscing about the revolution and free love of his youth, while spitefully informing Peter of Jan and Jules's burgeoning relationship. That Hardenberg later goes back on his promise not to call the police is perhaps emblematic of the older generation's abandonment of the causes of their youth. But in a similar sense, the twist in the film's tail—when Jan and Jule are reunited with Peter and make good on their escape to Spain—conveys a sense of hope for the future.

During breakfast, Jule tells Peter that she can't join him in Barcelona.

Year and place of birth
1970 Feldkirch, Austria
—
Lives and works in
Berlin, Germany
—
Education
Academy of Media Arts,
   Cologne, Germany
—
Filmography
1993 J-Cam (short)
1995 Der Dreifachstecker
   (short)
1999 Frank (short)
2001 The White Sound
   (Das weisse Rauschen)

2004 The Edukators (Die fetten
   Jahre sind vorbei)
2007 Reclaim Your Brain
   (Free Rainer)
2009 Deutschland '09
   ("Gefährder")
—
Director's awards
The White Sound
First Steps Awards
   (First Steps Award, 2001)
German Film Critics
Association Awards
   (Best Feature Film Debut,
   2001)
Max Ophüls Festival
   (Max Ophüls Award, 2001)
— —

Release date
2004
—
Country of release
Austria, Germany
—
Language
German
—
Running time
126 min.
—
Genre
Drama
—

Producers
Hans Weingartner,
Antonin Svoboda
—
Writers
Hans Weingartner,
Katharina Held
—
Cinematographers
Daniela Knapp,
Matthias Schellenberg
—
Score
Andreas Wodraschke

Key cast
Daniel Brühl: Jan
Julia Jentsch: Jule
Stipe Erceg: Peter
Burghart Klaussner: Hardenberg
—
Filming locations
Achenkirch, Austria
Berlin, Germany
Brandenburg, Germany
Hendaye, France
Lequeitio, Spain
—
Format
DVCPRO50
—

Awards for The Edukators
Munich International
Film Festival
   (Young German Cinema
   Awards – Best Actor,
   Best Direction,
   Best Screenwriting, 2004)
Bavarian Film Awards
   (Best Young Actress, 2005)
German Film Awards
   (Film Award in Gold for Best
   Performance by an Actor in
   a Supporting Role, Film Award
   in Silver for Outstanding
   Feature Film, 2005)
German Film Critics
Association Awards
   (Best Actress, Best Film,
   2005)
— —

HARDENBERG: Do you guys want to know what I really think of you?

The three nod, half amused, half curious.

HARDENBERG (Blows out the inhaled smoke): I admire you.

Jan, Jule and Peter try to not show how surprised they are by this comment. Peter sarcastically raises his eyebrows.

PETER: Oh, really?

Hardenberg continues.

HARDENBERG: Well, of course I don't agree with everything you do. Or how you do it. But truthfully you are doing something that I always dreamed of.

Jan, Jule, and Peter listen to Hardenberg's story.

The three sit outside the mountain hut.

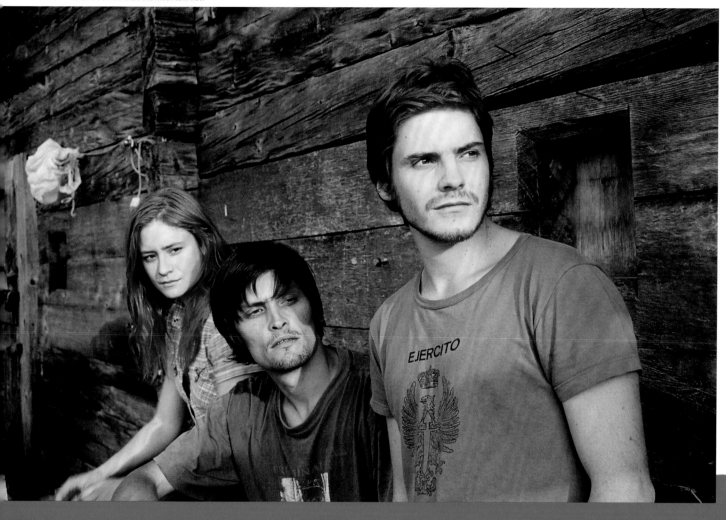

Peter thinks that Hardenburg is trying to flee, but finds him admiring the mountain view.

Maggy (Kim Schnitzer) is a single mother but also an ordinary teenager without a clear idea of what she wants from life. She can still hang out with friends, because her mother helps take care of her baby, Lucy. After meeting Gordon (Gordon Schmidt) at a disco, she falls in love and moves in with him. At first Gordon takes pride in his new role as a father, but living together is a bigger strain for both than either expected.

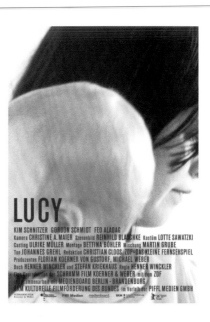

HENNER WINCKLER
LUCY

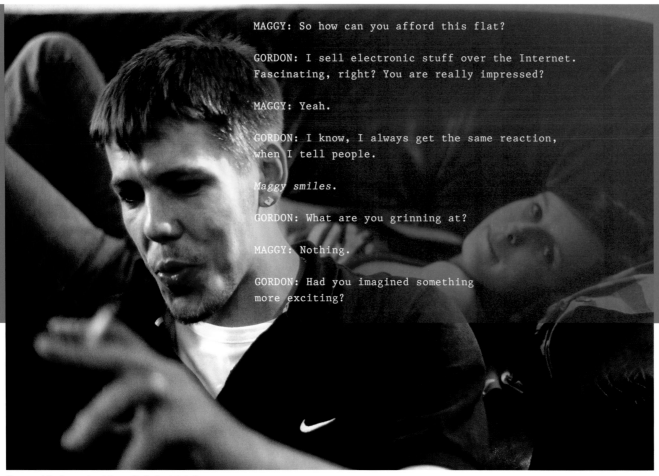

MAGGY: So how can you afford this flat?

GORDON: I sell electronic stuff over the Internet. Fascinating, right? You are really impressed?

MAGGY: Yeah.

GORDON: I know, I always get the same reaction, when I tell people.

Maggy smiles.

GORDON: What are you grinning at?

MAGGY: Nothing.

GORDON: Had you imagined something more exciting?

Maggy and Gordon smoke a joint and talk about their lives.

Henner Winckler is often associated with a group of filmmakers for whom the term Berliner Schule was coined. The label delineates a stylistic movement in German cinema operating far away from sensationalism or melodrama. Emerging during the 1990s, it can be identified by its stripped-down images that are used to tell realistic stories from day-to-day life. But the label ends up obscuring the differences between the filmmakers whose work falls under it.

Angela Schanelec, Thomas Arslan, and Christian Petzold belong to the first generation of the Berliner Schule, while Maren Ade, Ulrich Köhler, and Henner Winckler are the key representatives of the second generation. These last three maintain a close relationship, having known each other for a long time, and still exchange ideas on script development to this day. Despite this, however, their work is only similar up to a certain point, their alleged homogeneity not really standing up to closer inspection. Ade's debut feature, *The Forest for the Trees* (*Der Wald vor lauter Bäumen*, 2003) has a pronounced external drama, as the protagonist finds herself struggling with the outside world for the entire film. By contrast, Köhler's way of telling a story is characterized by a much more pared-down approach to dramatization. His characters are phlegmatic, much like Winckler's. But while Köhler's characters are constantly rebelling, the youth in Winckler's films are trapped within themselves, their concerns directed inward.

Lucy (2006) tells the story of Maggy, who has just turned eighteen, lives with her mother, and is no longer with the father of her child. At a disco, she meets Gordon and falls in love with him. She's impressed that he earns his own money and has his own flat. Following an argument with her mother, she decides to move in with him. Although Maggy hasn't had to take care of her child to any great extent until now, she takes Lucy with her, looking after her with Gordon. Initially, he likes playing the father role, but living together turns out to be more exhausting than either of them anticipated. As Gordon becomes more and more withdrawn, Maggy is increasingly left to her own devices.

Realism and art, real life and its dramatized form—how do you bring these things together? Winckler tells Maggy's story like a neutral observer would, from a distance that is transformed into intimacy in a barely perceptible manner. There is no one overarching drama to propel the plot forward, but lots of inconspicuous ones. Maggy finds herself caught between childhood and adulthood, between the drama of puberty and the disappointments of adult life. Her dilemma doesn't manifest itself in an attempt to go against her mother's generation, but rather in her attempts to imitate its behavior. Whether barbecuing on the balcony or buying a washing machine, she turns being an adult into a demonstration, intent on showing that she is more grown-up than even her mother. She seeks salvation in simulation, finding happiness in a game. But when it comes down to it, the moments of happiness she finds are always fleeting, disintegrating into disappointment as soon as the game is over.

Maggy wants to do it better. But she has no ideals of her own, looking instead to the idyllic images of family that she knows from the media. She watches programs about disasters on television, the big events taking place across the globe in sharp contrast to her own tiny world. Mixing laconicism and intensity, Winckler illustrates how dramas both large and small generate a similar momentum in qualitative terms, with neither being subordinate to the other. In doing so, he constantly undermines the audience's need for the big emotional moment without diminishing his subject. While his drama may be less vehement in its impact on a superficial level, it has all the more substance for it.

Characters given an opulent biography demand psychological explanations. Winckler impresses by having the courage to leave things out. He always chooses a detail or a section rather than focusing on the whole. Before and after are insignificant; his characters are always anchored to the here and now. *Lucy* doesn't retreat into psychology, gripping and confronting the audience instead with the moments that lead the characters to take action. And they take action without ever really saying much—one of Winckler's greatest strengths as a director.

The secret of *Lucy* lies in how discreetly Winckler is able to stage events. He shows the audience emotional states by allowing it to feel, to empathize. His characters are touching because they appear understandable and transparent in equal measure, much like the numerous panes of glass and window through which his camera observes them. The camera perspective ends up making the impossible possible, relating fundamental aspects of human relationships as if simultaneously from a distance and close up.

Gordon sits across from Maggy and the baby, unaware that she is the mother.

Maggy visits her mother and falls asleep.

Year and place of birth
1969 Hünfeld, Germany
—
Lives and works in
Berlin, Germany
—
Education
Academy of Art and Design,
    Offenbach, Germany
University of Fine Arts,
    Hamburg, Germany
—
Filmography
1998 *Tip Top* (short)
2002 *School Trip* (*Klassenfahrt*)
2006 *Lucy*
—

Director's awards
School Trip
Cinéma Tous Ecrans
    (Best Directing, 2002)
Entreveus Film Festival
    (Grand Prix, 2002)
Sochi International Film Festival
    (Special Jury Award, 2002)
— —

Release date
2006
—
Country of release
Germany
—
Language
German
—
Running time
92 min.
—
Genre
Drama
—

Producers
Florian Koerner von Gustorf,
Michael Weber
—
Writers
Henner Winckler,
Stefan Kriekhaus
—
Cinematographer
Christina A. Maier
—

Key cast
Kim Schnitzer: Maggy
Gordon Schmidt: Gordon
Feo Aladag: Eva
Polly Hauschild: Lucy
Ninjo Borth: Mike
—
Filming location
Berlin, Germany
—
Format
Super 16 mm
—

Awards for *Lucy*
European Cinema Festival
    (Special Jury Award, 2006)
Schwerin Art of Film Festival
    (DEFA Grant, 2006)
Undine Awards
    (Best Young Character
    Actress, 2006)
— —

Gordon and Maggy in bed after a quarrel.

Maggy's mother, Eva, visits Maggy's new home.

Maggy navigates the city with Lucy.

Having dreamt of being a pilot ever since she was a child, Park Kyung-won (Jang Jin-young) goes to Imperial Japan to fulfill her dream. While she braves hardships in an aviation school as a colonial woman, Kyung-won becomes friends with a famous Japanese female pilot, Masako Kibe (Yuko Fueki), and meets her love, Han Ji-hyeok (Kim Joo-hyuck), a Korean in the Japanese Army. She loves him, but hesitates to accept his marriage proposal because flying comes before love. Their love faces danger when Ji-hyeok is falsely accused as a traitor, and Kyung-won, as his lover, suffers, too.

JONG-CHAN YOON
BLUE SWALLOW

Kyung-won and Ji-hyeok flirt at the dance with their classmates.

Kyung-won and Jeong-hui ride their bicycles together and attend flight school.

There is a lot of pain in the films of Jong-Chan Yoon. Many audiences expect to see a reality as harsh as the one they experience in their own lives, but the suffering is also an expression of the director's own worldview. In his work, characters who are haunted by their pasts set a dark tone, and their gloomy circumstances refuse to brighten in spite of their best efforts. But the despair is offset by moments that can only be described as celebrations of pain. Yoon's films portray a reality that is clearly agonizing, yet the agony paradoxically triggers his characters, and his audiences, to continue fighting for a better world.

Yoon's first film, *Sorum* (2001), is about a traumatized woman living in an apartment building that will soon be demolished. The choice of setting is insightful, because construction is a good symbol of modern-day Korea. Across the country, older buildings are constantly being torn down and replaced by sky-high apartment complexes, reflecting the cultural emphasis placed on wealth and status. Although *Sorum* is usually categorized as a horror film, it is not a typical one. Its most chilling element is the horror that the decrepit building evokes.

Yoon's second feature, *Blue Swallow* (*Cheong yeon*, 2005), is set during the Japanese occupation (1910–45). Life in Korea during this period became progressively more restricted, especially for women, even though modernity brought about some changes in society. Set against this historical backdrop, the story centers on Park Kyung-won, a woman aspiring to be an aviator. For a woman to become a pilot then meant overcoming not only the obstacles of the colonial era,

but also the conservative ideology and patriarchal system of Korean society. Kyung-won meets these challenges by going to Japan to attend an aviation school while working as a taxi driver to make ends meet. At school she meets Han Ji-hyeok, a Korean student who is also studying abroad. Destiny separates the two, and while they are apart, Kyung-won succeeds in becoming a renowned pilot and cultivates a sisterly bond with Jeong-hui, another woman who wants to learn to fly. Kyung-won and Ji-hyeok are eventually reunited when he is sent to the aviation school as a commissioned officer, and the two rekindle their love.

The drama is intensified through Kyung-won's relationship with Masako Kibe, a famous model whose father is Japan's secretary of state. Kyung-won is unable to complete an aviation competition because she has to save Masako from an accident, and the experience leads Masako to become her patron. The film effectively uses these dramatic moments to portray the difficulty that Kyung-won continues to experience in the journey to fulfill her heart's desires.

Blue Swallow, which uses elaborate computer graphics, is much larger in scale and investment than the rest of Yoon's work. However, the film failed to be a commercial success and instead gave rise to a heated debate regarding the historical accuracy of Park Kyung-won's life. The director's ambition was perhaps to create a politically ambiguous character much like the hero of *Lawrence of Arabia* (1962), and to reinterpret a period in Korean history that requires a great deal of sensitivity. By using a flawed female figure as the main character instead of a heroic man,

Yoon explores the ambiguity of modernity and gender, while offering an alternate account of life during a contentious historical period.

Yoon's films are unique because his distinct portrayal of reality does not preclude other interpretations. He achieves this openness by refusing to exaggerate or glamorize the pain and suffering of life. Instead, he simply accepts pain and suffering as a part of life, and that acceptance distinguishes him from other Korean directors of his generation. While the majority of his contemporaries strive to fulfill viewer expectations by using the safe formulas of genre or fantastic elements, Yoon is stubbornly consistent in his approach: he quietly follows his characters and taps into the enigmatic depths of life. His main concern is not national ideology or historical accuracy. Instead, what truly concerns Yoon is the desire of the individual, and how that desire motivates the individual to confront and overcome the weight of history. *Blue Swallow* is his fearless exploration of this terrain.

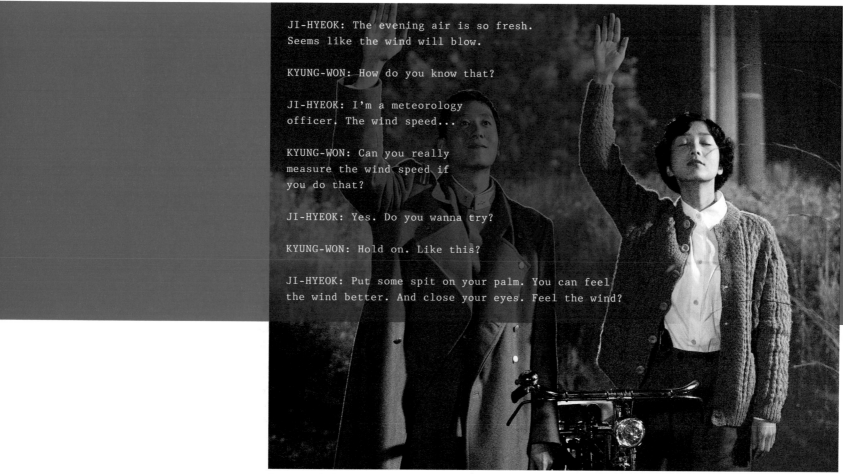

Kyung-won and Ji-hyeok raise their arms up to measure the wind speed.

Year and place of birth
1963   Seoul, South Korea
—

Lives and works in
Seoul, South Korea
—

Education
Syracuse University,
    New York, N.Y., USA
—

Filmography
2001   Sorum
2005   Blue Swallow
           (Cheong yeon)
2009   I am Happy (Naneun
           Haengbok-habnida)
—

Director's awards
Sorum
Pusan Film Critics
Association Awards
    (Best New Director Award,
    2001)
Baeksang Arts Awards
    (Best New Director Award,
    2002)
Fantasporto – The Oporto
International Film Festival
    (Best Direction, Special Jury
    Prize Award, 2002)
— —

Release date
2005
—

Country of release
South Korea
—

Language
Korean, Japanese
—

Running time
133 min.
—

Genre
Drama
—

Producers
Daniella Na, Verne Nobles,
Seok Myeong-hong
—

Writer
Jong-Chan Yoon
—

Cinematographer
Yoon Hong-sik
—

Score
Michael Staudacher
—

Key cast
Jang Jin-young: Park Kyung-won
Kim Joo-hyuck: Han Ji-hyeok
Han Ji-min: Lee Jeong-hui
Nakamura Toru: Tokuda
Yuko Fueki: Masako Kibe
—

Filming locations
Los Angeles, Calif., USA
Changchun, China
Ueda, Japan
Jebu Island, South Korea
Siheung, South Korea
Damyang, South Korea
Yangsoori, South Korea
—

Format
Super 35mm
—

Awards for Blue Swallow
Association of Korean Film
Critics Awards
    (Best Cinematography,
    Best Actress, 2006)
Daejong Film Festival
    (Best Music, 2006)
Icheon Chunsa Film Festival
    (Best Cinematography,
    Best Costume Design,
    2006)
Fajr International Film Festival
    (Best Screenplay Award,
    2007)
— —

Kyung-won and Gibe wait to be introduced as contestants for Japan's National Flight Tournament.

Kyung-won is ready for her first long flight, from Japan to China.

Kyung-won encounters a storm during her flight to Korea.

As a single Korean-Chinese mother, Cui Shunji (Liu Lianji) supports herself and her son by selling pickles as an unlicensed vendor. Shunji and Kim (Zhu Guangxuan) fall in love, but since Kim is married, they must keep their affair a secret. Life seems promising for Shunji when Sergeant Wang (Wang Tonghui), a regular customer, takes pity on her and helps her obtain a business permit for her pickle cart. Shunji's good fortune, however, quickly takes a tragic turn for the worse, and she considers the ultimate form of revenge.

ZHANG LU
GRAIN IN EAR

Shunji, next to the abandoned factory.

Shunji sells kimchi at the edge of the city for a living.

Like the main character in *Grain in Ear* (*Mang Zhong*, 2005), the director, Zhang Lu, is Korean Chinese. Born in Jilin in northern China, he was a professor in the Chinese Department of Yanbian University in Jilin before teaching himself filmmaking. In 2001, his short film *Eleven* (*Shiyi sui*) was screened at the Venice Film Festival. In his first feature-length film, *Tang Poetry* (*Tang shi*, 2003), he explored a minimalist film style that approached the suggestiveness of the titular art form, though the overall effect was less than fluid. *Grain in Ear* places greater emphasis on emotion and character-driven drama, and features understated acting and static camerawork. The result has won him awards at festivals ranging from Cannes to Pusan. Funded mostly from sources in South Korea and the West, his subsequent works target the international art-house circuit rather than the official distribution network within China.

Grain in Ear is the story of Cui Shunji, a downtrodden woman who has taken all the hard knocks that life has to deliver. Shunji is Korean Chinese and lives with her son in a small town in northern China, selling kimchi (pickled vegetables) by the roadside. The two are struggling but surviving, and they live in a tiny concrete home next door to four prostitutes. But Shunji's brief relationships with three men—a married man of Korean descent, a young policeman, and a chef at the factory cafeteria—lead to catastrophe. Betrayed by the Korean man (with whom she has had an affair), she is arrested as a prostitute and then raped by the policeman while in custody. The accidental death of her son finally

drives her over the edge, and she commits a destructive act of revenge.

There are more than two million ethnic Koreans in China, and they are not granted the special treatment received by other minorities such as Tibetans and Mongolians. Shunji may not be very conscious of her status as an ethnic minority, but cultural differences must have reinforced her feeling of isolation and marginalization on the lowest rung of the social ladder. She is a woman of few words and even fewer Korean words. She attempts to make her son learn Korean, but his impatience with the futile exercise and her desperation suggest the increasing distance between the ethnic group to which she belongs and its cultural roots.

For Shunji as a single mother, the immediate source of oppression comes from the selfish, greedy, and aggressive nature of the men around her. Shunji accepts the advances of the married Korean man, perhaps only out of an unarticulated feeling of ethnic affinity, but when his wife discovers the affair, he accuses Shunji of being a prostitute to save his own skin. Sergeant Wang, who helps her to obtain a vendor's license early in the film, is not devoid of human decency, but under the influence of the debasing environment of the police station, he too sides with her oppressors. By contrast, the women in the film stand together in hardship. Not only do the four prostitutes look out for her (roughhousing with her son and celebrating with her for getting her license), but the women who process the license show goodwill in asking to learn a Korean dance.

The request brings a rare smile to Shunji's face, but bright moments like this, alas, do not last.

When Shunji adds rat poison to the kimchi for Wang's wedding banquet, it is reminiscent of a similar episode in Aki Kaurismäki's *The Match Factory Girl* (Tulitikkutehtaan tyttö, 1990). Yet the film comes closer to the world of Rainer Werner Fassbinder in expressing sympathy for the socially humiliated and indicting the despicability of human nature and the ways in which society fosters alienation. It is not an exaggeration to say that Zhang, in his formal rigor, is worthy of these two European masters.

The characters in *Grain in Ear* speak and act lethargically, conveying the disintegration of an agri-cultural society which may be bankrupt before it can even benefit from industrialization. The fixed camera positions emphasize the compressed living space of the characters and suggest a daily rhythm that has almost come to a standstill. After the poisoning scene, however, the camera comes to life. It follows Shunji as she walks out of her bare apartment, and into the boundless expanses of wheat fields. When the screen goes black and the credits begin to roll, the sound of her footsteps and her breathing come to the fore.

This final long shot not only captures the eruption of Shunji's rage but also underlines the director's affection for her. Zhang has said that the Chinese title of the film, *Mang Zhong*, implies a sense of hope, because it refers to the growth of crops, the harvest, and the sowing and planting that follow. The concluding shot of the wheat fields echoes this theme—but not without a trace of irony.

Changhao stares angrily at the strange man pestering his mom.

Year and place of birth
1962 Yanji, China

—

Lives and works in
Beijing, China

—

Filmography
2001 Eleven (Shiyi sui) (short)
2003 Tang Poetry (Tang shi)
2005 Grain in Ear (Mang Zhong)
2007 Desert Dream (Hyazgar)
2008 Iri
2009 Dooman River

—

Director's awards
Desert Dream
**Cinefan Festival of Asian and
Arab Cinema
    (Asian and Arab Competition
    Award – Best Film, 2007)**

— —

Release date
2005

—

Country of release
South Korea

—

Language
Korean, Mandarin

—

Running time
109 min.

—

Genre
Drama

—

Producer
Choi Dooyoung

—

Writer
Zhang Lu

—

Cinematographer
Liu Yonghong

—

Key cast
Liu Lianji: Cui Shunji
Jin Bo: Changhao
Zhu Guangxuan: Kim
Wang Tonghui: Sergeant Wang

—

Filming location
Beijing, China

—

Format
35 mm

—

Awards for Grain in Ear
**Cannes International
Film Festival
    (ACID Award, 2005)**
**Pesaro International
Film Festival
    (Grand Prix, 2005)**
**Pusan International Film Festival
    (New Currents Prize, 2005)**
**Barcelona Asian Film Festival
    (Gold Durian Award, 2006)**
**Black Movie Film Festival
    (Young Critics Award, 2006)**

**Cinema Novo Film Festival
    (Best Film, 2006)**
**Durban International
Film Festival
    (Best Actress, Best Direction,
    2006)**
**Seattle Film Festival
    (Special Jury Prize, 2006)**
**Tours Asian Film Festival
    (Grand Prize, 2006)**
**Vesoul Asian Film Festival
    (Golden Wheel, 2006)**

— —

SERGEANT WANG: Name? Asking what you are called?

SHUNJI: Cui Shunji.

SERGEANT WANG: Age?

SHUNJI: Thirty-two. Korean minority.

SERGEANT WANG: Who asked you what minority?
Only answer what's asked. Place of birth?

SHUNJI: City of Yianyi in Jilin Province.

SERGEANT WANG: Ethnicity? Hey, answer the question. Ethnicity?

SHUNJI: I just said.

SERGEANT WANG: Say it again.

Shunji is arrested on grounds of prostitution and questioned by Sergeant Wang.

Shunji watches her son prior to the accident.

Alex (Konstantin Lavronenko), his wife Vera (Maria Bonnevie), and their two children move from their home in the city to stay in his father's old house in the countryside. As the family adjusts to this new environment, Vera reveals to Alex that she is pregnant by another man. Alex forces Vera to terminate the pregnancy and confronts the man he believes to be the father.

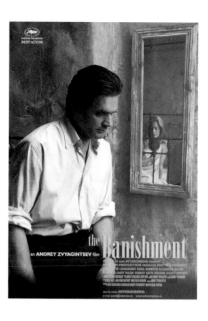

ANDREI ZVYAGINTSEV
THE BANISHMENT

KIR: Dad, why isn't the creek flowing?

ALEX: God only knows.

KIR: Did it get dry?

ALEX: It dried up. It used to flow down here, under the house, and to the ravine.

KIR: Did you see it?

ALEX: I saw it.

The family in the walnut garden after arriving in the countryside.

The decade following the breakup of the Soviet Union saw Russian cinema virtually disappear as a major artistic presence. The incomparable Aleksandr Sokurov had inherited the mantle of Andrei Tarkovsky, but his singular career straddled the Soviet and post-Soviet eras. *The Return* (*Vozvrashcheniye*, 2003) marked the arrival of a new voice—Andrei Zvyagintsev—who unquestionably belongs to the post-glasnost, post-Soviet generation.

The Return displays the kind of authority rarely seen in a first feature. Shot by the brilliant Mikhail Krichman, it is a visually striking, at times heartbreaking, film about an enigmatic father who suddenly appears in the lives of his teenage sons after twelve years. *The Banishment* (*Izgnanie*, 2007), also shot by Krichman, tells the tale of two brothers as well; they could well be the boys of *The Return*, now fully grown men. Zvyagintsev transposes the tale, based on a William Saroyan novel, to his native Russia.

Central to *The Banishment*, and what determines the lives of both men, are cultures and landscapes in conflict. As if to evoke Tarkovsky, the opening shot presents a lone tree, a reference to a famous scene in the master's final film, *The Sacrifice* (*Offret*, 1986). The tree—beautiful, defiant, solitary—is an iconic symbol of nature, and perhaps more deeply, of Russia itself. It is a silent witness, immutable, its secrets unknown.

From this shot of nature we move to a very different world. A car sweeps through the landscape. The driver, Mark, has been wounded. He speeds through an industrial landscape of factories and smokestacks, and stops at a house, where another man, Alex, removes the bullet. The two turn out to be brothers who appear to share a past of violence, but their history is as murky as that of the father in *The Return*. The wounded Mark is an outsider, estranged from his family. Alex, by contrast, is a family man, happily married with two children.

What follows is largely the story of Alex, who decides to take his wife and two children to their country house, which they have not visited for twelve years. This decision is given no context, but it seems a form of escape—a flight from the blight of industry and from a violent past. Visually, it is depicted as a return to the glories of unspoiled nature. The house is a refuge on first sight. Beauty lies in the fields, the light, and the grove of walnut trees on a hill, where the children play hide-and-seek. A dried-up creek that used to run through these trees is rich with symbolism.

The film is composed around a group of antinomies: violence and the city versus nature and country, and, ultimately, man in counterpoint with woman. The first half of *The Banishment* is pastoral in tone. Much of this is due to the landscape, but Alex's wife, Vera, further brings a calming presence and powerful aura. She also acts as the film's catalyst. This rural Eden, reveals her to be Eve to his Adam. She is pregnant, but not by Alex, and this shock casts a shadow over their attempt to escape the violence evoked in the film's opening moments. Vera is a strong, crystalline presence at first, associated with silence and her children, but the second half of the film sees her subsumed and overwhelmed by masculine forces.

The shadowy Mark, who stays at the periphery of the couple's lives, not wanting to see their children, now re-enters the picture. Alex has decided that an abortionist is needed, and Mark is the person who knows how to arrange these things. The male presence comes to the fore, and the mood darkens; the children effectively disappear from the story at this point.

Alex's jealousy pushes him to find the father of Vera's unborn child. As flashbacks flesh out the story of Alex and Vera's relationship, the film touches on the mystical—a prominent leitmotif in Russian culture, and a powerful thread through the careers of Tarkovsky and Sokurov. Against the backdrop of a thunderstorm, Alex confronts her lover; a new truth emerges, and the barren creek flows again. But it is too late to prevent a final tragedy involving Vera.

Zvyagintsev's achievements in *The Banishment* are multiple. The timelessness of Russia comes through not just in the film's landscape (the lone tree, the walnut grove, the creek), but also in its people, as in the final shot of peasants forking hay in the fields, set to music by Arvo Pärt. Yet all these in turn are starkly contrasted with time-specific things: industrial cities, cars, guns. And if woman represents fecundity, acceptance, and family, while man evokes violence and jealousy, Zvyagintsev conjoins them through an otherworldly sensibility that moves the human drama into the realm of myth. Elusive and illusive, mystical and transcendent, Zvyagintsev's films are paeans not just to Tarkovsky's magnificent legacy but also to Dostoevsky's incandescent and troubling canon.

Vera and Alex awake after a night of discussing their relationship.

Year and place of birth
1964   Novosibirsk, USSR
—

Lives and works in
Moscow, Russia
—

Education
**Moscow State Theater School,
Russia**
—

Filmography
**2003   *The Return*
(*Vozvrashcheniye*)
2007   *The Banishment*
(*Izgnanie*)**
—

Director's awards
The Return
**European Film Awards
(European Discovery
of the Year, 2003)
Film Festival Cottbus
(Award of the Ecumenical
Jury, Special Prize for
Best Direction, 2003)
Gijón International Film Festival
(Special Jury Award, 2003)**

**Russian Guild of Film Critics
(Golden Aries Best Debut,
2003)
Venice International Film Festival
(Best First Film Award,
Golden Lion, Luigi De
Laurentiis Award, SIGNIS
Award, Sergio Trasatti Award,
2003)
Mexico City International
Contemporary Film Festival
(Best Film, 2004)
Nika Awards
(Best Film, 2004)
Palm Springs International
Film Festival
(FIPRESCI Prize, 2004)
Thessaloniki International
Film Festival
(FIPRESCI Prize, 2004)**
— —

Release date
2007
—

Country of release
Russia
—

Language
Russian
—

Running time
157 min.
—

Genre
Drama
—

Producer
Dmitri Lesnevsky
—

Writer
Oleg Negin
—

Cinematographer
Mikhail Krichman
—

Score
**Andrei Dergachev,
Arvo Pärt**
—

Key cast
**Konstantin Lavronenko: Alex
Aleksandr Baluyev: Mark
Maksim Shibayev: Kir
Maria Bonnevie: Vera
Katya Kulkina: Eva
Yelena Lyadova: Vera (voice)
Andrey Shibarshin: Max
Dmitri Ulyanov: Robert**
—

Filming locations
**Charleroi, Belgium
Tourcouan, France
Roube, France
Vulcanesti, Moldova
Moscow, Russia**
—

Format
35 mm
—

Awards for *The Banishment*
**Cannes International
Film Festival
(Palme d'Or, Best Actor,
2007)
Moscow International
Film Festival
(Best Film in Russian
Program, 2007)**
— —

Alex and Vera take the children to their grandfather's grave.

Mark consoles Alex after the death of his wife.

Alex returns from his wife's funeral.

10 FILM CLASSICS

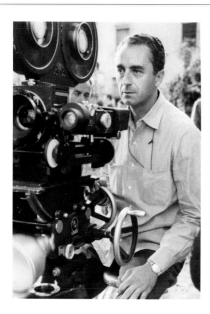

MICHELANGELO ANTONIONI
THE PASSENGER (1975)

The first thing we see in *The Passenger* (*Professione: reporter*) is a man walking across a desert in Africa. Neither mythical nor geographically tied to the character, this is not the desert of Pier Paolo Pasolini. It is marked out within a specific time and space, but never explicitly identified. The man does not understand the language spoken there; the English he speaks is not understood by the people he encounters. He is there for some reason unknown to us. When a camel passes by, he hides among the rocks. Presumably some danger awaits him. Then, suddenly, he is shown going to a hotel. Since the events leading up to these moments remain concealed from us, we do not initially know whether he is coming from somewhere or heading someplace else. But we realize that the man stands at a defining moment in his life, like a figure carved into some incongruous landscape.

The Passenger begins in media res and finishes before a classic resolution is reached—i.e., the hero's transformation—thus maintaining an ambiguous narrative structure. Yet the idea of the protagonist's transformation remains intact. Indeed, it becomes a dramatic motif when the character, David Locke, exchanges his identity with someone named David Robertson, who has died in the same hotel; Locke effectively becomes another man. A story of sorts still ensues: once he has made this decision, we follow the path that he has appropriated, a journey marked by fatality. But only a slender thread of a traditional plot remains, because Antonioni's focus lies within the character himself—in the way that he interacts with the world and in how the contours of fiction can be shaped

into a setting of resounding reality. As a director he is more interested in showing than telling, and here showing Africa is tantamount to showing his central character. We shall never truly know either; we are barely able to see them.

Antonioni therefore does away with the usual psychological justifications that allow the viewer to understand why a character does something or stops doing something. These would prevent us from experiencing the loss of direction that is the indelible hallmark of modernity. Since the passing of time requires a palpable density, Antonioni employs brutal ellipses to compress our sense of it. In the same way, flashbacks disrupt the flow of the film, not to clarify anything but more to act as footnotes, serving as digressions rather than explanations of the central character's behavior.

Locke seems to let himself be guided by chance, and the film adopts the same method. Although, paradoxically, the shadow of tragedy hangs over him, Antonioni chooses to disengage us from the foreseeable consequences of the ending and to resolve everything in one extraordinary continuous shot. Today, it is not unusual that the entire theoretical argument between classicism and modernity should be based upon the distinction between the story in this shot and the shot itself, though it may well have been strange when Antonioni did it more than thirty years ago. For the filmmaker, the shot evidently contains both the story and everything that the story could be. If all that has come before should fail to answer the question of what modernity is, this moment in the film yields the answer.

In this, the penultimate shot, all the storylines are resolved out of frame and in real time. The camera slowly pans away from Locke during his final dialogue with the nameless girl, closing off any possibility of their future relationship. We hear a door open and people entering and leaving, apparently the arms buyers who are looking for Locke. At the same time, the camera appears to lose interest in him, turning away to show a dusty street through the bars of the window. As it moves outside and swivels round to focus on the lifeless body of Locke—reaching the climax of this seven-minute shot—everything converges: the cries of the girl and his ex-wife trying to get into the room, the political intrigue, the inner story of a lonely man, the search for those who formed the story of his past, and the illusion of his future love. We may think that we know all this, but Antonioni gives the last word to Locke's ex-wife: "I never knew him." And with this, the world reclaims its enigmatic character. *The Passenger* is destined to stand the test of time, for it bears witness to an important fact: that our sense of who and what we are form part of what we call—for want of a better word—reality.

FEI MU
SPRING IN A SMALL TOWN (1948)

What accounts for the greatness of *Spring in a Small Town* (*Xiao cheng zhi chun*)—apart from the fact that it is composed like a Chinese poem—is the originality of its narrative voice. It is not unusual to find an off-screen narrator in Chinese cinema, but no film equals this one in its ambiguity of narrative voice and its experimentation with the form. In this respect, it is arguably the first modernist work in Chinese cinema.

In most Chinese films, the narrator, like ancient storytellers, serves to disclose selected elements of the plot. In *Spring in a Small Town*, however, the rules associated with narration are completely overthrown. The narrator does not initially tell us what is to follow; rather, she expresses herself in the first person, as the wife who introduces the four protagonists. Until the young doctor Zhishen appears, the narrator does not identify what she says as memory or as a figment of her imagination. Her monologue is outwardly not even addressed to the audience, which in turn has no choice but to enter her interior world and experience the story with her, thereby breaking the traditional boundary between subjective and objective voiceovers.

Moreover, the narrator who delivers these internal monologues is presented as being omniscient. She comments on scenes in which she plays no part, but at times she also expresses ignorance of certain things: "I don't know that Liyan is his friend." It could be that the scenes take place in the past, and the monologue relates her feelings at the time. However, in Chinese, verbs have no tense, and the same applies here to the images. If there is nothing to indicate that what we see or hear has happened in the past, then it could be occurring in the present. It might be

a personal flashback or a figment of the imagination; the line between the real and the imaginary is blurred, evoking stream-of-consciousness techniques from Western literary tradition.

A commonly held view is that the masterpieces of Chinese cinema belong to the realist school. *Spring in a Small Town* does not fit that classification. There are only five characters, and the film shows us nothing of the little town where they live except for the ruined walls. But the environment is rich in symbolism. It may even be said that the house and garden are a microcosm of the little town and, more generally, of all China. The walls represent, on the one hand, a barrier erected by reason and morality, since this is a film about the conflict between passion and morality, desire and reason. But on the other hand, their dilapidated state also signifies the ground that Chinese culture is losing to Western culture. The house is no doubt ancestral property; the books and the incense burner within are symbols of Chinese tradition. When Zhishen visits Yuwen and her husband Liyan, he brings from the outside world a belief in modern medicine; he wears Western clothes, whereas Liyan's family wears traditional garments. Yuwen for her part has a hard time choosing between the two men, and this too reveals the director's ambivalence.

The acting in *Spring in a Small Town* is exceptional. The influence of modern drama is apparent; the actors all came from the theater and do not have the look of everyday living. Possibly because of extensive rehearsals, there is a sort of tacit rapport among them. The dialogue flows smoothly, with rhythmic pauses and breaks, creating a realistic

effect but with a knowing smile. For once, the actors have overcome the opposition between naturalism and stylization so frequently found in Chinese cinema.

Fei Mu's aesthetic of long takes, which result in serene, two-dimensional compositions, also seems indebted to the theater. His techniques naturally work to the benefit of the acting and to the detriment of cinematic possibilities. However, the filmmaker's genius lies in integrating the performances into a unique style with artistic devices that belong wholly to the domain of cinema, such as voiceovers, camera placement, dissolves, and plays of light and shadow. Wong Kar-wai's *In the Mood for Love* (2000) is a notable and formidable descendant of Fei Mu's pioneering masterpiece, in its theme of repression of adulterous passion, its exploration of unfulfilled love, and its sensitive, subtle treatment of mood and feelings. Wong also uses monologues in narration, as well as documentary footage, to evoke a cinematic experience that is uniquely Chinese.

That the film ends with the couple's reunion is, to some viewers, a pity. Some say this resolution is what prevents the film from achieving perfection, but perfect works of art are not always great works, just as great works need not be perfect. If anything, the imperfect ending is in line with the Chinese literary tradition in which endings are happy and entail reconciliation, even in tragedies. Viewed from any artistic perspective—cinema, poetry, drama, or narrative literature—*Spring in a Small Town* both is rooted in and goes beyond Chinese tradition. Yet its cultural vision is Chinese in every sense. It is a veritable masterpiece of Chinese cinema.

WERNER HERZOG
<u>STROSZEK</u> (1977)

When reporting on crime stories, German newspapers follow the somewhat unusual convention of abbreviating surnames in order to protect those involved. ("Convicted criminal Karl F. broke into the house of the W. family by force at around midnight.") That's how Bruno Schlierstein ended up making film history as Bruno S. in the 1970s, having previously spent a large portion of his life in various psychiatric institutions and prisons. Werner Herzog had already given the Berlin street musician a leading role in his film *The Enigma of Kaspar Hauser* (*Jeder für sich und Gott gegen alle*, 1974), and was so thrilled with his discovery that he made the rash promise to also cast him as Woyzeck in his forthcoming film of the same name. When the role went to Klaus Kinski instead, Bruno S. became inconsolable. Herzog quickly wrote another role tailor-made for him, giving him a new name at the same time. Bruno S. ended up becoming Stroszek. The 1977 film was shot in his flat, in his Berlin milieu, Herzog's story appropriating both his dreams and his fears.

Bruno only ever refers to himself in the third person, as "the Bruno,"—the "I" has long been driven out of him. At the beginning of the film, Stroszek is released from prison. How many times must he have had to listen to the warden's speech about how he "never wants to see him again" and to promise that he'd "never touch even a drop of alcohol ever again"? The next scene takes Bruno to his local pub, Bierhimmel on Potsdamer Strasse, where he comforts prostitute Eva (Eva Mattes, the only professional actor in the film), who is being hassled by her pimps. Bruno's eccentric neighbor Mr. Scheitz (Clemens Scheitz) completes the trio. The three of them decide to leave their lives and the depressing Berlin winter behind and to take a ship to New York. From there, they set out in a rusty cruiser on their way to Wisconsin in order to live their American dream: a mobile home, television, limitless freedom.

Herzog discovered the location in which the second half of the film unfolds while researching serial killer Ed Gein with Errol Morris for a documentary that never got made. In *Stroszek*, however, Herzog emphasizes the friendliness of the place rather than any sinister qualities, focusing on the warm reception that these strange figures from Germany receive and the down-to-earth nature of the farmers, craftsmen, hunters, truckers, and waitresses. The fact that it all goes wrong for Bruno, Eva, and Mr. Scheitz can't be attributed to America but to the fact that their relationship of convenience begins to dissolve once out of Berlin. Bruno is forced to recognize that Eva does not return his love, and Mr. Scheitz's long-standing persecution complex only intensifies in the face of their mobile home being seized. The bank robbery that they then try to carry out is the perfect mixture of pure American slapstick and German melancholy.

Most audiences remember the film for its sad ending. Bruno winds up alone in a Cherokee reservation in North Carolina, where he forlornly goes around and around in an abandoned cable car as chickens and other small livestock perform a desperate dance of despair almost like a living music box. Herzog later stated what a great metaphor it was, even if he didn't know for what exactly.

With *Stroszek*, the extravagant director succeeded in creating one of the most moving films in the history of German cinema. At the same time, he set an example for the European and American independent scene in the following decades: *Stroszek* was written swiftly in a largely spontaneous manner and mixed professional actors with nonprofessionals, upon whose personal experiences the story was based. The film was improvised in large sections, open to the coincidences that came about during the shoot, not forcing a particular rhythm onto the actors but rather allowing them to follow their own. The film's dramatic structure is generally loose: the crew consisted of just a handful of people, the production costs remained low in the interest of artistic freedom. Herzog's approach to film is that of a pioneer, an adventurer. *Stroszek* is to this day a shining example for truly independent filmmakers, and the work of an artist who has always avoided the easiest, most commonly traveled route.

ABBAS KIAROSTAMI
<u>TEN</u> (2002)

First shown internationally at the 2002 Cannes Film Festival, *Ten* is already a classic, one that marks a turning point, even a revolution, in the way we think about cinema. It prefigured the current stylistic developments in which the boundaries of genres and formats, and between fiction and documentary, are increasingly blurred. Why might one prefer this film to Jean-Luc Godard's *Contempt* (*Le mépris*, 1963), Roberto Rossellini's *Rome, Open City* (*Roma, città aperta*, 1945), or John Ford's *The Searchers* (1956)? Quite simply because since 1989, when Abbas Kiarostami's *Where Is the Friend's Home?* (*Khane-ye doust kodjast?*) won three awards at the Locarno International Film Festival, the Iranian director has been confirming himself as the equal to any one of these great figures, and because, with the radical challenges his films pose, he has been influencing many of his fellow directors.

Consisting entirely of alternating static video shots filmed from within one car, *Ten* takes daring risks. One camera remains fixed on the driver, a fortyish divorcée, the other focuses on the various passengers who get in and out of the car. Her son (demanding, pretentious, and spoiled by a father who appears to be setting him against his mother) is followed by a series of women: her sister, an unidentified old lady on her way to pray at a mausoleum, a prostitute, an abandoned woman who has shaved her head, and so on. The film is divided into episodes depicting ten journeys (hence the title) made around the city of Tehran at various points throughout the day and night. The result is an astonishing distillation of contemporary Iranian society, especially in terms of its women and their relationship with men (the son, the husband, the father). It's a portrait of women that holds equally true in other countries and in other sociocultural contexts. So, in extension, it's a view of the world in general—a world that here is seen up close in the confined setting of an automobile.

And in Kiarostami's works, we are used to the car interior (see *Life and Nothing More* [*Zendegi va digar hich*, 1991] and *Taste of Cherry* [*Ta'm e guilass*, 1997], which was awarded the Palme d'Or at Cannes in 1997), and to witnessing the world from this vantage point. In those earlier films, the camera was a kind of protected frame, from behind which the director could film the outside surroundings. In *Ten*, the former observation point has become the stage, a miniature theater where anything can happen.

Kiarostami is known to have devised this method of filmmaking. The use of video made it possible to shoot long sequences without having to cut. Much of the time he was hidden in the back seat of the car, feeding the actors their lines as shots progressed. Other times he said nothing, allowing the actors to let go and make up their own dialogue as they went along. Or, because it's important to Kiarostami that he occasionally let his actors feel completely free of his "direction," he wasn't there at all. And this new method allowed him to do precisely that. The result is a focused, controlled form of improvisation, with no limits.

Beyond what the film describes, visually or figuratively, *Ten* explores the very meaning of representation, of the role and function of a director, and even the disappearance of direction. As Kiarostami says, "I didn't make the car, I didn't create this woman, and this kind of dialogue is the sort of thing you often hear. But when they appear at a given moment in a specific image, then it's a form of creation." The director brings external reality and his own experiences together in such a way that makes them wholly credible to the viewer.

A film somewhere between fiction and documentary, *Ten* captures a great deal more than mere images. The power and simplicity of the way Kiarostami tells his story—and all that goes on between the passengers in the car—in some way prevents the visuals revealing anything beyond their emotional affects. All the things through which they are filtered (settings, costumes, distance, etc.) seem secondary, leaving the suspended moments of truth to be savored—like the feelings of a woman who begins to weep, and not those of an actress playing the same role.

KIM KI-YOUNG
THE HOUSEMAID (1960)

In spring 2008, *The Housemaid* (*Hanyo*) by Kim Ki-young was digitally remastered and shown at the Cannes Film Festival. *The Housemaid* was one of only three classics chosen to be restored that year, along with the 1973 Senegalese film *Touki Bouki* and the 1964 Turkish film *Dry Summer* (*Susuz yaz*). Through this re-introduction to the world, *The Housemaid* has found its place not only as a masterpiece that represents 1960s Korean cinema, but also as an influential work in the scheme of world film history.

The Housemaid is frequently mentioned by the new generation of Korean directors when citing influences on their work. Park Chan-wook, the director of *Oldboy* (2003), often refers to Kim Ki-young and *The Housemaid* in interviews. He once said, "If Kim Ki-young was born in a country other than Korea, he'd be acknowledged as a worldwide auteur and master in today's film industry." South Korean films released after the Korean War have been virtually unknown to the world, although they were received well domestically. Both the adoration from the new generation of Korean directors and the international efforts to restore *The Housemaid* after half a century attest to the potency of Kim's artistic vision and the depths to which he went to explore human desire.

The plot unfolds as a housemaid is brought into a bourgeois family. The dramatic crosscurrents between the husband, the wife, and the infatuated housemaid are the microcosm through which Kim exposes hypocrisy and vulgarity under modernizing forces, and the problems that arise when individuals attempt to express their sexuality and gender identity under these circumstances. When the housemaid becomes

pregnant by the husband and tries to overthrow his wife's position, the family starts to unravel.

The Housemaid thus tapped into the realities of Korea's postwar society while illuminating the universal desire for power. The head of the household is desired not only by the housemaid and his wife, but also a third female figure, who introduced the housemaid to the family. She is a factory worker who continues to visit the house under the guise of receiving piano lessons from the husband. The conflict between these three women is investigated over the course of the film, yielding a study of how their desires erupt as they each strive to possess the bourgeois man.

Kim repeated variations on this narrative in two later films, *Fire Woman* (*Hwanyeo*, 1970) and *The Woman of Fire '82* (*Hwanyeo '82*, 1982). The key feature that is consistent throughout all three is Kim's exploration of female sexuality by bringing their desire to the foreground—needless to say, a groundbreaking accomplishment at the time. In these films, it is the women who take initiative in pursuing their desires, unlike the men, who are inactive and relatively incompetent. The male figure serves as a medium through which the female characters fulfill their bourgeois desires, or as the object of their sexual desire. He is stripped of his agency to make choices and solve problems, a state of affairs that expresses Kim's vision of masculinity as weighed down by inertia, in contrast to a femininity embodied through the aggressive pursuit of desires.

What also distinguishes *The Housemaid* is the array of stylistic features that we now recognize as uniquely characteristic of Kim Ki-young. The

exaggerated sound and clear contrast between light and shade in this black-and-white film, techniques that are not uncommon today, were revelatory back then. However, these elements went against the current of practiced norms of the time, thereby isolating Kim's films from his contemporaries. Korean public opinion pigeonholed Kim as no more than a cult director who produced eccentric and bizarre works. Kim himself used the term "master artisan" to describe his activities as a director, unlike his contemporaries who referred to themselves as artists. Kim's mastery of the craft is related to his ability to make films faster than any other director of the time. His skill at adapting to and accommodating the demands of his commercial investors brought his films favorable reception during the 1970s in Korea, a period which cannot be summarized as anything but a dark and repressive period in which the production of film, and all art, was heavily censored.

Despite his commercial successes, Kim is still regarded as the preeminent director of Korean classical films. This is a testament to the creativity and persistence with which he marked his films with his own unique voice, despite the limitations of working in a commercially demanding environment, much like the case of Alfred Hitchcock. Even before his untimely death in a fire in 1998, shortly after the Pusan International Film Festival mounted his career retrospective, Kim was preparing to make another film. Until the Pusan survey, Kim's films were virtually unknown outside of Korea, and it was through this retrospective that he gained the worldwide recognition and respect that had hitherto eluded his work.